Glossa

Here's a l..t respect
in Costa Rica:

birra (***bee***-rah): Slang for beer.

boca (***boh***-cah): Literally means "mouth," but also a term to describe a small appetizer served alongside a drink at many bars.

bomba (***bohm***-bah): Translates literally as "pump," but is used in Costa Rica for "gas station."

brete (***breh***-teh): Work, or job.

casado (cah-***sah***-doh): Literally means "married," but is the local term for a popular restaurant offering, featuring a main dish and various side dishes.

Chepe (***cheh***-peh): Slang term for the capital city, San José.

chunche (***choon***-cheh): Knicknack; thing, as in "whatchamacallit."

con mucho gusto (con ***moo***-choh ***goo***-stoh): With pleasure.

diay (dee-***eye***): An untranslatable but common linguistic punctuation, often used to begin a sentence.

La Sele (lah ***seh***-leh): Short for *La Selección*, the Costa Rican national soccer team.

macha or machita (***mah***-chah; mah-***chee***-tah): A blond woman.

mae (***mah***-eh): Not gender specific, this translates like "man" or "dude": used by many Costa Ricans, particularly teenagers, as frequent verbal punctuation.

mejenga (meh-***hen***-gah): An informal, or pickup, soccer game.

pachanga or pelón (pah-***chahn***-gah); peh-***lon***): Both terms used to signify a big party or gathering.

Ponga la mária, por favor (***pon***-gah la mah-***ree***-ah, por ***fah***-vor): Please put on the meter (you should direct taxi drivers to do this when first entering a cab).

pulpería (pool-peh-***ree***-ah): The Costa Rican version of the "corner store" or small market.

pura vida (***poo***-rah ***vee***-dah): Literally, "pure life"; translates as "everything's great."

soda (***soh***-dah): A casual diner-style restaurant serving cheap Tico meals.

Tico (***tee***-koh): Costa Rican.

Tiquicia (tee-***kee***-syah): Costa Rica.

tuanis (***twah***-nees): Means the same as *pura vida* (see earlier) but is used by a younger crowd.

una teja (***teh***-ha): 100 colones.

un rojo (***roh***-ho): 1,000 colones.

un tucán (too-***cahn***): 5,000 colones.

Upe! (***oo***-peh): Common shout to find out if anyone is home; used frequently because doorbells are so scarce.

zarpe (***zar***-peh): Last drink of the night, or "one more for the road."

Costa Rica For Dummies,
3rd Edition

Cheat Sheet

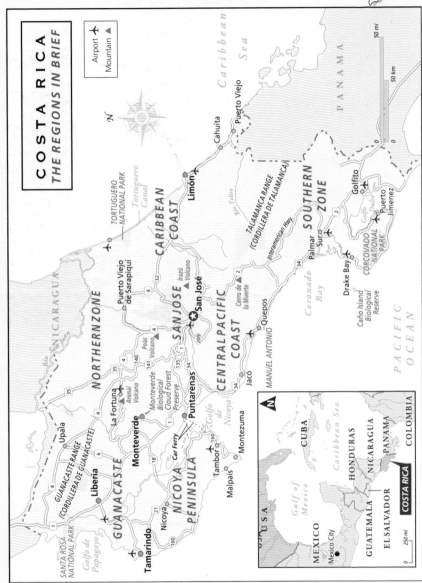

COSTA RICA
THE REGIONS IN BRIEF

Airport ✈
Mountain ▲

50 mi

50 km

Caribbean Sea

PANAMA

TORTUGUERO NATIONAL PARK

Tortuguero Canal

Cahuita

Puerto Viejo

CARIBBEAN COAST

Limón

Río Telire

TALAMANCA RANGE (CORDILLERA DE TALAMANCA)

Golfito

Puerto Jiménez

SOUTHERN ZONE

Palmar Sur

CORCOVADO NATIONAL PARK

Interamerican Hwy.

NORTHERN ZONE

Puerto Viejo de Sarapiquí

Río San Juan

NICARAGUA

SAN JOSE

Irazú Volcano

San José

Poás Volcano

Cerro de la Muerte

CENTRAL PACIFIC COAST

Quepos

MANUEL ANTONIO

Jacó

Drake Bay

Coronado Bay

Caño Island Biological Reserve

PACIFIC OCEAN

Upala

La Fortuna

Arenal Volcano

GUANACASTE RANGE (CORDILLERA DE GUANACASTE)

Monteverde Biological Cloud Forest Preserve

Puntarenas

Gulfo de Nicoya

Liberia

GUANACASTE

Monteverde

Car Ferry

Tambor

Montezuma

NICOYA PENINSULA

Nicoya

Malpaís

Tamarindo

SANTA ROSA NATIONAL PARK

Golfo de Papagayo

USA

Gulf of Mexico

CUBA

Caribbean Sea

MEXICO

Mexico City

HONDURAS

NICARAGUA

PANAMA

COSTA RICA

GUATEMALA

EL SALVADOR

COLOMBIA

250 mi

For Dummies: Bestselling Book Series for Beginners

Costa Rica
FOR
DUMMIES®
3RD EDITION

by Eliot Greenspan

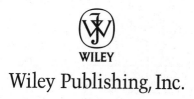

WILEY

Wiley Publishing, Inc.

Costa Rica For Dummies®, 3rd Edition

Published by
Wiley Publishing, Inc.
111 River St.
Hoboken, NJ 07030-5774
www.wiley.com

Copyright © 2010 by Wiley Publishing, Inc., Indianapolis, Indiana

Published simultaneously in Canada

For general information on our other products and services, please contact our Customer Care Department within the U.S. at 877-762-2974, outside the U.S. at 317-572-3993, or fax 317-572-4002.

For technical support, please visit www.wiley.com/techsupport.

Wiley also publishes its books in a variety of electronic formats. Some content that appears in print may not be available in electronic books.

ISBN: 978-0-470-48215-5

Manufactured in the United States of America

10 9 8 7 6 5 4 3 2 1

WILEY

About the Author

Eliot Greenspan is a poet, journalist, musician, and travel writer who took his backpack, mandolin, and typewriter the length of Mesoamerica before settling in Costa Rica in 1992. Since then, he has worked steadily as a travel writer, freelance journalist, and translator, and continued his travels in the region. He is also the author of *Frommer's Costa Rica, Frommer's Belize, Frommer's Guatemala, Frommer's Ecuador,* and *The Tico Times Restaurant Guide to Costa Rica,* as well as the chapter on Venezuela in *Frommer's South America.*

Dedication

As with previous editions, I'd like to again dedicate this book to Allen Ginsberg, Fielding Dawson, and Jane Faigao — three dear friends and teachers whom I treasure and miss.

Author's Acknowledgments

Here's to all the industry insiders, longtime locals, and everyday tourists, whose thoughts and impressions add immeasurably to my own wanderings, adventures, test runs, and site inspections. I'd also like to thank Mayling Charpentier for her help on the road and phones, as well as Myka Carroll and Jennifer Reilly for their editorial diligence.

Publisher's Acknowledgments

We're proud of this book; please send us your comments through our Dummies online registration form located at www.dummies.com/register/.

Some of the people who helped bring this book to market include the following:

Editorial

Editors: Myka Carroll, Development Editor; Lindsay Conner and Suzanna R. Thompson, Production Editors

Copy Editor: Elizabeth Kuball

Cartographer: Anton Crane

Editorial Assistant: Jessica Langan-Peck

Senior Photo Editor: Richard Fox

Cover Photos:
Front: © Roy Toft / National Geographic / Getty Images
Back: © Ken Welsh / AGE Fotostock, Inc. / PhotoLibrary

Cartoons: Rich Tennant
(www.the5thwave.com)

Composition Services

Project Coordinator: Patrick Redmond

Layout and Graphics: Carl Byers

Proofreaders: Melissa Cossell, Leeann Harney

Indexer: Slivoskey Indexing Services

Publishing and Editorial for Consumer Dummies

Diane Graves Steele, Vice President and Publisher, Consumer Dummies

Kristin Ferguson-Wagstaffe, Product Development Director, Consumer Dummies

Kelly Regan, Editorial Director, Travel

Publishing for Technology Dummies

Andy Cummings, Vice President and Publisher, Dummies Technology/ General User

Composition Services

Gerry Fahey, Vice President of Production Services

Debbie Stailey, Director of Composition Services

Contents at a Glance

Introduction.. 1

Part I: Introducing Costa Rica................................. 7
Chapter 1: Discovering the Best of Costa Rica.............................9
Chapter 2: Digging Deeper into Costa Rica................................18
Chapter 3: Deciding Where and When to Go...............................26
Chapter 4: Following an Itinerary: Five Great Options.............35

Part II: Planning Your Trip to Costa Rica........... 45
Chapter 5: Managing Your Money...47
Chapter 6: Getting to Costa Rica...58
Chapter 7: Getting Around Costa Rica......................................64
Chapter 8: Booking Your Accommodations 67
Chapter 9: Catering to Special Travel Needs or Interests.........73
Chapter 10: Taking Care of the Remaining Details.....................79

Part III: San José and the Central Valley 89
Chapter 11: Settling into San José...91
Chapter 12: Exploring San José 120

Part IV: Guanacaste and Environs 145
Chapter 13: Going for Gold in Guanacaste..............................147
Chapter 14: Exploring Guanacaste...169

Part V: Manuel Antonio and Environs 181
Chapter 15: Enjoying Magnificent Manuel Antonio...................183
Chapter 16: Living the Lush Life on the
    Central Pacific Coast 205

Part VI: Monteverde and Environs 233
Chapter 17: Visiting the Cloud Forests of Monteverde............235
Chapter 18: La Fortuna and the Arenal Area 255

Part VII: Touring the Rest of Costa Rica 279
Chapter 19: Seeking Solitude in Southern Nicoya.....................281
Chapter 20: Exploring Southern Costa Rica.............................299
Chapter 21: Chilling on Costa Rica's Caribbean Coast.............324

Part VIII: The Part of Tens................................. 353
Chapter 22: Ten Myths about Costa Rica.................................355
Chapter 23: Ten Costa Rican Moments 358

Appendix: Quick Concierge 361

Index.. 369

Maps at a Glance

Exploring Costa Rica in One Week 36
Exploring Costa Rica in Two Weeks 38
Costa Rica with Kids 40
Best Costa Rica Adventures 42
San José 96
Guanacaste 156
Tamarindo 158
Playa del Coco 160
Playa Hermosa 162
Manuel Antonio 189
Manuel Antonio National Park 197
Central Pacific Playas 207
Playa Jacó 209
Monteverde 239
Monteverde Cloud Forest Reserve 247
La Fortuna and the Arenal Volcano 256
Along the Shores of Lake Arenal 271
Montezuma 283
Malpaís and Santa Teresa 293
Osa Peninsula 302
Puerto Jiménez 309
Southern Costa Rica 310
Corcovado National Park 314
Cahuita 327
Puerto Viejo 341
Tortuguero 345

Table of Contents

Introduction *1*

   About This Book 1
   Conventions Used in This Book 1
   Foolish Assumptions 2
   How This Book Is Organized 3
      Part I: Introducing Costa Rica 3
      Part II: Planning Your Trip to Costa Rica....3
      Part III: San José and the Central Valley 3
      Part IV: Guanacaste and Environs 3
      Part V: Manuel Antonio and Environs...........4
      Part VI: Monteverde and Environs 4
      Part VII: Touring the Rest of Costa Rica 4
      Part VIII: The Part of Tens 4
      Appendix: Quick Concierge.........................4
   Icons Used in This Book..................................5
   Where to Go from Here 5

Part I: Introducing Costa Rica *7*

   Chapter 1: Discovering the Best of Costa Rica 9
   The Best High-End Hotels and Luxury Resorts 9
   The Best Accommodations Values 11
   The Best Ecolodges 12
   The Best Restaurants 13
   The Best Beaches...14
   The Best Adventures and Activities 15
   The Best Family Spots 17

   Chapter 2: Digging Deeper into Costa Rica 18
   History 101: The Main Events..........................18
      The early years 18
      Colonizing Costa Rica................................19
      Staking out independence 19
      Growing democracy in Central America.........20
   Building Blocks: Local Architecture 21
   A Taste of Costa Rica: Local Cuisine 21
      Getting the most out of eating in Costa Rica:
        Bocas and fresh fruit 22
      Enjoying a cup of joe 23
   A Word to the Wise: The Local Language............23

Background Check: Recommended Books and Movies ...24
Costa Rica on paper 24
Costa Rica on film...25

Chapter 3: Deciding Where and When to Go 26

Going Everywhere You Want to Be.....................................26
Seeking the center: San José and
the Central Valley 26
Going for gold in Guanacaste 27
Enjoying magnificent Manuel Antonio 27
Living the luxe life on the central Pacific coast 28
Visiting the cloud forests of Monteverde 28
Watching the lava flow from Arenal volcano 29
Seeking solitude on the Nicoya Peninsula...............29
Exploring southern Costa Rica 30
Chilling on the Caribbean coast................................30
Scheduling Your Time 31
Revealing the Secrets of the Seasons 31
Understanding Costa Rica's climate.........................32
Avoiding the crowds 33
Perusing a Calendar of Events...33
January..33
March 33
April...33
July...33
August 33
September...34
October 34
December...34

Chapter 4: Following an Itinerary: Five Great Options...35

Seeing Costa Rica's Highlights in One Week 35
Day 1..35
Day 2..35
Day 3..35
Day 4..36
Day 5..36
Day 6..37
Day 7..37
Touring the Best of Costa Rica in Two Weeks 37
Days 1 and 2 37
Day 3..37
Day 4..37
Day 5..38
Day 6..38

Day 7...38
Days 8, 9, and 10 39
Days 11, 12, and 13 39
Day 14...39
Discovering Costa Rica with Kids 39
Day 1...39
Day 2...40
Day 3...40
Day 4...40
Day 5...41
Day 6...41
Day 7...41
Having a High-Octane Week of Adventures 41
Day 1...41
Day 2...41
Day 3...41
Day 4...42
Day 5...42
Day 6...42
Day 7...42
Getting the Most out of a Week on the Gold Coast........43
Day 1...43
Day 2...43
Day 3...43
Day 4...43
Day 5...43
Day 6...44
Day 7...44

Part II: Planning Your Trip to Costa Rica 45

Chapter 5: Managing Your Money................................47

Planning Your Budget...47
Transportation 48
Lodging...49
Dining 50
Sightseeing...50
Shopping and nightlife 50
Cutting Costs — But Not the Fun...............................51
Getting the best airfares 51
Avoiding paying full price for your hotel room 51
Cutting other costs...52
Handling Money 53
Unlocking the mystery of the colón 53
Exchanging money...54
Using ATMs and carrying cash.......................55

Charging ahead with credit cards 55
Toting traveler's checks 56
Taking Taxes into Account 56
Dealing with a Lost or Stolen Wallet....................................57

Chapter 6: Getting to Costa Rica......................................58

Flying to Costa Rica 58
Getting the best airfare..59
Booking your flight online 60
Cruising to Costa Rica 61
Joining an Escorted Tour..61
Choosing a Package Tour..62

Chapter 7: Getting Around Costa Rica 64

Flying Is Fastest..64
Renting a Car 65
Busing It Around Costa Rica..66

Chapter 8: Booking Your Accommodations..................67

Getting to Know Your Options 67
Relaxing at a large resort 68
Hanging at a hotel..69
Enjoying intimacy at a boutique hotel or B&B........69
Getting close to nature at an ecolodge 69
Choosing a cabina..70
Finding the Best Room Rate 70
Surfing the Web for Hotel Deals 71
Reserving the Best Room...72

Chapter 9: Catering to Special
Travel Needs or Interests 73

Traveling with the Brood: Advice for Families................73
Making Age Work for You: Tips for Seniors.......................74
Accessing Costa Rica: Advice for
Travelers with Disabilities 75
Following the Rainbow: Resources for
Gay and Lesbian Travelers 75
Planning a Costa Rican Wedding 76
Volunteering and Studying in Costa Rica.........................77

Chapter 10: Taking Care of the Remaining Details 79

Getting a Passport..79
Applying for a U.S. passport.......................................79
Applying for other passports 79
Playing It Safe with Travel and Medical Insurance...........80

Staying Healthy When You Travel 82
    What to do if you get sick away from home............84
Staying Connected 85
    Voice over Internet protocol (VOIP)........................86
    Accessing the Internet away from home 86
Keeping Up with Airline Security Measures 86

Part III: San José and the Central Valley 89

Chapter 11: Settling into San José 91

Getting There...92
    Arriving by air 92
    Getting from the airport to your hotel.....................92
    Arriving by bus..94
    Arriving by car 94
Orienting Yourself in San José 94
    Introducing the neighborhoods................................95
    Finding information after you arrive........................99
Getting Around San José..99
    By taxi...99
    By bus..100
    By car 100
    On foot 101
Where to Stay in San José..101
    Runner-up hotels 107
Where to Dine in San José..109
Fast Facts: San José 116

Chapter 12: Exploring San José 120

Seeing San José by Guided Tour 120
The Top Attractions: Gold Underground
    and Jade in the Skies..121
More Cool Things to See and Do.......................................124
    Visiting attractions just outside the city 125
    Suggested one-, two-, and three-day
        sightseeing itineraries...129
Shopping: Gold Beans and Painted Oxcarts 130
    Best shopping areas 130
    What to look for and where to find it.....................131
Living It Up After Dark: From the
    Theaters to a Bitter Street 135
    The performing arts 136
    Dance clubs and discos 137
    The bar scene..138

Hanging out in San Pedro 138
Casinos...139
Taking a Day Trip out of San José...................................140
Guided tours and adventures 140
Bungee jumping 140
Canopy tours and the rain-forest aerial tram 141
Day cruises 141
Mountain-biking 142
Rafting, kayaking, and river trips............................142
Choosing the volcano trip that's right for you 143

Part IV: Guanacaste and Environs *145*

Chapter 13: Going for Gold in Guanacaste.................147
Getting There..148
By air 148
By bus..149
By car 150
Orienting Yourself in Guanacaste 151
Introducing the beaches and neighborhoods.......151
Finding information after you arrive......................153
Getting Around Guanacaste..154
By taxi...154
By car 154
By foot 154
By bus..155
Where to Stay in Guanacaste..155
Where to Dine in Guanacaste 164
Fast Facts: Guanacaste 168

Chapter 14: Exploring Guanacaste 169
Seeing Guanacaste by Guided Tour....................................169
The Top Attractions 170
More Cool Things to See and Do...173
Visiting some of the lesser-known beaches 173
Going under: Scuba diving......................................174
Hoisting sail..175
Hanging ten: Surfing and surf lessons...................175
Landing a big one...176
Teeing off: Golf in Guanacaste...............................176
Canopy tours 177
Horseback riding...178
Shopping for Local Treasures 178
Living It Up After Dark..178

Part V: Manuel Antonio and Environs............... *181*

Chapter 15: Enjoying Magnificent
Manuel Antonio...**183**

Getting There...184
    By air..184
    By car.......................................184
    By bus.......................................185
Orienting Yourself in Manuel Antonio.............186
Getting Around Manuel Antonio.......................186
Spending the Night...187
Dining Locally..192
Exploring Manuel Antonio..............................196
    Enjoying the beaches outside the park.................199
    Getting muddy on an all-terrain vehicle.............199
    Getting up close and personal
        with a mangrove.................................199
    Landing a big one.................................199
    Playing Tarzan....................................200
    Going local...200
    Playing tropical cowboy.....................201
    Riding the back roads on a mountain bike...........201
    Riding the wild white water of a jungle river........201
    Setting out to sea...............................201
    Snorkeling and scuba-diving...............202
    Taking a break to rejuvenate body and soul.........202
Shopping for Local Treasures..........................202
Living It Up After Dark...................................203
Fast Facts: Manuel Antonio.............................204

Chapter 16: Living the Lush Life on the
Central Pacific Coast..**205**

Jacó and Playa Herradura...............................206
    Getting there......................................206
    Orienting yourself in and around
        Jacó and Playa Herradura..................209
    Getting around....................................210
    Spending the night..............................210
    Dining locally.....................................215
    Exploring Jacó and Playa Herradura....................216
    Shopping for local treasures...............221
    Living it up after dark in Jacó
        and Playa Herradura..........................221

Fast Facts: Jacó and Playa Herradura 222
Dominical and the Beaches South of Dominical 223
    Getting there...223
    Orienting yourself in and around Dominical........224
    Getting around 225
    Spending the night...225
    Dining locally...227
    Exploring Dominical and the
        beaches south of Dominical 228
    Getting wet in Dominical and the
        beaches south of Dominical 230
    Shopping for local treasures 231
    Living it up after dark in Dominical......................231
Fast Facts: Dominical and the Beaches
    South of Dominical...231

Part VI: Monteverde and Environs.....................**233**

**Chapter 17: Visiting the Cloud Forests
of Monteverde**...**235**
    Getting There...236
        By car 236
        By bus..237
        Orienting yourself in Monteverde 238
        Getting around 240
    Spending the Night 240
    Dining Locally...244
    Exploring Monteverde...246
        The top attractions..246
        Other attractions in Monteverde..........................248
        Canopy tours and suspended bridges 249
        More cool things to see and do 251
    Shopping for Local Treasures 252
    Living It Up After Dark in Monteverde 253
    Fast Facts: Monteverde 253

Chapter 18: La Fortuna and the Arenal Area.............**255**
    La Fortuna and the Arenal Volcano...............................255
        Getting there...256
        Orienting yourself in La Fortuna
            and around the volcano 258
        Getting around and getting information 259
        Spending the night...259
        Dining locally...263
        Exploring La Fortuna and the
            Arenal volcano area...264

Shopping for local treasures 269
Living it up after dark in La Fortuna
     and around the Arenal volcano...........................269
Fast Facts: La Fortuna and the Arenal Volcano 270
Along the Shores of Lake Arenal 270
     Getting there..............................272
     Orienting yourself along the shores
          of Lake Arenal......................272
     Getting around and getting information 272
     Spending the night.........................273
     Dining locally...............................274
     Exploring along the shores of Lake Arenal...........275
     Shopping for local treasures 276
Fast Facts: Lake Arenal.........................276

Part VII: Touring the Rest of Costa Rica 279

Chapter 19: Seeking Solitude in Southern Nicoya ...281

Montezuma 281
     Getting there.........................282
     Orienting yourself in Montezuma...........283
     Getting around and getting information 284
     Spending the night.........................284
     Dining locally............................286
     Exploring Montezuma 287
     Shopping in Montezuma 289
     Living it up after dark in Montezuma...............289
Fast Facts: Montezuma........................290
Malpaís and Santa Teresa 291
     Getting there.........................292
     Spending the night.........................294
     Dining locally............................296
     Exploring Malpaís and Santa Teresa.............297
     Living it up after dark in Malpaís
          and Santa Teresa.....................297
Fast Facts: Malpaís and Santa Teresa.............297

Chapter 20: Exploring Southern Costa Rica............299

Drake Bay............................300
     Getting there.........................300
     Orienting yourself in Drake Bay...........301
     Spending the night.........................301
     Dining locally............................304
     Exploring Drake Bay 304
     Living it up after dark in Drake Bay................306

Puerto Jiménez and the Osa Peninsula............................306
Getting there.............................307
Orienting yourself in Puerto Jiménez
and the Osa Peninsula.............................308
Getting around and getting information...............308
Spending the night.............................311
Dining locally.............................312
Exploring Puerto Jiménez and
the Osa Peninsula.............................312
Golfito and the Golfo Dulce.............................316
Getting there.............................317
Orienting yourself in Golfito
and along the Golfo Dulce.............................318
Getting around.............................318
Spending the night.............................318
Dining locally.............................321
Exploring Golfito and the Golfo Dulce.............321
Fast Facts: Southern Costa Rica.............................323

Chapter 21: Chilling on Costa Rica's Caribbean Coast...324

Cahuita.............................325
Getting there.............................325
Orienting yourself in Cahuita.............................326
Getting around.............................327
Spending the night.............................327
Dining locally.............................329
Exploring Cahuita.............................330
Shopping for local treasures in Cahuita...............332
Living it up after dark in Cahuita.............................333
Puerto Viejo and the Southernmost Beaches.............333
Getting there.............................333
Orienting yourself in Puerto Viejo
and the southernmost beaches.............................334
Getting around.............................335
Spending the night.............................335
Dining locally.............................338
Exploring Puerto Viejo and the
southernmost beaches.............................339
Shopping for local treasures.............................343
Living it up after dark in Puerto Viejo.............343
Tortuguero.............................344
Getting there.............................344
Orienting yourself in Tortuguero.............................347
Getting around.............................347

Spending the night.....................................347
Dining locally...349
Exploring Tortuguero................................350
Fast Facts: The Caribbean Coast...............352

Part VIII: The Part of Tens *353*

Chapter 22: Ten Myths about Costa Rica 355

Costa Rica Is Just for the Adventurous...........................355
Costa Rica Isn't for Families 355
Bugs Are Bad 355
Costa Rica Is an Ecological Eden 356
You Can't Drink the Water...356
The Caribbean Coast Is Dangerous 356
It's Okay to Feed the Monkeys 356
It's Always Raining in the Rain Forest.............................356
Everybody Speaks English...356
Costa Rican Coffee Is the Best..357

Chapter 23: Ten Costa Rican Moments.....................358

Pouring Salsa Lizano on Your Gallo Pinto 358
Waking Up to the Sound of Howler Monkeys.................358
Catching Your First Wave 358
Zipping among Treetops on a Canopy Tour....................359
Watching a Sea Turtle Come Ashore to Nest 359
Enjoying a Pacific Ocean Sunset 359
Marveling at the City Lights at a Mirador......................359
Soaking in the Pool of a Jungle Waterfall.......................359
Catching the Glint of Sunlight
off a Quetzal's Feathers...359
Watching Arenal Volcano Blow Its Top 360

Appendix: Quick Concierge............... *361*

Fast Facts 361
Toll-Free Numbers and Web Sites....................................366
Where to Get More Information 368

Index...*369*

Introduction

osta Rica is one of the top vacation destinations in the Americas. Aside from sun-drenched beaches, steamy jungles, and abundant wildlife, Costa Rica has a wealth of attractions and adventures to please a wide range of travelers. Whether you're a family looking for something new, a snow bunny working on a winter tan, or an avid naturalist itching to delve into the wonderful world of the tropical rain forest, there's a Costa Rican vacation waiting just for you.

Costa Rica For Dummies, 3rd Edition, makes planning a vacation easy. Instead of an endless list with encyclopedic entries, this book focuses on the best that Costa Rica has to offer.

About This Book

Costa Rica For Dummies is a concise and precise guide to the top vacation options in Costa Rica. I've done the legwork for you and weeded out the unnecessary and overrated. I've tried to anticipate your every question, without bogging you down with superfluous details.

I give honest and accurate descriptions of Costa Rica's various hotels, restaurants, and attractions. I'm not afraid to take a stand to help you decide what to include in your Costa Rican vacation — and, even more important, what *not* to include.

Feel free to jump around or skip certain sections altogether. Use the index and table of contents — and the brief intro that I include here — to zero in and find the information most important to help you plan and enjoy a perfect vacation.

Please be advised that travel information is subject to change at any time — and this is especially true of prices. You may want to write or call ahead for confirmation when making your travel plans.

Conventions Used in This Book

In this book, hotels and restaurants are listed alphabetically with actual prices and frank evaluations. I include lists of hotels, restaurants, and attractions. As I describe each one, I often include abbreviations for commonly accepted credit cards:

AE: American Express

DC: Diners Club

MC: MasterCard

V: Visa

I also include some general pricing information to help you as you decide where to unpack your bags or dine on the local cuisine. I've used a system of U.S. dollar signs to show a range of costs for one night in a hotel (double occupancy) or a full meal for one at a restaurant (including a soup or salad, an entree, a dessert, and a nonalcoholic drink).

Check out the following table to decipher the dollar signs.

Cost	Hotel	Restaurant
$	Less than $75	Less than $10
$$	$75–$125	$10–$20
$$$	$126–$200	$21–$30
$$$$	$201–$350	$31–$45
$$$$$	More than $350	More than $45

The dollar-sign ratings allow you to make quick comparisons of the costs of various establishments. However, I also list specific and detailed pricing information in every listing.

Throughout this book, I use the exchange rate of 560 colones to $1. However, the Costa Rican colón is in a steady rate of devaluation, while the dollar and British pound also are in flux. To check the very latest exchange rates before you leave home, point your browser to www. xe.com/ucc.

For those hotels, restaurants, and attractions that are plotted on a map, a page reference is provided in the listing information. If a hotel, restaurant, or attraction is outside the city limits or in an out-of-the-way area, it may not be mapped.

Foolish Assumptions

As I wrote this book, I made some assumptions about you and what your needs as a traveler may be. Here's what I assumed about you:

- ✔ You may be an experienced traveler who hasn't had much time to explore Costa Rica and wants expert advice when you finally do get a chance to enjoy the country.

- ✔ You may be an inexperienced traveler looking for guidance when determining whether to take a trip to Costa Rica and how to plan for it.

> ✔ You're not looking for a book that provides all the information available about Costa Rica or that lists every hotel, restaurant, or attraction available to you. Instead, you're looking for a book that focuses on the places that will give you the best or most unique experiences in Costa Rica.

How This Book Is Organized

Costa Rica For Dummies contains eight parts. Parts I and II provide the nuts-and-bolts information to help you choose where and when to go and how to plan your trip. Parts III, IV, V, VI, and VII give detailed information on the best hotels, restaurants, and attractions to be found at the various destinations across Costa Rica. Part VIII provides some quick and clear final recommendations and important facts.

Part 1: Introducing Costa Rica

Part I is an overview of Costa Rica's various destinations and attractions. There is an easy-to-scan list of the very best of the best — my personal picks of Costa Rica's top hotels, nature lodges, restaurants, beaches, adventures, and more. I take a quick look into Costa Rica's history, culture, and cuisine, and offer straightforward advice on how to budget your time and decide where and when to visit.

Part 11: Planning Your Trip to Costa Rica

Here is where I lay out everything you need to make all the arrangements for your trip. I get down to the serious trip preparation, including how much you can expect your trip to cost. I weigh the pros and cons of planning your trip on your own, using a travel agent, and buying an all-inclusive package deal. I also offer special trip-planning advice for families, singles, gay and lesbian travelers, seniors, and travelers who are physically challenged. Finally, I take you through all the ins and outs of other vacation essentials, from getting a passport and considering travel insurance to staying safe.

Part 111: San José and the Central Valley

A vast majority of visitors to Costa Rica spend some time in San José (Costa Rica's capital city) and its environs, whether as a transportation hub or as an initial base for their trip. Part III tells you all you need to know about settling in and dining in style in San José and the surrounding Central Valley. It also includes advice on must-see attractions and exciting day trips.

Part 1V: Guanacaste and Environs

Costa Rica's "Gold Coast" is where to discover the beaches of the northwestern province of Guanacaste. Part IV delves into a variety of these beach towns and nearby destinations, with recommendations for everything from small boutique hotels to large, full-scale resorts. I describe the many tour and adventure options available in Guanacaste, including side trips to the inland Rincón de la Vieja National Park.

Part V: Manuel Antonio and Environs

Part V explores Costa Rica's most popular ecotourism destination, the lovely Manuel Antonio National Park. It also covers the surrounding central Pacific coast, both north and south of Manuel Antonio, touching on the beach destinations of playas Jacó, Herradura, and Hermosa, as well as Dominical.

Part VI: Monteverde and Environs

Monteverde, with its misty cloud forests, and Arenal, with its active volcano, are Costa Rica's principal inland attractions. This part covers both of these major attractions, while also introducing you to the area surrounding Lake Arenal. You'll find ample information about nature hikes, rafting trips, volcano viewing, hot springs, and more in this rich region.

Part VII: Touring the Rest of Costa Rica

If you want to explore the farther flung and less visited — although no less spectacular or interesting — Costa Rican destinations Part VII is where to find information. I give you recommendations and planning advice for trips to the remote beach destinations of the southern Nicoya Peninsula, the lush rain forests of southern Costa Rica, and the country's unique Caribbean coast.

Part VIII: The Part of Tens

Every *For Dummies* book has a Part of Tens. These two fun and pithy chapters are a little gift to you. Chapter 22 dispels some common myths and misconceptions about Costa Rica. Chapter 23 provides a concise list of some of the top experiences, attractions, and activities to be had in this beautiful country.

Appendix: Quick Concierge

In the back of this book, I've included an appendix — your Quick Concierge — containing lots of handy information you may need when traveling in Costa Rica. This one-stop reference section includes important phone numbers and Web addresses, as well as the inside scoop on issues running from safety to water quality. Check out this appendix when searching for answers to lots of little questions that may come up as you plan or travel. You can find the Quick Concierge easily because it's printed on yellow paper.

Icons Used in This Book

Think of the following icons as signposts. I use them to highlight especially useful advice, to draw your attention to things you won't want to miss, and to introduce a variety of topics.

 Keep an eye out for the Bargain Alert icon as you seek out money-saving tips and/or great deals.

 The Best of the Best icon highlights the best the destination has to offer in all categories — hotels, restaurants, attractions, activities, shopping, and nightlife.

 Watch for the Heads Up icon to identify annoying or potentially dangerous situations such as tourist traps, unsafe neighborhoods, budgetary rip-offs, and other things to beware.

 Find out useful advice on things to do and ways to schedule your time when you see the Tip icon.

 Look to the Kid Friendly icon for attractions, hotels, restaurants, and activities that are particularly hospitable to children or people traveling with kids.

 This icon points out secret little finds or useful resources that are worth the extra bit of effort to get to or track down.

Where to Go from Here

A Costa Rican vacation can be many things to many people. Options range from bird-watching and rain-forest hiking to high-octane adventuring to simply settling into a chaise lounge on a quiet beach and sipping cool cocktails.

Don't think of choosing your Costa Rican destinations and solidifying the details as a burden or a bore. Let this book help make the process an exciting time of discovery and opportunity. Enjoy and savor the planning. And then have a great trip!

Part I

Introducing Costa Rica

"He said this was the first thing he wanted to do when he got to Costa Rica."

In this part . . .

So you want to begin finding out about Costa Rica? In this part, I provide all the basic information you need to start planning a perfect vacation particularly suited to your needs and interests.

Chapter 1 tells you briefly about the best places, experiences, and attractions in Costa Rica. Additional information and detailed descriptions can be found later on, but this is the place to come for a condensed listing of the highlights.

If you want some historical background, cultural insight, or local language tips, Chapter 2 offers that up, and more.

Chapter 3 describes the various regions and destinations to help you choose where to go. In addition, if you want to find out about the local weather patterns and seasons, and some interesting Costa Rican holidays, celebrations, and events, this chapter is for you.

Finally, Chapter 4 lays out several potential itineraries that you can either follow to the letter or use as a rough draft in designing your perfect trip to Costa Rica.

Chapter 1

Discovering the Best of Costa Rica

In This Chapter
- Scoping out Costa Rica's top accommodations
- Finding the finest restaurants
- Exploring the best beaches, adventures, and attractions

*F*or such a compact country, Costa Rica is a marvelous and multifaceted destination. You can visit rain forests, cloud forests, and active volcanoes. You can walk along miles of beautiful beaches on either the Pacific or the Caribbean coast. And, you can stay at luxurious large resorts or romantic little getaways.

Adventure hounds will have their fill choosing from an exciting array of activities, and those just looking for some rest and relaxation can grab a chaise lounge or hammock and a good book.

 This chapter is designed as an at-a-glance reference to the absolute "best of the best" that Costa Rica has to offer, which are listed in the order they appear in the book. These attractions are highlighted by — what else — a Best of the Best icon when they appear elsewhere in this book.

The Best High-End Hotels and Luxury Resorts

Not too long ago, finding anything to fit in this category was difficult. Now, it's a breeze. Costa Rica boasts quite a few top-notch luxury properties ranging from isolated and unique boutique hotels to large beach resorts. The following are the best of the best:

- **Costa Rica Marriott (San José):** The Marriott is hands down the best of the large resort and business-class hotels in the San José area. Everything is in great shape, the service is bend-over-backwards, the restaurants are excellent, and the hotel features all the facilities and amenities you could want, save a golf course. See Chapter 11.

✔ **Finca Rosa Blanca Country Inn (Heredia):** My favorite boutique hotel in the San José metropolitan area. If the cookie-cutter rooms of large hotels leave you cold, then the unique rooms of this artistic inn may be up your alley. Finca Rosa Blanca is set among the lush hillsides and coffee plantations of Heredia, just 20 minutes from San José. See Chapter 11.

✔ **Peace Lodge (north of Varablanca):** The rooms here abound in beautiful design touches, and the bathrooms in the deluxe units are the most spectacular in the country. Each room comes with at least one custom-tiled Jacuzzi on a private balcony. The hotel adjoins the popular La Paz Waterfall Gardens. See Chapter 11.

✔ **Arenas del Mar (Manuel Antonio):** This boutique resort combines beautiful views with easy beach access, a rare commodity in Manuel Antonio. With large and ample rooms, excellent service and amenities, a fabulous restaurant, and a beautiful little spa, this place has a lot to offer. See Chapter 13.

✔ **Four Seasons Resort (Papagayo Peninsula):** The Four Seasons is currently the only major resort to really address the ultra-high-end luxury market in Costa Rica. Brad Pitt and Angelina Jolie, Madonna, and Michael Jordan are just a few of the notable guests who have come here. A beautiful setting, wonderful installations, a world-class golf course, and stellar service make this the current king of the hill in the upscale market. See Chapter 13.

✔ **JW Marriott Guanacaste Resort & Spa (Hacienda Pinilla):** With beautiful rooms, ample facilities, top-notch service, and the largest pool in Central America, this new resort has quickly established itself as one of the top upscale properties in the country. The ocean is just steps away, and there are several other excellent beaches nearby. See Chapter 13.

✔ **Makanda by the Sea (Manuel Antonio):** The large and luxurious villas here are superbly decorated and set on a forested hillside with wonderful views out to the sea. The overall vibe here is intimate and romantic, and the service and food are excellent. See Chapter 15.

✔ **Villa Caletas (north of Jacó):** Spread out over a steep hillside, high above the Pacific Ocean, these large and luxurious individual villas have a Mediterranean feel. The "infinity pool" here was one of the first in Costa Rica and is still my favorite. Sitting in a lounge chair at the pool's edge, you'll swear that it joins the sea. See Chapter 16.

✔ **Tabacón Grand Spa Thermal Resort (Arenal volcano):** In addition to having the most lush and luxurious natural hot springs and adjacent spa, this resort offers up stylish rooms with excellent views and proximity to the active Arenal volcano. Service and food here are top-notch as well. See Chapter 18.

✔ **The Springs Resort & Spa (Arenal volcano):** This new resort features opulent rooms with extravagant bathrooms, a series of sculpted hot-spring pools, excellent restaurants, extensive facilities, and fabulous views. See Chapter 18.

✔ **Hotel Punta Islita (Nicoya Peninsula):** Perched on a high, flat bluff overlooking the Pacific Ocean, Punta Islita is very popular with honeymooners, and rightly so. The rooms are large and luxurious, the food is excellent, and the setting is stunning. If you venture beyond your room and the hotel's inviting hillside pool, there's a long, almost always deserted beach for you to explore, as well as a wealth of activities for the more adventurous. See Chapter 19.

✔ **Flor Blanca Resort (Playa Santa Teresa):** The individual villas at this boutique resort are some of the largest and most beautiful in the country. The service and food are outstanding, and the location is breathtaking, spread over a lushly planted hillside just steps off Playa Santa Teresa. See Chapter 19.

✔ **Tree House Lodge (Punta Uva):** A unique and beautifully designed collection of private houses offers one of the most creative and luxurious accommodations on the Caribbean coast. I like the namesake Tree House suite, where a live tree occupies a central part of the living area, although the Beach House suite is also quite spectacular. See Chapter 21.

The Best Accommodations Values

Not looking to spend a fortune? No problem. Costa Rica is chock-full of excellent hotel and lodging values. Get the most for your accommodations dollar by booking into one of these fine establishments:

✔ **Hotel Grano de Oro (San José):** San José boasts dozens of old homes that have been converted into hotels, but few offer the luxurious accommodations or professional service that can be found at the Grano de Oro — and all at a great price. See Chapter 11.

✔ **Hotel Le Bergerac (San José):** This classy little hotel has been pleasing diplomats, dignitaries, and other discerning travelers for years. Ask for one of the garden rooms, or get the old master bedroom with its small private balcony. See Chapter 11.

✔ **Hotel Aranjuez (San José):** True budget seekers should look no further when looking to crash in San José. Great location, clean rooms, ample common areas, and plenty of perks make this a perennially popular choice. See Chapter 11.

✔ **El Velero Hotel (Playa Hermosa):** Set right on the beach, this little hotel offers cozy, upbeat rooms at a great price. A small pool and excellent restaurant round out the offerings here. See Chapter 13.

✔ **Hotel Verde Mar (Manuel Antonio):** One of Manuel Antonio's few true beachfront hotels is also one of its best bargains. Rooms are large and attractive and, most important, just a short walk from the surf. See Chapter 15.

- **Hotel Fonda Vela (Monteverde):** Many of the cozy and contemporary rooms here have views of the Nicoya Gulf. The restaurant here is excellent, and this is one of the closest lodgings to the famed Monteverde Cloud Forest Preserve. See Chapter 17.

- **Amor de Mar (Montezuma):** The rooms here are simple, but they're also clean, comfortable, and well maintained. And the setting is superb. A long, grassy lawn leads down to the rocky coast, where you'll find a swimming-pool-size tide pool carved into a coral rock outcropping. See Chapter 19.

- **Cabinas Sol y Mar (Playa Zancudo):** These beachfront rooms are a real bargain. Cozy and well-equipped, they're set just steps from the surf, surrounded by lush gardens and shady palm trees. The bar and restaurant here are excellent, lively, and justifiably popular. See Chapter 20.

- **Casa Verde Lodge (Puerto Viejo):** Lush gardens, tidy rooms, amiable hosts, and great prices make this my favorite hotel in the tiny town of Puerto Viejo. The refreshing pool and close proximity to everything are nice perks as well. See Chapter 21.

- **La Costa de Papito (Playa Cocles):** This place features large and lovely independent and duplex wooden bungalows spread around lush grounds. Just 90m (295 ft.) or so away, however, are the warm waves of the Caribbean Sea. See Chapter 21.

The Best Ecolodges

Costa Rica is a major ecotourism destination, and you'll find a wealth of wonderfully run ecolodges and nature resorts. Some of them, including several listed here, make a strong case for being listed among the top luxury hotels in the country:

- **Monteverde Lodge (Monteverde):** Run by the folks at Costa Rica Expeditions, this was one of the first ecolodges to open in Monteverde, and it remains one of the best. Beyond the comfortable accommodations and great food, the excellent guides are the greatest asset here. See Chapter 17.

- **Arenal Observatory Lodge (La Fortuna):** Originally a rustic research facility, this lodge has upgraded quite a bit over the years and now features comfortable rooms with impressive views of the Arenal volcano. There are also excellent trails to nearby lava flows and a beautiful waterfall. Toucans frequent the trees near the lodge, and howler monkeys provide the wake-up calls. See Chapter 18.

- **La Paloma Lodge (Drake Bay):** If your idea of the perfect nature lodge is one where your front porch provides some prime-time viewing of flora and fauna, this place is for you. If you decide to leave the comfort of your porch, the Osa Peninsula's lowland rain forests are just outside your door. See Chapter 20.

✔ **Bosque del Cabo Rainforest Lodge (Osa Peninsula):** Large and comfortable private cabins perched on the edge of a cliff overlooking the Pacific Ocean and surrounded by lush rain forest make this one of my favorite spots in the country. There's plenty to do, and there are always great guides here. See Chapter 20.

✔ **Lapa Rios (Osa Peninsula):** Costa Rica's first upscale ecolodge has aged well. The duplex bungalow rooms all have spectacular views and are set into a lush forest. A number of tours are available for guests, and the guides are often local residents who are intimately familiar with the environment. See Chapter 20.

✔ **Playa Nicuesa Rainforest Lodge (Golfo Dulce):** This lodge is by far the best option on the Golfo Dulce. Set in deep forest, the individual bungalows here are a beguiling blend of rusticity and luxury. See Chapter 20.

✔ **Selva Bananito Lodge (inland from the Caribbean coast):** This is one of the few lodges providing direct access to the southern Caribbean lowland rain forests. There's no electricity here, but that doesn't mean it's not plush. Hike along a riverbed, ride horses through the rain forest, climb 30m (100 ft.) up a ceiba tree, or rappel down a jungle waterfall. See Chapter 21.

✔ **Tortuga Lodge (Tortuguero):** Run by pioneering ecotourism operator Costa Rica Expeditions, this is the most comfortable and best equipped lodge in the Tortuguero area. The hotel has lush grounds, a beautiful pool, and excellent naturalist guides. See Chapter 21.

The Best Restaurants

Although Costa Rica is not known for its fine food, you'll have no trouble dining well. The following restaurants run the gamut in terms of cuisine and ambience, from local fresh seafood served on plastic lawn chairs set in the sand to top-notch Pacific Rim fusion served in an elegant and refined setting. If your travels take you near any of these restaurants, don't pass up the chance for a meal:

✔ **Park Café (San José):** The creative cooking of a 2-star Michelin chef combine with elegant décor and a romantic ambience in this courtyard treasure. The menu changes regularly, but never disappoints. See Chapter 11.

✔ **Grano de Oro Restaurant (San José):** This elegant little hotel has a similarly elegant restaurant serving delicious Continental dishes and decadent desserts. The open-air seating in the lushly planted central courtyard is delightful, especially for lunch. See Chapter 11.

✔ **Bacchus (Santa Ana):** Set in a wonderfully restored and updated ancient adobe home, this restaurant serves up the best Italian fare in the metropolitan area. The setting is elegant and the service is refined. See Chapter 11.

✔ **Dragonfly Bar & Grill (Tamarindo):** It's almost always packed at this popular Tamarindo eatery. Southwestern American and Pacific Rim fusion cuisines are the primary culinary influences here. Portions are massive, service excellent, and the prices fair. See Chapter 13.

✔ **Lola's (Playa Avellanas):** Fresh fruit juices, flash-grilled tuna, excellent salads, crisp Belgian fries, and more are served up at this delightful beachfront restaurant. Hammocks are hung from coconut trees, and the waves are just steps away. See Chapter 13.

✔ **Ginger (Playa Hermosa):** Serving an eclectic mix of traditional and Pan-Asian-influenced tapas, this sophisticated little joint is taking this part of Guanacaste by storm. Ginger even has a list of creative cocktails to match the inventive dishes. See Chapter 13.

✔ **Sunspot Bar & Grill (Manuel Antonio):** The menu changes regularly at this elegant restaurant housed under canvas tents poolside at one of Manuel Antonio's top hotels. There are precious few tables here, so be sure to reserve in advance. See Chapter 15.

✔ **El Patio Bistro Latino (Quepos):** This casual but elegant little place is a welcome oasis in the somewhat seedy city of Quepos. The chef's creative concoctions take full advantage of fresh local ingredients. See Chapter 15.

✔ **Sophia (Monteverde):** This place serves excellent Latin fusion fare in an intimate setting about halfway along the rough dirt road between Santa Elena and the Monteverde Cloud Forest Preserve. See Chapter 17.

✔ **Nectar (at Flor Blanca Resort, Santa Teresa):** Guanacaste's best boutique resort also has one of its best restaurants. The menu changes nightly but always has a heavy Pan-Asian-fusion flavor to it. The setting is romantic and subdued, in open-air space just steps from the sand. See Chapter 19.

✔ **Playa de los Artistas (Montezuma):** Whether you choose a seat on a tatami mat on the sand or one of their more traditional tables, this place is the perfect blend of refined cuisine and beachside funkiness. Fresh grilled seafood is the specialty here, and it's done to perfection. See Chapter 19.

✔ **La Pecora Nera (Puerto Viejo):** I'm not sure that a tiny surfer town on the remote Caribbean coast deserves such fine Italian food, but it's got it. Your best bet here is to allow yourself to be taken on a culinary roller-coaster ride with a mixed feast of the chef's nightly specials and suggestions. See Chapter 21.

The Best Beaches

With more than 1,200km (750 miles) of shoreline on its Pacific and Caribbean coasts, Costa Rica offers beachgoers an embarrassment of riches:

- ✔ **Playa Tamarindo:** Although some people may find Tamarindo overdeveloped, crowded, and chaotic, it's still one of Costa Rica's best beach destinations. Tamarindo has ample lodgings to suit every budget, as well as excellent restaurants at almost every turn. The beach here is long and broad, with sections calm enough for swimmers and others just right for surfers. Located about midway along the beaches of Guanacaste province, Tamarindo also has one of the liveliest nightlife scenes on this coast. See Chapters 13 and 14.

- ✔ **Playa Nacascolo:** This narrow band of soft white sand is a rare treasure on this coast, which is typified by coarser dark-sand beaches. Although it's within the grounds of the massive Four Seasons Resort, it's public property and open to all. See Chapter 14.

- ✔ **Playa Manuel Antonio:** Costa Rica's original rain forest–meets–beach destination retains its charms despite burgeoning crowds and mushrooming hotels. The beaches inside the national park are idyllic, and the views from the hills outside the park are enchanting. This is one of the few remaining habitats for the endangered squirrel monkey. See Chapter 15.

- ✔ **Playa Montezuma:** This little beach town at the southern tip of the Nicoya Peninsula has weathered fame and infamy and yet retains a funky sense of individuality. The nearby waterfalls are what set it apart from the competition, but the beach stretches for miles, with plenty of isolated spots to plop down your towel or mat. Also nearby are the Cabo Blanco and Curu wildlife preserves. See Chapter 19.

- ✔ **Malpaís:** If you're looking to visit Costa Rica's newest hot spot before the throngs discover it, head out to Malpaís. Here you'll find miles of nearly deserted beaches, great surf, and just a smattering of lodges, surf camps, and simple *cabinas.* If Malpaís is too crowded for you, head farther on down the road to Santa Teresa, Playa Hermosa, or Manzanillo. See Chapter 19.

- ✔ **Punta Uva and Manzanillo:** Below Puerto Viejo, the beaches of Costa Rica's eastern coast take on true Caribbean splendor, with turquoise waters, coral reefs, and palm-lined stretches of nearly deserted white-sand beach. Punta Uva and Manzanillo are the two most sparkling gems of this coastline. Tall coconut palms line the shore, providing shady respite for those who like to spend a full day on the sand, and the water is usually quite calm and good for swimming. See Chapter 21.

The Best Adventures and Activities

Costa Rica is a top-notch destination for adventure travel. The options and activities are many. Here are some of the best activities and adventures awaiting you:

✔ **Rafting the Pacuare River (near Turrialba):** This class III and IV river passes through primary and secondary forests and a beautiful steep gorge that, sadly, may be dammed soon. Get there quick! **Ríos Tropicales** can take you on this river. See Chapter 12.

✔ **Surfing Guanacaste Province:** This northwestern province has dozens of respectable beach and reef breaks, from Witch's Rock up near the Nicaraguan border to Playa Nosara more than 100km (62 miles) away. In addition to these two prime spots, try a turn at **Playa Grande** and **playas Negra** and **Avellanas.** Or, find your own secret spot. Rent a 4×4 with a roof rack, pile on the boards, and explore. If you want to learn, most of the popular surf beaches up here have surf schools. See Chapter 14.

✔ **Battling a billfish off the Pacific coast:** Billfish are plentiful all along Costa Rica's Pacific coast, and boats operate from most coastal beach and port towns. Go to **Quepos** (just outside Manuel Antonio) for the best fish scene, or head down to **Drake Bay,** the **Osa Peninsula,** or **Golfo Dulce,** if you want some isolation. See Chapters 15 and 20.

✔ **Swinging through the treetops on a canopy tour:** This unique adventure is becoming quite the rage. In most cases, after a strenuous climb using ascenders, you strap on a harness and zip from treetop to treetop while dangling from a cable. There are canopy tours all around Costa Rica. Check the various destination chapters to find a canopy tour operation near you.

✔ **Mountain-biking the back roads of Costa Rica:** The lack of paved roads that most folks bemoan is a huge boon for mountain bikers. There are endless back roads and cattle paths to explore. Tours of differing lengths and all difficulty levels are available. The area around Lake Arenal and the Arenal volcano is a perfect place to ride some fat-track bikes. Contact **Bike Arenal.** See Chapter 18.

✔ **Trying the sport of canyoning:** A new and nonstandardized adventure sport, canyoning usually involves hiking along and through the rivers and creeks of steep mountain canyons, with periodic breaks to rappel down the face of a waterfall, jump off a rock into a jungle pool, or float down a small rapid. **Pure Trek Canyoning** and **Desafío Expeditions** in La Fortuna, and **Psycho Tours** near Puerto Jiménez, are the prime operators. See Chapters 18 and 20.

✔ **Kayaking around the Golfo Dulce:** Slipping through the waters of the Golfo Dulce by kayak gets you intimately in touch with the raw beauty of this underdeveloped region. In addition to the open gulf waters where dolphins often frolic, **Escondido Trex** takes folks on trips into mangrove swamps and into river estuaries. See Chapter 20.

The Best Family Spots

Costa Rica's rugged reputation should not discourage family travel. Here are a few of the ample attractions and activities available to please tourists of all ages, as well as some of the hotels, resorts, and destinations perfectly suited to family travel:

- ✔ **La Paz Waterfall Gardens:** This multifaceted attraction features paths and suspended walkways alongside a series of impressive jungle waterfalls. Kids love the variety of natural attractions, from the immense butterfly garden to the hummingbird garden. The rooms at the **Peace Lodge** here are some of the best in the country. See Chapter 12.

- ✔ **Playa Tamarindo:** This lively surf town has a bit of something for everyone. This is a great spot for teens to learn how to surf or boogie-board, and there are a host of tours and activities to please the entire family. **Hotel Capitán Suizo** has an excellent location on a calm section of beach, spacious rooms, and a great pool for kids and adults alike. See Chapters 13 and 14.

- ✔ **Manuel Antonio:** Manuel Antonio has a little bit of everything: miles of gorgeous beaches, tons of wildlife (with monkey sightings almost guaranteed), and plenty of active tour options. Numerous lodging options are available, but **Hotel Sí Como No** with its large suites, two pools, water slide, and nightly movies, is probably your best bet. See Chapter 15.

- ✔ **Playa Hermosa:** The broad stretch of sand and protected waters of this Pacific beach make it a family favorite. However, just because the waters are calm doesn't mean it's boring here. I recommend staying at **Hotel Playa Hermosa Bosque del Mar** and checking in at **Aqua Sport,** where you can rent sea kayaks, sailboards, paddleboats, beach umbrellas, and bicycles. See Chapter 16.

- ✔ **Monteverde:** Monteverde not only boasts the country's most famous cloud forest but also sports a wide variety of related attractions and activities. After hiking through the reserve, you should be able to keep most kids happy and occupied riding horses; squirming at the local serpentarium; or visiting the butterfly farm, frog pond, and hummingbird gallery. More adventurous families can take one of the local zip-line canopy tours. See Chapter 17.

Chapter 2

Digging Deeper into Costa Rica

In This Chapter

▶ Discovering Costa Rica's past

▶ Experiencing Costa Rican cuisine and the dining scene

▶ Finding additional background materials — in print and on film

*T*his chapter gives you some handy background information and a glimpse into *Tico* (Costa Rican) culture, cuisine, and idiomatic idiosyncrasies, so you can take better advantage of your time in this beautiful country. I also recommend a list of excellent books, if you want to delve deeper into Costa Rica.

History 101: The Main Events

Costa Rica enjoyed thousands of years of human occupation before it was "discovered" by Christopher Columbus in 1502. Its history includes a civil war, the abolition of its standing army, and the building of a banana exporting empire. The country's stability, adherence to the democratic process, and the staunch position of neutrality are a source of great pride to Costa Ricans, who like to think of their country as the "Switzerland of Central America."

The early years

Little is known of Costa Rica's history before its colonization by Spanish settlers. The pre-Columbian Indians who made their home in this region of Central America never developed the large cities or advanced culture that flowered to the north and south. Still, ancient artifacts demonstrating a strong sense of aesthetics have been found at excavations around the country, primarily in the northwest. Beautiful gold and jade jewelry, intricately carved grinding stones, and artistically painted terra-cotta objects point to a small but highly skilled population.

Colonizing Costa Rica

On his fourth and final voyage to the New World, in 1502, Christopher Columbus anchored just offshore from present-day Limón. Whether he actually gave the country its name is open to discussion, but it wasn't long before the moniker took hold.

The early Spanish settlers found that, unlike the Indians farther north, the native population of Costa Rica was unwilling to submit to slavery. Despite their small numbers, scattered villages, and tribal differences, they fought back against the Spanish until they were overcome by superior firepower and European diseases. When the fighting was finished, however, very few Indians were left for the settlers to force into servitude. The few settlers who braved this outpost were often forced to till their own lands, a situation unheard of in other parts of Central America. Costa Rica was nearly forgotten, as the Spanish crown looked elsewhere for riches to plunder and souls to convert.

It didn't take long for Costa Rica's few Spanish settlers to head for the hills, where they found rich volcanic soil and a climate that was less oppressive than in the lowlands. Cartago, the colony's first capital, was founded in 1563, but it was not until the 1700s that additional cities were established in this agriculturally rich region. In the late 18th century, the first coffee plants were introduced. These plants thrived in the highlands, and Costa Rica had its first and foremost cash crop.

Staking out independence

In 1821, Spain granted independence to its colonies in Central America. Costa Rica joined with its neighbors to form the Central American Federation, but in 1838, it withdrew to form a new nation and pursue its own interests. By the mid-1800s, coffee was the country's main export. Free land was given to anyone willing to plant coffee on it, and plantation owners soon grew wealthy and powerful, creating Costa Rica's first elite class. Coffee plantation owners were powerful enough to elect their own representatives to the presidency.

This period was a stormy one in Costa Rican history. In 1856, the country was invaded by William Walker, an ambitious Tennessee mercenary who, with the backing of U.S. President James Buchanan and prominent early industrialists, was attempting to fulfill his grandiose dreams of presiding over a slave state in Central America. (Before his invasion of Costa Rica, he had invaded Nicaragua and Baja California.) The people of Costa Rica, led by their own president, Juan Rafael Mora, rose up against Walker and chased him back to Nicaragua. In 1860, Walker was defeated and captured for the last time in Honduras, where he was promptly executed.

In the 1870s, Costa Rica began construction of a railway from San José to the Caribbean coast, in order to facilitate the transport of coffee to

European markets. It took nearly 20 years and cost more than 4,000 workers their lives constructing the railway. Partway through the project, as funds were dwindling, the second chief engineer, Minor Keith, proposed an idea that not only enhanced his fortunes but also changed the course of Central American history. Banana plantations would be developed along the railway right of way (land on either side of the tracks). The export of this crop would help to finance the railway, and, in exchange, Keith would get a 99-year lease on the land with a 20-year tax deferment. The Costa Rican government gave its consent, and, in 1878, the first bananas were shipped from the country. In 1899, Keith and a partner formed the United Fruit Company, a business that eventually became the largest landholder in Central America and was the cause of political disputes and wars throughout the region.

Growing democracy in Central America

In 1889, Costa Rica held what is considered the first free election in Central American history. The opposition candidate won the election, and the control of the government passed from the hands of one political party to those of another without bloodshed or hostilities. This pattern of peaceful democracy continued for the next 60 years.

In 1948, however, Rafael Angel Calderón, who had served as the country's president from 1940 to 1944, refused to concede the country's leadership to the rightfully elected president, Otillio Ulate. Civil war ensued. Calderón was defeated by forces led by José "Pepe" Figueres. Following the civil war, a new constitution was drafted; among other changes, it abolished Costa Rica's army, so that such a revolution could never happen again.

In 1994, history seemed to repeat itself — peacefully this time — when José María Figueres took the reins of government from the son of his father's adversary, Rafael Angel Calderón.

In 2001, the Partido Acción Ciudadana (Citizens' Action Party, or PAC) forced the presidential elections into a second round, opening a crack in a two-party system that had become seemingly entrenched for good.

In 2004, major corruption scandals landed two former presidents, Miguel Angel Rodriguez and Rafael Angel Calderón, in jail; another, José Maria Figueres, remains abroad, avoiding calls for his return to face corruption allegations. These former presidents, as well as a long list of other high-level government employees and deputies, are implicated in various financial scandals and bribery cases. However, justice moves slowly in Costa Rica, and at press time only Calderón had been brought to trial.

In 2006, former president Oscar Arias Sánchez, who is a Nobel Peace Prize laureate and was president during the mid-1980s, was reelected. The election was historic on two fronts. First, Arias needed to amend national law prohibiting reelection — it still prohibits consecutive terms. But, perhaps more important, runner-up Otton Solis's upstart PAC, which placed second by an extremely slim margin, forever changed a seemingly entrenched two-party system, which had shared governance of Costa Rica for decades.

The most dramatic event during the early years of Arias's presidency was the October 2007 national referendum on whether to allow approval of a free trade agreement between Costa Rica and the United States and other Central American nations. That approval was passed by a very slim margin.

The global economic crisis of 2008 was slow to hit Costa Rica. Because credit here has historically been so tight, there was no major mortgage or banking crisis in the country. Still, early anecdotal reports show tourism down substantially in 2009, and it's unclear how profound an impact on the economy this and other global factors will have.

Building Blocks: Local Architecture

Costa Rica lacks the grand cities and distinctive Spanish-influenced architecture of other former Spanish colonial cities. You can still find some old examples of adobe buildings with high doorways and large windows, all topped with red tile roofs, especially in Liberia, Cartago, and some of the country's older, smaller cities.

Modern Costa Rica is being overrun with strip malls and commercial centers and nondescript housing built of concrete block and other modern materials. Perhaps the most noticeable and striking architectural feature you'll find almost universally across the country is the use of metal grating over all exterior windows and doors. Unfortunately, though occasionally ornate, this metal grating is a direct response to rampant petty crime and theft.

A Taste of Costa Rica: Local Cuisine

Simply put, Costa Rican cuisine is unspectacular. Rice and beans are standard Tico fare and are often served at all three meals a day. Mixed together, they're called *gallo pinto.* Either as *gallo pinto,* or served separately, rice and beans are an integral part of most Costa Rican meals.

If you're looking for typical (and cheap) eats, you'll find them in little restaurants known as *sodas,* which are the equivalent of diners in the United States. Your best bet at a *soda* is a *casado* (which translates as "married" and is the name for the local version of a blue-plate special). A *casado* usually consists of cabbage-and-tomato salad; fried plantains; and a chicken, fish, or meat dish of some sort. A *casado* also often comes with a hard-boiled egg and/or a slab of fresh cheese.

Costa Rica has two coasts, and, as you'd expect, plenty of seafood is available everywhere in the country. *Corvina* (sea bass) is the most commonly served fish. You'll also come across *pargo* (red snapper), *dorado* (mahimahi), and *atún* (tuna) on most menus, especially along the coasts. Although Costa Rica is a major exporter of shrimp and lobster, both are less common and more expensive than you may expect.

Corvina is one of my least favorite fish options. Costa Rican corvina is a distant cousin to the cold-water Chilean and other sea basses served in restaurants across the United States and Europe. In many cheaper restaurants, particularly in San José, shark meat is sometimes even sold as corvina. I highly recommend sticking with red snapper, mahimahi, and tuna, whenever possible.

Costa Rica is a major producer and exporter of beef. Unfortunately, quantity doesn't mean quality. Unless you go to one of the better restaurants or steakhouses, you'll probably be served rather tough steaks, cut rather thin.

Still, all is not lost. With an increase in international tourism, not to mention the need to please more sophisticated palates, some local chefs have begun to create a "nouvelle Costa Rican cuisine," updating time-worn recipes and using traditional ingredients in creative ways. At many of the better hotels and local restaurants, you'll find chefs doing interesting and tasty things with the local fruits and vegetables and fresh seafood, meats, and poultry.

You can also get good international cuisine at a host of Italian, Peruvian, Mexican, Pan-Asian, and other restaurants across the country.

Getting the most out of eating in Costa Rica: Bocas and fresh fruit

Appetizers, known as *bocas,* are served with drinks in most bars. Often the *bocas* are free, but even if they aren't, they're very inexpensive. Popular *bocas* include *gallos* (tortillas piled with meat, chicken, cheese, or beans), *ceviche* (a marinated seafood salad), *tamales* (stuffed cornmeal patties wrapped and steamed inside banana leaves), *patacones* (fried green plantain chips), and fried yuca. Tacos, tamales, and *empanadas* (turnovers) also are quite common. Making an evening and a full meal out of a long list of *bocas* is easy and enjoyable.

Costa Rica has a wealth of delicious tropical fruits. The most common are mangoes (the season begins in May), papayas, pineapples, melons, and bananas. Other fruits include the *marañón,* which is the fruit of the cashew tree and has orange or yellow glossy skin; the *granadilla,* or *maracuyá* (passion fruit); the *mamón chino,* which Asian travelers will immediately recognize as the rambutan; and the *carambola* (star fruit).

All these fruits are readily available in markets across the country and are sold at roadside stands on most major highways and thoroughfares.

Fresh fruits are also served in drinks made in a blender *en agua* (with water) or *con leche* (with milk). Named *frescos, refrescos,* or *jugos naturales,* these drinks are my favorites in Costa Rica. Among the more common fruits used are mangoes, papayas, blackberries *(mora),* and pineapples *(piña)*; you'll also come across passion fruit *(maracuyá)* and star fruit juices.

Enjoying a cup of joe

If you're a coffee drinker, you may be surprisingly disappointed in Costa Rica. Most of the best coffee has traditionally been saved for export, and Ticos tend to prefer their coffee weak and sugary. The better hotels and restaurants cater to gringo and European tastes and serve up superior blends.

If you want black coffee, ask for *café negro;* if you want it with milk, order *café con leche.* Most restaurants serve the milk warmed and in a separate container. If you want to ensure your milk comes separately, ask for *con leche aparte.*

If you want to try something different for your morning beverage, ask for *agua dulce,* a warm drink made from melted sugar cane and served with milk or lemon, or straight.

A Word to the Wise: The Local Language

Spanish is the official language of Costa Rica. Most hotel and restaurant staff have some functional knowledge of English, and all guides and higher-level tourism workers speak respectable English.

Costa Rican Spanish is neither the easiest nor the most difficult dialect to understand. Costa Ricans speak at a relatively relaxed speed and tend to enunciate clearly, without dropping too many final consonants. The *y* and *ll* sounds are very subtly pronounced — almost inaudible. Perhaps the most defining idiosyncrasy of Costa Rican Spanish is the way Ticos have of overemphasizing — almost chewing — their *r*'s.

For a glossary of Costa Rican terms, see the Cheat Sheet in the front of this book, or check out *Spanish For Dummies,* by Susana Wald (Wiley Publishing).

Throughout the book you'll see the term *Tico.* This is the common local slang for a Costa Rican and, by inference, all things Costa Rican. The name comes from the Costa Rican habit of adding a diminutive suffix to the end of many words and phrases. *Poquito* becomes *poquitico. Chiquito* becomes *chiquitico.* A Costa Rican woman is a *Tica.* Never use the term *Tican,* though; it's just wrong.

Background Check: Recommended Books and Movies

If you're looking to find out more on Costa Rica, a wealth of excellent resources is available. In this section, I list some of my favorite books, as well as a couple of films you should check out to round out your understanding of Costa Rica.

Costa Rica on paper

A couple of the books mentioned in this section may be difficult to track down in U.S. bookstores, but you'll find them all in abundance in Costa Rica. If you're in San José, a good place to peruse is **Seventh Street Books,** on Calle 7 between avenidas 1 and Central (☎ **2256-8251**).

For a readable look into Costa Rican society, check out *The Ticos: Culture and Social Change,* by Mavis Hiltunen Biesanz, Richard Biesanz, and Karen Zubris Biesanz (Lynne Rienner Publishers), an examination of the country's politics and culture, by the authors of the out-of-print *The Costa Ricans.*

Another good choice is *The Costa Rica Reader: History, Culture, Politics,* a broad selection of stories, essays, and excerpts edited by Steven Palmer and Iván Molina (Duke University Press).

To find out more about the life and culture of Costa Rica's Talamanca coast, an area populated by Afro-Caribbean people whose forebears emigrated from Caribbean islands in the early 19th century, pick up a copy of *What Happen: A Folk-History of Costa Rica's Talamanca Coast,* by Paula Palmer (Zona Tropical).

If you're looking for literature, *Costa Rica: A Traveler's Literary Companion,* edited by Barbara Ras, with a foreword by Oscar Arias (Whereabouts Press), is a collection of short stories by Costa Rican writers, organized by country regions. If you're lucky, you may find and pick up a copy of *Stories of Tatamundo,* by Fabian Dobles (University of Costa Rica Press); this collection of short stories is based on the character Tata Mundo, a rural peasant, who has come to embody and represent much of Costa Rica's national identity, or at least the idealized version of that identity — simple, kind, open, joyful, and wise.

Young adults will enjoy Kristin Joy Pratt's *A Walk in the Rainforest* (Dawn Publications), while younger children will like the beautifully illustrated *The Forest in the Clouds,* by Sneed B. Collard III and illustrated by Michael Rothman (Charlesbridge Publishing), and *The Umbrella* by Jan Brett (Putnam Juvenile).

Pachanga Kids (www.pachangakids.com) has published several illustrated bilingual children's books with delightful illustrations by Ruth Angulo, including *Mar Azucarada/Sugar Sea,* by Roberto Boccanera, and *El Coyote y la Luciernaga/The Coyote and the Firefly,* by Yazmin Ross, which (full disclosure) I translated, and which includes a musical CD that features your humble author's singing.

A host of field guides are available for wildlife enthusiasts. Perhaps, the best all-around option is *Costa Rica: Traveller's Wildlife Guides,* by Les Beletsky (Interlink Books). Most ecolodges have a copy or two of one of the major bird books. Still, avid bird-watchers will want to pick up a copy of *A Guide to the Birds of Costa Rica,* by F. Gary Stiles and Alexander Skutch (Cornell University Press), or the more recent *Birds of Costa Rica,* by Richard Garrigues and Robert Dean (Cornell University Press).

I think that everyone coming to Costa Rica should read *Tropical Nature: Life and Death in the Rain Forests of Central and South America,* by Adrian Forsyth and Ken Miyata, with a foreword by Dr. Thomas Lovejoy (Touchstone Books). My all-time favorite book on tropical biology, this is a wonderfully written and lively collection of tales and adventures by two Neotropical biologists who spent quite some time in the forests of Costa Rica.

Costa Rica on film

Be forewarned: Even though it is set in Costa Rica, *Jurassic Park* was not filmed here. For a glimpse of Costa Rica on film, you can check out Ridley Scott's *1492,* which was filmed here but is set in Hispaniola.

For films in which Costa Rica plays a more prominent role, you can look for *The Blue Butterfly,* starring William Hurt, or either of the small independent films *Tropix* or *Caribe,* both of which were written, set, and shot in the country. The former is in English, while the latter is in Spanish.

Chapter 3

Deciding Where and When to Go

In This Chapter

▶ Figuring out where to go
▶ Decoding the secrets of the travel seasons and climate
▶ Zeroing in on special events you may want to catch

Although not an especially large country, Costa Rica offers a wealth of distinct destinations. Understanding a bit about the climate, as well as the geography, will help you choose where and when to go and how much to try to fit into your time here. In addition to giving you the lowdown on Costa Rican life during the distinct wet and dry seasons (which coincide nearly exactly with high and low tourism seasons) and a description of the different regions and the various attractions to be found around the country, this chapter also includes a calendar of events if you'd like to plan your visit around a particular activity.

Going Everywhere You Want to Be

Visitors to Costa Rica come for a variety of reasons. Some come to just crash on a beautiful beach and unwind, others want to experience the wonders of the tropical rain forests and cloud forests, and some come to partake in an adventure or two. Combining one or more of these options into a perfect and personalized vacation is easy.

But first you'll want to know a little something about the country's geography and what each destination has to offer.

Seeking the center: San José and the Central Valley

Unless you're flying in and out of Liberia, San José will serve as a default hub or transfer point. In many ways and for most visitors, San José is little more than a rough-and-tumble, overcrowded, Central American metropolis. The downtown area is a congested mess — for pedestrians and drivers alike. Sidewalks are poorly maintained and claustrophobic, and street crime is a problem. Most visitors quickly seek the sanctuary of their hotel rooms and the first chance to escape the city.

Still, San José is one of the most cosmopolitan cities in Central America, with several decent museums, some very good restaurants, and a handful of excellent hotel options.

San José also makes a great base for a variety of day trips and excursions. Within an hour or two, you can climb a volcano, go white-water rafting, hike through a cloud forest, and stroll through a butterfly garden — among many, many other activities.

San José sits in the center of the *Valle Central* (Central Valley). The climate is mild and springlike year-round, and this is Costa Rica's primary agricultural region, with coffee farms making up the majority of landholdings. However, the Central Valley is also densely populated, containing three of the country's largest cities: San José, Alajuela, and Heredia.

The rolling green hills and peaks that form the rim of this valley rise to heights between 900m and 1,200m (2,952–3,936 ft.) above sea level. Several of these are volcanoes, including Poás and Irazú, which are both active.

Going for gold in Guanacaste

Guanacaste province occupies the northwestern corner of Costa Rica. It is home to many of the country's sunniest and most popular beaches and has earned its reputation as Costa Rica's Gold Coast.

With about 165cm (65 in.) of rain a year, this region is by far the driest in the country and has been likened to west Texas, with much better beaches and more monkeys. Guanacaste province borders Nicaragua and is named after the shady trees that still shelter the herds of cattle that roam the dusty savanna here. In addition to the beaches and cattle ranches, Guanacaste boasts several volcanoes and one of the last remnants of tropical dry forest left in Central America.

Guanacaste is the only place in Costa Rica where you'll find several large-scale resort hotels. However, you'll also find scores of excellent smaller beach resorts and hotels, and I list the best of each category in the chapters that follow. Guanacaste currently boasts four championship golf courses, and more are allegedly in the works.

Guanacaste also has the country's only other international airport, aside from San José. The number of direct flights and charters arriving here increases every year. If you want to spend your entire vacation in this area, be sure to book a direct flight into and out of Liberia.

Enjoying magnificent Manuel Antonio

Manuel Antonio is the name of a coastal national park, as well as the resort area that surrounds it. Many first-time visitors to Costa Rica plan their vacation around a visit here. The hills just outside the national park are covered in thick rain forest. The whole thing seems to gently tumble down to the sea. The views from these hills are spectacular, and the beaches are beautiful.

There's no real town of Manuel Antonio. The closest thing is the small fishing and port city of Quepos. Between Quepos and the national park entrance runs a 7km (4⅓-mile) stretch of narrow road that winds through the forested green hills here. Along this road, and in Quepos, you'll find all the area's hotels, restaurants, and shops.

However, Manuel Antonio's popularity has brought with it more crowds and a growing sense of overdevelopment. On weekends, the beaches are filled with people, and the dance club near the park entrance blares its music until early morning.

Living the luxe life on the central Pacific coast

Costa Rica's central Pacific coast lies relatively close to San José and is, for the most part, less developed than the northern province of Guanacaste. The beaches here are long, wide, and often nearly deserted. Most are backed by densely forested hills and mountains.

Although Manuel Antonio is the crown jewel of Costa Rica's central Pacific coast, the nearby beaches to the north and south are beginning to come into their own.

To the north of Manuel Antonio, the beach towns of Jacó and Playa Herradura are two of the closest to San José. Jacó is a bustling surf town popular with itinerant surfers, foreign snowbirds, and young Ticos and Costa Rican families looking for a close and inexpensive getaway.

Playa Herradura is home to a large and luxurious Marriott resort, featuring the area's only 18-hole golf course. On the hills above Playa Herradura sits Villa Caletas, one of the country's top boutique hotels.

Meanwhile, toward the southern end of this coast lies the funky little surfer town of Dominical, which is the gateway to Ballena National Marine Park and several barely discovered beautiful beaches.

Visiting the cloud forests of Monteverde

Monteverde sits high on the mountainous spine that runs down the center of Costa Rica. *Monteverde* translates as "green mountain," and this is an area of lush and luxurious rain and cloud forests.

Cloud forests are a unique phenomenon. The mountaintops and forests of Monteverde are blanketed almost daily in dense clouds. For reasons that I explain in more detail in Chapter 17, this unique climatic phenomenon forms an ecosystem that is incredibly rich in biodiversity. Within this small area are more than 2,500 species of plants, including 400 types of orchids, 400 species of birds (including the spectacular Resplendent Quetzal), and 100 different species of mammals.

The tiny villages of Santa Elena and Monteverde are gateways to the Monteverde Cloud Forest Reserve. You won't find any large resorts in Santa Elena or Monteverde. What you will find here are scores of small mountain lodges and ecolodges that run the gamut from decidedly rustic to nearly luxurious.

In addition to hiking and visiting the cloud forest, a host of activities are offered in the area, including horseback riding, canopy tours, ATV outings, and canyoning.

Watching the lava flow from Arenal volcano

Rising to a near-perfect cone, Arenal volcano is Costa Rica's most consistently active and pyrotechnically impressive volcano. Volcano viewing is the major attraction and activity here, although there's plenty more to do.

La Fortuna is a small rural town set at the foot of the volcano. La Fortuna has several hotels and is the base for most of the area's tour and adventure companies. From here, a road skirts along the edge of the base of the volcano heading toward Lake Arenal. You'll find the best hotels and restaurants along this stretch of road.

Lake Arenal sits below the volcano and is the country's largest body of fresh water. It's a great spot for fishing and boating. During the winter months, it's also a world-class and world-renowned windsurfing destination.

Also near the foot of the volcano are several beautiful and soothing hot springs, as well as the impressive La Fortuna waterfall. All around the lake and volcano are large expanses of rain forest and cloud forest, with ample opportunities for myriad tours and activities.

Because they're both located in the north-central part of the country, combining a couple of days each at Monteverde and Arenal is easy and common.

Seeking solitude on the Nicoya Peninsula

South of Guanacaste lies the Nicoya Peninsula. Although this area is similar in terms of geography and climate, and has nearly as many beautiful beaches, it's much less developed and populated.

This is a great place to come for some solitude and a true sense of getting away from it all. You'll find several very lovely boutique hotels along the southern coasts of the Nicoya Peninsula.

The two main beach towns and vacation destinations in this area are Montezuma and Malpaís. Between them lies the Cabo Blanco Absolute Nature Reserve, Costa Rica's oldest official nature reserve.

Montezuma is a long-standing beach destination popular with backpackers and adventurous travelers. Montezuma sits just on the inside of the Golfo de Nicoya (Nicoya Gulf), and its beaches are relatively calm and protected. It also features two lovely waterfalls.

Malpaís, Santa Teresa, and a series of neighboring beaches are Costa Rica's up-and-coming hot spots. Both Malpais and Santa Teresa boast long expanses of white-sand beaches backed by lush forests, and both are popular with surfers.

Farther north up the Nicoya Peninsula coast lies Punta Islita, one of the country's most exclusive, isolated, boutique beach resorts.

Exploring southern Costa Rica

The hot, humid southern region of Costa Rica is remote and undeveloped. It's characterized by dense rain forests and rugged coastlines. Much of the area is protected in Corcovado National Park, the largest single expanse of lowland tropical rain forest in Central America, and its nearby sister the Piedras Blancas National Park.

On the inside of the Osa Peninsula lies the Golfo Dulce, or "Sweet Gulf." This large and beautiful body of water is a great place for fishing, kayaking, and dolphin spotting.

Several wonderful remote ecolodges are spread around the shores of the Golfo Dulce and on the Osa Peninsula, bordering Corcovado National Park. Some people find the area solitary, but if you like your ecotourism raw, pure, and challenging, you'll want to visit this region.

Chilling on the Caribbean coast

Most of the Caribbean coast is wide, steamy lowland laced with rivers and blanketed with rain forests and banana plantations. The culture here is predominantly Afro-Caribbean, with many residents speaking English or a Caribbean dialect as their first language. The northern section of this coast is accessible only by boat or small plane and is home to Tortuguero National Park, which is known for its nesting sea turtles and riverboat trips through its network of jungle canals and lagoons.

The towns of Cahuita and Puerto Viejo, on the southern half of the Caribbean coast, are popular beach destinations. They're home to, or close to, some of the best and least crowded beaches in the country. Small coral reefs also dot the coastlines off each town, giving this region some of the best snorkeling in Costa Rica.

No large resorts are yet to be found here, and although the towns of Cahuita and Puerto Viejo can bustle at times, this area is remote and isolated and will really give you a sense of getting away from it all.

Scheduling Your Time

Although visiting several destinations during one trip is certainly possible, Costa Rica doesn't lend itself well to stringing together, say, five destinations in a week. If you want to visit several destinations, you have to factor in travel time. It takes four to eight hours to drive between San José and most popular destinations and approximately the same amount of time to drive between these different spots.

Commuter flights cut down the travel time considerably, but they add on cost and some logistical challenges because you often have to fly in and out of San José as a hub. So, if the flights don't line up, you may end up adding an extra overnight in San José.

Many folks are content to spend a week or more at one resort, and this is a good option in Costa Rica, especially up in Guanacaste, where you can enjoy the comforts of a beach resort combined with the ability to take day trips that range from horseback rides near the Rincón de la Vieja volcano to rafting trips on the Corobicí River to sailboat outings, hikes, and canopy tours. A similar amount of activities and tour options are available in Manuel Antonio and, to a slightly lesser extent, from the remote ecolodges of the Osa Peninsula.

If you're looking for some unadulterated beach time and plenty of sun and fun, Guanacaste is often your best choice. If you want to mix your beach time with a bit more adventure and a trip into the rain forest, Manuel Antonio is a great option.

For a more intense exploration of the tropical rain forests and cloud forests, you should visit one or more of the following destinations: Monteverde, the Osa Peninsula and Golfo Dulce, or Tortuguero.

For a simple loop that hits three major and distinct destinations, I always recommend that folks head straight for La Fortuna and the Arenal volcano, then head over to Monteverde, and finish by dropping down to the coast at Manuel Antonio.

In Chapter 4, I outline several possible itineraries to help you plan the perfect trip to Costa Rica, given your particular interests, budget, and time constraints.

Revealing the Secrets of the Seasons

Costa Rica's high season runs from mid-December to late April, which coincides almost perfectly with the chill of winter in the United States, Canada, and Europe. The high season also coincides almost perfectly with the country's dry season. If you want some unadulterated time on a tropical beach and less rain during your rain-forest experience, this is the time to come. During this period (and especially around the Christmas holidays), tourism is in full swing — prices are higher, attractions are more crowded, and reservations need to be made in advance.

In order to drum up business during the rainy season, locals sometimes refer to it as the *green season.* The adjective is appropriate. At this time of year, even brown and barren Guanacaste becomes lush and verdant. I love traveling around Costa Rica during the rainy season (but then again, I'm not trying to flee winter in Chicago); finding (or at least negotiating) reduced rates is easy, there are far fewer fellow travelers, and the rain is often limited to a few hours each afternoon (although you can occasionally get socked in for a week at a time).

Understanding Costa Rica's climate

Costa Rica is a tropical country with distinct wet and dry seasons. However, some regions receive rain all year, and others are very dry and sunny for most of the year. Temperatures in Costa Rica are rarely as extreme. The average annual daytime temperature for much of the country ranges between 71°F and 81°F (22°C–27°C). Moreover, temperatures vary primarily with elevation, not with seasons: On the coasts, it's hot all year, with daytime temperatures hovering between 90°F and 96°F (32°C–36°C). But up in the mountains, it can be cool at night any time of year, with temperatures dipping into the mid-60s (15°C–17°C). At the highest elevations (3,000–3,600m/9,840–11,808 ft.), frost is common.

The dry season, considered summer by Costa Ricans, is from mid-November to April. In Guanacaste, the dry northwestern province, the dry season lasts several weeks longer than in other places. Even in the rainy season, days often start sunny, with rain falling in the afternoon and evening. The wet or rainy season (or green season) is from May to mid-November. Costa Ricans call this time of year their winter.

For most of the wet season, the rains are often limited to a brief but substantial downpour during the late afternoon. However, from mid-August through October, the rain can be hard, heavy, and seemingly relentless for long stretches.

In general, the best time of year to visit weather-wise is in December and early January, when everything is still green from the rains, but the sky is clear.

Costa Rica's Caribbean coast breaks all the rules mentioned in this section. It can rain pretty much any time of the year here. However, the one semi-dependable period, when the Caribbean coast often enjoys clear skies and calm seas, is between mid-September and late October, when the rest of the country is experiencing some of the worst effects of the rainy season.

Some of the country's rugged dirt roads become downright impassable without four-wheel-drive during the rainy season.

Avoiding the crowds

Keep in mind that tourism in Costa Rica peaks during the Christmas holidays, spring break, and Easter week. Stay at home during these seasons if you don't want to fight crowds and pay top dollar. However, you'll generally get good weather, uncrowded beaches and resorts, and decent price breaks, if you visit from late April through early June, or from late November through mid-December.

Perusing a Calendar of Events

Some of the events listed here may be considered more of a *happening* than a well-organized event — there's not, for instance, a Virgin of Los Angeles PR committee that readily dispenses information. If I haven't listed a contact number, your best bet is to call the **Costa Rican Tourist Board** (Instituto Costarricense de Turismo, or ICT) at ☎ **800-343-6332** in the United States, 2223-1733 in Costa Rica, or visit www.visitcostarica.com.

January

Some of the best young tennis players from around the region and around the world come to San José and the **Copa del Café (Coffee Cup).** Matches are held at the Costa Rica Country Club (☎ **2228-9333**). First week in January.

March

Orchid growers throughout the world gather to show their wares, trade tales and secrets, and admire the hundreds of species on display at the **National Orchid Show.** The show takes place at a different venue each year in the Central Valley. Contact the Costa Rican Tourist Board for precise location and dates.

April

Costa Rica is a predominantly Roman Catholic country and **Holy Week** is celebrated with fervor. Religious processions are held in cities and towns throughout the country. The week before Easter.

July

Annexation of Guanacaste Day is celebrated each year in Liberia with Tico-style bullfights, folk dancing, horseback parades, rodeos, concerts, and other events. On and around July 25.

August

Over 100,000 people make the annual pilgrimage from San José to the basilica in Cartago every year in honor of the **Fiesta of the Virgin of Los**

Angeles. Even those who don't make the 24km (15-mile) trek take the day off to honor the country's virgin saint. August 2.

September

School children across the country take to the streets in marching bands heavy on xylophones and snare drums to celebrate **Costa Rica's Independence Day.** Many of the parades are nighttime affairs, replete with fireworks. September 15.

If you're visiting Costa Rica this time of year, **International Coastal Cleanup Day** is a good excuse to chip in and help clean up the Costa Rican shoreline. Third Saturday of September.

October

Limón's **Carnaval,** or **Día de la Raza,** is a miniature Mardi Gras, complete with floats and dancing in the streets, which commemorates Columbus's dropping anchor off this Caribbean port city in 1502. The weekend closest to October 12.

December

The streets of downtown San José belong to horses and their riders for **El Tope,** each December 26. The next day, those same streets are taken over by carnival floats, marching bands, and street dancers, for **Carnaval.**

Costa Rican bullfights and a hodgepodge of carnival rides, games of chance, and fast-food stands are set up at the fairgrounds in Zapote, a San José neighborhood. The **Festejos Populares (Popular Fiestas)** are a rowdy and raucous affair. Last week in December.

Chapter 4

Following an Itinerary: Five Great Options

In This Chapter
▶ Seeing Costa Rica's top sights in one or two weeks
▶ Traveling around Costa Rica with children
▶ Planning an all-out adventure vacation

Costa Rica boasts a veritable bounty of things to see and do. You can use the following itineraries as precise guides or as rough outlines to help you structure your time and plan your trip.

Seeing Costa Rica's Highlights in One Week

The timing is tight, but this itinerary packs a lot into a weeklong vacation.

Day 1

Arrive and get settled in San José. If you have time, visit the **Centro Nacional de Arte y Cultura (National Arts and Culture Center),** the **Museo de Oro Banco Central (Gold Museum),** and/or the **Teatro Nacional (National Theater).** Have dinner at **Café Mundo** in Barrio Amón. See Chapters 11 and 12.

Day 2

Rent a car and head to the **Arenal volcano.** Settle into your hotel and spend the afternoon at the hot springs of the **Tabacón Grand Spa Thermal Resort,** working out the kinks from the road. In the evening, either sign up for a volcano-watching tour or view it yourself (from the comfort of your hotel room balcony or from one of the better volcano-viewing spots I lay out for you in Chapter 18).

Day 3

Spend the morning doing something adventurous, such as **white-water rafting, mountain-biking, canyoning,** or **horseback-riding** and then

Exploring Costa Rica in One Week

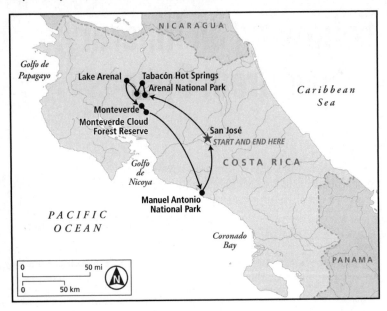

hiking to the **La Fortuna waterfall.** Make sure you give yourself at least four hours of daylight, though, to drive around **Lake Arenal** to **Monteverde.** Stop to shop for gifts, artwork, and souvenirs at the **Lucky Bug Gallery,** which is located just outside of Nuevo Arenal. After you get to Monteverde, settle into your hotel and head for a sunset drink at **El Sapo Dorado.** See Chapters 17 and 18.

Day 4

Wake up early and take a guided tour of the **Monteverde Cloud Forest Reserve.** Be sure to stop in at the **Hummingbird Gallery** next-door to the entrance after your tour. Spend the afternoon visiting several of the area's attractions, which include the **Butterfly Garden, Bat Jungle, Orchid Garden, Monteverde Serpentarium, Frog Pond of Monteverde,** and **World of Insects.** See Chapter 17.

Day 5

Use the morning to take one of the zip-line **canopy tours** here, but be sure to schedule it early enough that you can hit the road by noon for your drive to **Manuel Antonio.** Settle into your hotel and head for a sunset drink at one of the several roadside restaurants with **spectacular views over the rain forest to the sea.** You can drop off your car at any point now and just rely on taxis and tours. Adobe, Alamo, Economy, Hertz, National, and Payless all have offices in downtown Quepos, but check with your car-rental company in advance about any drop-off fees. See Chapter 15.

Day 6

In the morning, take a boat tour of the **Damas Island Estuary,** and then reward yourself for all this hard touring with an afternoon lazing on one of the beautiful beaches inside **Manuel Antonio National Park.** If you just can't lie still, be sure to hike the loop trail through the rain forest here and around **Cathedral Point.** See Chapter 15.

Day 7

Fly back to **San José** in time to connect with your departing flight home.

Touring the Best of Costa Rica in Two Weeks

If you have two weeks, you'll be able to hit all the highlights mentioned in the preceding section and more, all at a more relaxed pace, to boot.

It's a real judgment call, but you may want to substitute a two- to three-day trip to Tortuguero for either the Guanacaste or southern zone section listed here, or whittle down a day here or there along the way in order to squeeze in Tortuguero.

Days 1 and 2

Spend these days the same as you would in days 1 and 2 of "Seeing Costa Rica's Highlights in One Week," earlier in this chapter.

Day 3

Spend the morning doing something adventurous, such as **white-water rafting, mountain biking, canyoning,** or **horseback riding** and then **hiking** to the **La Fortuna waterfall.** If you're really active, you can schedule a second adventure for the afternoon or simply take some time to stroll around the little town of La Fortuna. In the evening, return to the Hot Springs, spend more time watching the volcano, or combine both. See Chapters 17 and 18.

Day 4

Drive around **Lake Arenal** to **Monteverde.** Stop to shop for gifts, artwork, and souvenirs at **Casa Delagua** and the **Lucky Bug Gallery,** both of which are located on the road between Tabacón and Tilaran. After you get to Monteverde, settle into your hotel and head to **El Sapo Dorado** for a sunset drink. See Chapters 17 and 18.

Exploring Costa Rica in Two Weeks

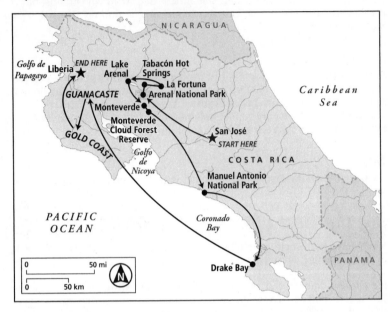

Day 5

Wake early and take a guided tour of the **Monteverde Cloud Forest Reserve.** Be sure to stop in at the **Hummingbird Gallery** next-door to the entrance after your tour. Spend the afternoon visiting several of the area's attractions, which include the **Butterfly Garden, Bat Jungle, Orchid Garden, Monteverde Serpentarium, Frog Pond of Monteverde,** and **World of Insects.** See Chapter 17.

Day 6

Use the morning to take one of the zip-line **canopy tours** here, but be sure to schedule it early enough that you can hit the road by noon for your drive to **Manuel Antonio.** Settle into your hotel and head for a drink or dinner at one of the several roadside restaurants with **spectacular sunset views over the rain forest to the sea.** You can drop off your car at any point now and just rely on taxis and tours. Adobe, Alamo, Economy, Hertz, National, and Payless all have offices in downtown Quepos, but check with your car-rental company in advance about any drop-off fees. See Chapters 15 and 17.

Day 7

In the morning, take a boat tour of the **Damas Island Estuary,** and then reward yourself for all this hard touring with an afternoon lazing on one of the beautiful beaches inside **Manuel Antonio National Park.** If you just can't lie still, be sure to hike the loop trail through the rain forest here and around **Cathedral Point.** See Chapters 15 and 16.

Days 8, 9, and 10

Fly from **Quepos** and **Manuel Antonio** to Golfito, Puerto Jiménez, or **Drake Bay,** and settle into one of the remote **ecolodges** of the **southern zone.** You'll need these three days to really experience the many natural wonders of this region. Aside from **hiking in the rain forest,** you'll be able to take **scuba or snorkel outings, sportfishing trips, kayak adventures,** and **surfing lessons.** See Chapter 20.

Days 11, 12, and 13

You've had enough nature and adventure — it's time to enjoy some pampering. From the southern zone, fly straight up to **Guanacaste** and spend your final days enjoying the pleasures of one of Costa Rica's **Gold Coast** beaches. If just lying on the beach or poolside is too mellow, you can take advantage of the scores of tour and activity options. Otherwise, break out that novel you've been too busy to open, and enjoy. See Chapters 13 and 14.

Day 14

Fly back to **San José** in time to connect with your departing flight home.

Discovering Costa Rica with Kids

Costa Rica is becoming a more kid-friendly destination every year. Still, very few attractions or activities are geared toward the very young, and the country has precious few resorts with well-developed children's programs. Youngsters and teens, especially those with strong adventurous and inquisitive traits, will do great here.

The biggest challenges for families traveling with children are travel distances and the time it takes to move around within the country, which is why I recommend flying in and out of Liberia, and basing yourself in Guanacaste. The Guanacaste area is ripe with activities, adventures, and attractions for the entire family. And everyone will enjoy the fact that this option drastically cuts down on travel time.

Day 1

Fly into Liberia. From here, it's a 30- to 45-minute drive to any of the many area beach resorts. I recommend either the **Four Seasons** or the **Hilton Papagayo.** Both have excellent children's programs, as well as tons of activity and tour options. See Chapter 13.

Costa Rica with Kids

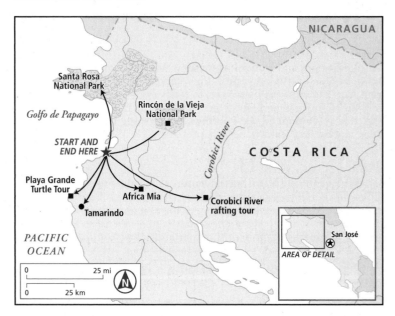

Day 2

Get to know and enjoy the facilities and activities offered up at your hotel or resort. Check out the **children's program** and any scheduled activities or tours that particularly appeal to anyone in your family. Feel free to adapt the following days' suggestions accordingly. See Chapters 13 and 14.

Day 3

The entire family will enjoy a rafting tour on the gentle **Corobicí River.** This trip is appropriate for all ages except infants. There'll be plenty of opportunities to watch birds and other wildlife along the way. If you schedule this properly, you can combine it with a visit to **Africa Mia,** an African-themed open-air animal park. See Chapter 14.

Day 4

Drop off the kids with the **children's program** at your hotel or resort for at least one full day, and treat yourselves to a **sailboat cruise.** You'll spend some time cruising the coast, take a break or two to snorkel, and probably stop for lunch at a deserted beach. See Chapter 14.

Day 5

It's time to head for the hills, which are mostly volcanoes in this neck of the woods. Book a full-day outing to **Hacienda Guachipilin,** near the **Rincón de la Vieja volcano.** Older and more adventurous children can sign up for a **horseback ride** or **canopy tour.** Younger children should get a kick out of visiting this working farm and cattle ranch. See Chapter 14.

Day 6

Use this day to satisfy any lingering whims. Some will want to just laze on the beach or by the pool. Others may want to try a **surf or boogie-board lesson.** If the kids feel left out, taking the whole brood out on a boat may be a good idea. You won't want for options. See Chapter 14.

Day 7

Use any spare time you have before your flight to buy last-minute **souvenirs** at your resort or in town, or just laze on the beach or by the pool. Fly home out of Liberia.

Having a High-Octane Week of Adventures

Costa Rica is a major adventure-tourism destination. Adventure opportunities range from white-water rafting and kayaking to zip-line canopy tours and canyoning adventures. The following itinerary packs a lot of punch into one week but doesn't even scratch the surface. You can also find excellent mountain biking, windsurfing, kiteboarding, and sportfishing. Feel free to modify the following itinerary to include any of these activities.

Day 1

Arrive and get settled in San José. If you have time, visit the **Centro Nacional de Arte y Cultura (National Arts and Culture Center),** the **Museo de Oro Banco Central (Gold Museum),** and/or the **Teatro Nacional (National Theater).** See Chapter 12.

Day 2

Begin a two-day white-water rafting expedition on the **Pacuare River,** and then camp out at a rustic lodge on the river's edge. See Chapter 12.

Day 3

Finish running the **Pacuare River,** and arrange for a transfer to **La Fortuna** at the end of your rafting trip. Settle into your hotel and head to the hot springs at the **Tabacón Grand Spa Thermal Resort** for a soothing soak and to watch the volcano. See Chapter 18.

Best Costa Rica Adventures

Day 4

Go **canyoning** with **Pure Trek Canyoning** in the morning, and then hop on some horses or mountain bikes in the afternoon and be sure to stop at the **La Fortuna Waterfall.** Take the short hike down to the base of the falls, and take a dip in one of the pools there. See Chapter 18.

Day 5

Arrange a **taxi-to-boat-to-horse** transfer over to **Monteverde.** Settle in quickly at your hotel and take a zip-line **canopy tour** in the afternoon. See Chapter 17.

Day 6

Wake up early and take a guided tour of the **Monteverde Cloud Forest Reserve.** Be sure to bring a packed lunch. After the guided tour, spend the next few hours continuing to explore the trails through the cloud forest here. See if you can spot a **Quetzal** on your own. Take a late-afternoon bus or transfer back to San José. See Chapter 17.

Day 7

Unfortunately, you'll most likely be on an early flight home from San José. If you have a few hours to kill, head for a hike or jog around the **La**

Parque Sabana (La Sabana Park) downtown, or, better yet, try to get yourself in a pickup soccer game. See Chapter 12.

Getting the Most out of a Week on the Gold Coast

Face it, for many people, the idea of touring around from place to place and checking in and out of a different hotel every day or two is just too much work for a vacation.

If you want to be able to settle into one hotel or resort, yet still have an adventure-packed, fun, and relaxing vacation, the following itinerary should be right up your alley.

Day 1

Fly into Liberia. From here it's a 30- to 45-minute drive to any of the area's many beach resorts. Choose one according to your budget, making sure to plan on taking a variety of tours during your stay. Check into your hotel, and use the rest of the day to unwind and shake off the weariness of travel. See Chapter 13.

Day 2

Get to know and enjoy the facilities and activities offered up at your hotel or resort. Take advantage of any free classes or water-sports equipment, and be sure to take a nice long walk on the beach. If your hotel is near a town, spend the afternoon exploring the local scene, and scope out a good spot for a sunset drink. See Chapter 13.

Day 3

It's time to head for the hills, which are mostly volcanoes in this neck of the woods. Book a full-day outing to the **Rincón de la Vieja volcano.** Be sure to hike the short loop trail around the bubbling mud pots here, and sign on for either a **horseback ride** or **canopy tour.** See Chapter 14.

Day 4

Shopping options are very limited in Costa Rica, but one of the most interesting outings is to the small Guanacaste village of **Guaitil,** where the locals have developed a unique ceramic style, using local mud, dyes, and wood-burning kilns. In the afternoon, rent a scooter and **explore some of the other beaches** near your resort. See Chapter 14.

Day 5

Take a **rafting trip** on the gentle **Corobicí River.** You'll have plenty of opportunities to watch birds and other wildlife on this outing. If it's

turtle nesting season, take a night tour to **Playa Grande** to see the giant leatherback turtles nest. See Chapter 14.

Day 6

You're at the ocean, so take advantage of it. Book a **sailing tour, sport-fishing outing,** or **surf lesson,** or just laze on the beach or by the pool. See Chapter 14.

Day 7

Use any spare time you have before your flight home from Liberia to buy last-minute **souvenirs,** or continue to laze on the beach or by the pool. See Chapter 13.

Part II
Planning Your Trip to Costa Rica

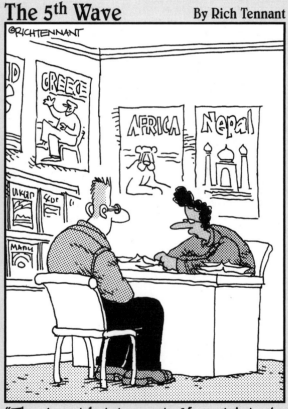

The 5th Wave   By Rich Tennant

@RICHTENNANT

"The closest hotel room to Manuel Antonio I could get you for that amount of money would be in Boca Raton."

In this part . . .

This is the place to come when you finally decide to take the plunge and book your trip. You'll find all the nuts-and-bolts information necessary to actually make arrangements. From planning a budget, to managing your money and changing cash into colones, to scoring a deal, this part has it all. You'll also find information on how to get to Costa Rica, and then how to get around after you're there.

Later on, you'll find suggestions and recommendations for a variety of travelers with particular needs, from families traveling with children, to disabled travelers, to gay and lesbian tourists looking for the inside scoop, to lovers looking to tie the knot in a tropical paradise.

Chapter 5

Managing Your Money

• •

In This Chapter

▶ Planning a budget
▶ Solving the mystery of the colón
▶ Zeroing in on cost-cutting tips

• •

"**S**o, how much is this trip to Costa Rica going to cost me, anyway?" is an important question, and one you'll want to address before packing your bags. As far as destinations go, Costa Rica is neither a budget hound's paradise nor a break-the-bank budget killer. In fact, you can tailor your vacation to meet just about any budget here. Although bargains can be found, and moderately prices hotels and resorts abound, there are also plenty of places to lap up the luxury.

In this chapter, I tell you how much things cost and offer you tips that can help you save big on some of the major expenses.

Planning Your Budget

With a little planning, mapping out a trip to Costa Rica to fit any budget is easy. Airfare and hotels will probably end up being your largest cash outlays. Other things, like rental cars and dining, are relatively inexpensive in Costa Rica.

Your choice of activities will also determine how much you spend: Relaxing on the beach and taking self-guided hikes in one of Costa Rica's national parks are both easy on the wallet. But guided tours and organized activities — such as white-water rafting trips, sportfishing outings, and zip-line canopy tours — can quickly add substantial costs to your vacation (see Table 5-1).

Table 5-1	What Things Cost in Costa Rica
Item/Activity	*Price*
Taxi from the airport to downtown San José	$18
Cup of coffee	$1
Bottle of beer	$1.50
Compact rental car (per day)	$35–$45
Four-wheel-drive rental car (per day)	$60–$90
White-water rafting trip on the Pacuare River	$75–$95
Zip-line canopy tour	$35–$60
Admission to the Gold Museum	$9
Admission to most national parks	$10
A day at the beach	Free!
A sunset cruise	$35–$55
Luxury room for two at the Four Seasons (Papagayo)	$815–$955
Rain-forest bungalow for two at Bosque del Cabo (Osa Peninsula), all meals and taxes included	$350–$390
Oceanview condo for four at Villas Nicolas (Manuel Antonio)	$190–$310
Moderate room for two at Hotel Grano de Oro (San José)	$115–$165
Budget room for two at Casa Verde Lodge (Puerto Viejo)	$38–$50
Gourmet dinner for two at Park Cafe (San José)	$60
Oceanfront dinner for two at El Pelicano (Playa Herradura)	$30
Costa Rican *casado* (blue-plate special)	$3.50

Transportation

The cost of your flight to Costa Rica will be one of your major expenses, especially during the high season. Airfares are almost impossible to predict and can change at the drop of a hat. Still, to give you an idea of what to expect, here's a sampling of potential fares from season to season: If you're going to Costa Rica in the off season — say, May or anytime between September and November — you may be able to snag a round-trip ticket for as little as $400 or $450 from any major U.S. hub. If you're traveling in the high season (late Dec–Apr, July–Aug), you'll pay more — probably in the $500 to $800 range.

Expect to pay a little more if you're departing from a city that's not a major airline hub. If you're traveling to Costa Rica over the Christmas holidays or during other peak periods, expect to pay full fare. After you get to Costa Rica, your in-country transportation costs should be low.

You can score any number of money-saving deals, especially if you consider an all-inclusive package. See Chapter 6 for more details on travel packages. I also tell you how to save on airfares in that chapter.

Internal Costa Rican flights

Many popular destinations inside Costa Rica are a four- to eight-hour drive from San José. Luckily, the country is served by a dependable network of internal commuter flights. One-way fares from San José to most other destinations run from $75 to $120. See Chapter 7 for details.

Rental cars

Rental cars are relatively inexpensive in Costa Rica. You can often get a compact for as little as $35 to $45 a day, or even less if you visit during the off season. If you need a larger car, or a four-wheel-drive vehicle, expect to pay more like $60 to $90 per day. Weekly rates almost always save you a bundle.

Because driving distances to most destinations are substantial, don't forget to factor in the cost of gas. Currently, a liter of premium gas costs 435 colones, or roughly $2.95 per gallon.

You'll seldom save by waiting to rent your car; generally, prices only go up as your pickup date approaches — especially in the busy travel seasons. Book as far in advance as possible for the best rate. Also, see "Cutting Costs — But Not the Fun," later in this chapter, as well as Chapter 7, for additional money-saving tips.

Lodging

Although Costa Rica has a few luxury resorts and several excellent high-end boutique hotels, its strong suit is affordable small to midsize hotels. Real budget hounds will have no problem finding clean and comfortable accommodations for under $75 per night. The best deals, though, can be found in the per-night range of $80 to $140.

In this book, I recommend a range of lodging choices in each destination to suit just about any budget. I also include many helpful tips on how to save money, regardless of your budget. For one thing, booking a package deal can be a huge money saver when it comes to hotels. For more information on packages, see Chapter 6. For additional cost-cutting measures, see "Cutting Costs — But Not the Fun," later in this chapter.

So that you don't encounter any unwanted surprises at checkout time, be sure to account for the 13 percent in taxes that will be added to your final hotel bill when planning your budget.

Dining

As tourism has boomed, dining options and quality have improved dramatically in Costa Rica. What's more, prices remain relatively low to downright cheap when compared to those found in the United States and Europe.

Even at some of the best restaurants in Costa Rica, main dishes rarely cost over $20, and most average between $10 and $15. Things get much more affordable at the local Tico restaurants, where full meals can often be had for under $7.

At any of the beach destinations, fresh seafood is plentiful and cheap. A grilled whole snapper should run you only $10 to $15 at most seaside restaurants.

If you're staying in one spot for an extended stay, a good way to save on dining expenses is to book a room with a kitchenette. Kitchen facilities are a virtual must if you're traveling with kids.

Sightseeing

This is an area where you have to budget carefully. Most of the tours and activities in Costa Rica require an individual guide or guided tour. Options include guided hikes through the rain forests or cloud forests, white-water rafting tours, sail and snorkel outings, and zip-line canopy tours. Rates on these range from $30 to $55 for a half-day outing, to $60 to $120 for full-day tours.

Other popular attractions found at various destinations include butterfly farms, serpentariums, and botanical gardens. Admission fees to these attractions run from $5 to $15 per person. Admission to most national parks costs $10, although there are a few exceptions, with the actual range running from $6 to $15.

The only real museums in the country are found in San José, and admission to these is generally between $3 and $8.

This book lists exact prices for activities, entertainment, admission fees, and the like, so you can budget your money realistically. If there's a way to land a bargain, I include that information, too.

Shopping and nightlife

These two areas are the most flexible parts of your budget. Your shopping options will be very limited in Costa Rica. Most of what you'll be able to buy are simple souvenirs and inexpensive handcrafts.

Costa Rica also has very limited nightlife options. There are virtually no major shows or theaters to tempt you. And tickets to those shows are very inexpensive, in any case. Most bars and dance clubs charge a very modest admission fee, or none at all.

Cutting Costs — But Not the Fun

I don't care how much money you have — you don't want to spend more than you have to. In this section, I give you some tips on how to avoid spending more of your hard-earned cash than is necessary.

Getting the best airfares

Getting the best airfare to Costa Rica is such a huge topic that I dedicate the better part of a chapter to it. Before you even start scanning for fares, see Chapter 6. That chapter also discusses how to find money-saving package deals.

Avoiding paying full price for your hotel room

A huge gap often exists between hotels' official *rack rates* (the published, full-price rates) and what you actually pay, so don't be scared off at first glance. What's more, savvy travelers can find ways to further widen the margin.

 The best way to avoid paying the full rack rate when booking your hotel is stunningly simple: Book directly with the hotel and ask for a cheaper or discounted rate. You may be pleasantly surprised — I have been, many times. *Remember:* Hotels sell the majority of their rooms for far below their rack rates. Moreover, they're accustomed to paying travel agents and wholesalers hefty commissions. If you book directly, they're saving that commission (as much as 30 percent). But you have to take the initiative and ask because no one is going to *volunteer* to save you money.

 Here are a few more potentially money-saving tips on hotels:

- ✔ **Rates are generally lowest in spring and fall.** The time of year you decide to visit may affect your bargaining power more than anything else. During the peak seasons — basically mid-December through mid-April and throughout the summer — demand is high and hotels are less likely to offer discounted rates. In the slower seasons — generally mid-April through mid-June and September through mid-December — when demand is down, they're often very willing to negotiate. In fact, many places drop rates by 10 percent to 30 percent automatically in the less-busy times of year. (If you haven't decided when you want to visit Costa Rica yet, see Chapter 3.)

- ✔ **Inquire about the hotel's own package deals.** Even if you're not traveling on an all-inclusive package (see Chapter 6), you may be able to take advantage of packages offered by hotels, resorts, and condos directly. Properties often list these deals on their Web sites, but not always, so it never hurts to ask additional questions about available specials.

- ✔ **If you're booking a hotel that belongs to a chain, contact the hotel directly in addition to going through central reservations.**

See which one gives you the better deal. Sometimes, the local reservationist knows about packages or special rates, but the hotel may neglect to tell the central booking line.

- ✔ **Reserve a hotel room with a kitchenette, or a condo with a full kitchen, and do your own cooking.** You may miss the pampering that room service provides, but you can save lots of money. Even if you prepare only breakfast and an occasional picnic lunch in the kitchen, you'll save significantly in the long run. Plus, if the beach is right outside your door, you won't ever have to leave it to go on restaurant runs.

- ✔ **Surf the Web to save.** A surprising number of hotels advertise great packages via their Web sites, and some even offer Internet-only special rates. In addition to surfing the hotel's own sites, you may want to try using a general travel-booking site such as **Expedia** (www.expedia.com), **Hotels.com, Orbitz** (www.orbitz.com), or **Travelocity** (www.travelocity.com) to book your hotel or a pay-one-price package that also includes airfare. Acting much like airline consolidators, these sites can sometimes offer big discounts on rooms as well. See Chapter 8 for a more complete discussion of how to use the Web to find a great hotel bargain.

Cutting other costs

Here are a few more useful money-saving tips:

- ✔ **Surf the Web to save on your rental car.** In addition to surfing car-rental agencies' own sites, you may want to try comparing rates through a general travel booking site such as **Expedia.com, Travelocity.com, Orbitz.com, or Sidestep.com.** This one-stop-shopping method can save you more than money — it can save you time, too.

- ✔ **Travel midweek.** If you can travel on a Tuesday, Wednesday, or Thursday, you may find cheaper flights to your destination. When you ask about airfares, see if you can get a cheaper rate by flying on a different day. For more tips on getting a good fare, see Chapter 6.

- ✔ **Reserve a room with a refrigerator and coffeemaker.** You don't have to slave over a hot stove to cut a few costs; many hotels have minifridges and coffeemakers. Buying supplies for breakfast will save you money — and probably calories.

- ✔ **Always ask for discount rates.** Membership in AAA, frequent-flier plans, trade unions, AARP, or other groups may qualify you for savings on rental cars, plane tickets, hotel rooms, and even meals. Ask about everything; you may be pleasantly surprised.

Handling Money

You're the best judge of how much cash you feel comfortable carrying or what alternative form of currency is your favorite. That's not going to change much on your vacation. True, you'll probably be moving around more and incurring more expenses than you generally do (unless you happen to eat out every meal when you're at home), and you may let your mind slip into vacation gear and not be as vigilant about your safety as when you're in work mode. But, those factors aside, the only type of payment that won't be quite as available to you away from home is your personal checkbook.

Unlocking the mystery of the colón

The unit of currency in Costa Rica is the **colón.** In mid-2009, there were approximately 560 colones to the U.S. dollar, but because the colón is in a constant state of devaluation, you can expect this rate to change. Because of this devaluation and accompanying inflation, this book lists prices in U.S. dollars. To check the very latest exchange rates before you leave home, point your browser to www.xe.com/ucc.

There are paper notes in denominations of 1,000; 2,000; 5,000; and 10,000 colones. Currently, two types of coins are in circulation. The older and larger nickel-alloy coins come in denominations of 5, 10, and 20 colones. There are even smaller denominations, but because of their evaporating value, you'll probably never see or have to handle them. In 1997, the government introduced gold-hued 5-, 10-, 25-, 50-, 100-, and 500-colón coins. They're smaller and heavier than the older coins, and the government is supposed to eventually phase out the other currency, although that plan has seemingly stalled. See Table 5-2 for currency conversions for the colón, U.S. dollars, Euro, and British pound.

Table 5-2	The Colón, the U.S. Dollar, the Euro, and the British Pound		
Colones	*U.S. $*	*E.U. €*	*British £*
10	0.02	0.01	0.01
25	0.05	0.03	0.03
100	0.18	0.13	0.12
500	0.89	0.66	0.62
5,000	8.90	6.65	6

(continued)

Table 5-2 *(continued)*

Colones	U.S. $	E.U. €	British £
10,000	18	13	12
25,000	45	33	31
50,000	89	66	62
100,000	179	133	123
500,000	893	666	617

 You'll hear people refer to a *rojo* or *tucán,* which are slang terms for the 1,000- and 5,000-colón bills, respectively. One-hundred-colón denominations are called *tejas,* so *cinco tejas* is 500 colones.

Exchanging money

If you fly into the Juan Santamaria International Airport in San José, you'll find a **Global Exchange** money-exchange booth just as you clear customs and immigration. However, these folks shave a good 10 percent off the official bank rate.

Several ATMs are available at the airport, including one inside the baggage-claim area. These will give you the current official bank exchange rate. However, the local machines charge between $1 and $2 per transaction, and, depending upon your card, bank, and type of account, you may face an additional charge from your home bank.

You can also change money at any bank in Costa Rica. I recommend the many private banks over the more cumbersome and crowded state-run banks.

Hotels will often exchange money and cash traveler's checks as well; there usually isn't much of a line, but they'll almost invariably give a less favorable exchange rate than you would get at a bank or ATM.

 When you change money, ask for some small bills and some 100-colón coins. Petty cash will come in handy for tipping and public transportation. Consider keeping the change separate from your larger bills so it's readily accessible and so you're less of a target for theft.

Unless you can secure a decent exchange rate, you really don't need to change dollars into colones in advance of your trip because the airport taxis all accept U.S. dollars.

 Be very careful about exchanging money on the streets; doing so is extremely risky. In addition to forged bills and short counts, street money-changers frequently work in teams that can leave you holding neither colones nor dollars. When receiving change in colones, checking the larger-denomination bills is a good idea; they should have protective bands or hidden images that appear when held up to the light.

Using ATMs and carrying cash

The easiest and best way to get cash away from home is from an ATM, sometimes referred to as a "cash machine" or "cashpoint." ATMs are quite common throughout Costa Rica, particularly in San José, and at most major tourist destinations around the country. You'll find them at almost all banks and most shopping centers. Still, make sure you have some cash at the start of your trip, never let yourself run totally out of spending money, and definitely stock up on funds before heading to any of the more remote destinations in the country. Outside San José and any of the more developed beach destinations, it's still best to think of your ATM card as a backup measure, because machines are not nearly as readily available or dependable as you may be accustomed to and you may encounter compatibility problems.

The **Cirrus** (☎ 800-424-7787; www.mastercard.com) and **PLUS** (☎ 800-843-7587; www.visa.com) networks span the globe. Look at the back of your bank card to see which network you're on; then call or check online for ATM locations at your destination. Be sure you know your personal identification number (PIN) before you leave home and be sure to find out your daily withdrawal limit before you depart. Also, keep in mind that many banks impose a fee every time your card is used at a different bank's ATM, and that fee can be higher for international transactions (up to $5 or more) than it is for domestic transaction (where fees are rarely more than $1.50). On top of this, the bank from which you withdraw cash may charge its own fee. To compare banks' ATM fees within the U.S., use www.bankrate.com. For international withdrawal fees, ask your bank.

In many international destinations, ATMs offer the best exchange rates, even taking into account the extra withdrawal fees you may be charged. Avoid exchanging money at commercial exchange bureaus and hotels, which often have the highest transaction fees.

In 2009, in response to a rash of "express kidnapping" in San José, in which folks are taken at gunpoint to an ATM to clean out their bank accounts, both Banco Nacional and Banco de Costa Rica stopped ATM service between the hours of 10 p.m. and 5 a.m. Other networks still dispense money 24 hours a day.

See the Quick Concierge for additional information on ATMs.

Charging ahead with credit cards

Credit cards are a safe way to carry money: They also provide a convenient record of all your expenses, and they generally offer relatively good exchange rates. You can also withdraw cash advances from your credit cards at banks or ATMs, provided you know your PIN. If you've forgotten yours, or didn't even know you had one, call the number on the back of your credit card and ask the bank to send it to you. It usually takes five to seven business days, though some banks will provide the number over the phone if you tell them your mother's maiden name or some other personal information.

Keep in mind that when you use your credit card abroad, many banks now assess a 1 percent to 3 percent transaction fee on *all* charges you incur abroad (whether you're using the local currency or your native currency).

Some credit card companies recommend that you notify them of any impending trip abroad so that they don't become suspicious when the card is used numerous times in a foreign destination and block your charges. Even if you don't call your credit card company in advance, you can always call the card's toll-free emergency number if a charge is refused — a good reason to carry the phone number with you. But perhaps the most important lesson here is to carry more than one card with you on your trip; a card might not work for any number of reasons, so having a backup is the smart way to go.

Toting traveler's checks

In Costa Rica, traveler's checks are accepted only by the larger hotels and restaurants, and primarily in the principal tourist destinations. Moreover, some hotels and restaurants even charge a service fee for the use of traveler's checks.

You can buy traveler's checks at most banks. They're offered in denominations of $20, $50, $100, $500, and sometimes $1,000. Generally, you'll pay a service charge ranging from 1 percent to 4 percent. The most popular traveler's checks are offered by **American Express** (☎ **800-807-6233** or ☎ **800-221-7282** for card holders — this number accepts collect calls, offers service in several foreign languages, and exempts Amex gold and platinum cardholders from the 1 percent fee); **Visa** (☎ **800-732-1322**); and **MasterCard** (☎ **800-223-9920**).

If you choose to carry traveler's checks, be sure to keep a record of their serial numbers separate from your checks in case they're stolen or lost. You'll get a refund faster if you know the numbers.

Taking Taxes into Account

There is a 13 percent tax on most goods and services in Costa Rica. Restaurants charge 13 percent tax and also add on a 10 percent service charge, for a total of 23 percent more on your bill. On restaurant menus, look for the letters *i.v.i.* next to the prices, which means the tax is included or factored into the listed price. Otherwise, tax may be added onto your bill later. All hotels charge 16.3 percent tax, which is the 13 percent tax, plus a 3.3 percent special hotel tax.

There is a $26 departure tax (payable in cash at the airport) for all visitors leaving Costa Rica by air.

Dealing with a Lost or Stolen Wallet

Be sure to contact all your credit card companies the minute you discover your wallet has been lost or stolen and file a report at the nearest police precinct. Your credit card company or insurer may require a police report number or record of the loss. Most credit card companies have an emergency toll-free number to call if your card is lost or stolen; they may be able to wire you a cash advance immediately or deliver an emergency credit card in a day or two. Call the following emergency numbers in Costa Rica:

- ✔ **American Express (for lost cards):** ☎ **0800-012-3211**
- ✔ **American Express (for lost traveler's checks):** ☎ **2242-8585**
- ✔ **MasterCard:** ☎ **0800-011-0184**
- ✔ **Visa:** ☎ **0800-011-0030**

For other credit cards, or for a local representative of these companies, call **Credomatic** (☎ **2295-9898**) in Costa Rica.

 Most credit cards carry a phone number you can call collect 24 hours a day from anywhere on the globe. Jotting down this number and keeping it in a safe place, separate from your wallet and valuables, before you travel is a good idea.

If your ATM card doesn't work and you need cash in a hurry, **Western Union** (☎ **800-777-7777** in Costa Rica; www.westernunion.com) has numerous offices around San José and in several major towns and cities around the country.

Identity theft and fraud are potential complications of losing your wallet, especially if you've lost your driver's license along with your cash and credit cards. Notify the major credit-reporting bureaus immediately; placing a fraud alert on your records may protect you against liability for criminal activity. The three major U.S. credit-reporting agencies are **Equifax** (☎ **800-766-0008**; www.equifax.com), **Experian** (☎ **888-397-3742**; www.experian.com), and **TransUnion** (☎ **800-680-7289**; www.transunion.com). Finally, if you've lost all forms of photo ID, call your airline and explain the situation; they might allow you to board the plane if you have a copy of your passport or birth certificate and a copy of the police report you've filed.

Chapter 6

Getting to Costa Rica

In This Chapter

▶ Finding the best airfares and cruises

▶ Considering a tour

▶ Taking advantage of package deals

Getting there may not *really* be half the fun, but it's a necessary step — and a big part of the planning process. How can you beat the high cost of international airfares? Should you reserve a package deal or book the elements of your vacation separately?

In this chapter, I give you all the information you need to make the trip decision that's right for you.

Flying to Costa Rica

The majority of international flights arrive at San José's Juan Santamaria International Airport, but an increasing number are landing in Liberia at the Daniel Olduber International Airport in the northern province of Guanacaste.

The following major airlines fly between mainland North America and one of Costa Rica's two airports.

✔ **Air Canada** (☎ 888-247-2262; www.aircanada.ca) flies from Toronto to San José.

✔ **American Airlines** (☎ 800-433-7300; www.aa.com) flies direct to San José from Fort Lauderdale, Miami, and Dallas–Ft. Worth and, direct from Miami and Dallas–Ft. Worth to Liberia.

✔ **Continental Airlines** (☎ 800-231-0856; www.continental.com) has direct flights from Houston and Newark to both San José and Liberia.

✔ **Delta Air Lines** (☎ 800-221-1212; www.delta.com) flies from Atlanta to both San José and Liberia.

- ✔ **Frontier** (☎ **800-432-1359;** www.frontierairlines.com) flies daily direct from Denver to San José.

- ✔ **JetBlue Airways** (☎ **800-538-2583;** www.jetblue.com) flies once daily direct from Orlando to San José.

- ✔ **Spirit Air** (☎ **800-772-7117;** www.spiritair.com) flies once daily direct between Ft. Lauderdale and San José.

- ✔ **US Airways** (☎ **800-622-1015;** www.usairways.com) has direct flights between both Phoenix, Arizona, and Charlotte, North Carolina, and San José, one weekly flight between Charlotte and Liberia.

- ✔ **United Airlines** (☎ **800-538-2929;** www.united.com) flies direct from Los Angeles, Miami, and New York's JFK to San José, and once weekly direct from Chicago to Liberia.

Getting the best airfare

Competition among the major airlines is unlike that of any other industry. Every airline offers virtually the same product (basically, a coach seat is a coach seat is a . . .), yet prices can vary by hundreds of dollars.

Business travelers who need the flexibility to buy their tickets at the last minute and change their itineraries at a moment's notice — and who want to get home before the weekend — pay (or at least their companies pay) the premium rate, known as the *full fare.* But if you can book your ticket far in advance and stay over Saturday night, and if you're willing to travel midweek (Tues–Thurs), you can qualify for the least expensive price — usually a fraction of the full fare. Obviously, planning ahead pays.

The airlines also periodically hold sales, in which they lower the prices on their most popular routes. These fares have advance-purchase requirements and date-of-travel restrictions, but you can't beat the prices. As you plan your vacation, keep your eyes open for these sales, which tend to take place in seasons of low travel volume — mid-April through mid-June and September through mid-December. You almost never see a sale around the peak summer vacation months of July and August, or around Thanksgiving or Christmas, when many people fly, regardless of the fare they have to pay.

Consolidators, also known as *bucket shops,* are great sources for international tickets, although they usually can't beat the Internet on fares within North America. Start by looking in Sunday newspaper travel sections; U.S. travelers should focus on the *New York Times, Los Angeles Times,* and *Miami Herald.* For a less-developed destination such as Costa Rica, small travel agencies that cater to immigrant communities in large cities often have the best deals.

Bucket-shop tickets are usually nonrefundable or rigged with stiff can-cellation penalties, often as high as 50 percent to 75 percent of the ticket price, and some put you on charter airlines with questionable safety records.

One consolidator specializing in travel to Latin America is **Latin Air Discount** (☎ 213-383-8906; www.latindiscountair.com). **STA Travel** (☎ 800-781-4040; www.statravel.com), the world's leader in student travel, offers good fares for travelers of all ages.

Booking your flight online

Search the Internet for cheap fares. The most popular online travel agen-cies are **Expedia** (www.expedia.com); **Orbitz** (www.orbitz.com), and **Travelocity** (www.travelocity.com). In the U.K., go to **travelsupermarket** (☎ 0845-345-5708; www.travelsupermarket.com), a flight search engine that offers flight comparisons for the budget airlines whose seats often end up in bucket-shop sales. Other Web sites for booking airline tickets online include **Cheapflights** (www.cheapflights.com), **SmarterTravel.com, Priceline.com,** and **Opodo** (www.opodo.co.uk). Meta search sites (which find and then direct you to airline and hotel Web sites for booking) include **SideStep** (www.sidestep.com) and **Kayak** (www.kayak.com) — the latter includes fares for budget carriers like JetBlue and Spirit as well as the major airlines. **Lastminute.com** is a great source for last-minute flights and getaways. In addition, most **air-lines** offer online-only fares that even their phone agents know nothing about. Also, keep an eye on price fluctuations and deals at Web sites such as **Airfarewatchdog.com**.

Frommers.com: The complete travel resource

For an excellent travel-planning resource, we highly recommend **Frommers.com** (www.frommers.com), voted Best Travel Site by *PC Magazine*. We're a little biased, of course, but we guarantee that you'll find the travel tips, reviews, monthly vacation give-aways, bookstore, and online-booking capabilities thoroughly indispensable. Among the special features are our popular **Destinations** section, where you get expert travel tips, hotel and dining recommendations, and advice on the sights to see for more than 4,000 destinations around the globe; the **Frommers.com Newsletter,** with the latest deals, travel trends, and money-saving secrets; our **Community** area, featuring **Message Boards,** where Frommer's readers post queries and share advice (sometimes even our authors show up to answer questions); and our **Photo Center,** where you can post and share vacation tips. When your research is done, the **Online Reservations System** (www.frommers.com/book_a_trip) takes you to Frommer's preferred online partners for booking your vacation at affordable prices.

Frequent-flier membership doesn't cost a cent, but membership may entitle you to better seats, faster response to phone inquiries, and prompter service if your luggage is stolen or your flight is canceled or delayed, or if you want to change your seat (especially after you've racked up some miles). And you don't have to fly to earn points; **frequent-flier credit cards** can earn you thousands of miles for doing your everyday shopping. With more than 70 mileage rewards programs on the market, consumers have never had more options. To play the frequent-flier game to your best advantage, consult the community bulletin boards on **FlyerTalk** (www.flyertalk.com) or go to **InsideFlyer** (www.insideflyer.com).

Cruising to Costa Rica

Some 200 cruise ships stop each year in Costa Rica, calling at Limón on the Caribbean coast, and at Puerto Caldera and Puntarenas on the Pacific coast. Many are part of routes that cruise through the Panama Canal. Cruise lines that offer stops in Costa Rica include **Crystal Cruises** (☎ 888-722-0021; www.crystalcruises.com), **Celebrity Cruises** (☎ 800-760-0654; www.celebritycruises.com), **Holland America** (☎ 877-932-4259; www.hollandamerica.com), **Norwegian Cruise Line** (☎ 866-234-7650; www.ncl.com), **Royal Caribbean** (☎ 866-562-7625; www.rccl.com), **Radisson Seven Seas Cruises** (☎ 877-505-5370; www.rssc.com), and **Silver Sea Cruises** (☎ 800-722-9955; www.silversea.com).

It might pay to book through a travel agency that specializes in cruises; these companies buy in bulk and stay on top of the latest specials and promotions. Try the **Cruise Company** (☎ **800-289-5505**; www.thecruisecompany.com) or **World Wide Cruises** (☎ **800-882-9000**; www.wwcruises.com).

Joining an Escorted Tour

Pay-one-price discount package tours are one thing, but escorted tours are a different animal altogether. Costa Rica is a friendly and accessible country for independent travel, but in some instances an escorted tour can be helpful. Many escorted tours to Costa Rica are built around a specific theme or adventure — bird-watching or mountain biking, for example. They're often led by knowledgeable and experienced guides.

You may be one of the many people who love escorted tours. The tour company takes care of all the details, and tells you what to expect at each leg of your journey. You know your costs upfront and, in the case of the tame ones, you don't get many surprises. Escorted tours can take you to the maximum number of sights in the minimum amount of time with the least amount of hassle.

If you decide to go with an escorted tour, I strongly recommend purchasing travel insurance, especially if the tour operator asks to you pay upfront. But don't buy insurance from the tour operator! If the tour operator doesn't fulfill its obligation to provide you with the vacation you paid for, there's no reason to think that it'll fulfill its insurance obligations either. Get travel insurance through an independent agency. (I tell you more about the ins and outs of travel insurance in Chapter 10.)

Depending on your recreational passions, I recommend one of the following tour companies:

- **Abercrombie & Kent** (☎ 800-554-7016; `www.abercrombiekent.com`) is a luxury-tour company that offers several tours to Costa Rica. It specializes in nine-day highlight tours hitting Monteverde, Arenal, and Tortuguero. Service is personalized and the guides are top-notch.

- **Caravan Tours** (☎ 800-227-2826; `www.caravan.com`) is a large wholesaler specializing in fully escorted tours. A ten-day fully escorted tour around the country begins at around $995 per person, not including airfare.

- **Costa Rica Expeditions** (☎ 2257-0766; `www.costaricaexpeditions.com`) is a Costa Rica–based company that offers everything from a ten-day escorted tour covering the whole country, to three-day/two-night and two-day/one-night tours of Monteverde Biological Cloud Forest Reserve and Tortuguero National Park, where it runs its own lodges. It also offers one- to two-day white-water rafting trips and other excursions.

- **Overseas Adventure Travel** (☎ 800-493-6824; `www.oattravel.com`) offers good-value natural history and soft adventure itineraries, with optional add-on excursions. Tours are limited to 16 people and are guided by naturalists. All accommodations are in small hotels, lodges, or tent camps. The "Real Affordable Costa Rica" 13-day package lives up to its name beginning at $1,895 per person (including round-trip airfare from Miami).

For more information on Escorted General-Interest Tours, including questions to ask before booking your trip, see `www.frommers.com/planning`.

Choosing a Package Tour

For lots of destinations, package tours can be a smart way to go. In many cases, a package tour that includes airfare, hotel, and transportation to and from the airport costs less than the hotel alone on a tour you book yourself. That's because packages are sold in bulk to tour operators, who resell them to the public. It's kind of like buying your vacation at a buy-in-bulk store — except the tour operator is the one who buys the 1,000-count box of garbage bags and resells them 10 at a time at a cost that undercuts the local supermarket.

The quality of package tours can vary widely. Every destination, including Costa Rica, usually has a few packagers that are better than the rest because they buy in even bigger bulk. The time you spend shopping around is likely to be well rewarded. The following is a list of top packagers to explore:

- ✔ **Costa Rica Experts** (☎ **800-827-9046** or 773-935-1009; www.crexpert.com) offers a large menu of a la carte and scheduled departures, as well as day trips and adventure packages.

- ✔ **Liberty Travel** (☎ **888-271-1584**; www.libertytravel.com) is one of the biggest packagers in the Northeast. Liberty offers several value packages, with or without air, to various upscale all-inclusive and boutique properties in Costa Rica. Calling the toll-free number immediately connects you to the Liberty Travel store nearest your home.

- ✔ **Vacation Express** (☎ **800-309-4717**; www.vacationexpress.com) is a large packager with excellent deals on air-only, air-and-hotel, and all-inclusive options to Costa Rica.

Several of the big **online travel agencies** — Expedia (www.expedia.com), Orbitz (www.orbitz.com), Travelocity (www.travelocity.com) — also do a brisk business in packages. If you're unsure about the pedigree of a smaller packager, check with the Better Business Bureau in the city where the company is based, or go online to www.bbb.org. If a packager won't tell you where it's based, walk away.

If you're booking a last-minute getaway, you may be able to score a stellar deal through **Lastminute.com,** which books all-inclusive travel packages as much as 60 percent off what the major packagers charge. The catch? You can only price and purchase your trip between 3 hours and 14 days before your departure, and all destinations are not available from all departure points. Still, if you're just dying to get away on the spur of the moment, it's worth checking out. You may also want to check out **Travel HUB** (www.travelhub.com) for last-minute package deals.

Be aware that some travel packagers are likely to book you on their own charter flights rather than on commercial flights on major airlines. Which airline the packager uses doesn't really make a difference, unless you have a particular allegiance to a specific airline (or to collecting miles in a frequent-flier program). Be sure that you know which airline you're flying when you book. If you really do want to fly with a specific airline, that doesn't rule out a packager. In fact, just about any packager will be happy to book you a land-only vacation that lets you book your own airfare separately (even the airline packagers will do this; see the list of packagers mentioned earlier).

For more information on package tours and for tips on booking your trip, see www.frommers.com/planning.

Chapter 7

Getting Around Costa Rica

In This Chapter

▶ Flying to your destination

▶ Renting a car

▶ Busing it around Costa Rica

Getting around Costa Rica is pretty simple and you have plentiful options. In this chapter, I give you the general lowdown on how to book and save money on rental cars, as well as the scoop on commuter airlines and local buses.

To visit many of the top spots in Costa Rica, taking a quick little commuter flight is the best, and sometimes only, option. Luckily, an excellent network of commuter flights is serviced by two reliable local airlines.

If you're going to crash on the beach for the week or visit just one area, you probably won't need to rent a car. But if you want to travel around the country and explore a few different destinations, renting a car is inexpensive and easy.

Finally, if you really want to keep your budget in line, local buses, and a couple of regularly scheduled minivan lines, are the way to go. That said, buses are by far the slowest and least comfortable means of transportation.

Flying Is Fastest

Many of Costa Rica's most popular destinations are a four- to eight-hour drive from San José. Luckily, excellent and affordable commuter airline service is offered to all these spots.

One-way fares from San José to most popular destinations run between $75 and $120. Flight times are generally between 20 minutes and a little over an hour.

Costa Rica's two principal local commuter airlines are

- ✔ **Sansa** (☎ 877-767-2672 in the U.S. and Canada, 2290-4100 in Costa Rica; www.flysansa.com)

- ✔ **Nature Air** (☎ 800-235-9272 in the U.S. or Canada, 2299-6000 in Costa Rica; www.natureair.com)

Sansa operates from a separate terminal at San José's Juan Santamaría International Airport, and offers a free shuttle bus from its downtown San José office to the airport. **Nature Air** operates from the small **Tobís Bolaños International Airport** in Pavas, 6.4km (4 miles) from San José. The ride from downtown to Pavas takes about ten minutes, and a metered taxi fare should cost $10 to $20.

Renting a Car

Renting a car in Costa Rica is no idle proposition. The roads are riddled with potholes, most rural intersections are unmarked, and, for some reason, sitting behind the wheel of a car seems to turn peaceful Ticos into homicidal maniacs.

This reality check isn't meant to scare you off from driving in Costa Rica. If you plan to visit more than one destination, and you're comfortable facing the aforementioned challenges, renting a car is a great way to go.

 Despite what you may have heard, you probably don't absolutely need a four-wheel-drive vehicle in Costa Rica. Monteverde is the only major destination where four-wheel-drive is more or less mandatory, because roads generally aren't paved there. The rest of the country can be reached by paved roads.

Still, many visitors enjoy the extra clearance afforded by a four-wheel-drive vehicle. Moreover, a four-wheel-drive vehicle does allow you more freedom to venture off the beaten path.

The following companies rent cars in Costa Rica:

- ✔ **Adobe:** ☎ 800-769-8422; www.adobecar.com

- ✔ **Alamo:** ☎ 877-222-9075; www.alamo.com

- ✔ **Avis:** ☎ 800-331-1212; www.avis.com

- ✔ **Budget:** ☎ 800-472-3325; www.budget.com

- ✔ **Dollar:** ☎ 800-800-3665; www.dollar.com

- ✔ **Hertz:** ☎ 800-654-3001; www.hertz.com

- ✔ **National:** ☎ 800-227-9058; www.nationalcar.com

- ✔ **Payless:** ☎ 800-729-5377; www.paylesscarrental.com

- ✔ **Thrifty:** ☎ 800-847-4389; www.thrifty.com

Before driving off with a rental car, be sure that you inspect the exterior and point out every tiny scratch, dent, tear, or any other damage. It's a common practice with many Costa Rican car-rental companies to claim that you owe payment for minor dings and dents that the company finds when you return the car.

Although rental cars no longer bear special license plates, they're still readily identifiable to thieves and frequently targeted. (Nothing is ever safe in a car in Costa Rica, although parking in guarded parking lots helps.) Transit police also sometimes target tourists. Never pay money directly to a police officer who stops you for any traffic violation.

Busing It Around Costa Rica

Buses are by far the most economical way to get around the country, but they can be slow, uncomfortable, and a hassle if you have a lot of luggage. Costa Rican buses are inexpensive and they go nearly every-where. There are two types:

- ✔ **Local buses** are the cheapest and slowest; they stop frequently and are generally a bit dilapidated.

- ✔ **Express buses** run between San José and most beach towns and major cities; these tend to be newer units and more comfortable, although very few are so new or modern as to have bathroom facilities.

Gray Line (☎ 2220-2126; www.graylinecostarica.com) and **Interbus** (☎ 2283-5573; www.interbusonline.com) run regularly scheduled departures in passenger vans and small buses to and from most of the major tourist destinations in the country. Both charge between $27 and $45 for a one-way trip, depending on the distance to your destination.

For more detailed information on how to get to various destinations, see the various destination chapters that follow.

Both Gray Line and Interbus offer pickup and drop-off at a wide range of hotels. This means that if you're the first person picked up or the last person dropped off, you may have to sit through a long period of subse-quent stops before finally hitting the road or reaching your destination. I've heard some horror stories about both lines concerning missed or severely delayed connections and rude drivers.

Be very careful with your bags and belongings on public buses and around public bus stations. Tourists are prime targets for thieves and pickpockets, and these are places where they're easy picking. Try to always keep an eye on your belongings. If you must store your luggage out of sight, check on it during intermediary stops when others are load-ing and offloading more baggage, just to be safe.

Chapter 8

Booking Your Accommodations

In This Chapter

▶ Figuring out what kind of accommodations are right for you
▶ Checking out prices
▶ Getting the best room at the best rate

*H*otel choices in Costa Rica are extensive and extremely varied. You can spend a week of utter luxury at a full-service beach resort, or some time trekking through the cloud forest while staying at an isolated ecolodge. You can even sleep in deluxe tent on the edge of a deserted beach surrounded by rain forest. This chapter helps you zero in on the type of accommodation best suited to your needs and tastes.

Costa Rica offers excellent options for every budget if you just know where to look — and I include the best of them in the chapters that follow. At the end of this chapter, I give specific tips on how to find the best rate and best room, no matter what your budget is. For more general tips on how to save, check out Chapter 5.

Getting to Know Your Options

Before you book your accommodations, you need to figure out what kind of place you want and how much you want to spend. Your options range from large-scale luxury resorts to basic budget *cabinas* (simple, rustic, Costa Rican hotels). In between these extremes, you'll find numerous small to midsize hotels, ranging from moderate to downright decadent, as well as a whole host of ecolodges in remote, wild destinations.

Table 8-1 gives you an idea of what you can expect to pay in each price category.

Table 8-1		Key to Hotel Dollar Signs*
Dollar Sign(s)	*Price Range*	*What to Expect*
$	Less than $75 per night	Budget — in this range you'll find everything from very basic to quite comfortable options, but sometimes lacking amenities such as air-conditioning, televisions, and in-room telephones.
$$	$75–$124	Moderate — a midpriced room, often in a charming small to midsize hotel. You'll start to get more amenities in this price range, but air-conditioning, televisions, and in-room phones may still be missing.
$$$	$125–$199	Expensive — a high-quality hotel room with plenty of amenities.
$$$$	$200–$349	Very expensive — a high-quality room in a full-service resort, or intimate boutique hotel.
$$$$$	$350 or more per night	Ultraluxurious — only a few properties in Costa Rica charge this much. For this price, you'll get a huge room, suite, or private bungalow; an impressive view; and excellent service.

* Each range of dollar signs, from one ($) to five ($$$$$), represents the median rack-rate price range for a double room, per night, during the high season; this does not factor in the 13 percent hotel tax.

Relaxing at a large resort

Relatively few large-scale resorts exist in Costa Rica. Only the Four Seasons and JW Marriott resorts cater to the ultra-high-end traveler.

Aside from a few exceptions in San José, most of the large resorts are beach resorts. (There are still none in the remote rain-forest and cloud-forest destinations.) Most are located in the northwestern province of Guanacaste.

A resort (or resort hotel) offers everything that your average hotel offers — plus much more. Every resort hotel is different, of course, but you can expect such amenities as pools (often more than one) with poolside bar service; an activities desk; a fitness center and often a full-service spa; a variety of restaurants, bars, and lounges; a 24-hour front desk; concierge, valet, and bell services; twice-daily maid service; room service; tennis and sometimes golf; a business center; extensive children's programs; and more comforts. Beach resorts all offer direct beach access, with beach chairs and umbrellas, and often beach-toy rentals and a host of ocean activities.

Many luxury resorts also boast an increasing slate of in-room extras, such as CD players and big TVs with Nintendo systems, on-screen Web access, VCRs or DVD players, and Internet access.

Although large resorts often carry the heftiest rack rates, you can often score good deals if you book these as part of a package (see Chapter 6) because the large resorts often presell a chunk of their rooms in bulk to packagers and wholesalers. Many large resorts also feature special offers and package deals on their own Web sites.

Hanging at a hotel

Most hotels in Costa Rica tend to be smaller and have fewer facilities than your typical resort. In many cases, midpriced hotels don't offer air-conditioning. Still, most are very comfortable and feature a whole host of facilities, amenities, and activity options. Although many have a small swimming pool, in general, you shouldn't expect more than one restaurant or bar, or the myriad amenities that come with a full-fledged resort.

Unless otherwise noted, hotel pools and tennis courts are outdoors.

You'll find proportionally few chain hotels in Costa Rica, although Barceló, Best Western, Clarion, Comfort, Crowne Plaza, Hilton, Holiday Inn, InterContinental, Marriott, Meliá, Occidental, Radisson, and Ramada are all represented.

Enjoying intimacy at a boutique hotel or B&B

Boutique hotels are smaller — with maybe 10 to 40 rooms — and more intimate than your average hotel. Bed-and-breakfasts are usually even smaller still. In both cases, the rooms are often more stylish and less cookie-cutter and usually have more amenities than those found at similarly priced hotels. The service also tends to be more attentive and personalized.

Throughout the book, I list the best boutique hotels Costa Rica has to offer. Several of these have banded together under the banner of **Small Distinctive Hotels of Costa Rica** (☎ **2258-0150;** www. distinctivehotels.com).

Getting close to nature at an ecolodge

Costa Rica is one of the world's great natural destinations. Bird-watchers, neophyte naturalists, and professional biologists flock here to spot wildlife and learn about the natural wonders of Costa Rica's many national parks and bioreserves. Ecosystems range from the high-altitude cloud forests of Monteverde, to the lowland rain forests of Manuel Antonio and the Osa Peninsula, to the jungle canals of Tortuguero. In all these remote destinations, you'll find small, isolated nature lodges or ecolodges. Some rival any accommodation in the country for a sense of style and personal attention, with a fair amount of luxury thrown in besides. (However, very few have air-conditioning or televisions in the rooms. In general, you shouldn't need the former and should be able to do without the latter here.) All have on-staff naturalist guides and a host of tour and hiking options.

Choosing a cabina

Cabinas are Costa Rica's cut-rate accommodations. Many are simple cinder-block rooms, with concrete floors, and no air-conditioning. The better ones, however, can be quite cozy, and may have wood or tile floors, firm beds, plenty of space, an overhead fan, and perhaps even air-conditioning and/or a television. Many *cabinas* feature either communal or private cooking areas, or laundry facilities. *Cabinas* are also great places to mingle with Costa Ricans. Throughout the book, I only include the cream of the crop of the *cabina* field.

An ever increasing number of hotels are offering Wi-Fi connections, usually for free. In most instances, I mention this in the review, but more and more hotels are adding this perk all the time. If staying connected is important to you, be sure to ask before booking.

Finding the Best Room Rate

The **rack rate** is the maximum rate a hotel charges for a room. It's the rate you get if you walk in off the street and ask for a room for the night. You sometimes see these rates printed on the fire/emergency exit diagrams posted on the back of your door.

Hotels are happy to charge you the rack rate, but you can almost always do better. Perhaps the best way to avoid paying the rack rate is surprisingly simple: Just ask for a cheaper or discounted rate. You may be pleasantly surprised.

In all but the smallest accommodations, the rate you pay for a room depends on many factors — chief among them being how you make your reservation. A travel agent may be able to negotiate a better price with certain hotels than you can get by yourself. (That's because the hotel often gives the agent a discount in exchange for steering his business toward that hotel.)

Reserving a room through the hotel's toll-free number may also result in a lower rate than calling the hotel directly. On the other hand, the central reservations number may not know about discount rates at specific locations. For example, a local franchise may offer a special group rate for a wedding or family reunion, but it may neglect to tell the central booking line. Your best bet is to call both the local number and the toll-free number and see which one gives you a better deal.

Room rates (even rack rates) change with the season, as occupancy rates rise and fall. But even within a given season, room prices are subject to change without notice, so the rates quoted in this book may be different from the actual rate you receive when you make your reservation. Be sure to mention membership in AAA, AARP, frequent-flier programs, and any other corporate rewards programs you can think of — or your Uncle Joe's Elks lodge in which you're an honorary inductee, for that matter — when you call to book. You never know when the affiliation may be worth a few dollars off your room rate.

A great way to get a great deal on a hotel room, especially at the large resorts, is to book it as part of an all-inclusive travel package that includes airfare and hotel, and sometimes other extras, in one low price. For details on how to find the best package deals, see Chapter 6.

Surfing the Web for Hotel Deals

Shopping online for hotels is generally done one of two ways: by booking through the hotel's own Web site or through an independent booking agency (or a fare-service agency like Priceline). These Internet hotel agencies have multiplied in mind-boggling numbers of late, competing for the business of millions of consumers surfing for accommodations around the world. This competitiveness can be a boon to consumers who have the patience and time to shop and compare the online sites for good deals — but shop they must, for prices can vary considerably from site to site. And keep in mind that hotels at the top of a site's listing may be there for no other reason than that they paid money to get the placement.

In addition to the online travel booking sites **Expedia** (www.expedia.com), **Hotwire** (www.hotwire.com), **Orbitz** (www.orbitz.com), **Priceline.com,** and **Travelocity** (www.travelocity.com), you can book hotels through **Hotels.com, Quikbook** (www.quikbook.com), and **Travelaxe** (www.travelaxe.net).

HotelChatter (www.hotelchatter.com) is a daily webzine offering smart coverage and critiques of hotels worldwide. Go to **TripAdvisor** (www.tripadvisor.com), or **hotelshark** (www.hotelshark.com) for helpful independent consumer reviews of hotels and resort properties.

It's a good idea to **get a confirmation number** and **make a printout** of any online booking transaction.

Your best bet in Costa Rica may be negotiating directly with the hotels themselves, especially the smaller hotels. In this day and age, almost every hotel in Costa Rica has e-mail, if not its own Web site, and you'll find the contact information right there. However, be aware that response times may be slower than you'd like, and many of the smaller hotels may have some trouble communicating back and forth in English.

Reserving the Best Room

After you make your reservation, asking one or two more pointed questions can go a long way toward making sure you get the best room in the house.

- ✔ **Always ask for a corner room.** They're usually larger, quieter, and have more windows and light than standard rooms, and they don't always cost more.

- ✔ **Ask if the hotel is renovating.** If it is, request a room away from the renovation work.

- ✔ **Inquire about the location of the restaurants, bars, and discos in the hotel — all sources of annoying noise.**

If you aren't happy with your room when you arrive, talk to the front-desk staff. If they have another room, they should be happy to accommodate you, within reason.

Chapter 9

Catering to Special Travel Needs or Interests

In This Chapter
▶ Bringing the kids along
▶ Finding travel tips for seniors, folks with disabilities, and gays and lesbians
▶ Tying the knot in Costa Rica
▶ Exploring volunteer and educational travel

osta Rica is an exotic and diverse destination that is well suited to all sorts of travelers. Travelers come in a variety of ages, sizes, and types. You may wonder how Costa Rica is for families traveling with kids. What will it be like for same-sex couples? Is it hospitable to older travelers or those with disabilities? Can I get married there? If you have any of these questions, you've turned to the right chapter. In the following pages, I give you the details of what to expect and how best to prepare for any or all of these circumstances.

Traveling with the Brood: Advice for Families

Costa Rica is an excellent destination for children, especially those who are inquisitive and adventurous. Most children will be fascinated by the wildlife. Imagine: This is a place where grown adults come to study and collect insects, frogs, and snakes. So kids will feel right at home. Older children can learn to surf and fly through the air on a zip-line canopy tour.

Most hotels in Costa Rica give discounts for children under 12, and children under 3 or 4 are usually allowed to stay for free. Discounts for children and the cutoff ages vary according to the hotel. In general, don't assume that your kids can stay in your room for free, but be sure to ask.

Many hotels, villas, and *cabinas* come equipped with kitchenettes or full kitchen facilities. These can be a real money saver for those traveling with children, and I list many of these accommodations in the destination chapters that follow.

Cabinas are Costa Rica's version of cheap lodging. They're very inexpensive and very basic — often just cinder-block buildings divided into small rooms. They cater primarily to Tico families on vacation. (See Chapter 8 for more information.)

Hotels offering regular, dependable baby-sitting service are few and far between. If you'll need baby-sitting, make sure that your hotel offers it, and be sure to ask whether the baby sitters are bilingual. In many cases, they aren't; this language difference usually isn't a problem with infants and toddlers, but it can cause problems with older children.

Look for the Kid Friendly icon as you flip through this book. I use it to highlight hotels, restaurants, and attractions that are particularly welcoming or suited to families traveling with kids. Zeroing in on these listings can help you more efficiently plan your trip.

All visitors to Costa Rica, including children, need to have a current passport.

For a list of more family-friendly travel resources, visit www.frommers. com/planning.

Making Age Work for You: Tips for Seniors

Although senior citizens are respected and honored in Costa Rican society, they're seldom offered official discounts or perks. Still, mention the fact that you're a senior citizen when you make your travel reservations. Although all the major U.S. airlines except America West have cancelled their senior discount and coupon-book programs, many hotel chains still offer discounts for seniors.

Always carry an ID card with you, especially if you've kept your youthful glow.

Members of **AARP,** 601 E St. NW, Washington, DC 20049 (☎ **888-687-2277** or 202-434-2277; www.aarp.org), get discounts on hotels (including chains represented in Costa Rica), airfares, and rental cars. AARP offers members a wide range of benefits, including *AARP: The Magazine* and a monthly newsletter. Anyone over 50 can join.

Many reliable agencies and organizations target the 50-plus market. **Elderhostel** (☎ **800-454-5768;** www.elderhostel.org) arranges Costa Rica study programs for those ages 55 and older, as well as intergenerational trips good for families. **ElderTreks** (☎ **800-741-7956,** or 416-558-5000 outside North America; www.eldertreks.com) offers small-group tours to Costa Rica, restricted to travelers 50 and older.

For more information and resources on travel for seniors, see www.frommers.com/planning.

Accessing Costa Rica: Advice for Travelers with Disabilities

Most disabilities shouldn't stop anyone from traveling. There are more options and resources out there than ever before. Still, Costa Rica does present specific challenges to travelers with disabilities. Although Costa Rica has an Equality of Opportunities for People with Disabilities law, and some facilities have been adapted, in general, there are relatively few wheelchair-accessible buildings. In San José or elsewhere, sidewalks are crowded and uneven. Only a small number of hotels offer wheelchair-accessible accommodations, and there are no public buses thus equipped. In short, people with disabilities often have difficulty getting around in Costa Rica.

Many travel agencies offer customized tours and itineraries for travelers with disabilities. **Flying Wheels Travel** (☎ **507-451-5005;** www.flyingwheelstravel.com) offers escorted tours and cruises that emphasize sports and private tours in minivans with lifts. Another good operator offering tours in Costa Rica is **Accessible Journeys** (☎ **800-846-4537** or 610-521-0339; www.disabilitytravel.com). **Access-Able Travel Source** (☎ **303-232-2979;** www.access-able.com) offers extensive access information and advice for traveling around the world with disabilities.

One local agency specializes in tours for travelers with disabilities and restricted mobility. **Vaya Con Silla de Ruedas** (☎/fax **2454-2810;** www.gowithwheelchairs.com) has a ramp- and elevator-equipped van and knowledgeable, bilingual guides. It charges very reasonable prices and can provide anything from simple airport transfers to complete multiday tours.

For more on organizations that offer resources to disabled travelers, go to www.frommers.com/planning.

Following the Rainbow: Resources for Gay and Lesbian Travelers

Costa Rica is a conservative Catholic country where public displays of same-sex affection are rare and considered somewhat shocking. Aside from the large resort hotels, some smaller hotels, a handful of bars and clubs, and one section of beach in Manuel Antonio, there are few places where same-sex shows of affection and contact are widely accepted. Still, gay and lesbian tourism to Costa Rica is robust, and gay and lesbian travelers are generally treated with respect. If you take into account the local mores, you should not experience any harassment.

A note for female travelers

For lack of better phrasing, Costa Rica is a typically "macho" Latin American nation. Single women can expect a nearly constant stream of catcalls, hisses, whistles, and car horns, especially in San José. The best advice is to ignore the unwanted attention rather than try to come up with a witty rejoinder. Women should also be careful walking alone at night, both in San José and in more remote destinations. I definitely don't recommend hitchhiking. You may want to check out the award-winning Web site **Journeywoman** (www.journeywoman.com), a women's travel information network where you can sign up for a free e-mail newsletter and get advice on everything from etiquette and dress to safety.

For a general overview of the current situation, news of any special events or meetings, and up-to-date information, www.gaycostarica.com is your best bet, especially for gays, and to a much lesser extent for lesbians.

The **International Gay and Lesbian Travel Association** (IGLTA; ☎ 800-448-8550 or 954-776-2626; www.iglta.org) is the trade association for the gay and lesbian travel industry, and offers an online directory of gay- and lesbian-friendly travel businesses and tour operators.

Two agencies specializing in gay and lesbian travel are **Gay Adventure Tours, Inc.** (☎ 207-239-6559; www.gayadventuretours.com), which focuses solely on tours to Costa Rica, and **Above and Beyond Tours** (☎ 800-397-2681; www.abovebeyondtours.com), which offers gay and lesbian tours worldwide and is the exclusive gay and lesbian tour operator for United Airlines.

For more gay and lesbian travel resources visit www.frommers.com/planning.

Planning a Costa Rican Wedding

Getting married in Costa Rica is simple and straightforward. In most cases, all you need are current passports. You'll have to provide some basic information, including a copy of each passport, your dates of birth, your occupations, your current address, and the names and addresses of your parents. Two witnesses are required to be present at the ceremony. If you're traveling alone, your hotel or wedding consultant will provide the required witnesses.

Things are slightly more complicated if one or more of the partners was previously married. In such a case, the previously married partner must provide an official copy of the divorce decree.

Most travelers who get married in Costa Rica do so in a civil ceremony officiated by a local lawyer. After the ceremony, the lawyer records the marriage with Costa Rica's National Registry, which issues an official marriage certificate. This process generally takes between four and six weeks. Most lawyers or wedding coordinators then have the document translated and certified by the Costa Rican Foreign Ministry and at the embassy or consulate of your home country within Costa Rica before mailing it to you. From here, it's a matter of bringing this document to your local civil or religious authorities, if necessary.

Because Costa Rica is more than 90 percent Roman Catholic, arranging for a church wedding is usually easy in all but the most isolated and remote locations. To a lesser extent, a variety of denominational Christian churches and priests are often available to perform or host the ceremony. If you're Jewish, Muslim, Buddhist, or a follower of some other religion, bringing your own officiant is a good idea.

Officially, the lawyer must read all or parts of the Costa Rican civil code on marriage during your ceremony. This is a rather uninspired and somewhat dated legal code that, at some weddings, can take as much as 20 minutes to slog through. Most lawyers and wedding coordinators are quite flexible and can work with you to design a ceremony and text that fits your needs and desires. Insist on this.

Most of the higher-end and romantic hotels in Costa Rica have ample experience in hosting weddings. Many have an in-house wedding planner. Narrowing the list is tough, but I'd say the top choices include **Hotel Punta Islita** (Chapter 19), **Villa Caletas** (Chapter 16), **Makanda-by-the-Sea** (Chapter 15), **Flor Blanca Resort** (Chapter 19), and the **Four Seasons** (Chapter 13). If you want a remote, yet luxurious, rain-forest lodge to serve as host and backdrop, try **La Paloma Lodge** (Chapter 20), **Bosque del Cabo Rainforest Lodge** (Chapter 20), or **Lapa Ríos** (Chapter 20). Another interesting option is **Punta Coral,** a private reserve owned by Calypso Tours (☎ **800-887-1969;** www.calypsotours.com).

If you're looking for service beyond what your hotel can offer, or if you want to do it yourself, check out www.weddings.co.cr, www.weddingscostarica.net, www.liquidweddings.com, or www.tropicaloccasions.com.

Volunteering and Studying in Costa Rica

"Working" vacations have become more and more popular over the last few years and several ecologically oriented volunteer and study programs are available throughout Costa Rica. These programs can be a unique and rewarding way to spend your vacation time.

Be warned: These "volunteer" experiences do not come cheap. You must pay for your transportation and there is sometimes a program fee, which can be hefty. (The cost will be the same as, or more than, a traditional vacation.)

If you'd like to explore ways to spend your vacation time a little differently, here is a list of some institutions and organizations that are working on ecology and sustainable development projects:

- ✔ **Association for the Preservation of the Wild Flora and Fauna** (APREFLOFAS; ☎ 2574-6816; www.preserveplanet.org) is a pioneering local conservation organization that accepts volunteers and runs environmentally sound educational tours around the country.

- ✔ **Asociación de Voluntarios para el Servicio en las Areas Protegidas** (ASVO; ☎ 2258-4430; www.asvocr.com) organizes volunteers to work in Costa Rican national parks. A two-week minimum commitment is required, as is a basic ability to converse in Spanish. Housing is provided at a basic ranger station, and there is a $17 daily fee to cover food, which is basic Tico fare.

- ✔ **Earthwatch Institute** (☎ 800-776-0188 in the U.S.; www.earthwatch.org) organizes volunteers to go on research trips to help scientists collect data and conduct field experiments in a number of scientific fields and a wide range of settings. Expeditions to Costa Rica range from studies of the nesting habits of leatherback sea turtles to research into sustainable coffee-growing methods.

- ✔ **Global Volunteers** (☎ 800-487-1074 in the U.S.; www.globalvolunteers.org) is a U.S.-based organization that offers a unique opportunity to travelers who've always wanted a Peace Corps–like experience but can't make a two-year commitment. For two to three weeks, you can join one of its working vacations in Costa Rica.

- ✔ **Habitat for Humanity International** (☎ 2296-3436; www.habitatcostarica.org) has several chapters in Costa Rica and sometimes runs organized Global Village programs here.

- ✔ **Vida** (☎ 2221-8367; www.vida.org) is a local nongovernmental organization working on sustainable development and conservation issues; it can often place volunteers.

Chapter 10

Taking Care of the Remaining Details

In This Chapter

▶ Getting a passport and buying travel insurance

▶ Keeping safe and healthy when you travel

▶ Staying connected in Costa Rica

▶ Dealing with airline security

---

*T*his chapter helps you shore up the final details — from getting a passport to purchasing travel insurance to mapping out strategies to stay connected while you're in Costa Rica.

Getting a Passport

A valid passport is required of all travelers entering Costa Rica.

Applying for a U.S. passport

The U.S. State Department Web site (http://travel.state.gov) provides downloadable passport applications as well as the current fees for processing applications. *Note:* Children are required to present a passport when entering the United States at airports. More information on obtaining a passport for a minor can be found at http://travel.state.gov.

 Allow plenty of time before your trip to apply for a passport; processing normally takes four to six weeks (3 weeks for expedited service) but can take longer during busy periods (especially spring). And keep in mind that if you need a passport in a hurry, you'll pay a higher processing fee.

Applying for other passports

The following list offers more information for citizens of Australia, Canada, New Zealand, and the United Kingdom.

✔ **Australians** can pick up an application from their local post office or any branch of Passports Australia, but they must schedule an interview at the passport office to present their application materials. Call the **Australian Passport Information Service** at ☎ **131-232,** or visit the government Web site at www.passports.gov.au.

✔ **Canadians** can pick up applications at travel agencies throughout Canada or from the central **Passport Office,** Department of Foreign Affairs and International Trade, Ottawa, ON K1A 0G3 (☎ **800-567-6868;** www.ppt.gc.ca). *Note:* Canadian children who travel must have their own passports. However, if you hold a valid Canadian passport issued before December 11, 2001, that bears the name of your child, the passport remains valid for you and your child until it expires.

✔ Residents of **Ireland** can apply for a ten-year passport at the **Passport Office,** Setanta Centre, Molesworth Street, Dublin 2 (☎ **01-671-1633;** www.irlgov.ie/iveagh). Those under age 18 and over 65 must apply for a three-year passport. You can also apply at 1A South Mall, Cork (☎ **21-494-4700**) or at most main post offices.

✔ **New Zealanders** can pick up a passport application at any New Zealand Passports Office or download it from their Web site. Contact the **Passports Office** at ☎ **0800-225-050** in New Zealand or 04-474-8100, or log on to www.passports.govt.nz.

✔ **United Kingdom** residents can pick up applications for a standard ten-year passport (5-year passport for children under 16) at passport offices, major post offices, or a travel agency. For information, contact the **United Kingdom Passport Service** (☎ **0870-521-0410;** www.ukpa.gov.uk).

Playing It Safe with Travel and Medical Insurance

The types of insurance travelers are most likely to need are trip-cancellation insurance and medical insurance. The cost of travel insurance varies widely, depending on the cost and length of your trip, your age and health, and the type of trip you're taking. You can get estimates from various providers through **InsureMyTrip.com.** Enter your trip cost and dates, your age, and other information, for prices from more than a dozen companies.

U.K. citizens and their families who make more than one trip abroad per year may find an annual travel insurance policy works out cheaper. Check **moneysupermarket.com,** which compares prices across a wide range of providers for single- and multi-trip policies.

Most big travel agents offer their own insurance and will probably try to sell you their packages when you book a holiday. Think before you sign. **Britain's Consumers' Association** recommends that you insist on seeing the policy and reading the fine print before buying travel insurance. **The Association of British Insurers** (☎ 020-7600-3333; www.abi.org.uk) gives advice by phone and publishes Holiday Insurance, a free guide to policy provisions and prices. You might also shop around for better deals: Try **Columbus Direct** (☎ 0870-033- 9988; www.columbusdirect.net).

Here is my advice on trip-cancellation and medical insurance:

✔ **Trip-cancellation insurance** will help retrieve your money if you have to back out of a trip or depart early, or if your travel supplier goes bankrupt. Trip cancellation traditionally covers such events as sickness, natural disasters, and State Department advisories. The latest news in trip-cancellation insurance is the availability of **expanded hurricane coverage** and the **"any-reason"** cancellation coverage, the latter of which costs more than other types of insurance but covers cancellations made for any reason. You won't get back 100 percent of your prepaid trip cost, but you'll be refunded a substantial portion. **TravelSafe** (☎ 888-885-7233; www.travelsafe.com) offers both types of coverage. **Expedia** (www.expedia.com) also offers any-reason cancellation coverage for its air-hotel packages. You can also try one of the following recommended insurers: **Access America** (☎ 866-807-3982; www.accessamerica.com); **Travel Guard International** (☎ 800-826-4919; www.travelguard.com); **Travel Insured International** (☎ 800-243-3174; www.travelinsured.com); and **Travelex Insurance Services** (☎ 888-457-4602; www.travelex-insurance.com).

For travel overseas, you may want to look into **medical insurance.** Most U.S. health plans (including Medicare and Medicaid) do not provide coverage, and the ones that do often require you to pay for services upfront and reimburse you only after you return home.

If you require additional medical insurance, try **MEDEX Assistance** (☎ 410-453-6300; www.medexassist.com) or **Travel Assistance International** (☎ 800-821-2828; www.travelassistance.com; for general information on services, call the company's **Worldwide Assistance Services, Inc.,** at ☎ 800-777-8710).

Canadians should check with their provincial health-plan offices or call **Health Canada** (☎ 866-225-0709; www.hc-sc.gc.ca) to find out the extent of their coverage and what documentation and receipts they must take home in case they're treated overseas.

Travelers from the U.K. should carry their European Health Insurance Card (EHIC), which replaced the E111 form as proof of entitlement to free/reduced-cost medical treatment abroad

(☎ **0845-606-2030;** www.ehic.org.uk). Note, however, that the EHIC only covers "necessary medical treatment"; for repatriation costs, lost money, baggage, or cancellation, you should buy travel insurance from a reputable company.

Staying Healthy When You Travel

Getting sick will ruin your vacation, so I *strongly* advise against it. (Of course, last time I checked, the bugs weren't listening to me any more than they probably listen to you.)

Staying healthy on a trip to Costa Rica is predominantly a matter of being a little cautious about what you eat and drink and using common sense. Know your physical limits, and don't overexert yourself in the ocean, on hikes, or in athletic activities. Respect the tropical sun and protect yourself from it.

For information on purchasing additional medical insurance for your trip, see the preceding section.

Talk to your doctor before leaving on a trip if you have a serious and/or chronic illness. For conditions such as epilepsy, diabetes, or heart problems, wear a **MedicAlert identification tag** (☎ **888-633-4298;** www.medicalert.org), which immediately alerts doctors to your condition and gives them access to your records through MedicAlert's 24-hour hotline. Contact the **International Association for Medical Assistance to Travelers** (IAMAT; ☎ **716-754-4883,** or 416-652-0137 in Canada; www.iamat.org) for tips on travel and health concerns in the countries you're visiting, and lists of local, English-speaking doctors. The U.S. **Centers for Disease Control and Prevention** (☎ **800-311-3435;** www.cdc.gov) provides up-to-date information on health hazards by region or country and offers tips on food safety. **Travel Health Online** (www.tripprep.com), sponsored by a consortium of travel medicine practitioners, may also offer helpful advice on traveling abroad. You can find listings of reliable clinics overseas at the **International Society of Travel Medicine** (www.istm.org)

Tropical illnesses

Your chance of contracting any serious tropical disease in Costa Rica is slim, especially if you stick to the beaches or traditional spots for visitors. However, malaria, dengue fever, and leptospirosis all exist in Costa Rica, so knowing what they are is a good idea.

Although not widespread, **malaria** is found in the lowlands on both coasts and in the northern zone. Although rarely found in urban areas, it's still a problem in some remote rural regions and along the Caribbean coast. Malaria prophylaxes are available, but several have side effects, and others are of questionable effectiveness. Consult your doctor regarding what is currently considered the best preventive treatment for malaria. Be sure to ask whether a recommended drug will cause you to be hypersensitive to the sun; it would be a shame to come down here for the beaches and then have to hide under an umbrella the entire time. Because malaria-carrying mosquitoes usually come out at night, you should do as much as possible to avoid being bitten after dark. If you are in a malarial area, wear long pants and long sleeves, use insect repellent, and either sleep under a mosquito net or burn mosquito coils (similar to incense, but with pesticide).

Of greater concern, perhaps, is **dengue fever,** which has had periodic outbreaks in Latin America since the mid-1990s. Dengue fever is similar to malaria and is spread by an aggressive daytime mosquito. This mosquito seems to be most common in lowland urban areas, and Puntarenas, Liberia, and Limón have been the worst-hit cities in Costa Rica. Dengue is also known as "bone-break fever" because it's usually accompanied by severe body aches. The first infection with dengue fever will make you very sick but should cause no serious damage. However, a second infection with a different strain of the dengue virus can lead to internal hemorrhaging and could be life threatening.

Many people are convinced that taking B-complex vitamins daily will help prevent mosquitoes from biting you. I don't think the American Medical Association has endorsed this idea yet, but I've run across it in enough places to think that there may be something to it.

One final tropical fever that I think you should know about (because I got it myself) is **leptospirosis.** There are more than 200 strains of *leptospiri,* which are animal-borne bacteria transmitted to humans via contact with drinking, swimming, or bathing water. This bacterial infection is easily treated with antibiotics; however, it can quickly cause very high fever and chills and should be treated promptly.

If you develop a high fever accompanied by severe body aches, nausea, diarrhea, or vomiting during or shortly after a visit to Costa Rica, consult a physician as soon as possible.

Costa Rica has been relatively free of the **cholera** epidemic that has spread through much of Latin America in recent years. This is largely due to an extensive public-awareness campaign that has promoted good hygiene and increased sanitation. Your chances of contracting cholera while you're here are very slim.

Dietary red flags

Because many folks experience minor gastrointestinal weirdness when visiting a foreign country, I recommend buying and drinking bottled water or soft drinks, but the water in San José and in most of the heavily visited spots in Costa Rica is safe to drink. If your stomach is very sensitive, drink straight from the bottle or can (wiping it off first), avoid drinks with ice, and don't eat fruits or vegetables that you don't peel first, except at the better hotels and restaurants.

Even though the water in San José and most popular destinations in Costa Rica is generally safe, and even though you've been careful to buy bottled water, order *frescos en leche* (fruit shakes made with milk rather than water), and drink your soft drink warm (without ice cubes — which are made from water, after all), you still might encounter some intestinal difficulties. Most of this is just due to tender northern stomachs coming into contact with slightly more aggressive Latin American intestinal flora. In extreme cases of diarrhea or intestinal discomfort, it's worth taking a stool sample to a lab for analysis. The results will usually pinpoint the amoebic or parasitic culprit, which can then be readily treated with available over-the-counter medicines.

Except in the most established and hygienic of restaurants, it's also advisable to avoid ceviche, a raw seafood salad, especially if it has any shellfish in it. It could be home to any number of bacterial critters.

Bugs, bites, and other wildlife concerns

Although Costa Rica has Africanized bees (the notorious "killer bees" of fact and fable) and several species of venomous snakes, your chances of being bitten are minimal, especially if you refrain from sticking your hands into hives or under rocks in the forest. If you know that you're allergic to bee stings, consult your doctor before traveling.

Snake sightings, much less snakebites, are very rare. Moreover, the majority of snakes in Costa Rica are nonpoisonous. If you do encounter a snake, stay calm, don't make any sudden movements, and don't try to handle it. Avoid sticking your hands under rocks, branches, and fallen trees.

Scorpions, black widow spiders, tarantulas, bullet ants, and biting insects of many types can all be found in Costa Rica. In general, they aren't nearly the danger or nuisance most visitors fear. Watch where you stick your hands. In addition, you might want to shake out your clothes and shoes before putting them on to avoid any unpleasant and painful surprises.

Tropical sun

Limit your exposure to the sun, especially during the first few days of your trip and, thereafter, from 11 a.m. to 2 p.m. Use a sunscreen with a high SPF, and apply it liberally. Remember that children need more protection than adults.

What to do if you get sick away from home

Your hotel front desk should be your best source of information and assistance if you get sick while in Costa Rica. In addition, your local consulate in Costa Rica can provide a list of area doctors who speak English. The local English-language newspaper, the *Tico Times,* is another good resource.

In general, Costa Rica has a high level of medical care and services for a developing nation. The better private hospitals and doctors in San José are very good. In fact, given the relatively low-cost nature of care and treatment, a sizeable number of Americans come to Costa Rica each year for elective surgery and other care.

Most state-run hospitals and walk-in clinics around the country have emergency rooms that can treat most conditions, although I highly recommend the private hospitals in San José if your condition is not life-threatening and can wait for treatment until you reach one of them.

In San José, try **Clínica Bíblica,** Avenida 14 between calles Central and 1 (☎ **2522-1000;** www.clinicabiblica.com), which offers emergency services to foreign visitors at reasonable prices, or the **Hospital CIMA** (☎ **2208-1000;** www.hospitalsanjose.net), which has the most modern facilities in the country and is located in Escazú on the Próspero Fernández Highway that connects San José and the western suburb of Santa Ana.

Staying Connected

Costa Rica primarily uses **GSM (Global System for Mobile Communications)** networks. If your cellphone is on a GSM system and you have a world-capable multiband phone such as many Sony Ericsson, LG, Motorola, or Samsung models, you can make and receive calls across civilized areas around much of the globe. Just call your wireless operator and ask for international roaming to be activated on your account. Per-minute charges can be high, though — up to $5 in Costa Rica, depending upon your plan.

Unfortunately, those with unlocked tri- and quad-band GSM phones still cannot simply buy a local SIM card in Costa Rica. However, a free trade agreement with the United States and other Central American nations is expected to open up the state monopoly on telecommunications during 2010, and this should change.

Several local firms rent cellphones to visiting tourists and business travelers. However, none of the rental companies has a booth or office at the airport, so you'll have to contact a rental company either beforehand or from your hotel. Most will deliver the phone to your hotel. **Cell Service** (☎ **2296-5553;** www.cellservicecr.com), **Costa Rica Cellular Connection** (☎ **800-372-3183** in the U.S. and Canada, 8876-1776 in Costa Rica; www.costaricacellularconnection.com), and **GSM Rent A Cell** (☎ **2231-5410;** www.gsmrentacell.com) all rent cellphones. Rates range from $5 to $10 per day or $30 to $50 per week for the rental, with charges of 50¢ to $1.50 per minute for local calls and $1 to $3 per minute for international calls.

In addition to these companies, most of the major car-rental agencies are offering cellphone rentals, for rates similar to those listed earlier.

Voice over Internet protocol (VOIP)

If you have Web access while traveling, consider a broadband-based telephone service (in technical terms, **voice over Internet protocol,** or **VOIP**) such as Skype (www.skype.com) or Vonage (www.vonage.com), which allow you to make free international calls from your laptop or in a cybercafe. Neither service requires the people you're calling to also have that service (though there are fees if they don't). Check the Web sites for details.

Accessing the Internet away from home

Most major tourist destinations in Costa Rica have one or more cyber-cafes, and in those destinations that don't, most hotels will let you check your e-mail and surf the Web either for free or for a nominal charge.

If you have your own computer, you can use the high-speed Wi-Fi access offered by more and more hotels, resorts, cafes, and retailers around Costa Rica, either free or for a small fee.

Costa Rica uses standard U.S.-style two- and three-prong electric outlets with 110-volt AC current, and standard U.S.-style phone jacks. Wherever you go, bring a **connection kit** with power and phone adapters, a spare phone cord, and a spare Ethernet network cable — or find out whether your hotel supplies them to guests.

Keeping Up with Airline Security Measures

With the federalization of airport security, security procedures at U.S. airports are more stable and consistent than ever. Generally, you'll be fine if you arrive at the airport **one hour** before a domestic flight and **two hours** before an international flight; if you show up late, tell an airline employee and she'll probably whisk you to the front of the line.

Bring a **current, government-issued photo ID** such as a driver's license or passport. Keep your ID at the ready to show at check-in, the security checkpoint, and sometimes even the gate. (Children under 18 do not need government-issued photo IDs for domestic flights, but they do for international flights to most countries.)

E-tickets have made paper tickets nearly obsolete. If you have an E-ticket, you can beat the ticket-counter lines by using airport **electronic kiosks** or even **online check-in** from your home computer. Online check-in involves logging on to your airline's Web site, accessing your reservation, and printing out your boarding pass — and the airline may even offer you bonus miles to do so! If you're using a kiosk at the airport, bring the credit card you used to book the ticket or your frequent-flier card. Print out your boarding pass from the kiosk and simply proceed to the security checkpoint with your pass and a photo ID. **Curbside check-in** is also a good way to avoid lines, although a few airlines still ban curbside check-in; call the airline or check the airline's Web site before you go.

Speed up security by **not wearing metal objects** such as big belt buckles. If you have metallic body parts, a note from your doctor can prevent a long chat with the security screeners. Keep in mind that only **ticketed passengers** are allowed past security, except for folks escorting disabled passengers or children.

Federalization has stabilized **what you can carry on** and **what you can't.** Travelers in the U.S. are allowed one carry-on bag, plus a "personal item" such as a purse, briefcase, or laptop bag. Carry-on hoarders can stuff all sorts of things into a laptop bag; as long as it has a laptop in it, it's still considered a personal item. The Transportation Security Administration (TSA) has issued a list of restricted items; check www.tsa.gov for details.

Airport screeners may decide that your checked luggage needs to be searched by hand. You can purchase luggage locks that allow screeners to open and relock a checked bag if hand-searching is necessary. Look for Travel Sentry–certified locks at luggage or travel shops and Brookstone stores (or online at www.brookstone.com). For more information on the locks, visit www.travelsentry.org.

Part III

San José and the Central Valley

"Nowhere have I seen such biodiversity of frogs, snakes, butterflies, and insects. And that's just in my coffee cup!"

In this part . . .

Located more or less in the geographic center of the country, San José is also the political, social, cultural, and transportation center of Costa Rica. This part tells you what to see and what to avoid in the city. It lists the best hotels and restaurants in San José in a range of price categories and a variety of locations.

After you're settled in, orientated, and well fed, you can take advantage of a wide range of attractions and day trips in the city and surrounding Central Valley to keep you busy. I fill you in on your numerous options in this part.

Chapter 11

Settling into San José

In This Chapter

▶ Arriving in San José and getting your bearings

▶ Finding your way around San José

▶ Choosing where to stay and where to dine

▶ Taking in the view from a *mirador*

*T*he prevailing rap is that San José is an unattractive, uninspiring, and somewhat dangerous city, and you should make every effort to get out of the city as quickly as possible. This is, in part, true: Streets are burdened by traffic in a near-constant state of gridlock, sidewalks are poorly maintained and claustrophobic, and street crime is a problem.

Still, San José is one of the most cosmopolitan cities in Central America. Several very respectable museums are in town. And you can find a broad selection of small, elegant hotels in renovated historic buildings, as well as innovative restaurants serving a wide range of international cuisines.

Things have been improving, however. Mayor Johnny Araya has led ambitious and controversial campaigns to rid the narrow sidewalks of illegal vendors, to reduce the clutter of billboards and overhead signs, and to bury a good share of the city's electrical and phone cables. A move to more efficiently regulate bus and commuter traffic has also begun, although much more needs to be done in this area.

San José makes a great base for a variety of day trips and excursions. Within an hour or two, you can climb a volcano, go white-water rafting, hike through a cloud forest, and stroll through a butterfly garden — among many, many other activities.

For many visitors to Costa Rica, San José invariably serves as a default hub or transfer point, unless you're flying in and out of Liberia (see Chapter 6 for more information). This chapter helps you plan your time in the capital and helps ease your way through the aforementioned pitfalls.

Getting There

With the increasing number of direct flights into Liberia, San José is no longer the de facto transportation hub for all tourists coming to Costa Rica. Still, a vast majority of travelers do fly in and out of the country's capital, because for most airlines, San José is the gateway to Costa Rica.

Flying is clearly the fastest and most comfortable way to get to San José. This section also covers arriving by bus and car. However, these options are far less common, given the long travel times involved and the often shabby conditions of the buses and roads.

Arriving by air

A great majority of international flights to Costa Rica land at the **Juan Santamaría International Airport** (☎ **2437-2626** for 24-hour airport information; www.alterra.co.cr; airport code: SJO), which is located near the city of Alajuela, about 20 minutes from downtown San José.

At press time the airport was still in the midst of a major renovation and expansion, a process that has been plagued by work stoppages, delays, contract disputes, bickering between the government and the international company in charge of the work, and financing problems. It's hard to be specific, but work is expected to be completed sometime in 2010.

So far, one of two new terminal buildings have been completed, and all the major airlines have moved their desks into this terminal. However, the new baggage claim and Customs and Immigration areas, which are modern and spacious, are not particularly fast and efficient. Moreover, despite the major remodeling, chaos and confusion continue to greet arriving passengers the second they step out of the terminal. As in the past, you must abandon your luggage carts just before exiting the building and then face a gauntlet of aggressive taxi drivers and people offering to carry your bags. Fortunately, all the major car-rental companies, and the official airport taxi service (see later in this section) have booths inside the terminal after you clear Customs.

Most porters or skycaps wear a uniform identifying them as such, but sometimes "improvised" porters will try to earn a few dollars by carrying your bags. (Because the line of waiting taxis and shuttles is just steps away, your bags probably won't have to be carried.)

Tip porters about 50¢ per bag.

Keep a watchful eye on your bags. In the past, thieves have preyed on newly arrived passengers and their luggage.

Getting from the airport to your hotel

You can get to and from the airport in several different ways, but I list them here, starting with what's easiest:

✔ **By taxi:** If you have a lot of luggage, a cab is your best option. Try to stick with **Taxis Unidos Aeropuerto** (☎ **2221-6865**; www. taxiaeropuerto.com), which operates a fleet of orange vans and sedans out of the airport. You no longer have to buy a prepaid voucher, as these taxis now use official meters. It costs between $18 and $22 to most hotels downtown.

In addition to Taxis Unidos, you'll also find regular cabs (marked red sedans) and *pirata* (pirate) cabs, freelance drivers using their own vehicles. A handful of these drivers and their touts await all arriving flights, and will be screaming "Taxi, my friend," or something similar, as you exit the terminal. You could use either of these latter options. *Piratas* tend to charge a dollar or two less, but I recommend using the official service for safety and standardized prices.

Don't worry if you haven't been able to exchange money for colones. The official taxi company, and most of the *piratas,* accept U.S. dollars.

✔ **By shuttle:** A couple of the large chain hotels, including the **Marriott** and **Hampton Inn,** have regular free shuttles to and from the airport.

You can also take the **Gray Line** (☎ **2220-2126**; www.grayline costarica.com) or **Interbus** (☎ **2283-5573**; www.interbus online.com) shuttle-bus services. Gray Line runs approximately every 30 minutes and charges $15 per person to most downtown hotels. You can either book in advance or catch the bus at the curb just beyond the exit for international arriving passengers. Interbus charges between $7 and $10 per person and will arrange specific pickup times. With Interbus, reserving in advance is best.

✔ **By bus:** Alajuela–San José buses stop right at the airport, run frequently, and will drop you off anywhere along Paseo Colón, or at a station downtown near Parque de la Merced (La Merced Park) between calles 12 and 14 and avenidas 2 and 4. You can take one of two separate lines: **Tuasa** buses are red; **Station Wagon** buses are beige/yellow. At the airport, you'll find the bus stop directly in front of the main terminal. Be sure to ask whether the bus is going to San José, or you may end up in Alajuela.

✔ **By rental car:** Quite a few car-rental agencies with desks and offices can be found at the airport, although if you're planning to spend a few days in San José itself, a car is a liability. (If you're heading immediately to the beach, though, picking up your car here is much easier than having to get it at a downtown office.)

Various car-rental agencies already have desks inside the new terminal, right where you exit Customs and Immigration; other agencies are still in limbo, awaiting completion of airport remodeling, so be sure to contact them first to confirm that they'll have an agent or an office at the airport when you arrive.

The airport sits right off the main Interamerican Highway, and the only exit will put you right on the highway. Follow signs to San José if you're going downtown. Follow signs to Alajuela and San Ramón if you're heading straight to the beach or to a hotel either in Alajuela or north of the Interamerican Highway.

Arriving by bus

San José is connected to all other major Central American hub cities by a couple of bus lines. **Transnica** (☎ 2223-4242; www.transnica.com; Calle 22, between avenidas 3 and 5) and **Tica Bus Company** (☎ 2221-0006; www.ticabus.com; Avenida 3 and Calle 26) both service San José directly from Panama City and Managua, with onward connections to most other major Central American cities. Buy your ticket in advance — several days in advance if you plan to travel on weekends or holidays.

Buses arriving from Panama pass first through Cartago and San Pedro before letting passengers off in downtown San José; buses arriving from Nicaragua generally enter the city on the west end of town, on Paseo Colón. If you're staying here, you can ask to be let off before the final stop.

Arriving by car

If you're intrepid enough to be arriving by car, you'll be entering San José via the Interamerican Highway. If you arrive **from Nicaragua and the north,** you'll find that the highway brings you first past the airport and the city of Alajuela, to the western edge of downtown, right at the end of Paseo Colón, where it hits Parque La Sabana (La Sabana Park). This area is well marked with large road signs, which direct you either to the downtown (centro) or to the western suburbs of Rhormerser, Pavas, and Escazú. If you're heading downtown, just follow the flow of traffic and turn left on Paseo Colón.

If you're entering **from Panama and the south,** things get a little more complicated. The Interamerican Highway first passes through the city of Cartago and then through the San José suburbs of Curridabat and San Pedro before reaching downtown. This route is relatively well marked, and if you stick with the major flow of traffic, you should find San José without any problem. If you get lost, feel free to stop and ask directions. If you don't speak any Spanish, repeating the phrase *San José centro* should get you pointed toward downtown.

Orienting Yourself in San José

Downtown San José is laid out on a grid. *Avenidas* (avenues) run east and west, while *calles* (streets) run north and south. The center of the city is at **Avenida Central** and **Calle Central.** To the north of Avenida Central, the *avenidas* have odd numbers beginning with Avenida 1; to the south, they have even numbers beginning with Avenida 2. Likewise, *calles* to the east of Calle Central have odd numbers, and those to the west have even numbers.

The main downtown artery is **Avenida 2,** which merges with Avenida Central on either side of the downtown area. West of downtown, Avenida Central becomes **Paseo Colón,** which ends at Parque La Sabana and feeds into the highway to Alajuela, the airport, and the Pacific coast. East of downtown, Avenida Central leads to San Pedro and then to Cartago and the Interamerican Highway heading south. **Calle 3** takes you out of town to the north and puts you on the Guápiles Highway out to the Caribbean coast.

Introducing the neighborhoods

San José is spread out and sprawling. It's divided into dozens of neighborhoods known as *barrios.* Only a handful of these are of any interest or concern for visitors. This section gives you a quick rundown of the major barrios or neighborhoods in San José. I mention only the best-known barrios — meaning the ones that you're most likely to stay in or visit. Most are close to the central downtown area, but some are located on the outskirts or are considered close-in suburbs.

Downtown

In San José's busy downtown, you'll find most of the city's museums, as well as a handful of small urban parks and open-air plazas. Many tour companies, restaurants, and hotels are also located here. Unfortunately, gridlocked traffic and heavy exhaust fumes make this one of the least pleasant parts of the city. Streets and avenues are usually bustling and crowded with pedestrians and vehicular traffic, and street crime is most rampant here. The sections of Avenida Central between calles 6 and 7, as well as Avenida 4 between calles 9 and 14, have been converted into a pedestrian malls, slightly improving things on these stretches.

Barrio Amón and Barrio Otoya

These two picturesque neighborhoods, just north and east of downtown, are the site of the greatest concentration of historic buildings in San José. Some of these have been renovated and turned into hotels and restaurants. If you're looking for character and don't mind the noise and exhaust fumes from passing cars and buses, this neighborhood makes a good base for exploring the city.

La Sabana/Paseo Colón

Paseo Colón, a wide boulevard west of downtown, is an extension of Avenida Central and ends at Parque La Sabana. It has several good, small hotels and numerous restaurants. This is also where several of the city's car-rental agencies have their in-town offices. Once the site of the city's main airport, the Parque La Sabana is San José's largest public park, with ample green areas, jogging paths, an urban "canopy tour," sport facilities, and a couple of small ponds. At the juncture of Paseo Colón and Parque La Sabana sits the Costa Rican Art Museum.

San José

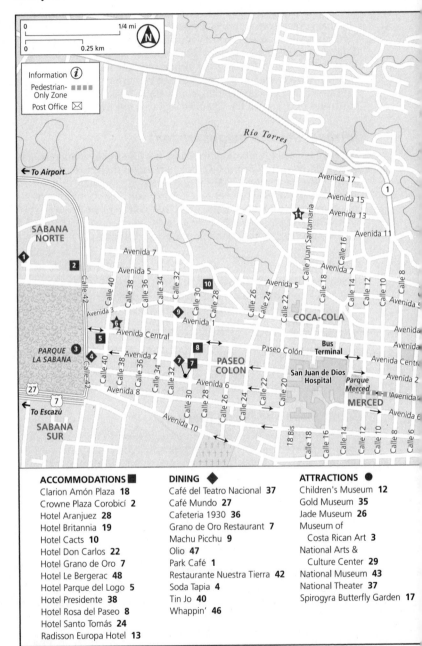

0   1/4 mi
0   0.25 km

Information ⓘ
Pedestrian-
Only Zone ▪▪▪▪
Post Office ✉

← To Airport

Río Torres

Avenida 17
Avenida 15
Avenida 13
Avenida 11

SABANA NORTE

Avenida 7
Avenida 7
Avenida 5
Avenida 5

Calle Juan Santamaria

COCA-COLA

Avenida 3
Avenida 1
Avenida Central

Bus Terminal
Paseo Colón

PARQUE LA SABANA

Avenida 2
PASEO COLON
San Juan de Dios Hospital
Parque Merced

Avenida 8
Avenida 2

27
7
← To Escazú

SABANA SUR

Avenida 10

MERCED

18 Bis

ACCOMMODATIONS ■
Clarion Amón Plaza **18**
Crowne Plaza Corobicí **2**
Hotel Aranjuez **28**
Hotel Britannia **19**
Hotel Cacts **10**
Hotel Don Carlos **22**
Hotel Grano de Oro **7**
Hotel Le Bergerac **48**
Hotel Parque del Logo **5**
Hotel Presidente **38**
Hotel Rosa del Paseo **8**
Hotel Santo Tomás **24**
Radisson Europa Hotel **13**

DINING ◆
Café del Teatro Nacional **37**
Café Mundo **27**
Cafeteria 1930 **36**
Grano de Oro Restaurant **7**
Machu Picchu **9**
Olio **47**
Park Café **1**
Restaurante Nuestra Tierra **42**
Soda Tapia **4**
Tin Jo **40**
Whappin' **46**

ATTRACTIONS ●
Children's Museum **12**
Gold Museum **35**
Jade Museum **26**
Museum of
    Costa Rican Art **3**
National Arts &
    Culture Center **29**
National Museum **43**
National Theater **37**
Spirogyra Butterfly Garden **17**

SHOPPING

Arte Latino **33**
Boutique Annemarie **22**
Boutique Kiosco **20**
Galería Amon **23**
Galería Jacobo Carpio **41**
Galería Namu **25**
Seventh Street Books **34**
TEORetica **21**

NIGHTLIFE

Casino Club Colonial **30**
Casino Del Rey **31**
Castro's **11**
Chelles **39**
Copacabana **15**
El Cuartel de la Boca del Monte **44**
El Observatorio **45**
El Pueblo **16**
El Tobogán **14**
Key Largo **32**
Vertigo **6**

San Pedro, Los Yoses, and Barrio Escalante

Located just east of downtown, Los Yoses and Barrio Escalante are upper-middle-class neighborhoods that are home to many diplomatic missions and embassies. San Pedro is a little farther east and is the site of the University of Costa Rica. There are numerous college-type bars and restaurants all around the edge of the campus, as well as several good restaurants and small hotels in both neighborhoods.

Escazú, Santa Ana, and Ciudad Colón

Located in the hills west of San José, Escazú, Santa Ana, and Ciudad Colón are fast-growing, mostly affluent suburbs. Although the area is only 10 to 20 minutes from San José by taxi, it feels much farther away because of its slightly more rural atmosphere. This area has a large expatriate community, with many bed-and-breakfast establishments and excellent restaurants.

"I know a number is here somewhere . . .": The arcane art of finding an address in San José

Finding an address is one of the most confusing aspects of visiting Costa Rica in general, and San José in particular. Although street addresses and occasional building numbers are often listed for locations in downtown San José, they're almost never used. Addresses are given as a set of coordinates such as "Calle 3 between avenidas Central and 1." It's then up to you to locate the building within that block, keeping in mind that the building could be on either side of the street.

Many addresses or directions forego street names and numbers altogether and rely on more colloquial information, such as the number of meters from a specified intersection or some other well-known landmark. (Don't get hung up on exact measurements; in Costa Rica, 100m = 1 block, 200m = 2 blocks, and so on.) The landmarks are what become truly confusing for visitors to Costa Rica because they're often simply restaurants, bars, and shops that would be familiar only to locals.

Things get even more confusing when the landmark in question no longer exists. The classic example of this is "the Coca-Cola," one of the most common landmarks used in addresses in the blocks surrounding San José's main market. The trouble is, the Coca-Cola bottling plant that it refers to is no longer there; the edifice is long gone, and one of the principal downtown bus depots stands in its place. Old habits die hard, though, and the address description remains.

You may also try to find some place near the *antiguo higuerón* (old fig tree) in San Pedro. This tree was felled years ago. In outlying neighborhoods, addresses can become long directions such as "50m south of the old church, then 100m east, then 20m south." Luckily for the visitor, most downtown addresses are more straightforward.

Heredia, Alajuela, and the airport area

Heredia and Alajuela are two colonial-era cities that lie closer to the airport than San José. Alajuela is the closest city to the airport, with Heredia lying about midway between Alajuela and the capital. Several quite beautiful high-end boutique hotels are found here. Several large, modern hotels are located on, or just off, the Interamerican Highway close to the airport.

Finding information after you arrive

The **Costa Rican Tourism Institute**, or **Instituto Costarricense de Turismo** (ICT; ☎ 2443-1535; www.visitcostarica.com) has a desk at the Juan Santamaría International Airport, located in the baggage claims area, just before Customs. You can pick up maps and browse brochures, and they may even lend you a phone to make or confirm a reservation. It's open daily from 9 a.m. to 10 p.m.

If you're looking for the **main ICT visitor information center** in San José, it's located below the Plaza de la Cultura, at the entrance to the Oro Museum (Gold Museum), on Calle 5 between avenidas Central and 2 (☎ 2222-1090). The people there are helpful, although the information they have to offer is rather limited. This office is open Monday through Friday from 9 a.m. to 5 p.m.

Getting Around San José

You've got plenty of options for getting around San José. In most instances, a taxi will be your best bet. But in this section, I also tell you how to navigate the city by bus, rental car, and foot.

By taxi

Taxis are an easy and inexpensive way to get around San José. Although taxis in San José have *marías* (meters), the drivers sometimes refuse to use them, particularly with foreigners, so you'll occasionally have to negotiate the price. Always try to get them to use the meter first (say, "Ponga la maría, por favor"). The official rate at press time is around 80¢ for the first kilometer (½ mile) and around 60¢ for each additional kilometer. If you have a rough idea of how far it is to your destination, you can estimate how much it should cost from these figures. After 10 p.m., taxis are legally allowed to add a 20 percent surcharge. Some of the meters are programmed to include the extra charge automatically, but be careful: Some drivers will use the evening setting during the daytime or to try to charge an extra 20 percent on top of the higher meter setting.

Tipping taxi drivers is not expected. Also, it's not uncommon for passengers to sit in the front seat with the driver.

Depending on your location, the time of day, and the weather (rain places taxis at a premium), it's relatively easy to hail a cab downtown. You'll always find taxis in front of the Teatro Nacional (National Theater) and around Parque Central (Central Park) at Avenida Central and Calle Central. Taxis in front of hotels and the El Pueblo tourist complex usually try to charge more than others, although this is technically illegal. Most hotels will gladly call you a cab, either for a downtown excursion or for a trip back out to the airport. You can also get a cab by calling **Coopetaxi** (☎ 2235-9966), **Coopeirazu** (☎ 2254-3211), or **Coopeguaria** (☎ 2227-9300). **Cinco Estrellas Taxi** (☎ 2228-3159) is another company that is based in Escazú, but it services the entire metropolitan area and airport and claims to always have an English-speaking operator on call.

By bus

Bus transportation around San José is cheap — the fare is usually somewhere around 10¢ to 50¢ (although the Alajuela/San José buses that run in from the airport cost 75¢). However, be forewarned: Costa Rica's urban buses tend to be overcrowded, slow, and in poor condition. Moreover, they're often frequented by pickpockets and petty thieves. So if you do opt to take the local public transportation, be alert and careful.

The most important buses are those running east along Avenida 2 and west along Avenida 3. The **Sabana/Cementerio** bus runs from Parque La Sabana to downtown and is one of the most convenient buses to use. You'll find a bus stop for the outbound Sabana/Cementerio bus near the main post office on Avenida 3 near the corner of Calle 2 and another one on Calle 11 between avenidas Central and 1. This bus also has stops all along Avenida 2. **San Pedro** buses leave from Avenida Central between calles 9 and 11, in front of the Cine Capri, and take you out of downtown heading east. **Escazú-** and **Santa Ana–**bound buses leave from the Coca-Cola bus station, as well as from Avenida 1 between calles 24 and 28. Alternatively, you can pick up both the Escazú and Santa Ana buses, as well as those bound for Alajuela and the airport, from the busy bus stop on Calle 42, just north of Gimnasio Nacional.

Board buses from the front. The bus drivers can make change, although they don't like to receive large bills. ***Remember:*** Be especially mindful of your wallet, purse, or other valuables because pickpockets often work the crowded buses.

By car

In general, I consider it a liability for visitors to rent a car while in San José. The city streets are poorly marked and congested, Costa Rican drivers tend to be aggressive, and traffic laws as well as basic norms of road courtesy are generally ignored. Relying on taxis is much easier and more economical.

Renting a car in San José will cost you between $45 and $140 per day (the higher prices are for four-wheel-drive vehicles). Many car-rental agencies have offices at the airport, as well as downtown. Regardless, almost all will either meet you at the airport or deliver the car to any San José hotel. See Chapter 7 for more information on renting a car in Costa Rica.

On foot

Downtown San José is quite compact. Even so, aside from touring a few heavily trafficked tourist areas in broad daylight, I don't recommend exploring San José by foot. Street crime is a real problem; because most visitors stand out prominently, they are targets. The best places to stroll around downtown are the two main plazas — Plaza de la Democracia and Plaza de la Cultura — and the pedestrian-only sections of Avenida Central between calles Central and 7, and Avenida 4 between calles 9 and 14.

Where to Stay in San José

You'll find a wide range of hotel options in San José, ranging from comfortable and homey budget lodgings to unique boutique hotels housed in restored colonial-era mansions to large modern resort hotels. Most hotels in San José are moderately priced, including some of the best of the bunch.

 If you're heading out to Guanacaste, the central Pacific, or the northern zone, you may want to consider a hotel either near or beyond the airport. Sure, you give up proximity to downtown, but you can cut as much as an hour off your travel time to any of these destinations.

 Apart from the large, modern hotels and chains, few hotels in San José come with air-conditioning. Even many of the more expensive boutique hotels lack air-conditioning. The good news, given the mild, temperate climate, is that this is really not a problem for most people. If you absolutely must have air-conditioning, be sure to inquire in advance whether your room will have it.

The following list features a wide range of choices to suit any budget. I also list a selection of hotels from various neighborhoods, including hotels close to the airport and others just slightly out of downtown.

Prices for recommended hotels are designated with dollar signs — the more you see, the more expensive the hotel. Check the introduction to this book for how the dollar-sign system works. Also, see Chapter 8 for tips on booking your accommodations.

Clarion Amón Plaza
$$$–$$$$ Barrio Amón

This business-class hotel is larger and more modern than the nearby boutique options. Nothing particularly stands out about the property or rooms here; however, in terms of service, location, and price, this hotel gets my nod over the nearby Holiday Inn. The rooms are all large and well kept, and they come with plenty of amenities, including wireless Internet connections. The hotel features a small exercise room, a casino, free Wi-Fi throughout and a lovely, open-air, sidewalk restaurant. You're also close to all the downtown action here.

See map p. 96. Avenida 11 and Calle 3 bis, San José. ☎ 877-424-6423 in the U.S., 2523-4600 in Costa Rica. Fax: 2523-4614. www.hotelamonplaza.com. Free parking. Rack rates: $130–$160 double, $220 suite. AE, DC, MC, V.

Finca Rosa Blanca Coffee Plantation & Inn
$$$$–$$$$$ Santa Bárbara de Heredia

Finca Rosa Blanca is an eclectic architectural confection set amid the lush, green hillsides of a coffee plantation. Square corners have seemingly been prohibited in the design of this beautiful hotel. Instead, you'll find turrets and curving walls of glass, arched windows, and a semicircular built-in couch. Everywhere the glow of polished hardwood blends with blindingly white stucco walls and brightly painted murals.

Inside, plenty of original artwork lines the walls, and each room is decidedly unique. El Guarumo (The Cecropia) has a delightful handcrafted tile tub built into a nook with great views, while La Ventana (The Window) features a hand-painted mural of a window over the room's queen-size bed. If breathtaking bathrooms are your idea of the ultimate luxury, consider splurging on the master suite, which has a stone waterfall that cascades into a tub in front of a huge picture window. This suite also has a spiral staircase that leads to the top of a turret, where the master bedroom is located. The separate villas have the same sense of eclectic luxury, with quite a bit of space and privacy. All rooms are nonsmoking and have free Wi-Fi.

The small outdoor pool sits on a gentle hillside, and a Jacuzzi rests on the roof of the main building. The hotel has 14 hectares of organic coffee under cultivation, and its in-house coffee tour is not to be missed. In 2008, the hotel added a full-service spa, and a large restaurant and outdoor dining area, with excellent views over the valley and city below.

Santa Bárbara de Heredia. ☎ 2269-9392. Fax: 2269-9555. www.fincarosa blanca.com. Free parking. Rack rates: $290–$450 double. Extra person $30. Rates include breakfast. AE, MC, V.

Hotel Aranjuez
$ **Barrio Amón**

This is the best budget option close to downtown. Located on a quiet and safe street on the outskirts of the Barrio Amón neighborhood, this humble hotel is made up of five contiguous houses. The rooms are all simple and clean, although some are a little dark. Both the rooms and bathrooms vary greatly in size, so be very specific when reserving, or ask to see a few rooms when you arrive. The cheapest rooms here share a couple of communal bathrooms. The best features, aside from the convivial hostel-like atmosphere, are the lush and shady gardens; the hanging orchids, bromeliads, and ferns decorating the hallways and nooks; and the numerous open lounge areas furnished with chairs, tables, and couches — great for lazing around and sharing travel tales with your fellow guests. The hotel has a couple of computers, as well as Wi-Fi throughout, and both are offered free.

See map p. 96. Calle 19, between avenidas 11 and 13, San José. ☎ **877-898-8663** *in the U.S., 2256-1825 in Costa Rica. Fax: 2223-3528.* www.hotelaranjuez.com. *Free parking. Rack rates: $26–$47. Rates include breakfast buffet. V.*

Hotel Britannia
$$ **Barrio Amón**

This is the most luxurious of the many boutique hotels that have been created from restored old houses in Barrio Amón. Built in 1910, the large, low building, with its wraparound veranda, is also one of the area's most attractive hotels. Along with the restored old home, a four-story addition is separated from the original building by a narrow atrium. Rooms in the old section have hardwood floors and furniture; high ceilings and fans help keep them cool. In the deluxe rooms and junior suites, you get air-conditioning, one king- or two queen-size beds, and, in the case of the junior suites, a minibar. The standards come with either one king or two twin beds. Although the street-side rooms have double glass, light sleepers will still want to avoid them. The quietest rooms are those toward the back of the newer addition. In what was once a wine cellar, you'll find a casual restaurant.

See map p. 96. Calle 3 and Avenida 11, San José. ☎ **800-263-2618** *in the U.S., 2223-6667 in Costa Rica. Fax: 2223-6411.* www.hotelbritanniacostarica.com. *Limited street parking. Rack rates: $89–$105 double, $117 junior suite. AE, MC, V.*

Hotel Don Carlos
$$ **Barrio Amón**

If you're looking for an affordable, small hotel that is unmistakably Costa Rican and hints at the days of the planters and coffee barons, this is the place for you. Located in an old residential neighborhood, only blocks from the heart of downtown, the Don Carlos is popular with both vacationers and businesspeople. A large reproduction of a pre-Columbian carved-stone human figure stands outside the front door of this gray inn, which was a former president's mansion. Inside you'll find many more such reproductions, as well as orchids, ferns, paintings, and parrots. The rooms are distinct and vary greatly in size, so be specific when you reserve, or ask if it's possible to see a few when you check in. You'll also find a soothing ten-person Jacuzzi and an outdoor orchid garden and atrium where breakfast is served. The gift shop here is one of the largest in the country, and guests have free use of the hotel's computers and Wi-Fi network.

See map p. 96. 779 Calle 9, between avenidas 7 and 9, San José. ☎ *2221-6707. Fax: 2255-1152.* www.doncarloshotel.com. *Free parking. Rack rates: $80–$90 double. Rates include continental breakfast. AE, MC, V.*

Hotel Grano de Oro
$$–$$$$ Paseo Colón

San José boasts dozens of old homes that have been converted into boutique hotels, but this one is my favorite. Located on a quiet side street off Paseo Colón, this small hotel offers a variety of room types to fit most budgets and tastes. I prefer the patio rooms, which have French doors opening onto private patios. However, if you want a room with more space, ask for one of the deluxe rooms, which also have large, modern, tiled bathrooms with big tubs. All rooms are nonsmoking. Throughout all the guest rooms, you find attractive hardwood furniture, including old-fashioned wardrobes in some rooms. For additional luxuries, you can stay in one of the suites, which have whirlpool tubs. If you don't grab a suite, you still have access to the hotel's two rooftop Jacuzzis. The hotel's gorgeous restaurant is set around a spacious interior courtyard and serves excellent international cuisine and some of the best desserts in the city.

See map p. 96. Calle 30, no. 251, between avenidas 2 and 4, 150m (1½ blocks) south of Paseo Colón, San José. ☎ *2255-3322. Fax: 2221-2782.* www.hotelgranode oro.com. *Free parking. Rack rates: $115–$165 double, $210–$305 suite. AE, MC, V.*

Hotel Le Bergerac
$$–$$$ Los Yoses

Charming and sophisticated, the Hotel Le Bergerac has ingratiated itself over the years with business travelers and members of various diplomatic missions. These guests have found a tranquil environment in a quiet suburban neighborhood, spacious and comfortable accommodations, personal service, and gourmet meals. Still, you don't have to be a diplomat or business traveler to enjoy this hotel's charms. Le Bergerac is composed of three houses with courtyard gardens in between. Almost all the rooms are quite large, and each is a little different. My favorite rooms are those with private patio gardens or balconies.

See map p. 96. Calle 35, no. 50, San José. ☎ *2234-7850. Fax: 2225-9103.* www.bergerachotel.com. *Free parking. Rack rates: $90–$145 double. Rates include full breakfast. AE, DC, MC, V.*

Hotel Presidente
$$–$$$ **Downtown**

This modern business-class hotel is a good midrange option in the dead center of downtown. Although the hotel's eight stories practically qualify it for skyscraper status, very few of the rooms have any view to speak of; those with north-facing windows are your best bet. Rooms are all clean and modern and feature the basic amenities you'd expect. Most rooms come with one double and one single bed. If you want more space, opt for one of the junior suites. The master suite is a massive two-bedroom, featuring a wide-screen TV in the living room and a private eight-person Jacuzzi. A popular, casual, cafe-style restaurant is located just off the street.

See map p. 96. Avenida Central and Calle 7, San José. ☎ **2222-3022.** *Fax: 2221-1205.* www.hotel-presidente.com. *Free parking. Rack rates: $101–$111 double, $135–$175 junior suite, $350–$360 suite. Rates include breakfast buffet. AE, MC, V.*

Hotel Santo Tomás
$–$$ **Downtown**

Even though it's on a busy downtown street that gets quite sketchy after dark, this converted mansion is a quiet oasis inside. Built over 100 years ago by a coffee baron, the house has been lovingly restored and maintained by its owner, Thomas Douglas. Throughout the hotel, you'll enjoy the deep, dark tones of well-aged and well-worked wood. The rooms vary in size, but most are fairly spacious and have a small table and chairs. All rooms are nonsmoking and feature free Wi-Fi. Skylights in some bathrooms will brighten your morning, and firm beds provide a good night's sleep. The hotel has a couple of patio areas, as well as a lounge and combination breakfast room and outdoor bar. A small kidney-shaped pool rests outside with a Jacuzzi above it; the two are solar heated and connected by a tiny waterslide. The staff and management are extremely helpful with tour arrangements and any other needs or requests, and the restaurant here is excellent.

See map p. 96. Avenida 7, between calles 3 and 5, San José. ☎ **877-446-0658** *in the U.S.,* ☎ *2255-0448 in Costa Rica. Fax: 2222-3950.* www.hotelsantotomas.com. *No parking. Rack rates: $80–$110 double. Rates include breakfast buffet. MC, V.*

Marriott Costa Rica Hotel
$$$$–$$$$$ **Near the Airport**

Hands down, the Marriott is the top large luxury resort hotel in the San José metropolitan area. The hotel is designed in a mixed colonial style, with hand-painted Mexican tiles; antique red-clay roof tiles; weathered columns; and heavy wooden doors, lintels, and trim. The centerpiece is a large open-air interior patio, which somewhat replicates Old Havana's Plaza de Armas. The rooms are all comfortable and well appointed, with either a king-size bed or two double beds, two telephones, a working desk, an elegant wooden armoire holding a large TV, plenty of closet space, a comfortable sitting chair and ottoman, and a Juliet balcony. The bathrooms are up to par but feel slightly small for this price. Amenities are plentiful, and service here reaches a level of attention to detail uncommon in Costa Rica. Kids love the two large pools, and this is one of the few San José options with dependable baby-sitting services.

San Antonio de Belén. ☎ **888-236-2427** *in the U.S. and Canada, 2298-0844 in Costa Rica. Fax: 2298-0033.* www.marriott.com. *Free parking. Rack rates: $260 double, $310 executive level, $450 master suite, $1,000 presidential suite. AE, DC, MC, V.*

Peace Lodge
$$$$–$$$$$ Varablanca

The rooms here are some of the most impressive in the country — the bathrooms in the deluxe units easily earn that distinction alone. The lodge is an outgrowth of the popular La Paz Waterfall Gardens, which features a host of attractions and activities to please the entire family (see Chapter 12 for more information). The rooms are large and feature sparkling wood floors and trim, handcrafted four-poster beds, beautiful stone fireplaces, intricately sculpted steel light fixtures, and a host of other creative touches and details. Each room has a private balcony fitted with a mosaic-tiled Jacuzzi. The aforementioned deluxe bathrooms come with a second oversize Jacuzzi set under a skylight in the middle of an immense room that features a full interior wall planted with ferns, orchids, and bromeliads and fed by a functioning waterfall system. The lodge is located about 45 minutes from the airport. Peace Lodge was right near the epicenter of a major 6.2 earthquake in January 2009. However, the installations here and at the Waterfall Gardens escaped with very minor damage.

6km (3¾ miles) north of Varablanca on the road to San Miguel. ☎ **954-727-3997** *in the U.S., 2482-2720 or 2225-0643 in Costa Rica.* www.waterfallgardens.com. *Free parking. Rack rates: $245–$305 double, $395 villa. Rates include breakfast and entrance to La Paz Waterfall Gardens. Rates lower in the off season, higher during peak weeks. AE, MC, V.*

Vista del Valle Plantation Inn
$$–$$$ Alajuela

If you have little need for San José and are looking for a comfortable base for exploring the rest of Costa Rica, consider this fine little country inn. The architecture has a strong Japanese influence. The rooms are all either independent or duplex villas. All are open and airy, with lots of windows letting in lots of light. You also find plenty of varnished woodwork, small kitchenettes (in some), and comfortable wraparound decks here. My favorites are the Mona Lisa and Ylang-Ylang suites, which are octagonal in shape and set on the edge of the bluff with impressive views over the Río Grande and its steep-walled canyon. The grounds are wonderfully landscaped, with several inviting seating areas set among a wealth of flowering tropical plants. You can lounge around the lovely outdoor pool, take a hike or horseback-ride, and even play tennis here. The hotel is located 20 minutes north of the Juan Santamaría International Airport, and staying here can cut as much as an hour off your travel time to the Pacific coast beaches, Arenal volcano, and the Monteverde cloud forest.

40km (27 miles) north of San José, just off the Interamerican Highway. ☎ **2450-0800** *or tel/fax 2451-1165.* www.vistadelvalle.com. *Free parking. Rack rates: $100 double, $150–$170 villa. Rates include full breakfast. Rates lower in the off season. AE, MC, V.*

Xandari Resort & Spa
$$$$ Alajuela

Xandari is yet another architecturally stunning small hotel not far from the airport. Set on a high hilltop above the city of Alajuela, Xandari commands wonderful views of the surrounding coffee farms and the Central Valley below. The villas are huge private spaces with high-curved ceilings, stained-glass windows, and handmade fine furniture. All come with both an outdoor patio with a view and a private covered *palapa* (straw umbrella), as well as a smaller interior terrace with chaise lounges. Most have king-size beds; the rest have two queens. All rooms boast spacious living rooms with rattan sofas and chairs, as well as small kitchenettes. The owners are artists, and their original works and innovative design touches abound. The hotel grounds contain several miles of trails that pass by at least five jungle waterfalls, as well as lush gardens and fruit orchards. The adjacent "spa village" features a series of private thatch-roofed treatment rooms, many with their own Jacuzzi, and most with stunning views. A wide range of spa and beauty treatments is offered, in addition to yoga and other fitness classes.

5km (3 miles) east of downtown Alajuela, off the road to Poás volcano. ☎ **866-363-3212** *in the U.S. or 2443-2020. Fax 2442-4847.* www.xandari.com. *Free parking. Rack rates: $230–$315 double. Rates include continental breakfast and airport shuttle. $25 for extra person; children 2 and under stay free in parent's room. Rates lower in the off season. AE, MC, V.*

Runner-up hotels

If all the hotels in the preceding section are full, try one of these very good hotels.

Alta Hotel

$$$–$$$$$ Santa Ana This small boutique hotel is infused with old-world charm. Most of the rooms here have wonderful views of the Central Valley from private balconies; the others have nice garden patios. *Alto de las Palomas, old road to Santa Ana.* ☎ ***888-388-2582*** *in the U.S. and Canada, 2282-4160 in Costa Rica. Fax: 2282-4162.* www.thealtahotel.com.

Courtyard by Marriott San José

$$$ Escazú A tidy and comfortable business-class hotel in the western suburb of Escazú, the Courtyard has the added bonus of having numerous dining and nightlife options in an adjacent strip mall. *Next to the Plaza*

Itzkatsu, off the Prospero Fernandez Highway, Escazú. ☎ **888-236-2427** *in the U.S. and Canada, 2208-3000 in Costa Rica. Fax: 2288-0808.* www.marriott.com.

Crowne Plaza Corobicí

$$$–$$$$ La Sabana   Located just past the end of Paseo Colón, the Corobicí offers all the amenities you would expect at a typical airport hotel, with one added bonus: It's much closer to downtown. Joggers will enjoy the nearby Parque La Sabana, and the Corobicí claims to have the largest health spa in Central America. *Autopista General Cañas, Sabana Norte.* ☎ **800-227-6963** *in the U.S., 2231-5698 in Costa Rica.* www.crowneplaza.com.

El Rodeo Country Inn

$$–$$$ San Antonio de Belen   If you want a small, boutique option close to the airport, this totally remodeled old inn is an excellent bet. Just ten minutes from the terminal, it has an excellent restaurant, tennis court, and peaceful country setting. *San Antonio de Belén.* ☎ **2293-3909.** *Fax: 2293-3464.* www.elrodeohotel.com.

Holiday Inn Express

$$$ Airport Area   This international chain is one of the closest hotels to the airport. It's very convenient if you're arriving late or leaving early. *Autopista General Cañas, by the airport.* ☎ **800-465-4329** *in the U.S., 2443-0043 in Costa Rica. Fax: 2442-9532.* www.hiexpress.com.

Hotel Bougainvillea

$–$$ Heredia   The views across the valley from this hillside hotel are wonderful, and the gardens are beautifully designed and well tended. In fact, the bird-watching is pretty good in the hotel's relatively expansive gardens. A complimentary hourly downtown shuttle bus will take you in and out of town. *In Santo Tomás de Santo Domingo de Heredia, 100m (1 block) west of the Escuela de Santo Tomás.* ☎ **2244-1414.** *Fax 2244-1313.* www.hb.co.cr.

Hotel Cacts

$ Paseo Colón   This interesting budget hotel is housed in an attractive tropical contemporary home. Rooms vary considerably in size, so it's always best to check out a few first, if possible. *Avenida 3 bis, no. 2845, between calles 28 and 30.* ☎ **2221-2928** *or 2221-6546. Fax: 221-8616.* www.hotelcacts.com.

Hotel Milvia

$ San Pedro   Artistic touches and original artwork abound in this cheerful little bed-and-breakfast in the eastern district of San Pedro. The hotel is housed in a classic old wooden home that has been beautifully restored. 1 block north and 2 blocks east of the Muñoz y Nanne Supermarket. ☎ **2225-4543.** *Fax: 2225-7801.* www.hotelmilvia.com.

Hotel Parque del Lago

$$$ **Paseo Colón**   Located on the western edge of busy Paseo Colón, right near the Costa Rican Art Museum and Parque La Sabana, this hotel is convenient to both downtown and the western suburbs of Escazú and Santa Ana, with easy access to the country's major highways. *Calle 40, between Avenida 2 and Paseo Colón, San José.* ☎ *2257-8787. Fax 2223-1617.* www. parquedellago.com.

Hotel Rosa del Paseo

$$$ **Paseo Colón**   This hotel is housed in a beautiful old stucco home built more than 110 years ago. Try to grab one of the rooms on the second floor, which feature wooden floors and front doors that open onto the open-air central courtyard. *2862 Paseo Colón, between calles 28 and 30.* ☎ *2257-3225. Fax: 2223-2776.* www.rosadelpaseo.com.

Orquídeas Inn

$$ **Alajuela**   This little boutique inn is just ten minutes from the airport on the road heading out of Alajuela to Grecia and the Poás volcano. The rooms are all spacious and comfortable, with tile floors, private bathrooms, and colorful Guatemalan bedspreads. *Alajuela.* ☎ *2433-7128. Fax 2433-9740.* www.orquideasinn.com.

Radisson Europa Hotel

$$$–$$$$ **Downtown**   This business-class hotel is a good choice for anyone looking for a big, dependable luxury hotel near downtown San José. The hotel features a very-well-equipped gym that is part of the local Multispa chain. *Calle Blancos, behind La República building.* ☎ *888-201-1718 in the U.S., 2257-3257 in Costa Rica. Fax: 2257-8221.* www.radisson.com.

Real InterContinental San José

$$$$–$$$$$ **Escazú**   This is a modern and luxurious large-scale business-class hotel. The hotel is located just across from a large, modern, shopping-mall complex, which is nice if you want access to the shopping, restaurants, and a six-plex movie theater. *Autopista Próspero Fernández, across from the Multiplaza mall, Escazú.* ☎ *800-424-6835 in the U.S. and Canada, 2208-2100 in Costa Rica. Fax: 2208-2101.* www.ichotelsgroup.com.

Where to Dine in San José

Although the Costa Rican cuisine and the local dining scene are easily disparaged and dismissed, still some creative chefs have been trying to educate and enlighten the Costa Rican palate, particularly in San José. Many have begun using fresh local ingredients in new and exciting ways. The early results are quite promising. In addition, many excellent restaurants now serve international cuisines ranging from Italian and Asian, to Peruvian and even Indian. I list the best of the local restaurant scene in this section, with options ranging from typical Tico fare to eclectic fusion cuisine.

Reservations are only necessary in a handful of upscale or very popular restaurants, and in these cases I note the fact in the restaurant's information section.

You'll find several good restaurants in the downtown, Barrio Amón, and San Pedro neighborhoods. Escazú and Santa Ana, two popular upscale suburbs, boast the greatest number of interesting, creative, and varied options.

See Chapter 2 for information on Costa Rican cuisine and Chapter 5 for information on budgeting for meals.

Bacchus
$$$–$$$$ Santa Ana   ITALIAN

This is my favorite Italian restaurant in the metro area. At first glance, you may not realize the restaurant is housed in a historic home that is over a century old. On closer inspection, you'll appreciate how the classic and contemporary blend seamlessly in an elegant atmosphere. The best tables are on the covered back patio, where you can watch the open kitchen and wood-burning pizza oven in action. The menu features a range of antipasti, pastas, pizzas, and main dishes. Everything is perfectly prepared and beautifully presented. The desserts are also excellent, and the wine list is extensive and fairly priced.

Downtown Santa Ana. ☎ *2282-5441. Reservations required. Main courses: $8–$24. AE, MC, V. Open: Tues–Sat noon to 3 p.m. and 6–11 p.m., Sun noon to 9 p.m.*

Café del Teatro Nacional
$$ Downtown   COFFEEHOUSE

Housed in a spacious room off the main lobby of the Teatro Nacional (National Theater), this is an elegant little coffeehouse. Even if there's no show on during your visit, you can enjoy a light meal, sandwich, dessert, or cup of coffee here, while soaking up the neoclassical atmosphere. The theater was built in the 1890s from the designs of European architects, and the Art Nouveau chandeliers, ceiling murals, and marble floors and tables are pure Parisian. The ambience is French-cafe chic, but the marimba music drifting in from outside the open window and the changing art exhibits by local artists will remind you that you're still in Costa Rica. On sunny days, outdoor seating opens up at wrought-iron tables on the side of the theater. In addition to the regular hours of operation, the cafe is open until 8 p.m. any evening that there is a performance in the theater.

See map p. 96. Avenida 2 between calles 3 and 5, in the Teatro Nacional. ☎ *2221-1329. Main courses: $5–$12, sandwiches $4–$7. AE, MC, V. Open: Mon–Sat 9 a.m.–4:30 p.m.*

Café Mundo
$$–$$$ **Barrio Amón   INTERNATIONAL**

This is a beautiful and lively spot to grab a meal. Wood tables and Art
Deco wrought-iron chairs are spread spaciously around several rooms
and open-air verandas in this former colonial mansion. The appetizers
include vegetable tempura, crab cakes, and chicken satay, alongside more
traditional Tico standards such as *patacones* (fried plantain chips) and
fried yuca. A long list of pastas and pizzas, as well as more substantial
main courses, round out the menu. One room here boasts colorful wall
murals by Costa Rican artist Miguel Cassafont. This place is almost always
filled to brimming with a broad mix of San José's bohemian, theater, arts,
gay, and university crowds.

*See map p. 96. Calle 15 and Avenida 9, 200m (2 blocks) east and 100m (1 block) north
of the INS building.* ☎ **2222-6190.** *Reservations recommended. Main courses:
$6–$14. AE, MC, V. Open: Mon–Thurs 11 a.m.–10:30 p.m., Fri 11 a.m. to midnight, Sat
5 p.m. to midnight.*

Cafeteria 1930
$–$$ **Downtown   INTERNATIONAL**

Fronting the Plaza de la Cultura, the open-air section of this simple hotel
restaurant is probably the best people-watching spot in the city. A
wrought-iron railing, white columns, and arches create an old-world atmosphere, and a marimba band often plays right in front. It's open 24 hours
a day. Stop by for breakfast and watch the plaza vendors set up their
booths, or peruse the *Tico Times* over coffee while you have your shoes
polished. The menu is basic and the food is unspectacular, but you won't
find a better place downtown to bask in the tropical sunshine while you
sip a beer or have a light lunch. This is also a great place to come just
before or after a show at the Teatro Nacional.

See map p. 96. In the Gran Hotel Costa Rica, Avenida 2 between calles 1 and 3.
☎ **2221-4011.** *Main courses: $7–$32, sandwiches $6.50–$12. AE, DC, MC, V. Open:
Daily 24 hours.*

Grano de Oro Restaurant
$$$–$$$$ **Paseo Colón   CONTINENTAL**

This is one of the most elegant and romantic restaurants in the city.
Tables are spread around several rooms ringing a small, open-air central
courtyard. When the weather's nice, you can also grab a seat inside the
courtyard. The menu features a wide range of meat and fish dishes. The
lomito piemontes is two medallions of filet mignon stuffed with Gorgonzola
cheese in a sherry sauce, while the *pernil de conejo* is a rabbit thigh stuffed
with a mushroom pâté, served with Dijon mustard sauce. If you opt for
fish, I recommend the macadamia-encrusted corvina, which is served with
a light and tangy orange sauce. Be sure to save room for the Grano de Oro
pie, a decadent dessert with various layers of chocolate and coffee
mousses and creams.

See map p. 96. Calle 30, no. 251, between avenidas 2 and 4, 150m (1½ blocks) south of Paseo Colón. ☎ *2255-3322. Reservations recommended. Main courses: $12–$44. AE, MC, V. Open: Daily 6 a.m.–10 p.m.*

La Cava Grill
$$–$$$ Escazú   COSTA RICAN/STEAKHOUSE

This is a cozy and casual joint housed underneath the popular, yet over-priced and overrated, Le Monastère restaurant. Although the décor is much less ornate, the service much less formal, and the menu much less French, the view is still just as spectacular. Grab one of the window seats here on a clear night and enjoy the sparkle of the lights below. The menu features a range of simply prepared meat, poultry, and fish. More-adventurous diners can try the *tepesquintl,* a large rodent that is actually quite tasty. You'll find live music and a festive party most weekend nights in the attached bar.

Escazú, 1.5km (1 mile) south of Centro Comercial Paco; follow the signs to Le Monastère. ☎ *2289-4404. Reservations recommended. Main courses: $6–$22. AE, MC, V. Open: Mon–Sat 6 p.m. to midnight.*

La Luz
$$$–$$$$ Santa Ana   FUSION

La Luz serves up excellent fusion cuisine, mixing fresh local ingredients with the best of a whole host of international ethnic influences. The fiery garlic prawns are sautéed in ancho-chile oil and sage and served over a roasted-garlic potato mash. Then the whole thing is served with a garnish of fried leeks and a tequila-lime butter and cilantro-oil sauce. I also enjoy the beef tenderloin in a strawberry-balsamic reduction, served over a champagne-infused risotto. The glass-walled dining room is one of the most elegant in town, with a view of the city lights. The wait staff is atten-tive and knowledgeable. On top of all this, you get nightly specials and a wide selection of inventive appetizers and desserts.

In the Hotel Alta, on the old road to Santa Ana. ☎ *2282-4160. Reservations recommended. Main courses: $12–$24. AE, DC, MC, V. Open: Daily 7 a.m.–3 p.m. and 6–10 p.m.*

La Mar Cebicheria
$$$ Santa Ana   PERUVIAN/FUSION

This is the latest outpost of famed Peruvian chef and restaurateur Gastón Acurio's growing international empire. A refined take on Lima's typical street food and ceviche restaurants, you can get a variety of marinated seafood concoctions here. I recommend the Nikkei, which features chunks of raw tuna in a tangy sesame-soy marinade. Though there are a host of main dishes on the menu, the strong suit here are fusion takes on a range of traditional Peruvian appetizers — *tiraditos, anticuchos, causas* — which makes this a great place to pick and share amongst friends, while enjoying the tasty (and strong) *pisco sours.*

Plaza Momentum, Santa Ana. ☎ **2282-6856**. *Reservations recommended. Main courses: $9–$18. AE, DC, MC, V. Open: Sun–Mon 11:45 a.m.– 4:30 p.m., Tue– Sat 11:45 a.m.–3:30 p.m. and 7–10 p.m.*

Machu Picchu
$$ Paseo Colón PERUVIAN

Machu Picchu is an unpretentious little hole in the wall that has become one of the most popular restaurants in San José. One of my favorite entrees is the *causa limeña,* lemon-flavored mashed potatoes stuffed with shrimp. The ceviche is excellent, as is the *ají de gallina,* a dish of shredded chicken in a fragrant cream sauce, and octopus with garlic butter. For main dishes, I recommend *corvina a lo macho,* sea bass in a slightly spicy tomato-based seafood sauce. Be sure to ask for a pisco sour, a classic Peruvian drink made from *pisco,* a grape liquor. These folks have a sister restaurant over in San Pedro (☎ **2283-3679**).

See map p. 96. Calle 32, between avenidas 1 and 3, 150m (1½ blocks) north of the KFC on Paseo Colón. ☎ **2222-7384**. *Reservations recommended. Main courses: $8–$16. AE, DC, MC, V. Open: Mon–Sat 11 a.m.–3 p.m. and 6–10 p.m.*

Olio
$–$$ Los Yoses TAPAS

Exposed brick walls, dark-wood wainscoting, and stained-glass lamps imbue this place with character and romance. Couples will want to grab a table in a quiet nook, while groups tend to gravitate toward the large main room or the bar. The extensive tapas menu features traditional Spanish fare, as well as bruschetta, antipasti, and a Greek *mezza* plate. For a main dish, I recommend the chicken Vesubio, which is marinated first in a balsamic vinegar reduction and finished with a creamy herb sauce, or the *arrollado siciliano,* which is a thin filet of steak rolled around spinach, sundried tomatoes, and mozzarella cheese and topped with a pomodoro sauce. The midsize wine list features fairly priced wines from Italy, France, Spain, Germany, Chile, Greece, and even Bulgaria.

See map p. 96. Barrio California, 200m (2 blocks) north of Bagelman's. ☎ **2281-0541**. *Main courses: $5–$12. AE, DC, MC, V. Open: Mon–Fri noon to midnight, Sat 6 p.m. to midnight.*

Park Café
$$$–$$$$ La Sabana FUSION

Having opened and run a Michelin 2-star restaurant in London and another 1-star joint in Cannes, Richard Neat now finds himself turning out his fusion cuisine in an intimate space spread around the interior patio courtyard of a stately old downtown mansion, which also doubles as an antiques and imported furniture store. The menu changes regularly but might feature roasted scallops with ricotta tortellini in a pumpkin *jus,* or some expertly grilled quail on a vegetable purée bed, topped with poached quail egg. Presentations are artfully done and often served in such a way as to encourage sharing. The well-thought-out and fairly priced wine list is a perfect complement to the cuisine.

See map p. 96. Sabana Norte, 1 block north of Rostipollos. ☎ **2290-6324.** *Reservations recommended. Main courses: $13–$22. V. Open: Tues–Sat noon to 3 p.m. and 7–10 p.m.*

Restaurante Nuestra Tierra
$ Downtown   COSTA RICAN

The décor at this two-story place seeks to imitate a humble country ranch kitchen, with heavy wooden tables, chairs, and paneling, and strings of fresh onions and bunches of bananas hung from the rafters and columns. Service is friendly and efficient, dressed in typical *campesino* dress, they periodically break out into traditional folkloric dances. Sure, it's touristy, but if you want a *casado* or some *gallo pinto,* anytime of the day or night, this is the place to come. The biggest downside here is that the restaurant fronts the very busy Avenida 2, so head for a second-floor table away from the traffic.

See map p. 96. Avenida 2 and Calle 15. ☎ **2258-6500.** *Main courses: $4–$8. MC, V. Open: Daily 24 hours.*

Soda Tapia
$ Paseo Colón   COSTA RICAN

The food is unspectacular, dependable, and quite inexpensive at this landmark local restaurant. Seating is offered inside the brightly lit dining room, as well as on the sidewalk-style patio fronting the parking area, which itself fronts a very busy city avenue. Dour but efficient wait staff take the order you mark down on your combination menu/bill. This place is great for late-night eats or for before or after visits to Parque La Sabana or the Museo de Arte Costarricense (Costa Rican Art Museum). These folks also have another site in a small strip mall in Santa Ana (☎ **2203-7174**).

See map p. 96. Calle 42 and Avenida 2, across from the Museo de Arte Costarricense. ☎ **222-6734.** *Main courses: $4.50–$9, sandwiches $2–$4. MC, V. Open: Daily 7 a.m. to midnight.*

Tin Jo
$$–$$$ Downtown   CHINESE/PAN-ASIAN

This is the best Pan-Asian restaurant in San José. A long-time local favorite, Tin Jo has a wide and varied menu, with an assortment of Cantonese and Szechuan staples; a range of Thai, Japanese, and Malaysian dishes; and even some Indian food. The delicious pineapple shrimp in coconut-milk curry is served in the hollowed-out half of a fresh pineapple. Other dishes not to miss include the salt-and-pepper shrimp, beef teriyaki, and Thai curries. Tin Jo is also a great option for vegetarians. For dessert, try the sticky rice with mango or the banana tempura. The waiters here are some of the most attentive in Costa Rica. The décor features artwork and textiles from across Asia, and you'll have real tablecloths and cloth napkins. The lively atmosphere, extensive menu, and excellent service also make this a great choice for families traveling with kids.

See map p. 96. Calle 11, between avenidas 6 and 8. ☎ 2221-7605 or 2257-3622. Reservations recommended. Main courses: $6–$15. AE, MC, V. Open: Mon–Sat 11:30 a.m.–3 p.m. and 5:30–10 p.m. (Fri–Sat kitchen open until 11 p.m.), Sun 11:30 a.m.–10 p.m.

Whappin'
$$ **Barrio Escalante   COSTA RICAN/CARIBBEAN**

You don't have to go to Limón or Cahuita to get good home-cooked Costa Rican Caribbean food. The menu features a range of regional chicken, beef, or fish dishes, and almost all come with a side of the classic Caribbean-style rice and beans cooked in coconut milk. I usually go with the whole red snapper covered in a spicy sauce of sautéed onions. A small bar rests at the entrance and some simple tables are spread around the restaurant, with an alcove here and there. Everything is very simple, and the prices are quite reasonable. After a dinner of fresh fish, with rice, beans, and *patacones* (fried plantain chips), the only letdown is that the beach is some four hours away.

See map p. 96. Barrio Escalante, 200m (2 blocks) east of El Farolito. ☎ 283-1480. Main courses: $6.50–$14. AE, MC, V. Open: Mon–Sat 11:30 a.m.–2:30 p.m. and 6–10 p.m.

Taking in the view

Although myriad unique experiences can be had in Costa Rica, one of my favorites is dining on the side of a volcano, with the lights of San José shimmering below. These hanging restaurants, called *miradores,* are a resourceful response to the city's topography. Because San José is set in a broad valley surrounded on all sides by volcanic mountains, people who live in these mountainous areas have no place to go but up — so they do, building roadside restaurants vertically up the sides of the volcanoes.

The food at most of these establishments usually isn't spectacular, but the views often are, particularly at night, when the wide valley sparkles in a wash of lights. The town of **Aserri,** 10km (6¼ miles) south of downtown San José, is the king of *miradores,* and **Mirador Ram Luna** (☎ 2230-3060) is the king of Aserri. Grab a window seat and, if you have the fortitude, order a plate of *chicharrones* (fried pork rinds). Live music — usually folk, pop, or jazz — is frequently played here. You can hire a cab for around $9, or take the Aserri bus at Avenida 6, between calles Central and 2. Just ask the driver where to get off.

You can also find *miradores* in the hills above Escazú and in San Ramón de Tres Ríos and Heredia. The most popular is **Le Monastère** (☎ 2289-4404; closed Sun), an elegant converted church serving somewhat overrated French and Belgian cuisine in a spectacular setting in the hills above Escazú. I recommend coming here just for the less formal **La Cava Grill** (see the listing earlier in this chapter), which often features live music, ranging from folk to pop to jazz. I also like **Mirador Tiquicia** (☎ 2289-5839), which occupies several rooms in a sprawling old Costa Rican home and has live folkloric dance shows on Thursdays.

Fast Facts: San José

American Express

American Express Travel Services is represented in Costa Rica by ASV Olympia (Oficentro La Sabana, Sabana Sur; ☎ 2242-8585), which can issue traveler's checks and replacement cards and provide other standard services. To report lost or stolen American Express traveler's checks within Costa Rica, call the above number or ☎ 2295-9000, or call collect to 336-393-1111 in the United States.

ATM Locators

ATMs are widely available around San José. Before you leave home, ask your bank to print out a list of ATMs that accept your bank card or MasterCard or Visa cards. Or check out the following sites: http://visa.via.infonow.net/usa_atm or www.mastercard.com/cardholderservices/atm.

Business Hours

Banks are usually open Monday through Friday from 9 a.m. to 4 p.m., although many have begun to offer extended hours. Offices are open Monday through Friday from 8 a.m. to 5 p.m. (many close for 1 hour at lunch). Stores are generally open Monday through Saturday from 9 a.m. to 6 p.m. (many close for 1 hour at lunch). Stores in modern malls generally stay open until 8 or 9 p.m. and don't close for lunch. Most bars are open until 1 or 2 a.m.

Currency Exchange

Although a Global Exchange money exchange office has opened in the area just beyond Customs and Immigration at the Juan Santamaría International Airport, it gives pretty unfavorable rates. In general, few true money-exchange operations exist in San José. However, you can change money at all state-owned banks and private banks. Hotels will often exchange money and cash traveler's checks as well, without much waiting involved. However, they may shave a few colones off the exchange rate.

Be very careful about exchanging money on the streets; it's extremely risky. In addition to forged bills and short counts, street money-changers frequently work in teams that can leave you holding neither colones nor dollars.

The best way to get cash in Costa Rica is with an ATM connected to your debit-card account at home.

Dentists

You can call your consulate and ask the duty officer to recommend a dentist. Many bilingual dentists also advertise in the *Tico Times*. Because treatments are so inexpensive in Costa Rica, dental tourism has become a popular option for people needing extensive work.

Doctors

Call your consulate and ask the duty officer to recommend a doctor in San José, or see "Hospitals" in this Quick Concierge.

Embassies/Consulates

If you have a passport, immigration, legal, or other problem, contact your consulate. The following embassies and consulates are located in San José: U.S. Embassy, in front of Centro Commercial, on the road to Pavas (☎ 2519-2000, or 2220-3127 after hours in case of emergency); Canadian Consulate, Oficentro Ejecutivo La Sabana, Edificio 5 (☎ 2242-4400); and British Embassy, Paseo Colón, between calles 38 and 40 (☎ 2258-2025). There are no Australian or New Zealand embassies in Costa Rica.

Emergencies

In case of any emergency, dial ☎ **911** (which should have an English-speaking operator); for an ambulance, call ☎ 128; and to report a fire, call ☎ 118. If 911 doesn't work, you can contact the police at ☎ 2222-1365 or 2221-5337, and they may be able to find someone who speaks English.

Hospitals

Clínica Bíblica, Avenida 14 between calles Central and 1 (☎ 2522-1000; www. clinicabiblica.com), is conveniently located close to downtown and has several English-speaking doctors. The Hospital CIMA (☎ 2208-1000; www.hospital sanjose.net), located in Escazú on the Próspero Fernández Highway, which connects San José and the western suburb of Santa Ana, has the most modern facilities in the country.

Information

The Costa Rican Tourism Institute, or Instituto Costarricense de Turismo (ICT; ☎ 2443-1535; www.visitcostarica.com) has a desk at the Juan Santamaría International Airport, located in the baggage-claims area, just before Customs. You can pick up maps and browse brochures, and they may even lend you a phone to make or confirm a reservation. It's open daily from 9 a.m. to 10 p.m.

If you're looking for the main ICT visitor information center in San José, it's located below the Plaza de la Cultura, at the entrance to the Oro Museum (Gold Museum), on Calle 5 between avenidas Central and 2 (☎ 2222-1090). The people there are helpful, although the information they have to offer is rather limited. This office is open Monday through Friday from 9 a.m. to 5 p.m.

Internet Access

Internet cafes can be found all over San José. Rates run between 50¢ and $2 per hour. Many hotels either have their own Internet cafe or Wi-Fi networks or allow guests to send and receive e-mail from their in-house computers. If your hotel doesn't provide the service, Racsa, Avenida 5 and Calle 1 (☎ 287-0087; www.racsa.co. cr), the state Internet monopoly, sells prepaid cards in 5-, 10-, and 15-hour denominations for connecting your laptop to the Web via a local phone call. Some knowledge of configuring your computer's dial-up connection is necessary. Be sure to factor in the phone-call charge if calling from a hotel.

Laundry and Dry Cleaning

Self-service laundromats are uncommon in Costa Rica, and hotel services can be expensive. Aqua Matic (☎ 2291-2847) and Tyson (☎ 2215-2362) are two dependable laundry and dry-cleaning chains with outlets all over town. The latter will even pick up and deliver your clothes free of charge.

Mail

The main *correo* (post office) is on Calle 2 between avenidas 1 and 3 (☎ 800-900-2000 toll-free in Costa Rica; www.correos. go.cr) and is open Monday through Friday from 8 a.m. to 5:30 p.m. and Saturday from 7:30 a.m. to noon. At press time, mailing a letter to the United States costs 170 colones (30¢), and mailing a letter to Europe costs 190 colones (35¢). Given the Costa Rican postal service's track record, I recommend paying an extra 500 colones ($1) to have anything of any value certified. Better yet, use an international courier service or wait until you get home to post it.

Maps

The Costa Rican Tourism Institute (see "Information" earlier in this section for locations) can usually provide you with decent maps of both San José and Costa Rica. Other sources in San José are Seventh Street Books, Calle 7 between avenidas Central and 1 (☎ 2256-8251); Librería

Lehmann, Avenida Central between calles 1 and 3 (☎ 2522-4848); and Librería Universal, Avenida Central between calles Central and 1 (☎ 2222-2222).

Police

Dial ☎ **911** or ☎ **2222-1365** for the police. They should have someone who speaks English.

Restrooms

Restrooms are known as *sanitarios* or *servicios sanitarios*. You may also hear them called *baños*. They're marked *damas* (women) and *hombres* or *caballeros* (men). Public restrooms are rare to nonexistent, but most big hotels and public restaurants will let you use their restrooms. If you're downtown, public restrooms are located at the entrance to the Museo de Oro.

Safety

Pickpockets and purse slashers are rife in San José, especially on public buses, in the markets, on crowded sidewalks, and near hospitals. Leave your passport, money, and other valuables in your hotel safe, and carry only as much as you really need when you go out. Making a photocopy of your passport's opening pages and carrying that with you is a good idea. If you do carry anything valuable with you, keep it in a money belt or special passport bag around your neck. Day packs are a prime target of brazen pickpockets throughout the city. One common scam involves someone dousing you or your pack with mustard or ice cream. Another scamster (or two) will then quickly come to your aid — they're usually much more interested in cleaning you out than cleaning you up.

Stay away from the red-light district northwest of the Central Market. Also, be advised that Parque Nacional is not a safe place for a late-night stroll. Other precautions include walking around corner vendors, not between the vendor and the building; the tight space

between the vendor and the building is a favorite spot for pickpockets. Never park a car on the street, and never leave anything of value in a car, even if it's in a guarded parking lot. Don't even leave your car unattended by the curb in front of a hotel while you dash in to check on your reservation. With these precautions in mind, you should have a safe visit to San José.

Taxes

All hotels charge 13 percent value-added tax. Restaurants also charge the 13 percent tax and add on a 10 percent service charge, for a total of 23 percent more on your bill. A $26 departure tax is charged to all visitors leaving by air.

Taxis

Taxis are plentiful in San José. Depending on your location, the time of day, and the weather (rain places taxis at a premium), hailing a cab downtown is relatively easy. You'll always find taxis in front of the Teatro Nacional and around Parque Central at Avenida Central and Calle Central. You can also get a cab by calling Coopetaxi (☎ 2235-9966), Coopeirazu (☎ 2254-3211), or Coopeguaria (☎ 2227-9300). Cinco Estrellas Taxi (☎ 2228-3159) is another option; though it's based in Escazú, it services the entire metropolitan area and airport and claims to always have an English-speaking operator on call.

Although taxis have *marías* (meters), the drivers sometimes refuse to use them, particularly with foreigners, so you'll occasionally have to negotiate the price. Always try to get them to use the meter first (say, "Ponga la maría, por favor"). The official rate at press time is around 80¢ for the first kilometer (½ mile) and around 60¢ for each additional kilometer. If you have a rough idea of how far it is to your destination, you can estimate how much it should cost from these figures. After 10 p.m., taxis are legally allowed to add a 20 percent surcharge. For more information, see "Getting Around San José," earlier in this chapter.

Telephone/Fax

Costa Rica has an excellent phone system, with a dial tone similar to that heard in the United States. A phone call within Costa Rica costs around 10 colones (20¢) per minute. Pay phones take either a phone card or 5-, 10-, or 20-colón coins. Phone cards are the way to go, as coin-operated phones are getting harder to find. You can purchase phone cards in a host of gift shops and pharmacies. However, there are several competing phone-card companies, and certain cards work only with certain phones. CHIP phone cards work with a computer chip and just slide into specific phones, although these phones aren't widely available. A better bet are the 197 and 199 phone cards, which are sold in varying denominations. These have scratch-off PINs and can be used from any phone in the country. In general terms, the 197 cards are sold in smaller denominations and are used for local calls, while the 199 cards are deemed international and are easier to find in larger denominations. Either card can be used to make any call, however, provided that the card can cover the costs. Another perk of the 199 cards is the fact that you can get the instructions in English. For local calls, calling from your hotel is often easiest, although you'll likely be charged around 100 to 300 colones (18¢–54¢) per call.

Numbers beginning with 0800 and 800 within Costa Rica are toll-free, but calling an 800 number in the States from Costa Rica is not toll-free. In fact, it costs the same as an overseas call.

Water

Tap water in San José is perfectly safe, but if you're prone to stomach problems, you may prefer to drink bottled water. If you aim to err on the side of caution, avoid ordering drinks with ice and eating uncooked fruits or vegetables, unless you peel them yourself.

Chapter 12

Exploring San José

In This Chapter

▶ Taking a guided tour of San José
▶ Checking out the top attractions in San José
▶ Finding the best places to shop
▶ Experiencing San José's nightlife
▶ Heading out of town for a day trip

Most visitors try to get out of San José as fast as possible so they can spend more time on the beach or off in the rain forests and cloud forests. But if you'll be in San José for longer than an overnight stay, there are plenty of sights and activities to keep you busy. Some of the best and most modern museums in Central America are here, with a wealth of fascinating pre-Columbian artifacts. Several great things to see and do also lie just outside San José in the Central Valley.

Seeing San José by Guided Tour

You shouldn't have any reasons to take a guided tour of San José. It's so compact that you can easily visit all the major sights on your own. The best attractions are all described later in this chapter, and I give you a few suggested itineraries later in this chapter as well. However, if you want to take a city tour, which will run you between $20 and $50, try one of these companies: **Costa Rica Sun Tours** (☎ **2296-7757;** www.crsuntours.com); **Horizontes Travel** (☎ **2222-2022;** www.horizontes.com); **Gray Line Tours** (☎ **2220-2126;** www.grayline costarica.com); or **Swiss Travel Service** (☎ **2282-4898;** www.swiss travelcr.com). These same companies also offer a range of day trips out of San José (see "Taking a Day Trip out of San José," later in this chapter). Almost all the major hotels have tour desks, and most of the smaller hotels will also help arrange tours and day trips.

Be sure to check out the map in Chapter 11 for help in locating the following listings.

The Top Attractions: Gold Underground and Jade in the Skies

Centro Nacional de Arte y Cultura (National Arts and Culture Center)
Downtown

Occupying a full city block, this was once the National Liquor Factory. Now it houses the offices of the Cultural Ministry, several performing arts centers, and the Museum of Contemporary Art and Design. The latter has done an excellent job of promoting cutting-edge Costa Rican and Central American artists while also featuring impressive traveling international exhibits, including large retrospectives by Mexican painter José Cuevas and Ecuadorian painter Oswaldo Guayasamín. If you're looking for modern dance, experimental theater, or a lecture on Costa Rican video, this a good place to check. Allow around two hours to take in all the exhibits here.

See map p. 96. Calle 13, between avenidas 3 and 5. ☎ **2257-7202** *or 2257-9370.* www. madc.ac.cr. *Bus: Any downtown bus. Admission: $1, 60¢ for students with a valid ID, free for seniors and children 11 and under. Free for everybody on Mon. Open: Mon–Sat 9:30 a.m.–4:45 p.m.*

Museo de Arte Costarricense (Museum of Costa Rican Art)
La Sabana

Originally the country's first major airport terminal, this museum houses a collection of works in all media by Costa Rica's most celebrated artists. On display are some exceptionally beautiful pieces in a wide range of styles, demonstrating how Costa Rican artists have interpreted and imitated the major European movements over the years. In addition to the permanent collection of sculptures, paintings, and prints, regular temporary exhibits are staged here. If the second floor is open during your visit, be sure to go up and have a look at the conference room's bas-relief walls, which chronicle the history of Costa Rica from pre-Columbian times to the present. My favorite feature here is the outdoor sculpture garden, with works by José Sancho, Jorge Jiménez Deredia, Max Jiménez, and Francisco Zuñiga. The museum closed for renovations in 2009, but it's expected to be open again by early 2010. You can easily spend an hour or two here — more if you take a stroll through the neighboring park.

See map p. 96. Calle 42 and Paseo Colón, Parque La Sabana Este. ☎ **2222-7155.** *Bus: Sabana-Cementerio. Admission: $5 adults, $3 children and students, free for everyone on Sun. Open: Tues–Fri 9 a.m.–5 p.m., Sat–Sun 10 a.m.–4 p.m.*

Museo de Jade Marco Fidel Tristán (Jade Museum)
Downtown

Jade was the most valuable commodity among the pre-Columbian cultures of Mexico and Central America, worth more than gold. This modern museum displays a huge collection of jade artifacts dating from 500 b.c. to a.d. 800. Many are large pendants that were parts of necklaces and are primarily human and animal figures. An extensive collection of pre-Columbian polychromed terra-cotta vases, bowls, and figurines is also on display. Some of these pieces are amazingly modern in design and exhibit a surprisingly advanced technique. Particularly fascinating is a vase that incorporates real human teeth and a display that shows how jade was embedded in human teeth merely for decorative reasons. All the explanations are in English, as well as Spanish. Allot yourself at least an hour to tour this museum.

See map p. 96. Avenida 7 between calles 9 and 9B, 1st floor, INS Building. ☎ **2287-6034.** *Bus: Any downtown bus. Admission: $7 adults, free for children 11 and under. Open: Mon–Fri 8:30 a.m.–3:30 p.m., Sat 9a.m–1p.m.*

Museo de los Niños (Children's Museum)
Downtown

A former army barracks and then prison, this museum houses an extensive collection of exhibits designed to edify and entertain children of all ages. Many of the exhibits encourage hands-on play. Kids can experience a simulated earthquake or make music by dancing across the floor. If you're traveling with children, you'll definitely want to come here; you may want to visit even if you don't have kids with you. This museum sometimes features limited shows of "serious" art in a side gallery and is also the home of the National Auditorium, where gala concerts and recitals are often held. You can spend anywhere from one to four hours here, depending on how much time your children spend at each exhibit. Be careful, though: The museum is large and spread out, and losing track of a family member or friend is easy.

This museum is located a few blocks north of downtown, on Calle 4. It's within easy walking distance of downtown sites, but you may want to take a cab because you'll have to walk right through the worst part of the red-light district to get here.

See map p. 96. Calle 4 and Avenida 9. ☎ **2258-4929.** *www.museocr.com. Bus: Any downtown bus. Admission: $2 adults, $1.20 students and children 17 and under. Open: Tues–Fri 8 a.m.–4:30 p.m., Sat–Sun 10 a.m.–5 p.m.*

Museo de Oro Banco Central (Gold Museum)
Downtown

Located directly beneath the Plaza de la Cultura, this unusual underground museum houses one of the largest collections of pre-Columbian gold in the Americas. On display are more than 20,000 troy ounces of gold, in more than 2,000 objects. The sheer number of small pieces can be overwhelming and seem redundant, but the unusual display cases and complex lighting systems show off every piece to its utmost. This museum complex also includes a gallery for temporary art exhibits, separate coin and stamps museums, a modest gift shop, and a branch of the Costa Rican Tourist Institute's information center. Plan to spend between one and two hours here.

See map p. 96. Calle 5, between avenidas Central and 2, underneath the Plaza de la Cultura. ☎ **243-4202.** www.museosdelbancocentral.org. *Bus: Any downtown bus. Admission: $9 adults, $4 students, 80¢ children 11 and under. Open: Daily 9:30 a.m.–5 p.m.*

Museo Nacional de Costa Rica (National Museum)
Downtown

Costa Rica's most important historical museum is housed in a former army barracks that was the scene of fighting during the civil war of 1948. You can still see hundreds of bullet holes on the turrets at the corners of the building. Inside this traditional Spanish-style courtyard building, you find displays on Costa Rican history and culture from pre-Columbian times to the present. In the pre-Columbian rooms, you see a 2,500-year-old jade carving that is shaped like a seashell and etched with an image of a hand holding a small animal.

Among the most fascinating objects unearthed at Costa Rica's numerous archaeological sites are many *metates* (grinding stones). This type of grinding stone is still in use today throughout Central America; however, the ones on display here are more ornately decorated than those you'll see anywhere else. Some of the *metates* are the size of a small bed and are believed to have been part of funeral rites. A separate vault houses the museum's collection of pre-Columbian gold jewelry and figurines. In the courtyard, you'll be treated to a wonderful view of the city and see some of Costa Rica's mysterious stone spheres. Taking in the lion's share of the collection here takes about two hours.

See map p. 96. Calle 17, between avenidas Central and 2, on the Plaza de la Democracia. ☎ **2257-1433.** www.museocostarica.go.cr. *Bus: Any downtown bus. Admission: $6 adults, $3 students and children 11 and under. Open: Tues–Sat 8:30 a.m.–4 p.m., Sun 9 a.m.–4 p.m. Closed Jan 1, Holy Thursday, Good Friday, Easter Sunday, May 1, and Dec 25.*

Spirogyra Butterfly Garden
Downtown

This butterfly garden is smaller and less elaborate than the Butterfly Farm (see the listing later in this chapter), but it provides a good introduction to the life cycle of butterflies. Moreover, it's a calm and quiet oasis in a noisy and crowded city, quite close to downtown. You'll spend anywhere from a half-hour to several hours here, depending on whether you have lunch or refreshments at the small coffee shop and gallery. You'll be given a self-guided tour booklet when you arrive, and an 18-minute video is shown continuously throughout the day. You'll find Spyrogyra near El Pueblo, a short taxi ride from the center of San José.

See map p. 96. 100m (1 block) east and 150m (1½ blocks) south of El Pueblo Shopping Center. ☎/fax **2222-2937.** www.infocostarica.com/butterfly. *Bus: Calle Blancos bus from Calle 3 and Avenida 5. Admission: $6. Open: Daily 8 a.m.–4 p.m. (cafe open until 7:30 p.m.).*

More Cool Things to See and Do

San José has several pleasant and inviting downtown parks and plazas. Most are very close to one or more major attractions, and they make excellent spots to take a break and soak in the sunshine and local color.

The largest of these is **Parque La Sabana (La Sabana Park)** on the western edge of downtown. This sprawling park has a network of trails and paths used by bikers, joggers, and pedestrians, as well as basketball and tennis courts, *fútbol* (soccer) fields, and baseball diamonds. You'll also find a small outdoor sculpture garden, but this is not to be confused with the sculpture garden found at the neighboring **Museo de Arte Costarricense (Museum of Costa Rican Art).** The park boasts excellent spots to have a picnic, particularly on the banks of the small ponds, and even is home to a small zip-line canopy tour.

In the heart of downtown, the **Plaza de la Cultura** occupies the space between the **Teatro Nacional (National Theater)** and busy Avenida Central. Stepped down on several levels, you'll find ample park benches, which are great places to sit and people-watch. If you have some spare change, buy a handful of popcorn to feed the pigeons. Underneath this plaza, you'll find the **Museo de Oro Banco Central (Gold Museum).** On the western edge of this plaza sits the Gran Hotel Costa Rica, with its inviting outdoor **Cafeteria 1930** (see Chapter 11).

A few blocks east of the Plaza de la Cultura, the **Plaza de la Democracia** occupies a full city block. This concrete affair is a bit stark and dour, with just a few undersized trees and a massive bronze sculpture of Don Pepe Figueres. Moreover, it's often very run-down and unkempt. However, the plaza does offer a few well-placed benches. The plaza is bordered on one side by the **Museo Nacional de Costa Rica (National Museum)** and an extensive **outdoor market** of handicrafts and other assorted souvenirs.

Parque Central (Central Park) is a full city block located off Avenida 2. The park is fronted on one side by the **Teatro Melico Salazar (Melico Salazar Theater)** and on another by the **Catedral Nacional (National Cathedral).** In the center of this park is a large gazebo, which on rare occasions hosts live music concerts. This park is a very popular lunchtime spot for local workers.

Set between the Legislative Assembly and the National Library, the **Parque Nacional (National Park)** is perhaps the shadiest and most lush of the downtown city parks, forgetting the Parque La Sabana, which is in another class. At the northeast corner of this park sits the main entrance to the **Museo Nacional de Arte y Cultura (National Arts and Culture Center).** This park is delightful on a sunny day, with numerous benches and a series of bronze busts of famous historical figures. Be careful at night, however — this park is taken over by prostitutes and transvestites after dark.

Finally, **Parque Morazán (Morazán Park)** is another popular downtown park, featuring a central gazebo and a series of benches and small patches of grass. With several major governmental offices and businesses nearby, this is also a popular lunchtime meeting spot for local workers. I actually prefer the neighboring diminutive **Parque España (Spain Park),** which is shadier, with large stands of bamboo and other mature trees. Parque España fronts the INS Building, which houses the **Museo de Jade Marco Fidel Tristán (Jade Museum),** as well as an alternative entrance to the **Museo Nacional de Arte y Cultura** (see earlier in this section).

Be especially on guard for pickpockets and street crime while in downtown San José.

Visiting attractions just outside the city

Several wonderful attractions lie within easy reach of downtown San José. Most are able to provide transportation at a reasonable rate. Others can be reached by public transportation. Or most can be reached by taxi for between $15 and $30 each way.

In addition to the places listed here, other exciting adventures and day trips are available out of San José. For a rundown of these, see "Taking a Day Trip out of San José," later in this chapter.

Butterfly Farm
Alajuela

This is the best butterfly farm and exhibit in the metropolitan area. At any given time, you may see around 30 of the 80 different species of butterflies raised here. The butterflies live in a large enclosed garden similar to an aviary and flutter about the heads of visitors during tours of the gardens. You should be certain to spot glittering blue morphos (a large fleet-winged butterfly with iridescent blue pigment on its wings) and a large butterfly that mimics the eyes of an owl.

The admission includes a two-hour guided tour. In the demonstration room, you see butterfly eggs, caterpillars, and pupae. There are cocoons trimmed in a shimmering gold color and cocoons that mimic a snake's head to frighten away predators. The last guided tour of the day begins at 3 p.m.

If you reserve in advance, the Butterfly Farm has three daily bus tours that run from many major San José hotels. The cost, including round-trip transportation and admission to the garden, is $35 for adults, $30 for students, and $20 for children 11 and under. Buses pick up passengers at more than 20 different hotels in the San José area.

In front of Los Reyes Country Club, La Guácima de Alajuela. ☎ *2438-0400.* www. butterflyfarm.co.cr. *Admission: $15 adults, $10 students, $7 children 5–11, free for children 4 and under. Open: Daily 8:45 a.m.–3 p.m.*

Café Britt Farm
Heredia

Café Britt is one of the leading coffee exporters in Costa Rica, and the company has put together a wonderful tour and stage production at its farm. Here, you can see how coffee is grown. You also visit the roasting and processing plant to learn how a coffee "cherry" is turned into a delicious roasted bean. Tasting sessions are offered for visitors to experience the different qualities of coffee. A restaurant and a store are on-site, so you can buy coffee and coffee-related gift items. The entire tour, including transportation, takes about three to four hours. Allow some extra time and an extra $10 for a visit to their nearby working plantation and mill. You can even strap on a basket and go out coffee picking during harvest time. The folks here offer several full-day options that combine a visit to the Britt Farm with a stop at Poás volcano, the Butterfly Farm (see the preceding listing), or the Rain Forest Aerial Tram Caribbean (see "Canopy tours and the rain-forest aerial tram," later in this chapter). They've also begun offering mountain-bike tours in the hills of Heredia above their farm, ending with lunch or refreshments at their restaurant.

North of Heredia on the road to Barva. ☎ *2277-1600.* www.coffeetour.com. *Admission: $20 adults, $16 children 6–11; $37 adults and $33 children, including transportation from downtown San José and a coffee drink. Add $15 for a full buffet lunch. Open: Store and restaurant daily 8 a.m.–5 p.m., tour daily 11 a.m.*

Else Kientzler Botanical Garden
Sarchi

Located on the grounds of an ornamental flower farm, on the outskirts of the tourist town Sarchí, these are extensive, impressive, and lovingly laid-out botanical gardens. Over 2.5km (1½ miles) of trails run through a collection of more than 2,000 species of flora. All the plants are labeled with their Latin names, with some further explanations around the grounds in both English and Spanish. The grounds include a topiary labyrinth, as well as a variety of lookouts, gazebos, and shady benches. A children's play area features some water games, jungle-gym setups, and a child-friendly little zip-line canopy tour. Over 40 percent of the gardens are wheelchair accessible.

Tuan (☎ **2258-2004**) buses leave San José about five times throughout the day for Sarchí from Calle 18 between avenidas 5 and 7. The fare is $1.25. Alternatively, you can take any Grecia bus from this same station. In Grecia, they connect with the Alajuela-Sarchí buses, leaving every 30 minutes from Calle 8 between avenidas Central and 1 in Alajuela.

About 6 blocks north of the central fútbol (soccer) stadium in the town of Sarchí, Alajuela. ☎ *2454-2070.* www.elsegarden.com. *Admission: $14 adults, $6 students with valid ID and children 5–12. A guided tour costs an extra $15 per guide per hour, for a group of up to 15 persons. Advance reservations are necessary for guided tours. Open: Daily 8 a.m.–4 p.m.*

INBio Park
Heredia

Run by the National Biodiversity Institute (Instituto Nacional de Biodiversidad, or INBio), this place is part museum, part educational center, and part nature park. In addition to watching a 15-minute informational video, visitors can tour two large pavilions explaining Costa Rica's biodiversity and natural wonders, and hike on trails that re-create the ecosystems of the forests. A two-hour guided hike is included in the entrance fee, and self-guided tour booklets are also available. Other features are a good-size butterfly garden, as well as a Plexiglas viewing window into the small lagoon. One of my favorite attractions here is the series of wonderful animal sculptures donated by one of Costa Rica's premiere artists, José Sancho. If you get hungry, try the simple cafeteria-style restaurant for lunch or the on-site coffee shop. You can easily spend two to three hours here.

400m (4 blocks) north and 250m (2½ blocks) west of the Shell station in Santo Domingo de Heredia. ☎ *2507-8107.* www.inbio.ac.cr. *Admission: $23 adults, $13 children 12 and under. Open: Daily 8 a.m.–6 p.m. INBio Park can arrange round-trip transportation from downtown for $18 per person.*

Lankester Gardens
Cartago

Costa Rica has more than 1,400 varieties of orchids, and no fewer than 800 species are on display at this botanical garden in Cartago province. Created in the 1940s by English naturalist Charles Lankester, the gardens are now administered by the University of Costa Rica. The primary goal is to preserve the local flora, with an emphasis on orchids and bromeliads. Paved trails meander from open, sunny gardens into shady forests. In each environment, different species of orchids are in bloom. An information center and gift shop round out the offerings, and the trails are well tended and well marked. Plan to spend one to three hours here if you're interested in flowers and gardening; you can run through it more quickly if you're not.

Paraíso de Cartago. ☎ *2552-3247.* www.jardinbotanicolankester.org. *Take the Cartago bus from San José, and then the Paraíso bus from a stop 100m*

(1 block) south and 75m (¾ block) west of the Catholic church ruins in Cartago (ride takes 30–40 minutes). Admission: $5 adults, $3.50 children 6–16. Open: Daily 8:30 a.m.–5:30 p.m. Closed all national holidays.

La Paz Waterfall Gardens
Varablanca, Heredia

The namesake attraction here consists of a series of trails through primary and secondary forest alongside the La Paz River, with lookouts over a series of powerful falls, including the namesake La Paz Fall. The trails include lookouts and suspended walkways that give you an intimate, and sometimes wet, view of the falls. An orchid garden, a hummingbird garden, and a huge butterfly garden — they claim it's the largest in the world — are some of the other attractions here. There's also a small serpentarium, featuring a mix of venomous and nonvenomous native snakes, and several terrariums containing various frogs and lizards. A large artificial trout pond, which you can also swim in, rounds out the official attraction offerings here. Although the admission fee is a little steep, the trails and waterfalls are beautiful, everything is wonderfully done, and there's a lot to do and see here. A buffet lunch will run you an extra $15 at the large cafeteria-style restaurant. This is a good stop after a morning visit to the Poás volcano. Plan to spend between two and four hours here.

6km (3¾ miles) north of Varablanca on the road to San Miguel, Heredia. ☎ 2225-0643. www.waterfallgardens.com. Take a Puerto Viejo de Sarapiquí bus from Calle 12 and Avenida 9 (make sure it passes through Varablanca and La Virgen), and ask to be let off at the entrance. These buses are infrequent and coordinating your return can be difficult, so coming in a rental car or arranging transport is best. Admission: $32 adults, $20 children and students with valid ID. Open: Daily 8:30 a.m.–5:30 p.m.

Zoo Ave
Alajuela

This zoo is, by far, the best-run one in the country. The zoo began as a bird sanctuary and rescue center. Dozens of scarlet macaws, reclusive owls, majestic raptors, several different species of toucans, and a host of brilliantly colored birds from Costa Rica and around the world make this one exciting place to visit. Bird-watching enthusiasts will be able to get a closer look at birds that they may have seen in the wild. But there is much more to see here. There are also large iguana, deer, tapir, puma, and monkey exhibits — and look out for the 3.6m (12-ft.) crocodile. Zoo Ave houses only injured, donated, or confiscated animals. Walking the paths and visiting all the exhibits here takes about two hours.

La Garita, Alajuela. ☎ 2433-8989. www.zooave.org. Catch one of the frequent Alajuela buses on Avenida 2 between calles 12 and 14. In Alajuela, transfer to a bus for Atenas and get off at Zoo Ave before you get to La Garita. Fare is 75¢. Admission: $15 adults, $13 children 11 and under. Open: Daily 9 a.m.–5 p.m.

Suggested one-, two-, and three-day sightseeing itineraries

San José is a compact city, with a limited number of major attractions. You can easily knock off almost all of them in a few days. Here are some sample itineraries covering one-, two-, and three-day stays in San José. (See Chapter 11 and earlier in this chapter for specific listing information.)

If you have one day

On **Day One,** start your day by having coffee and breakfast at the **Cafeteria 1930,** on the outdoor patio of the Gran Hotel Costa Rica, on the edge of the **Plaza de la Cultura.** After breakfast, visit the **Museo de Oro Banco Central (Gold Museum),** and see if you can get tickets for a performance that night at the **Teatro Nacional (National Theater).** From the Plaza de la Cultura, stroll up Avenida Central to the **Museo Nacional (National Museum).** Have lunch at **Café Mundo.** If it's a nice day, be sure to grab one of the outdoor tables near a flowing fountain.

After lunch, head over to the nearby **Centro Nacional de Arte y Cultura (National Arts and Culture Center),** but only if you have the energy for another museum. After all this culture, some shopping at the open-air stalls at the **Plaza de la Democracia** is in order. Try dinner at **Bakea** before going to the **Teatro Nacional.** After the performance, let your day come full circle with a cup of coffee or a nightcap at the **Cafeteria 1930** before calling it a night.

If you have two days

On **Day Two,** you're probably best off taking one of the day trips outside of San José described in the "Taking a Day Trip out of San José" section, later in this chapter. Alternatively, you could spend the day further exploring the capital. Start by heading out on Paseo Colón to the **Museo de Arte Costarricense (Museum of Costa Rican Art)** and **Parque La Sabana (La Sabana Park).** Intrepid travelers can do some shopping at the **Mercado Central.** You can pick up the fixings for a **picnic lunch** at the Mercado Central or at any supermarket in town.

After lunch, if you've brought kids along, you'll want to visit the **Museo de Los Niños (Children's Museum)** or the **Spyrogyra Butterfly Garden.** Otherwise, this is a good time to tour the **Museo de Jade Marco Fidel Tristán (Jade Museum).** If you want to get more shopping in, be sure to save some time for the nearby **Galeria Namu.** For dinner, grab a taxi and head for one of the *miradores* (see Chapter 11) for dinner, and enjoy the spectacular view of the lights of San José twinkling below you.

If you have three days

On **Day Three,** head out early to the **Poás volcano** and then visit the **La Paz Waterfall Gardens,** returning through the hills of Heredia, with a stop at **INBio Park** if you have the time and energy. Alternatively, you could head to the **Irazú volcano, Lankester Gardens,** and the colonial city of **Cartago.** Start your day at the volcano and work your way back toward San José. If you want to try an organized tour, try a cruise to **Isla Tortuga** in the Gulf of Nicoya, a **white-water rafting** trip on the Pacuare River, or a visit to the **Rain Forest Aerial Tram Caribbean.**

Shopping: Gold Beans and Painted Oxcarts

Serious shoppers will probably be disappointed in Costa Rica. Aside from coffee and miniature reproductions of working oxcarts, you'll find few distinctly Costa Rican wares. To compensate for its own relative lack of goods, Costa Rica does a brisk business in selling crafts and clothing imported from Guatemala, Panama, and Ecuador.

Best shopping areas

San José's principal shopping district is bounded by avenidas 1 and 2, from about Calle 14 in the west to Calle 13 in the east. For several blocks west of the Plaza de la Cultura, **Avenida Central** is a pedestrian-only street mall where you can find store after store of inexpensive clothes for men, women, and children. Depending on the mood of the police that day, you may find a lot of street vendors as well.

Most shops in the downtown district are open Monday through Saturday from about 8 a.m. to 6 p.m. Some shops close for lunch, while others remain open (it's just the luck of the draw for shoppers, although fewer and fewer stores are closing for lunch these days). When you do purchase something, you'll be happy to find that the sales and import taxes have already been figured into the display price.

Do not buy any kind of sea-turtle products (including jewelry); wild birds; lizard, snake, or cat skins; corals; or orchids (except those grown commercially). International laws prohibit trade in endangered wildlife, and such goods will be confiscated at the airport. No matter how unique, beautiful, insignificant, or inexpensive it may seem, your purchase will directly contribute to the further hunting of endangered species.

Visiting a Costa Rican market

There are several large markets near downtown, but by far the largest is the **Mercado Central,** located between avenidas Central and 1 and calles 6 and 8. Although this crowded maze of stalls is primarily a food market, inside you'll find all manner of vendors, including a few selling Costa Rican souvenirs, leather goods, and musical instruments. Be especially careful about your wallet or purse and any prominent jewelry — very skilled pickpockets frequent this area. All the streets surrounding the Mercado Central are jammed with produce vendors selling from small carts or loading and unloading trucks. It's always a hive of activity, with crowds of people jostling for space on the streets. Your best bet is to visit on Sundays or on weekdays; Saturdays are particularly busy. In the hot days of the dry season, the aromas can get quite heady.

You'll also find a daily street market on the west side of the **Plaza de la Democracia.** The market boasts two long rows of outdoor stalls selling T-shirts, Guatemalan and Ecuadorian handicrafts and clothing, small ceramic *ocarinas* (small musical wind instruments), and handmade jewelry. The atmosphere here is much more open than at the Mercado Central, which I find just a bit too claustrophobic.

Finally, two other similar options downtown include **La Casona,** Calle Central between avenidas Central and 1 (☎ 2222-7999), a three-story warren of crafts and souvenir shops, and **El Pueblo,** a tourism complex built in the style of a mock colonial-era village, with a wide range of restaurants, gift shops, art galleries, bars, and discos.

Heading to a mall

With globalization and modernization taking hold in Costa Rica, much of the local shopping scene has shifted to large mega-malls. Modern multi-level affairs with cineplexes, food courts, and international brand-name stores are becoming more ubiquitous. The biggest and most modern of these malls include the **Mall San Pedro, Multiplaza, Terra Mall,** and **Mall Real Cariari.** Although they lack the charm of the small shops found around San José, they're a reasonable option for one-stop shopping; most contain at least one or two local galleries and crafts shops, along with a large supermarket, which is always the best place to stock up on local coffee, hot sauces, liquors, and other nonperishable foodstuffs.

What to look for and where to find it

If the large markets and malls don't have what you're looking for, perhaps one of the specialty shops or galleries listed in the following sections will fill the bill.

You may be able to negotiate prices down a little bit, but bargaining is not a traditional part of the vendor culture here, so you'll have to work hard to save a few dollars.

Art galleries

Arte Latino (Calle 5 and Avenida 1; ☎ 2258-7083) carries original artwork in a variety of media, featuring predominantly Central American themes. Some of it is pretty gaudy, but this is a good place to find Nicaraguan and Costa Rican "primitive" paintings. The gallery also has storefronts in the Multiplaza Mall in Escazú and at the Mall Cariari, which is located on the Interamerican Highway, about halfway between the airport and downtown, across the street from the Hotel Herradura.

For an outstanding gallery dealing mainly in high-end Costa Rican art, head to **Galería 11–12** (Plaza Itskatzu, off the Prospero Fernandez highway in Escazú; ☎ 2288-1975; www.galeria11-12.com). The collection here ranges from neoclassical painters such as Teodorico Quirós to modern masters such as Francisco Amighetti and Paco Zuñiga, to current stars such as Rafa Fernández, Fernando Carballo, and Fabio Herrera.

Galería Jacobo Karpio (Avenida 1, Casa 1352, between calles 11 and 13; ☎ 2257-7963) handles some of the more adventurous modern art to be found in Costa Rica. Karpio has a steady stable of prominent Mexican, Cuban, and Argentine artists, as well as some local talent.

TEORetica (Avenida 7 and Calle 11; ☎ 2233-4881; www.teoretica. org) is a small downtown gallery, run by Virginia Pérez-Ratton, one of the more adventurous and internationally respected collectors and curators in Costa Rica. You'll often find very interesting and cutting-edge exhibitions here.

Galería Amón (#937 Calle 7, between avenidas 7 and 9; ☎ 2223-9725; www.amon937.com) features contemporary artists from both Central and South America. Housed in a stylish old home in the historic Barrio Amón district, the spaces are ample and well lit, and there's almost a museum-like feel to the exhibitions.

Art lovers should check out Molly Keeler's one-day **Art Tour** (☎ 8359-5571 or 2288-0896; www.costaricaarttour.com), which includes scheduled visits to the studios and personal shops of prominent local artists working in a wide range of media.

Books

For English-language novels, field guides and general guidebooks, and natural history books, head to either **Seventh Street Books** (☎ 2256-8251; Calle 7 between avenidas 1 and Central), or **Librería Internacional** (☎ 2253-9553; www.libreriainternacional.com). Librería Internacional has several outlets around San José, including storefronts in most of the major modern malls.

You can also order a host of field guides and other Costa Rican–themed books in English online from www.zonatropical.net.

Handicrafts

The quality of Costa Rican handicrafts is generally very low, and the offerings are limited. The most typical items you'll find are hand-painted wooden **oxcarts.** These come in a variety of sizes, and the big ones can be shipped to your home for a very reasonable price.

Notable exceptions to the generally meager crafts offerings include the fine wooden creations of **Barry Biesanz** (☎ 2289-4337; www. biesanz.com). His work is sold in many of the finer gift shops around, but beware: Biesanz's work is often imitated, so make sure that what you buy is the real deal (he generally burns his signature into the bottom of the piece). **Lil Mena** is a local artist who specializes in working with and painting on handmade papers and rough fibers. You'll find her work in a number of shops around San José.

You may also run across **carved masks** made by the indigenous Boruca people of southern Costa Rica. These full-size balsa masks come in a variety of styles, both painted and unpainted, and run anywhere from $20 to $90, depending on the quality of workmanship. **Cecilia "Pefi" Figueres** makes practical ceramic wares that are lively and fun. Look for her brightly colored abstract and figurative bowls, pitchers, and coffee mugs at some of the better gift shops around the city.

Scores of shops around San José sell a wide variety of crafts, from the truly tacky to the divinely inspired. Here are some that sell more of the latter and fewer of the former.

Biesanz Woodworks (Escazú; ☎ 2289-4337; www.biesanz.com; call for directions and off-hour appointments) produces a wide range of high-quality items, including bowls, jewelry boxes, humidors, and some wonderful sets of wooden chopsticks. Biesanz Woodworks is actively involved in reforestation, so you can even pick up a hardwood seedling here.

Occupying two floors at the Hotel Don Carlos, **Boutique Annemarie** (Calle 9, between avenidas 7 and 9; ☎ 2221-6063) has an amazing array of wood products, leather goods, papier-mâché figurines, paintings, books, cards, posters, and jewelry. You'll see most of this stuff at the other shops, but not in such quantities or in such a relaxed and pressure-free environment. Don't miss this shopping experience.

Galería Namu (Avenida 7, between calles 5 and 7; ☎ 2256-3412; www.galerianamu.com) has some very high-quality arts and crafts, including excellent Boruca and Huetar carved masks and "primitive" paintings, many painted by rural women. It also carries a good selection of the ceramic work of Cecilia "Pefi" Figueres. This place organizes tours to visit various indigenous tribes and artisans as well.

Boutique Kiosco (Calle 7 and Avenida 11, Barrio Amón; ☎ 2258-1829) features a range or original and one-off pieces of functional, wearable, and practical pieces made by contemporary Costa Rican and regional artists and designers. Though the offerings are regularly changing, you'll usually find a mix of jewelry, handbags, shoes, dolls, furniture, and knickknacks. Pieces are often made with recycled or sustainable materials.

Jewelry

The outgrowth of a jewelry-making school, **Studio Metallo** (650m/6½ blocks east of the Iglesia Santa Teresita, Barrio Escalante; ☎ 2281-3207; www.studiometallo.com) has some excellent hand-crafted jewelry made in a range of styles, using everything from 18-karat white and yellow gold and pure silver, to some less-exotic and -expensive alloys. Some works integrate gemstones, while many others focus on the metal work.

Part working jewelry factory, part shopping center, part tourist trap, **Plaza Esmeralda** (Sabana Norte, 800m/8 blocks north of Jack's, in Pavas; ☎ 2296-0312) is a good place to come to buy replicas of pre-Columbian jewelry. The several shops here carry a wide range of typical tourist souvenirs and locally produced arts and craftworks at fair prices. Visitors are treated to a 15-minute guided tour where you can see some of the jewelry being manufactured.

Leather goods

In general, Costa Rican leather products are not of the highest grade or quality, and prices are not particularly low — but take a look and see for yourself.

Del Río (☎ 2262-1415) is a local leather-goods manufacturer, with stores in most of the city's modern malls. It also offers free hotel pickups and transfers to its factory outlet in Heredia.

Liquor

The national drink is **guaro,** a rough, clear liquor made from sugar cane. The most popular brand is **Cacique,** which you'll find at every liquor store and most supermarkets. Costa Ricans drink their *guaro* straight or mixed with club soda or Fresca. When drinking it straight, it's customary to follow a shot with a bite into a fresh lime covered in salt.

Costa Ricans also drink a lot of rum. The premier Costa Rican rum is **Centenario,** but I recommend that you opt for the Nicaraguan **Flor de Caña** or Cuban **Havana Club,** which are both far superior rums.

Because of the trade embargo, bringing Havana Club into the United States is illegal.

Several brands and styles of coffee-based liqueurs are also produced in Costa Rica. **Café Rica** is similar to Kahlúa, and you can also find several types of coffee cream liqueurs. The folks at **Café Britt** produce their own line of coffee liqueurs, which are quite good. You can buy them in most supermarkets, liquor stores, and tourist shops.

Music

A CD of Costa Rican music makes a great souvenir. **Editus** is an inventive trio (guitar, violin, and percussion) that has several albums out. They've won two Grammy awards for their collaborations with Rubén Blades on the albums *Tiempos* and *Mundo.*

Taking a trip to Sarchí for some local crafts

Sarchí is Costa Rica's main artisan town. The colorfully painted miniature oxcarts that you see all over the country are made here. Oxcarts such as these were once used to haul coffee beans to market. Today, although you may occasionally see oxcarts in use, most are purely decorative. However, they remain a well-known symbol of Costa Rica. In addition to miniature oxcarts, many carved wooden souvenirs are made here with rare hardwoods from the nation's forests. Dozens of shops are located within a few blocks of each other in town, and all have similar prices.

If you're driving, take the Interamerican Highway north. After passing the airport and the turnoff for Jacó and Manuel Antonio, look for the marked exit for Grecia and Sarchí. It's about a 30-minute drive from the airport to Sarchí. A taxi should charge around $35 each way from downtown.

About five buses leave San José for Sarchí from Calle 18, between avenidas 5 and 7. The fare is $1.25. Alternatively, you can take any Grecia bus from this same station. In Grecia, they connect with the Alajuela–Sarchí buses, which leave every 30 minutes from Calle 8, between avenidas Central and 1 in Alajuela.

Jazz pianist **Manuel Obregón** has several excellent albums out, including *Simbiosis,* on which he improvises along with the sounds of Costa Rica's wildlife, waterfalls, and weather, as well as his work with the *Papaya Orchestra* and *Rio Infinito Orchestra,* collaborations and gatherings of musicians from around Central and South America.

Papaya Music (www.papayamusic.com) produces and distributes an excellent range of local music, including everyone from Obregon to **Malpais,** a local pop-rock band, to a broad selection of traditional folk music, including one of my favorite local discs, *Dr. Bombodee,* by the Costa Rican–born calypsonian Walter "Gavitt" Ferguson.

Many gift shops around the country carry a small selection of Costa Rican music. You can also find music stores in all the modern malls mentioned in the "Heading to a mall" section, earlier in this chapter.

Living It Up After Dark: From the Theaters to a Bitter Street

Catering to a mix of tourists, college students, and just everyday party-loving Ticos, San José has a host of options to meet the nocturnal needs of visitors and locals alike. You'll find plenty of interesting clubs and bars, a wide range of theaters, and some very hot dance clubs.

To find out what's going on in San José while you're in town, pick up either the *Tico Times* (English) or *La Nación* (Spanish), two local newspapers. The former is a good place to find out where local expatriates are hanging out; the latter's "Viva" and "Tiempo Libre" sections have extensive listings of discos, movie theaters, and live music.

The performing arts

Theater is very popular in Costa Rica, and downtown San José is studded with small theaters. However, tastes tend toward the burlesque, and the crowd pleasers are almost always simplistic sexual comedies. The **National Theater Company** (☎ 2221-1273) is an exception, tackling works from Lope de Vega to Lorca to Mamet. Similarly, the small independent group **Abya Yala** (☎ 2240-6071) also puts on several cutting-edge, avant-garde shows each year. Almost all the theater offerings are in Spanish, although the **Little Theatre Group** (www.littletheatre group.org) is a long-standing amateur group that periodically stages works in English. Check the *Tico Times* to see if anything is running during your stay.

Costa Rica has a strong modern dance scene. Both the **University of Costa Rica** (☎ 2207-4595) and the **National University** (☎ 2256-4838) have modern-dance companies that perform regularly in various venues in San José. In addition to the university-sponsored companies, check to see if any smaller independent companies are performing.

The **National Symphony Orchestra** (☎ 2240-0333; www.osn.go.cr) is a respectable orchestra by regional standards, although its repertoire tends to be rather conservative. The symphony season runs March through November, with concerts roughly every other weekend at the **Teatro Nacional** (National Theater; Avenida 2, between calles 3 and 5; ☎ 2221-5341; www.teatronacional.go.cr) and the **Auditorio Nacional** (National Auditorium; ☎ 2256-5876), located at the Museo de Los Niños (see the listing earlier in this chapter). Tickets cost between $3 and $30 and can be purchased at the box office.

Visiting artists also stop in Costa Rica from time to time. Recent concerts have featured hard rockers Iron Maiden, Argentine pop star Fito Paez, operatic legend Placido Domingo, and Brazilian maestro Caetano Veloso. Many of these concerts and guest performances take place in San José's two historic theaters, the **Teatro Nacional** (see earlier in this section) and the **Teatro Melico Salazar** (Avenida 2, between calles Central and 2; ☎ 2221-4952), as well as at the **Auditorio Nacional** (see earlier in this section). Really large shows are sometimes held at *fútbol* (soccer) stadiums or at the amphitheater at the Hotel Herradura.

Dance clubs and discos

Ticos love to dance, and you'll find plenty of places to hit the dance floor in San José. Salsa and merengue are the main beats that move people here, but you'll also find clubs specializing in more modern dance music such as house. Many of the dance clubs and salons feature live music on the weekends.

In general, bars open anywhere from mid- to late-afternoon and stay open to anywhere from midnight to 2 a.m. Most dance clubs follow similar hours, although a very few open as late as 8 p.m. Some bars and dance clubs do stay open as late as 4 a.m.

A good place to sample a range of San José's nightlife is in **El Pueblo,** a shopping, dining, and entertainment complex done up like an old Spanish village. It's just across the river to the north of town. The best way to get there is by taxi; all the drivers know El Pueblo well. Within the alleyways that wind through El Pueblo are a dozen or more bars and dance clubs — plus an indoor *fútbol* (soccer) playing field. In El Pueblo, **Fiesta Latina** (☎ 2222-8782), **Twister** (☎ 2222-5746), and **Friends** (☎ 2233-5283) are happening party spots. Across the street, **Copacabana** (☎ 2233-5516) is a popular dance spot. For a mellower option, inside El Pueblo, try **Café Art Boruca** (☎ 2221-3615).

Most of the places listed in this section demand a nominal cover charge; sometimes it includes a drink or two.

If you want to mingle with locals and visit a classic Costa Rican dance club, head to **Castro's** (Avenida 13 and Calle 22, Barrio Mexico; ☎ 2256-8789). The music varies throughout the night, from salsa and merengue to reggaeton and, occasionally, electronic trance. Spread over a couple of floors, you'll find several rooms and various types of environments here, including some intimate and quiet corners.

The dance floor at **El Tobogán** (2 blocks north and 1 block east of the La República main office, off the Guápiles Highway; ☎ 2257-3396) is about the size of a football field, yet it still fills up. This is a place where Ticos come with their loved ones and dance partners. The music is a mix of classic Latin dance rhythms — salsa, cumbia, and merengue. It's open only on the weekends (until about 2 a.m.), but a live band is always playing, and sometimes the music is very good.

Tucked inside a nondescript office building and commercial center on Paseo Colón, **Vertigo** (Edificio Colón, Paseo Colón; ☎ 2257-8424) has quickly become one of the more popular places for rave-style, late-night dancing, and partying. The dance floor is huge, the ceilings are high, and electronic music rules the roost. It's open daily until 4 a.m.

The bar scene

There seems to be something for every taste in San José. Lounge lizards will be happy in most hotel bars in the downtown area, while students and the young at heart will have no problem mixing in at the livelier spots around town, especially out in San Pedro.

Perhaps the best part of the San José bar scene is something called a *boca,* the equivalent of a *tapa* in Spain: a little dish of snacks that arrives at your table when you order a drink. Although this is a somewhat dying tradition, especially in the younger, hipper bars, you'll still find *bocas* alive and well in the older, more traditional Costa Rican drinking establishments. In most, the *bocas* are free, but in some, where the dishes are more sophisticated, you'll have to pay for the treats.

Chelles (Avenida Central and Calle 9; ☎ 2221-1369) makes up for its lack of style and ambience with plenty of tradition and its diverse and colorful clientele. The lights are bright, the chairs surround simple Formica-topped card tables, and mirrors adorn most of the walls. Simple sandwiches and meals are served, and pretty good *bocas* come with the drinks. Plus, this place is open 24 hours a day.

El Cuartel de la Boca del Monte (Avenida 1, between calles 21 and 23; ☎ 2221-0327) began life as an artist-and-bohemian hangout, and over the years, it has evolved into the leading meat market for the young and well heeled. However, artists still come, as do local and foreign-exchange students, young working stiffs, and tourists. Live music is usually offered here on Monday, Wednesday, and Friday nights, and when it's playing, the place is packed shoulder-to-shoulder.

You can easily miss the narrow entrance to **El Observatorio** (Calle 23, between avenidas Central and 1; ☎ 2223-0725). Owned by a local film-maker, the décor includes a heavy dose of cinema motifs. The space is large, with high ceilings, and one of the best (perhaps only) smoke extraction systems of any popular bar, making the air pleasant to breathe, despite the fact that 80 percent of the clientele are chain smokers. Regular live music and movie screenings are featured, and a pretty good menu of appetizers and main dishes, drawn from various world cuisines, is on hand.

Housed in a beautiful old mansion just off Parque Morazán in the heart of downtown, **Key Largo** (Calle 7, between avenidas 1 and 3; ☎ 2221-0277) is worth a visit if only to take in the scene and admire the dark-stained, carved-wood ceilings. However, be forewarned, this has historically been, and still is, one of the city's prime hangouts for prostitutes and their potential customers.

Hanging out in San Pedro

The 2-block stretch of **San Pedro** just south of the University of Costa Rica has been dubbed La Calle de Amargura (The Street of Bitterness), and it's the heart and soul of this eastern suburb and college town. Bars and cafes are mixed in with bookstores and copy shops. After dark, the streets here are packed with teens, punks, students, and professors bar-hopping and just hanging around. You can walk the strip until some-place strikes your fancy, or you can try one of the places listed in this section.

The **Jazz Café** (next to the Banco Popular on Avenida Central; ☎ 2253-8933; www.jazzcafecostarica.com) is consistently one of the more happening spots in San Pedro and one of my favorites, although low ceilings and poor air circulation make it almost unbearably smoky most nights. Wrought-iron chairs, sculpted busts of famous jazz artists, and creative lighting give the place ambience. Live music is featured here just about every night. These folks have also opened a sister Jazz Café Escazu (☎ 2288-4740) on the western end of town.

Set on a busy corner in the heart of the University district, **Terra U** (2 blocks east and 1½ blocks north of the church in San Pedro; ☎ 2225-4261) is quickly becoming one of the most popular bars in the area. Part of this is due to the inviting, open-air, street-front patio area, which provides a nice alternative to the all-too-common smoke-filled rooms found at most other trendy spots.

You can get here by heading out (east) on Avenida 2, following the flow of traffic. You'll first pass through the neighborhood of **Los Yoses** before you reach a big traffic circle with a big fountain in the center (La Fuente de la Hispanidad). The **Mall San Pedro** is located on this traffic circle. Heading straight through the circle (well, going around it and continuing on what would have been a straight path), you'll come to the **Church of San Pedro,** about 4 blocks east of the circle. The church is San Pedro's major landmark.

Casinos

Gambling is legal in Costa Rica; however, there are some idiosyncrasies involved in gambling a la *Tica*.

If blackjack is your game, you'll want to play rummy. The rules are almost identical, except that the house doesn't pay one and a half times on blackjack — instead, it pays double on any three of a kind or three-card straight flush, even if it pushes you over 21.

If you're looking for roulette, what you'll find here is a bingolike spinning cage of numbered balls. The betting is the same, but some of the glamour is lost.

You'll also find a version of five-card-draw poker, but the rule differences are so complex that I advise you to sit down and watch for a while, and then ask some questions before joining in. That's about all you'll find — no craps tables or baccarat are on hand.

Mechanical slot machines are currently outlawed — but you'll be able to play electronic slots and poker games. Most of the casinos here are quite casual and small by international standards. You may have to dress up slightly at some of the fancier hotels, but most are accustomed to tropical-vacation attire.

Casinos are located at several of the mid- to large-scale hotels, as well as some stand-alone casinos downtown. **Casino Club Colonial** (Avenida 1, between calles 9 and 11; ☎ 2258-2807) and **Casino Del Rey** (Avenida 1 and Calle 9, inside the Hotel Del Rey; ☎ 2257-7800) are two good options, virtually next door to each other.

Taking a Day Trip out of San José

San José makes an excellent base for exploring the beautiful Central Valley and the surrounding mountains. A wide range of organized day trips are offered, ranging from visits to some pre-Colombian ruins to a host of adventure activities.

Guided tours and adventures

For most visitors, the best way to take advantage of a day trip or adventure outside of San José is as part of a guided tour or outing.

A number of companies offer a wide variety of primarily nature-related day tours out of San José. The best of these include **Costa Rica Expeditions** (☎ 2257-0766; www.costaricaexpeditions.com), **Costa Rica Sun Tours** (☎ 2296-7757; www.crsuntours.com), and **Horizontes Tours** (☎ 2222-2022; www.horizontes.com).

Before signing on for a tour of any sort, find out how many fellow travelers will be accompanying you, how much time will be spent in transit and eating lunch, and how much time will actually be spent doing the primary activity. I've had complaints about tours that were rushed; that spent too much time in a bus or on secondary activities; or that had a cattle-car, assembly-line feel to them.

I've arranged the tours in this section by type of activity. In addition to these tours, many others exist, some of which combine two or three different activities or destinations.

Bungee jumping

Nothing is unique about bungee jumping in Costa Rica, but the sites here are quite beautiful. If you've always had the bug, **Tropical Bungee** (☎ 2248-2212; www.bungee.co.cr) helps folks jump off an 80m (262-ft.) bridge for $65 per person, and $30 for a second jump. Transportation is provided free from San José twice daily. These folks also offer para-gliding tours.

Canopy tours and the rain-forest aerial tram

Getting off the ground and up into the treetops is the latest fad, and it was arguably first developed in Costa Rica. Scores of so-called zip-line canopy tours abound around the country.

You have several options relatively close to San José. The quickest and easiest way to experience a zip-line canopy tour from San José is to head to the La Sabana park and take the **Urban Canopy Tour** (☎ 2215-2544). Given the fact that this tour is set on a relatively flat patch of city park, it's neither as extensive nor as exciting as the other options around the country. Still, the tour has eight zip-line cables, with the longest being some 200m (650 ft.) long. The tour costs $20.

The folks at the **Original Canopy Tours** (☎ 2291-4465; www.canopy tour.com) have their **Mahogany Park** operation, located about one hour outside of San José. The tour here features ten platforms and, at the end, you have the choice of taking a cable to a ground station or doing an 18m (60-ft.) rappel down to finish off. The tour takes about two hours and costs $45.

Another option is the **Rain Forest Aerial Tram Caribbean** (☎ 2257-5961; www.rainforesttram.com), built on a private reserve bordering Braulio Carillo National Park. The tramway takes visitors on a 90-minute ride through the treetops, where they have the chance to glimpse the complex web of life that makes these forests unique. These folks have several complimentary attractions, including a butterfly garden, serpentarium, and frog collection. They even have their own zip-line canopy tour. There are also well-groomed trails through the rain forest and a restaurant on-site, so a trip here can easily take up a full day. The cost for tours, including transportation from San José and either breakfast or lunch, is $105. Alternatively, you can drive or take one of the frequent Guápiles buses — they leave every half-hour throughout the day and cost $2 — from the Caribbean bus terminal (Gran Terminal del Caribe) on Calle Central, 1 block north of Avenida 11. Ask the driver to let you off in front of the *teleférico* (tram). If you're driving, head out on the Guápiles Highway as if driving to the Caribbean coast. Watch for the tram's roadside welcome center — it's hard to miss. For walk-ins, the entrance fee is $55; students and kids under 18 pay $28.

Because the Rain Forest Aerial Tram Caribbean is a popular tour for groups, I highly recommend that you have an advance reservation in the high season and, if possible, a ticket. Otherwise, you may end up waiting a long time for your tram ride or even be shut out. The tram can handle only about 80 passengers per hour, so scheduling is tight; the folks here try to schedule as much as possible in advance.

Day cruises

If you want to really enjoy the beach and the tropics, take a cruise to lovely Tortuga Island in the Gulf of Nicoya. These full-day tours entail an early departure for the two-and-a-half-hour chartered bus ride to Puntarenas, where you board your vessel for a one-and-a-half-hour cruise to Tortuga Island. Then you get several hours on the picturesque island, where you can swim, lie on the beach, play volleyball, or try a canopy tour, followed by the return journey.

The original and most dependable company running these trips is **Calypso Tours** (☎ 2256-2727; www.calypsotours.com). The tour costs $119) per person and includes round-trip transportation from San José, a basic continental breakfast during the bus ride to the boat, all drinks on the cruise, and an excellent buffet lunch on the beach at the island. The Calypso Tours main vessel is a massive motor-powered catamaran. A second vessel runs a separate tour to a private nature reserve at **Punta Coral.** The beach is much nicer at Tortuga Island, but the tour to Punta Coral is much more intimate, and the restaurant, hiking, and kayaking are all superior here.

Mountain-biking

The best bicycle riding is well outside of San José — on dirt roads where you're not likely to be run off the highway by a semi or run head-on into someone coming around a blind curve in the wrong lane. Several companies run a variety of one-day and multiday tours out of San José. The one-day tours usually involve a round-trip bus or van ride out of downtown to the primary destination. These destinations include the small towns of Sarchí and Turrialba, as well as the Irazú and Poás volcanoes. Several of these tours are designed to be either entirely or primarily descents. **Costa Rica Biking Adventure** (☎ 2225-6591; www.biking incostarica.com) offers a variety of mountain-biking tours using high-end bikes and gear. A one-day trip should cost between $95 and $150 per person.

A unique option is to take a **Railbike Tour** (☎ 8303-3300; www.rail bike.com). This tour involves a mountain bike rigged to a contraption that fits over abandoned railroad tracks, running through the countryside outside San José. The full-day tour costs $75 and includes all equipment, plus a light breakfast and full lunch.

Rafting, kayaking, and river trips

Dozens of tumultuous rivers cascade down from the Costa Rican mountains. Several have become very popular for white-water rafting and kayaking. If I had to choose just one day trip to do out of San José, it would be a white-water rafting trip. For between $75 and $120, you can spend a day rafting through lush tropical forests; multiday trips are also available. Some of the most reliable rafting companies are **Aventuras Naturales** (☎ 800-514-0411 in the U.S., 2225-3939 in Costa Rica; www.toenjoynature.com), **Exploradores Outdoors** (☎ 2222-6262; www.exploradoresoutdoors.com), and **Ríos Tropicales** (☎ 2233-6455; www.riostropicales.com). These companies all ply a number of rivers of varying difficulties, including the popular **Pacuare** and **Reventazón rivers.**

Of all of Costa Rica's white-water rivers, the **Pacuare River** is the most popular and arguably the most spectacular. Class III and IV rapids weave through predominantly uninhabited forest, and toucans fly overhead. Near the end of the run, the river passes through a narrow steep-walled canyon.

Choosing the volcano trip that's right for you

Poás, Irazú, and Arenal volcanoes are three of Costa Rica's most popular destinations, and the first two are easy day trips from San José. Although numerous companies offer day trips to Arenal, I don't recommend them because you'll spend at least three and a half hours on travel in each direction. You usually arrive when the volcano is hidden by clouds and leave before the night's darkness shows off its glowing eruptions. For more information on Arenal volcano, see Chapter 18.

Tour companies offering trips to Poás and Irazú include **Costa Rica Expeditions** (☎ 2257-0766; www.costaricaexpeditions.com), **Costa Rica Sun Tours** (☎ 2296-7757; www.crsuntours.com), and **Horizontes Tours** (☎ 2222-2022; www.horizontes.com). Prices range from $30 to $50 for a half-day trip, and from $60 to $120 for a full-day trip.

The 3,378m (11,080-ft.) **Irazú volcano** is historically one of Costa Rica's more active volcanoes, although it's relatively quiet these days. It last erupted on March 19, 1963, on the day that President John F. Kennedy arrived in Costa Rica. A good paved road passes right to the rim of the crater, where a desolate expanse of gray sand nurtures few plants and the air smells of sulfur. The landscape here is often compared to that of the moon. You'll get fabulous views of the fertile Meseta Central and Orosi Valley as you drive up from Cartago, and if you're very lucky, you may be able to see both the Pacific Ocean and the Caribbean Sea. Clouds usually descend by noon, so get here as early in the day as possible.

A visitor center with information on the volcano and natural history can be found at the entrance to the park, just off the parking lots. A short trail leads to the rim of the volcano's two craters, their walls a maze of eroded gullies feeding onto the flat floor far below. This is a national park, with an admission fee of $10 charged at the gate. Dress in layers; this may be the tropics, but it can be cold up at the top if the sun's not out. The park restaurant, at an elevation of 3,022m (9,912 ft.), with walls of windows looking out over the valley far below, claims to be the highest restaurant in Central America.

If you don't want to take an organized tour, buses leave for Irazú volcano daily at 8 a.m. from Avenida 2 between calles 1 and 3 (across the street from the entrance to the Gran Hotel Costa Rica). The fare is $7 round-trip, with the bus leaving the volcano at 12:30 p.m. To make sure that the buses are running, call ☎ **2530-1064.** If you're driving, head northeast out of Cartago toward San Rafael, and then continue driving uphill toward the volcano, passing the turnoffs for Cot and Tierra Blanca en route.

Poás volcano is 37km (23 miles) from San José on narrow roads that wind through a landscape of fertile farms and dark forests. As at Irazú, a paved road runs right to the top, although you'll have to hike in about 1km (½ mile) to reach the crater. The volcano stands 2,640m (8,659 ft.) tall and is located within a national park, which preserves not only the volcano but also dense stands of virgin forest. Poás's crater, said to be the second largest in the world, is more than a mile across. Geysers in the crater sometimes spew steam and muddy water 180m (590 ft.) into the air, making this the largest geyser in the world. An information center is located at the entrance to the park, just off the parking lots. Here you can see a slide show about the volcano, and you'll find well-groomed and well-marked hiking trails through the cloud forest that rings the crater. About 15 minutes from the parking area, along a forest trail, is an overlook onto beautiful Botos Lake, which has formed in one of the volcano's extinct craters.

Be prepared when you come to Poás: This volcano is often enveloped in dense clouds. If you want to see the crater, you'll want to come early and during the dry season. Moreover, it can get cool up here, especially when the sun isn't shining, so dress appropriately. Admission to the national park is $10 at the gate.

In case you don't want to go on a tour, a daily bus (☎ **2442-6900** or 2222-5325) leaves from Avenida 2, between calles 12 and 14, at 8 a.m. and returns at 2 p.m. The fare is $6 round-trip. The bus is often crowded, so arrive early. If you're driving, head for Alajuela, continue on the main road through town, and follow signs for Fraijanes. Just beyond Fraijanes, you'll connect with the road between San Pedro de Poás and Poasito; turn right toward Poasito, and continue to the rim of the volcano.

Part IV
Guanacaste and Environs

The 5th Wave   By Rich Tennant

In this part . . .

The northwestern province of Guanacaste is home to Costa Rica's greatest array of beach towns and resort destinations. This part gives you insights into choosing the right beach or resort to fit your travel needs and wants. From the quiet, isolated beaches of Playa Hermosa and Pan de Azúcar, to the bustling surfer town of Tamarindo, to the mega-resorts of the Papagayo Peninsula, this part helps you choose the perfect destination on Costa Rica's Gold Coast. This part also lists a wide range of activities to keep you busy while in Guanacaste.

Chapter 13

Going for Gold in Guanacaste

In This Chapter

▶ Arriving in Guanacaste

▶ Finding your way around Guanacaste

▶ Choosing where to stay and dine in Guanacaste

▶ Enjoying the many tour and activity options in Guanacaste

▶ Taking on the night in Guanacaste

*W*ith a long, beautiful, and varied shoreline, Guanacaste definitely deserves its designation as Costa Rica's "Gold Coast." Occupying the northwest corner of the country, Guanacaste is the driest and most consistently sunny region in Costa Rica. Not surprisingly, it is home to many of the country's most popular beaches and resorts.

Guanacaste province is named after the tall and broad shady trees that still shelter the herds of cattle that roam the dusty inland savanna here. In addition to the beaches, resorts, and cattle ranches, Guanacaste has several active volcanoes and one of the last remnants of tropical dry forest left in Central America.

Hotel options range from large, luxurious resorts and all-inclusives to isolated beachfront bed-and-breakfasts and small inns. Guanacaste currently boasts four regulation golf courses, and more are allegedly in the works.

 During the dry season, the hillsides in Guanacaste turn brown and barren. Dust from dirt roads blankets the trees in many areas, and the scenery seems far from tropical. Driving these dirt roads without air-conditioning and closed windows can be extremely unpleasant.

On the other hand, if you happen to visit this area in the rainy season, the hillsides are a beautiful, rich green, and the sun usually shines all morning, giving way to an afternoon shower — just in time for a nice siesta.

Getting There

Whether you fly directly to Liberia, or take a commuter flight from San José, the fastest and easiest way to get to Guanacaste is by air. I highly recommend it. If you want the freedom and flexibility of a car, you can always rent one in Guanacaste. However, if you're touring the country by car, or want to save money, you can also drive or take a bus. You'll find detailed information on all these options in the following sections.

By air

The **Daniel Oduber Airport** (☎ **2668-1010** or 2688-1117; airport code: LIR) in Liberia is a small, modern, international airport that receives a steady stream of scheduled commercial and charter flights throughout the year.

Following are the major commercial airlines with regularly scheduled service to Liberia:

- ✔ **American Airlines** (☎ **800-433-7300;** www.aa.com) has four weekly direct flights between Miami and Liberia, and twice weekly flights between Dallas–Ft. Worth and Liberia.

- ✔ **Continental** (☎ **800-231-0856;** www.continental.com) has daily direct flights between Houston and Liberia, twice-weekly flights between Newark and Liberia.

- ✔ **Delta** (☎ **800-221-1212;** www.delta.com) has daily direct flights between its Atlanta hub and Liberia, and a once-weekly direct flight between Los Angeles and Liberia.

- ✔ **United** (☎ **800-538-2929;** www.united.com) has a once-weekly direct flight between Chicago and Liberia.

- ✔ **US Airways** (☎ **800-622-1015;** www.usairways.com) has a once-weekly direct flight between Charlotte and Liberia.

In addition, numerous commercial charter flights arrive from various North American and European cities throughout the high season. Check with your travel agent.

A small, commuter airstrip also lies in Tamarindo. If you're going to Tamarindo (or Playa Grande), and coming from San José, flying into and out of Tamarindo is your best option.

Most of the beaches in Guanacaste are between a 25- and 55-minute drive from the Liberia airport. If you're going to Playa Hermosa, Playa Ocotal, or the Papagayo Peninsula, you're best off flying into Liberia. Playa Flamingo, Playa Brasilito, Playa Conchal, and Sugar Beach, are slightly closer to Tamarindo, but the differences are almost negligible.

Sansa (☎ **877-767-2672** in the U.S. and Canada, 2290-4100 in Costa Rica; www.flysansa.com) and **Nature Air** (☎ **800-235-9272** in the U.S. and

Canada, 2299-6000 in Costa Rica; www.natureair.com) are two local commuter airlines with daily service to both Liberia and Tamarindo. The flight takes about 50 minutes and costs between $114 and $126 each way.

By bus

Gray Line (☎ 2220-2126; www.graylinecostarica.com) and **Interbus** (☎ 2283-5573; www.interbusonline.com) are two private bus companies running fleets of modern minivans to all the major destinations in Costa Rica. Both service all the different beaches mentioned in this chapter. The fares run between $33 and $45 each way on either line.

Both companies will pick you up at most San José–area hotels and drop you off at any of the hotels in this region. However, if you're the first pickup, or last drop-off on the route, you may be in for a long and tedious wait.

You can also take inexpensive Costa Rican bus lines to many Guanacaste beaches. Tickets cost between $5.25 and $8, and the trips take between five and six hours. You can buy tickets on the bus or just prior to departing at the station. In most cases, getting a confirmed ticket in advance is very hard and usually unnecessary.

The following is a listing of the schedules, terminal locations, and contact information of the major bus companies servicing the major beach destinations of Guanacaste.

- ✔ **Playa del Coco:** Pulmitan buses (☎ 2222-1650) leave San José for Playa del Coco at 8 a.m., and 2 and 4 p.m. daily, departing from Calle 24, between avenidas 5 and 7.

- ✔ **Playa Hermosa and Playa Panamá:** Tralapa buses (☎ 2221-7202) leave San José daily at 3 p.m., departing from Calle 20, between avenidas 3 and 5, stopping first at Playa Hermosa and next at Playa Panamá.

- ✔ **Playa Brasilito, Playa Flamingo, and Playa Potrero:** Tralapa buses (☎ 2221-7202) leave San José daily at 8 and 10:30 a.m., and 3 p.m., departing from Calle 20, between avenidas 3 and 5, stopping at playas Brasilito, Flamingo, and Potrero, in that order.

- ✔ **Tamarindo:** Tracopa-Alfaro buses (☎ 2222-2160) leave San José for Tamarindo at 8:30 and 11:30 a.m., and 3:30 p.m., departing from Calle 14 between avenidas 3 and 5. **Tralapa** (☎ 2221-7202) also has one daily direct bus to Tamarindo, leaving at 4 p.m. from its main terminal at Calle 20, between avenidas 3 and 5.

Alternatively, Pulmitan express buses (☎ 2222-1650 in San José, 2666-0458 in Liberia) leave San José for Liberia roughly every hour between 6 a.m. and 8 p.m., from Calle 24 between avenidas 5 and 7. The ride to Liberia is four hours. After you're in Liberia, you can transfer to a local bus to your destination of choice at the main Liberia bus station. In general, at least three to four daily buses run between Liberia and each of the various Guanacaste beach destinations.

No direct bus service exists to either Playa Ocotal or Playa Grande. Playa del Coco is very close to Playa Ocotal, and a cab ride from the bus station there should be just about $5. Playa Grande is about a 20-minute ride from Tamarindo, and a taxi should charge you around $20 for this trip.

By car

Driving to Guanacaste from San José is a relatively easy and straight shot, with only two major routes.

If you're going to any of the more northern beaches, take the Interamerican Highway west from San José, and follow the signs for Nicaragua and the Guanacaste beaches. Turn left at the major crossroads at the entrance to Liberia. This intersection is very well marked, and will point you toward Santa Cruz and the various Guanacaste beaches. Driving to Liberia from San José takes approximately three and a half to four hours. From Liberia, it's another 25 to 55 minutes to most of the beaches in this area.

After the turnoff, the road to the Papagayo Peninsula is prominently marked 8km (5 miles) south of the Liberia airport. At the corner here, you'll see a massive Do It Center hardware store and lumberyard.

If you're going on to Playa Hermosa and Playa Panamá, continue on a little farther and, just past the village of Comunidad, turn right. In about 11km (6¾ miles), you'll come to a fork in the road; take the right fork. These roads are relatively well-marked, and a host of prominent hotel billboards should make it easy enough to find the beach.

If you continue farther on the road to Santa Cruz, just beyond the town of Belén you'll see the turnoff for Playa Conchal, Playa Flamingo, Playa Brasilito, Sugar Beach, and Tamarindo.

If you're going to Tamarindo, Playa Conchal, Playa Brasilito, or Sugar Beach, the most direct route is by way of the La Amistad bridge over the Tempisque River. Take the Interamerican Highway west from San José. Forty-seven kilometers (29 miles) past the turnoff for Puntarenas, you'll see signs for the turnoff to the bridge. After crossing the river, follow the signs for Nicoya and Santa Cruz. Continue north out of Santa Cruz until just before the village of Belén, where you'll find the turnoff for the various beaches. In another 20km (12 miles), you'll hit the village of Huacas. Take the left fork for Playa Tamarindo, and head straight for the road to Playa Flamingo, Playa Brasilito, Playa Conchal, and Sugar Beach.

Orienting Yourself in Guanacaste

The province of Guanacaste occupies the bulk of Costa Rica's northwestern land mass, from the northern section of the Nicoya Peninsula up to the Nicaraguan border. For tourists, most of Guanacaste's appeal lies with its miles and miles of beautiful beaches. The capital of Guanacaste is the city of Liberia, where you'll find the Daniel Oduber International Airport. The city itself holds little appeal for most tourists. In fact, although much of Guanacaste province is inland, the only major attraction here for visitors is the Rincón de la Vieja volcano and the surrounding Rincón de la Vieja National Park.

Introducing the beaches and neighborhoods

The beaches of Guanacaste come in various shapes and sizes. Some are protected and calm, while others feature strong surf. Some are quite developed, while others are home to just a few hotels and small resorts.

Here's a quick rundown of Guanacaste's principal beach destinations, running (more or less) from north to south.

Papagayo Peninsula

The turnoff for this long narrow peninsula is the first you'll hit heading west from the Liberia airport. So far, only two major hotels have opened up here, the Allegro Papagayo Resort and the Four Seasons Resort Costa Rica. However, more are on the drawing board. The peninsula features several stunning and often deserted beaches, including **Playa Nacascolo,** which is inside the property of the Four Seasons Resort — but all beaches in Costa Rica are public, so you cannot be denied entry. Almost all the beaches here are very well protected, with little or no wave action.

Playa Hermosa and Playa Panama

Surrounded by steep forested hills, **Playa Hermosa** is a curving gray-sand beach that is long and wide, with rocky bluffs at either end. It's also relatively protected and is consistently one of the region's calmest beaches for swimming. Fringing the beach is a swath of trees that stays surprisingly green right through the dry season. The shade provided by these trees, along with the calm protected waters, is a big part of the beach's appeal.

Beyond Playa Hermosa, you'll find the still underdeveloped **Playa Panamá** and, farther on, the calm waters of **Bahía Culebra,** a large protected bay dotted with small, semiprivate patches of beach and ringed with mostly intact dry forest. The large Hilton Papagay Resort sits on a point dividing Playa Panamá from Bahía Culebra.

Playa del Coco and Playa Ocotal

Playa del Coco was one of the first beaches in Guanacaste to be developed, and it has long been a popular destination with middle-class Ticos and weekend revelers from San José. It's also a prime scuba-diving spot. The beach, which has grayish-brown sand, is quite wide at low tide and almost nonexistent at high tide. In between high and low tides, it's just right.

Playa Ocotal is a tiny pocket cove featuring a small salt-and-pepper beach bordered by high bluffs. It's quite beautiful. When the water is calm, you'll find good snorkeling around some rocky islands close to shore here. You'll see a fair amount of residential development just inland here, as well as a couple of small hotels and resorts.

Playas Conchal, Brasilito, Flamingo, and Pan de Azúcar

Playa Conchal is the first in a string of beaches stretching north along this coast. For decades, this was the semiprivate haunt of a few beach cognoscenti. The Spanish word for shell is *concha.* The unique beach here is made up primarily of soft crushed shells. Nearly every place you could walk, turn, or lay down your towel was shell collectors' heaven. Unfortunately, as Conchal has developed and its popularity spread, unscrupulous builders have brought in dump trucks to haul away the namesake seashells for landscaping and construction, and the impact has been noticeable.

Just beyond Playa Conchal to the north, you'll come to **Playa Brasilito,** a tiny beach town and one of the few real villages in the area. The soccer field is in the center of the village, and around its edges you'll find a couple of little *pulperías* (general stores). Playa Brasilito is popular both with Ticos and budget travelers from abroad. You'll find a few hotels and a couple of campsites here.

Playa Flamingo is located on a long spit of land that forms part of Potrero Bay. The beach here is a beautiful stretch of white sand. For my money, Playa Flamingo has perhaps the prettiest stretch of sand up here, and the little town is starting to boom again after years of lying seemingly dormant.

If you continue along the road from Brasilito without taking the turn for Playa Flamingo, you'll soon come to **Playa Potrero.** The sand here is a hard-packed brownish gray, but the beach is long, deserted, and quite calm for swimming. You can see the hotels of Playa Flamingo across the bay. Drive a little farther north, and you'll find the still undeveloped **Playa La Penca** and, finally, **Playa Pan de Azúcar,** a beautiful little salt-and-pepper beach with one lone small resort hotel backing it, Hotel Sugar Beach (see the listing later in this chapter).

Playa Grande and Tamarindo

Playa Grande is a long, isolated, and sparsely developed stretch of beach with strong surf. It's very popular with surfers, which can make the beach unsuitable for swimming at times. Playa Grande is one of the principal nesting sites for the giant leatherback turtle, the largest turtle in the world. I almost hate to mention places to stay in Playa Grande because the steady influx of tourists and development could spell doom for this beach as a turtle nesting site.

 Tamarindo is a bustling boomtown and one of the most popular beaches on the Gold Coast. Tamarindo boasts a mixture of hotels in a variety of sizes and price ranges and an eclectic array of restaurants, as well as several seemingly out-of-place modern strip malls.

Rampant development continues to spread up the hills inland from the beach and south beyond to **Playa Langosta.** The beach itself is a long, wide swath of white sand that curves gently from one rocky headland to another. Behind the beach are low, dry hills that can be a dreary brown in the dry season, but they instantly turn green with the first brief showers of the rainy season. Fishing boats bob at their moorings at the south end of the beach, and brown pelicans fish just outside the breakers.

The southernmost beaches

The beaches south of Tamarindo are some of the least developed on this coast. All are fairly exposed to the open ocean and, thus, popular with surfers. In order, heading south, you'll find the beaches of **Avellanas, Playa Negra,** and **Junquillal.** All feature just a few small hotels and simple restaurants. These are great places to get away from it all.

Rincón de la Vieja National Park

This national park begins on the flanks of the Rincón de la Vieja volcano and includes this volcano's active crater. Down lower, you'll find an area of geothermal activity with *fumaroles* (cracks where volcanic gases escape), geysers, and hot mud pools that create a bizarre, otherworldly landscape. In addition to hot springs and mud pots, you can explore waterfalls, a lake, and volcanic craters. The bird-watching here is excellent, and the views across the pasturelands to the Pacific Ocean are stunning.

Finding information after you arrive

A small information kiosk greets you at the Liberia airport, but invariably your best bet for information will be your hotel front desk, concierge, or tour desk. Almost every hotel in the region has a tour desk; you can also find them at tour offices in most major beach towns.

Getting Around Guanacaste

The best way to get around Guanacaste is by taxi or rental car, or as part of an organized tour. (For information on the many available tour options, see Chapter 14.)

By taxi

Taxis are available at the airport and in all the major beach towns. Any hotel in the area can call you a taxi. Rates range from $3 to $6 for short rides, to $25 to $50 for longer jaunts between more distant towns and destinations.

By car

Many of the major car-rental agencies have offices at the Liberia airport and around Guanacaste. Reserving in advance with a company's U.S. or international reservations office is probably best, but you can also rent a car for a day or more by calling after you're in Costa Rica. Any of the following car-rental companies will deliver your car to any Guanacaste-area hotel:

- ✔ **Adobe** (☎ **800-769-8422** in the U.S. and Canada, 2667-0608 in Liberia, 2653-0031 in Tamarindo; www.adobecar.com)

- ✔ **Alamo** (☎ **877-222-9075** in the U.S. and Canada, 2668-1111in Liberia, 2653-0727 in Tamarindo; www.alamo.com)

- ✔ **Avis** (☎ **800-331-1212** in the U.S. and Canada, 2668-1138 in Liberia; www.avis.com)

- ✔ **Budget** (☎ **800-472-3325** in the U.S. and Canada, 2668-1118 in Liberia, 2436-2000 in Tamarindo; www.budget.com)

- ✔ **Dollar** (☎ **800-800-3665** in the U.S. and Canada, 2668-1061 in Liberia; www.dollar.com)

- ✔ **Hertz** (☎ **800-654-3001** in the U.S. and Canada, 2221-1818 central reservation number in Costa Rica, 2653-1358 in Tamarindo; www.hertz.com)

- ✔ **Payless** (☎ **800-729-5377** in the U.S. and Canada, 2667-0511 in Liberia, 2653-0015 in Tamarindo; www.paylesscarrental.com)

- ✔ **Thrifty** (☎ **800-847-4389** in the U.S. and Canada, 2665-0787 in Liberia, 2653-0829 in Tamarindo; www.thrifty.com)

By foot

Most of the beach destinations here are small and easily navigable — in and of themselves — by foot. You can even sometimes walk between two beach towns or destinations — say, from Playa Conchal to Playa Brasilito or from Tamarindo to Playa Langosta. However in most cases, you'll need to find some sort of motorized transportation to get between the different beach destinations.

By bus

Public buses are not a practical means for most tourists to get around Guanacaste. Although regular local buses connect most of the major beach towns and destinations with Liberia, you'll find virtually no connections among the different beach towns and destinations.

Where to Stay in Guanacaste

Guanacaste is Costa Rica's fastest-developing tourist destination, and the region boasts hotel options to suit any budget and any vacation style. Here are the best choices in a broad range of categories.

El Velero Hotel
$$ Playa Hermosa

This longstanding little hotel is a great choice right on the beach in Playa Hermosa. White walls and polished tile floors give El Velero a Mediterranean flavor. The guest rooms are large, and those on the second floor have high ceilings. All have free Wi-Fi. The furnishings are simple, though, and some of the bathrooms are a bit small. The hotel has its own popular little restaurant, which offers a good selection of meat, fish, and shrimp dishes, as well as weekly barbecue fests. Various tours, horseback-riding, and fishing trips can be arranged through the hotel; however, the most popular excursions are the full-day and sunset cruises on the hotel's namesake sailboat.

See map p. 156. Playa Hermosa. ☎ **2672-1017.** *Fax: 2672-0016.* www.costarica hotel.net. *Rack rates: $89 double. Rates lower in the off season, higher during peak periods. AE, MC, V.*

Four Seasons Resort Costa Rica
$$$$$ Papagayo Peninsula

The Four Seasons is by far the most luxurious and impressive large-scale resort in Costa Rica. The resort is set near the very end of a long peninsula on a narrow spit of land between two white-sand beaches. The majority of the rooms are in three long, four-story, oceanfront buildings. The architecture here is stunning, with most buildings featuring flowing roof designs and other touches imitating the forms of turtles, armadillos, and butterflies.

All the rooms are very large, with wood floors, rich wood furnishings, tasteful fixtures and decorations from around the world, marble bathrooms with a deep tub and separate shower, luscious cotton sheets and bathrobes, and a large private balcony. The rooms on the third and fourth

Guanacaste

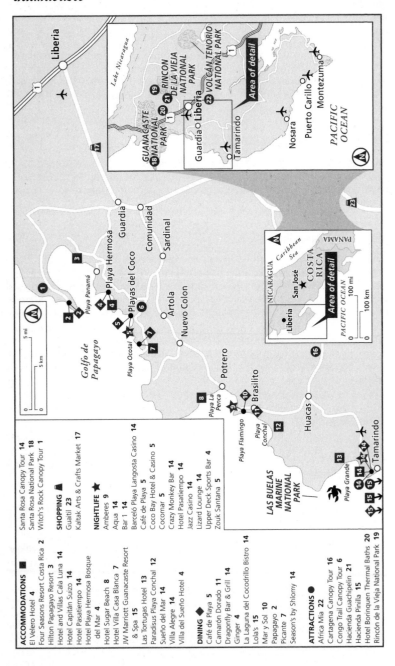

ACCOMMODATIONS ■
El Velero Hotel **4**
Four Seasons Resort Costa Rica **2**
Hilton Papagayo Resort **3**
Hotel and Villas Cala Luna **14**
Hotel Capitán Suizo **14**
Hotel Pasatiempo **14**
Hotel Playa Hermosa Bosque
  del Mar **4**
Hotel Sugar Beach **8**
Hotel Villa Casa Blanca **7**
JW Marriott Guanacaste Resort
  & Spa **15**
Las Tortugas Hotel **13**
Paradisus Playa Conchal **12**
Sueño del Mar **14**
Villa Alegre **14**
Villa del Sueño Hotel **4**

DINING ◆
Café de Playa **5**
Camarón Dorado **11**
Dragonfly Bar & Grill **14**
Ginger **4**
La Laguna del Cocodrillo Bistro **14**
Lola's **15**
Mar y Sol **10**
Papagayo **2**
Picante **7**
Season's by Shlomy **14**

ATTRACTIONS ●
Africa Mia **22**
Cartagena Canopy Tour **16**
Congo Trail Canopy Tour **6**
Hacienda Guachipelín **21**
Hacienda Pinilla **15**
Hotel Borinquen Thermal Baths **20**
Rincón de la Vieja National Park **19**

Santa Rosa Canopy Tour **14**
Santa Rosa National Park **18**
Witch's Rock Canopy Tour **1**

SHOPPING ▒
Guaitil **23**
Kaltak Arts & Crafts Market **17**

NIGHTLIFE ★
Amberes **9**
Aqua **14**
Bar 1 **14**
Barceló Playa Langosta Casino **14**
Café de Playa **5**
Coco Bay Hotel & Casino **5**
Cocomar **5**
Crazy Monkey Bar **14**
Hotel Pasatiempo **14**
Jazz Casino **14**
Lizard Lounge **14**
Upper Deck Sports Bar **4**
Zouk Santana **5**

floors have the best views and cost a little more. The others have either garden views or partial ocean views, even though every room faces the sea. On the rocky hill at the end of the peninsula are the resort's suites and villas. These are all similarly appointed, but with even more space and often a private pool, a Jacuzzi, or an open-air gazebo for soaking in the views.

The resort also features the renowned service of the Four Seasons (including family-friendly amenities such as kid-size bathrobes and childproof rooms), one of the best-equipped full-service spas in the country, a truly spectacular golf course that offers ocean views from 15 of its 18 holes, and several excellent dining options. Of the hotel's restaurants, **Papagayo** (see listing later in this chapter), serving Nuevo Latino cuisine, is my favorite.

See map p. 156. Papagayo Peninsula. ☎ **800-819-5053** *in the U.S., 2696-0000 in Costa Rica. Fax: 2696-0500.* www.fourseasons.com/costarica. *Rack rates: $815–$955 double, $1,480–$9,500 suites and villas. Rates lower in the off season, higher during peak weeks. Children stay free in parent's room. AE, DC, MC, V.*

Hilton Papagayo Resort
$$$$–$$$$$ Papagayo Peninsula

The very first all-inclusive resort in the Guanacaste region, this place was taken over by the Hilton group in 2008. A major overhaul ensued, and the resort is in very good shape. Most of the duplex villas can be separated into two rooms or shared by a family or two couples. Inside, one room is equipped with a king-size bed; the other has two queens. All rooms have marble floors, large bathrooms, and small private patios or balconies. The resort is quite spread out, so if you don't want to do a lot of walking or wait for the minivan shuttles, request a room near the main pool and restaurants. If you want a good view, ask for one on the hill overlooking the bay. The hotel has a large, modern, and plush spa facility. It also has its own small crescent-shape swath of beach, which is very calm and protected for swimming.

See map p. 156. Playa Panamá. ☎ **800-445-8667** *in the U.S. and Canada, 2672-0000 in Costa Rica. Fax: 2672-0181.* www.hilton.com. *Rack rates: $229–$579 double, $530–$630 junior suite. Rates include all food and drinks, a range of activities, and taxes. AE, DC, MC, V.*

Hotel and Villas Cala Luna
$$$–$$$$$ Tamarindo

If you're looking for serious luxury in Tamarindo, stay in one of the two- or three-bedroom villas here, which are the size of a small home and just as well equipped. The living rooms are huge, with high-peaked ceilings, couches, tables and chairs, satellite televisions, and complete sound systems. The full kitchens come with microwave ovens and cappuccino machines — even washing machines. If this isn't enough, each villa has its own private swimming pool. The bedrooms are spacious and elegant, with either a king-size bed or two double beds. Everything is done in soft

Tamarindo

To Airport

ACCOMMODATIONS ■
Hotel and Villas Cala Luna **4**
Hotel Capitán Suizo **5**
Sueño del Mar **3**
Villa Alegre **2**

DINING ◆
Dragonfly Bar & Grill **7**
La Laguna del
   Cocodrillo Bistro **13**
Season's by Shlomy **6**

NIGHTLIFE ★
Aqua **11**
Bar 1 **9**
Barceló Playa
   Langosta Casino **1**
Crazy Monkey Bar **12**
Hotel Pasatiempo **8**
Jazz Casino **10**

PACIFIC OCEAN

Playa
Tamarindo

NICARAGUA

Caribbean Sea

Monteverde

Tamarindo ★ San José

COSTA RICA

PACIFIC OCEAN

PANAMA

0   100 mi
0   100 km

Isla
Capitan

Punta
San Francisco

Playa Langosta

pastels with hand-painted accents, and the red-tile roofs and Mexican tile floors add elegance while keeping things cool. Rooms in the hotel are spacious and similarly well done, with their own terraces, but you'll have to share the hotel's main swimming pool with the rest of the guests. The hotel isn't right on the beach; you have to cross the street and walk a short path to reach the ocean. The hotel offers free Wi-Fi in most of its common areas.

See map p. 156. Playa Tamarindo. ☎ *800-503-5202 in the U.S. and Canada, 2653-0214 in Costa Rica. Fax: 2653-0213.* www.calaluna.com. *Rack rates: $185 double, $370–$470 villa. Rates for rooms, but not villas, include continental breakfast. Rates slightly higher during peak weeks. AE, MC, V.*

Hotel Capitán Suizo
$$$–$$$$$ Tamarindo

This well-appointed beachfront hotel is located on the quiet southern end of Tamarindo. The rooms are housed in a series of two-story buildings.

The lower rooms have air-conditioning and private patios; the upper units have plenty of cross ventilation and inviting balconies. All have large bathrooms and sitting rooms with fold-down futon couches. In effect, all the rooms are really junior suites, with separate sitting/living-room areas. The spacious individual bungalows are spread around the shady grounds; each comes with a tub in the bathroom and an inviting outdoor shower among the trees.

The hotel's free-form pool is the best I've found outside of a large resort. The shallow end slopes in gradually, imitating a beach, and a separate children's pool is nearby. Perhaps this hotel's greatest attribute is its location just steps from one of the calmer and more isolated sections of Playa Tamarindo.

See map p. 156. Playa Tamarindo. ☎ *2653-0353 or 2653-0075. Fax: 2653-0292.* www.hotelcapitansuizo.com. *Rack rates: $175–$195 double, $235–$275 bungalow, $360 suite. Rates include breakfast buffet. Rates lower in the off season, higher during peak periods. AE, MC, V.*

Hotel Playa Hermosa Bosque del Mar
$$$–$$$$ **Playa Hermosa**

Tucked away under shady trees, this sprawling beachfront spread has gotten a major remodel and upgrade and is now the premier beachfront boutique hotel on Playa Hermosa. The plush oceanfront suites feature outdoor Jacuzzis. The garden-view suites are very similar but an indoor sauna replaces the Jacuzzi. In both cases, second-floor units have better views and higher ceilings. The junior suites are all cozy and well-equipped. The whole complex was built around and amongst the lush existing gardens and trees, and employs sustainable practices wherever possible. Trees come up and through the main lobby and restaurant, and through some of the decks off the rooms. Three of the suites are handicapped accessible. The second-floor bar and lounge has great views through the trees to the sea. Free Wi-Fi is offered throughout the hotel.

See map p. 156. Playa Hermosa. ☎ *2672-0046. Fax: 2672-0019.* www.hotelplayahermosa.com. *Rack rates: $175 junior suite, $225–$275 suite. Rates lower in the off season, higher during peak periods. AE, MC, V.*

Hotel Sugar Beach
$$$–$$$$ **Playa Pan de Azúcar**

Hotel Sugar Beach is located on a beautiful, semiprivate, salt-and-pepper beach about a ten-minute drive north of Playa Flamingo along a rough dirt road. It's the only hotel in the area, and that's what gives it most of its charm, in my opinion — it boasts lots of seclusion and privacy. The beach is on a small cove surrounded by rocky hills. The hotel itself is perched above the water. Nature lovers will be thrilled to find wild howler monkeys and iguanas almost on their doorsteps. Snorkelers should be happy here, too; this cove has some good snorkeling in the dry season. The rooms, which come in a variety of sizes and configurations, are all neat,

Playa del Coco

modern, and comfortable. Some of the better suites are located on a high point of land, with wonderful views. However, I prefer the beachfront rooms and suites. If you don't land one of the rooms with a view, head to the main lodge and restaurant, which have a commanding view from their hillside perch.

See map p. 156. Playa Pan de Azúcar. ☎ **654-4242**. *Fax: 654-4239.* www.sugar-beach.com. *Rack rates: $125–$155 double, $195–$350 suite, $475–$660 villa. Rates include breakfast. Rates lower in the off season. AE, MC, V.*

Hotel Villa Casa Blanca
$$ Playa Ocotal

With a great hillside perch, beautiful gardens, and attractive rooms, this bed-and-breakfast is an excellent choice. Located about 500m (1,640 ft.) inland from the beach, all the guest rooms feature fine furnishings and are well kept. Some are a tad small, but others are quite roomy and some even have kitchenettes. The suites are higher up and have ocean views. My favorite has a secluded patio with lush flowering plants all around. A little rancho serves as an open-air bar and breakfast area, and beside this is a pretty little lap pool with a bridge over it. Another separate *rancho* serves as a sort of lounge/recreation area and has a satellite television. An inviting hot tub and sitting area awaits you near the pool, and free Wi-Fi is offered throughout. These folks manage several rental houses and condos in the area, so if you plan to stay for a week or more, or if you need lots of room, ask about these.

See map p. 156. Playa Ocotal. ☎ 2670-0518. Fax: 2670-0448. www.hotelvilla casablanca.com. *Rack rates: $105 double, $125 suite. Rates include breakfast buffet. Rates lower in the off season, higher during peak periods. AE, MC, V.*

JW Marriott Guanacaste Resort & Spa
$$$$–$$$$$ Hacienda Pinilla

The newest large-scale resort in Costa Rica is also one of its best. The rooms, facilities, restaurants, amenities, and service here are all top-of-the-line. All have large flat-screen televisions, separate tubs and showers, and a spacious balcony or patio with a cooling retractable shade screen. Of the limited number of beachfront rooms, the Marimba suite (no. 339), a corner unit, is probably the best in the house. The large spa is modern and luxurious. The Mansita beach in front of the resort is a bit rocky, but beautiful stretches of Playa Avellanas lie a short walk or shuttle ride away, and the hotel also boasts the largest pool in Central America, edging out the Paradisus Playa Conchal for the honor.

See map p. 156. Hacienda Pinilla, Guanacaste. ☎ 888-236-2427 in the U.S. and Canada, 2681-2000 in Costa Rica. Fax: 2681-2001. www.marriott.com. *Rack rates: $225–$369 double, $425–$769 suite, $1,625–$1,770 presidential suite. AE, DC, DISC, MC, V.*

Las Tortugas Hotel
$$ Playa Grande

Playa Grande is best known for the leatherback turtles that nest here, and much of the beach is now part of Las Baulas National Park, which was created to protect the turtles. However, this beach and this hotel are also very popular with surfers. Several of the rooms are quite large, and most have interesting stone floors and shower stalls. The upper suite has a curving staircase that leads to its second room. A few canoes on the nearby estuary are available for gentle paddling among the mangroves.

The owners here led the fight to have the area declared a national park and continue to do everything possible to protect the turtles. As part of the hotel's turtle-friendly design, a natural wall of shrubs and trees shields the beach from the hotel's light and noise, and the swimming pool is shaped like a turtle.

See map p. 156. Playa Grande. ☎ 2653-0423 or tel/fax 2653-0458. www.las tortugashotel.com. *Rack rates: $90 double, $120 suite. Rates lower in the off season, slightly higher during peak weeks. MC, V.*

Playa Hermosa

PACIFIC OCEAN

Soccer Field

To Playa Panama →

← To Playa del Coco

Playa Hermosa

San José ⊛

Caribbean Sea

COSTA RICA

PACIFIC OCEAN
0 ___ 50 mi
0 ___ 50 km

0 ___ 200 yds
0 ___ 200 m

ACCOMMODATIONS ■
El Velero Hotel **3**
Hotel Playa Hermosa
  Bosque del Mar **1**
Villa del Sueño **2**

DINING ◆
Ginger **4**

DINING ★
Upper Deck Sports
  Bar **5**

Paradisus Playa Conchal
$$$$–$$$$$ Playa Conchal

This sprawling all-suite, all-inclusive resort is large and luxurious. From the massive, open-air reception building down to the free-form swimming pool, everything here is on a grand scale. The rooms feature either one king-size bed or two queen-size beds in a raised bedroom nook. Down below, you can relax in a comfortable sitting area, with a couch, coffee table, and chairs with ottomans. The bathrooms are large and modern, with marble tiles, full tubs, bidets, and a telephone. Each unit has a garden patio or a small balcony. Only three of the buildings actually front the ocean, and in two of these you'll find the resort's two presidential suites, which have double the living area of the standard suites and even more luxurious appointments.

Unlike most all-inclusives, only one of the restaurants here is buffet; the others are sit-down where you can order a la carte, although these meals are decidedly mediocre. The hotel has a beautiful golf course, with broad, open holes; rolling hills; and the occasional sea view. Because of the golf course and its ponds and wetlands, good bird-watching is abundant here, with healthy populations of parrots, roseate spoonbills, and wood storks. The hotel also has an excellent children's program, as well as loads of activities, with both water- and land-based sports equipment for guest use.

See map p. 156. Playa Conchal. ☎ **888-336-3542** *in the U.S., 2654-4123 in Costa Rica. Fax: 2654-4181.* www.solmelia.com. *Rack rates: $319–$443 double, $419–$503 royal suites, $990 presidential suites. Rates include all meals, drinks, taxes, a wide range of activities, and use of nonmotorized land- and water-sports equipment. Golf and spa services extra. AE, MC, V.*

Sueño del Mar
$$$–$$$$ **Playa Langosta**

This small bed-and-breakfast has charming little touches and innovative décor: four-poster beds made from driftwood; African dolls on the windowsills; Kokopeli candleholders; and open-air showers with sculpted angelfish, hand-painted tiles, and lush tropical plants. Fabrics are from Bali and Guatemala. Somehow all this works well together, and the requisite chairs and lounges nestled under shade trees right on the beach add the crowning touch. The two casitas have their own kitchen, veranda, and sleeping loft. The honeymoon suite is a spacious second-floor room, with wraparound screened-in windows, a delightful open-air shower, and an ocean view. The beach right out front is rocky and a bit rough, but it does reveal some nice, quiet tidal pools at low tide; it's one of the better sunset-viewing spots in Costa Rica. Breakfasts are huge and elaborate. The entire, albeit tiny, complex is wired with free Wi-Fi. No children under 12 are allowed unless your party rents out the entire hotel.

See map p. 156. Playa Langosta. ☎/fax **2653-0284.** www.sueno-del-mar.com. *Rack rates: $195 double, $220–$295 suite or casita. Rates include full breakfast. Rates lower in the off season, higher during peak periods. MC, V.*

Villa Alegre
$$$–$$$$ **Playa Langosta**

This small bed-and-breakfast on Playa Langosta is well-run and homey. Each of the rooms is decorated in the theme of a different country. In the main house, Guatemala, Mexico, and the United States are all represented. Of these, Mexico is the biggest and best, with a large open-air bathroom and shower. Every room has its own private patio, courtyard, or balcony. The villas are quite spacious, with full kitchenettes. My favorite is the Japanese villa, with its subtle design touches and great woodwork. The Russian and the United States villas are truly wheelchair-accessible, with ramps and modified bathrooms. The smallest units are the Guatemala room and the California casita. The beach is just 90m (295 ft.) or so away through the trees, and a very pleasant little pool can be found here as well. Breakfasts are delicious and abundant.

See map p. 156. Playa Tamarindo. ☎ **2653-0270.** *Fax: 2653-0287.* www.villa alegrecostarica.com. *Rack rates: $170–$185 double, $230 villa. Rates include full breakfast. Rates lower in the off season. AE, MC, V.*

Villa del Sueño Hotel
$$–$$$$ Playa Hermosa

This small hotel provides excellent value and attentive service in a beautiful setting. Although Villa del Sueño is not right on the beach (it's about 90m/295 ft. from the sand), its well-groomed lawns and gardens feel like an oasis in the dust and heat of a Guanacaste dry season. All the rooms have cool tile floors, high hardwood ceilings, ceiling fans, and well-placed windows for cross ventilation. The second-floor superior rooms have more space, larger windows, and air-conditioning. A small pool and open-air bar are in the center courtyard. Meals are served in the main building's open-air restaurant, which has a stage for live music played here several nights a week throughout the high season. In addition, they have a separate open-air dinner theater, which has periodic gala performances, as well. The folks here manage a neighboring condominium development, which has additional apartment and efficiency units available for nightly and weekly rental.

See map p. 156. Playa Hermosa. ☎ **800-378-8599** *in the U.S. and Canada, 2672-0026 in Costa Rica. Fax: 2672-0021.* www.villadelsueno.com. *Rack rates: $75–$105 double, $130–$255 condo. Rates lower in the off season, higher during peak periods. AE, MC, V.*

Where to Dine in Guanacaste

Café de Playa
$$$ Playa del Coco   INTERNATIONAL

This hip restaurant has brought a bit of class and style to Playa del Coco. The creative menu covers a lot of ground, with influences from Italy and across Asia quite noticeable. Appetizers range from an octopus carpaccio to a cold Thai beef salad. There's a host of pasta choices and a very tasty oriental rice salad with smoked tuna, caviar, and avocado. Lobster is served several ways, as are tender filets of top grade meats. For dessert, be sure to try the passion fruit ice cream. Heavy teak tables and chairs are spread around the ample, open-air dining room, or out under the open sky. The bar, which is made from thick bamboo, and lounge are dimly lit, chic, and very inviting.

See map p. 156. Playa del Coco. ☎ **2670-1621.** *Reservations recommended in high season. Main courses: $12–$20. MC, V. Open: Daily 7 a.m.–10 p.m.*

Camarón Dorado
$$–$$$ Playa Brasilito SEAFOOD

With tables and kerosene torches set right in the sand just steps from the crashing surf, this is one of my favorite restaurants in the area. More tables are available in the simple, open-air dining room, for those who don't want sand in their shoes. The service is semiformal, with the attentive wait staff bringing you a bowl of flower-infused water so that you can wash your hands even before you order. The seafood is fresh, well-prepared, and reasonably priced. One time, when I asked to see the wine list, two waiters came over carrying about 12 different bottles between them.

See map p. 156. Playa Brasilito. ☎ **2654-4028.** *Reservations recommended in high season. Main courses: $6–$23. MC, V. Open: Daily 11 a.m.–10 p.m.*

Dragonfly Bar & Grill
$$$ Tamarindo INTERNATIONAL/FUSION

Tucked away on a back street, this restaurant has quickly become one of the top choices in Tamarindo, earning fast praise and a loyal following with its excellent food and cozy ambience. The menu mixes and matches several cuisines, with the Southwestern United States and Pacific Rim fusion as the strongest influences. There are daily fish and seafood specials, which may range from wood-fired red snapper to pistachio crusted mahimahi. If you're in the mood for meat, I recommend the thick chile-rubbed pork chop with chipotle mashed potatoes. The restaurant space itself is a simple open-air establishment, with a concrete floor and rough wood tree trunks as support columns. There's an open wood-fired grill and oven on one side, and a popular bar toward the back. They offer free Wi-Fi throughout the restaurant.

See map p. 156. Tamarindo ☎ **2653-1506.** *Reservations recommended. Main courses: $10–$16. AE, MC, V. Open: Mon–Sat 6–10 p.m.*

Ginger
$$ Playa Hermosa TAPAS

Ginger is one of the hippest and more creative restaurants in the region. The architecture and décor are stylish and modern, with sharp angles and loads of chrome and glass. The food is an eclectic mix of modern takes on wide-ranging international fare, all served as tapas, meant to be shared while sampling some of the many cocktails and wines served here. Still, you can easily make a full meal of a night here. Order the house special ginger-glazed chicken wings, along with some spring rolls, and a plate of fresh mahimahi marinated in vodka and Asian spices. You can also order more-traditional Mediterranean and Spanish-style tapas, as well as delicious desserts.

See map p. 156. Playa Hermosa, on the main road. ☎ **2672-0041.** *Tapas: $4.50–$8. AE, MC, V. Open: Tues–Sun 5–10 p.m.*

La Laguna del Cocodrillo Bistro
$$$$ Tamarindo FUSION

This small restaurant has impressed me every time I've eaten here. Beautiful presentations and a creative use of ingredients are the norm. Start things off with their crab bisque, which is served with a terrine of asparagus, avocado, and potato, or opt for the expertly spiced seared scallops. For a main dish, try the fresh red snapper, which is stuffed with a cognac-flavored mousse. Be sure to save room for dessert, which is always excellent. The open-air restaurant space is very small, but when the weather permits, more tables are set up under the trees in their beach-front garden area. Separate restaurateurs also serve breakfast and lunch in this space.

See map p. 156. Tamarindo, on the main road, toward the north end of town. ☎ **2653-3897.** *Reservations recommended. Main courses: $12–$29. MC, V. Open: Mon–Sat 7:30 a.m.–9 p.m.*

Lola's
$$–$$$ Playa Avellanas INTERNATIONAL

Long loved by locals, the secret is out about Lola's. Named after the owner's recently departed pet pig, this place serves up top-notch fresh fare in a beautiful open-air beachfront setting. Most of the heavy, homemade wooden tables and chairs are set in the sand, under the intermittent shade of palm trees and large canvas umbrellas. The fresh seared tuna, big healthy salads, and Belgian fries are the favorites here, alongside the fresh fruit smoothies and delicious sandwiches on just-baked bread. You'll have to come early on weekends to get a seat.

See map p. 156. On the beach, Playa Avellanas. ☎ **2652-9097.** *Main courses: $4.50–$13. No credit cards. Open: Tues–Sun 8 a.m to sunset.*

Mar y Sol
$$$$–$$$$$ Playa Flamingo INTERNATIONAL/SEAFOOD

Seventh-generation Catalan chef Alain Taulere has cooked for the likes of Henry Kissinger and Prince Rainier of Monaco. For the less well-known visitors to his hilltop restaurant in Flamingo Beach, he offers a small, well-executed menu of fresh seafood and meats. The ambience of the restaurant is casually formal, with the open-air main dining room dimly lit by old-fashioned lampposts and covered by a thatched roof. The many excellent seafood choices include rich and creamy lobster bisque and a hearty bouillabaisse. If you want meat or game, I recommend the duck served with passion fruit–cognac sauce. For dessert, try one of the homemade tropical fruit ice creams, which are sweet and refreshing. Call in advance and they'll provide free transportation from and back to your hotel.

See map p. 156. Playa Flamingo. ☎ **2654-4151.** *Reservations recommended. Main courses: $17–$39. AE, DC, MC, V. Open: Nov–Apr daily 10 a.m.–3:30 p.m. and 5–10 p.m.; May–Aug daily 2–10 p.m. Closed Sept–Oct.*

Papagayo
$$$$$ **Four Seasons Resort   NUEVO LATINO**

The luxurious Four Seasons (see listing earlier in this chapter) boasts one of the best Nuevo Latino (New Latin) restaurants in Costa Rica. The menu is always long and creative, but it changes regularly and features daily specials. I thoroughly enjoyed my ancho chile–crusted rack of lamb served with a *mole poblano* sauce. The tamarind-crusted ahi tuna is also excellent and comes with jalapeño corn pudding and mango salsa. The large dining room has high ceilings and low lighting, and it features some equally large artworks by renowned Costa Rican painters. However, the best seats, weather permitting, are those at the few outdoor garden tables.

See map p. 156. At the Four Seasons Resort, Papagayo Peninsula. ☎ *2696-0006. Reservations necessary. Main courses: $25–$40. AE, MC, V. Open: Daily 6–10 p.m.*

Picante
$$–$$$ **Playa Ocotal   INTERNATIONAL**

You'll enjoy excellent fresh fish and daily specials in the large, open-air, poolside restaurant at this modest little resort and condominium project. Beyond the pool and down a steep little hill, you can see the Pacific Ocean. The menu is pretty simple and straightforward, with a selection of fresh seafood dishes, big burgers, excellent fish sandwiches, and large creative salads. The daily chalkboard specials are usually more creative and eclectic, ranging from sesame-seared tuna to mahimahi topped with a home-made curry sauce.

See map p. 156. At Bahia Pez Vela resort, Playa Ocotal. ☎ *670-0901. Main courses: $9–$18. MC, V. Open: Daily 9 a.m.–9:30 p.m.*

Seasons by Shlomy
$$–$$$ **Tamarindo   INTERNATIONAL**

This is another of Tamarindo's standout restaurants. Chef and owner Shlomy Koren has earned a fond and faithful following for both his consistency and creativity. For years he held court at Pachanga. Now located in the poolside patio of the Arco Iris Hotel, he continues to please. The contemporary cuisine carries a heavy Mediterranean influence: The seared tuna in a honey-chili marinade is always a favorite, as is the seafood pasta with an unexpected lemon vinaigrette sauce. Desserts often feature home-made ice creams and sorbets.

See map p. 156. Inside the Arco Iris Hotel, Tamarindo. ☎ *8368-6983. Reservations recommended. Main courses: $13–$15. No credit cards. Open: Mon–Sat 6–10 p.m.*

Fast Facts: Guanacaste

Ambulance
Call ☎ **128.**

ATMs
You'll find ATMs in Liberia, and all of the major tourist beach towns of Guanacaste, as well as at the Daniel Oduber Airport in Liberia.

Country Code and City Code
The country code for Costa Rica is **506.** Costa Rica does not use city or area codes. To call from the United States, dial 011-506 plus the eight-digit number. From within Costa Rica, you simply dial the eight-digit number.

Currency Exchange
Most hotels will exchange money for you at decent rates. To get official rates, head to one of the banks in Tamarindo, Flamingo, Playa del Coco, or Liberia.

Fire
Call ☎ **118.**

Hospitals
The Liberia Hospital (☎ 2666-0011) is the best hospital in the area. A smaller hospital lies in the city of Santa Cruz. Most of the beach towns have some sort of health clinic.

Information
See "Orienting Yourself in Guanacaste," earlier in this chapter.

Internet Access
Internet cafes can be found in all the major beach towns of Guanacaste. Rates run between $1 and $3 per hour.

Pharmacies
Each of the beach towns and destinations has a pharmacy or two. Ask at your hotel for the nearest and best-stocked option.

Police
Call ☎ **911.**

Post Office
Small post offices are open in most of the major beach towns. Alternatively, most hotels can mail your letters and postcards for you.

Taxis
Taxis meet all incoming flights at the Daniel Oduber Airport in Liberia, and at the small airstrip in Tamarindo. Though taxi services can be found in all the beach towns, it's almost always better to have your hotel call a cab for you, instead of hoping to find one on the street.

Chapter 14

Exploring Guanacaste

* * *

In This Chapter

▷ Scoping out the many tour and activity options in Guanacaste

▷ Buying something beyond tourist trinkets

▷ Enjoying Guanacaste's nightlife

* * *

Guanacaste is vast. Tours and adventure opportunities are abundant. Though you may be content to pass your days soaking in the sun and taking the occasional dip in the ocean or pool, you'll have plenty to choose from if you're feeling more active.

Although most of the tours and adventures listed in this chapter are best done as part of a guided excursion, if you have your own rental car, or you want to hire a taxi or private guide, you can certainly set them up independently.

Seeing Guanacaste by Guided Tour

Nearly all the hotels and resorts in Guanacaste have a tour desk or can help you arrange a variety of popular day tours and activities. Prices range from $35 to $120 per person, depending on the length of the tour and the activity or activities involved.

 Be careful before signing up for a trip to a more distant destination. Find out how much time will be spent on travel and how much time will be spent enjoying the attraction and activities. I don't recommend the day trips to Arenal volcano or Monteverde, for example, because the drive is three to four hours each way in a bus or minivan. Still, some folks are willing to put up with that much travel time for the chance to visit these very worthwhile places. (See Chapters 17 and 18 for more information on Arenal and Monteverde.)

Finding out how many other folks will be on the tour with you is also a good idea. If you're going on a rafting trip, or any other tour where the group will be broken up into smaller units, group size is not critical. But on any nature tour, hike, or other guided activity, I recommend ten people per guide as a maximum, with six or fewer people per guide as optimal. If you're the last person in line on an overcrowded nature hike, you'll have difficulty hearing the guide's explanations and you're unlikely to see much of the wildlife pointed out to those at the front of the line.

Visits to other lodges and destinations, as well as rafting trips, are best done on guided tours. Other activities, including sportfishing and surfing, are best done on your own.

See the map in Chapter 13 for help in locating the following listings.

The Top Attractions

Africa Mia

Forget about howler monkeys, toucans, jaguars, and other new-world fauna, this place is filled with large mammals more identified with the ancient continent of Africa. The broad, open plains of Guanacaste are strikingly similar geographically to those found in Africa, especially in the dry season. So it shouldn't come as too much of a shock to see antelope, zebra, giraffe, and elands roaming the grassy plains of Guanacaste. **Africa Mia (My Africa)** offers safari-style, open-jeep tours through its 100-hectare private reserve, which is populated with a wide range of nonnative (predominantly African) species. All the animals are herbivores, so don't expect to see any lions, hyenas, or cheetahs. Still, the trip does provide some of the sense of being on the Serengeti or some other African plain, and it usually offers up some excellent photographic opportunities.

See map p. 156. On the Interamerican Highway. 8km (5 miles) south of Liberia. ☎ *2666-1111.* www.africamia.net. *Admission: $16 adults, $11 children 11 and under. Make reservations in advance.*

Hacienda Guachipelin

This working cattle and horse ranch is located 23km (14 miles) northeast of Liberia on the edge of Rincón de la Vieja National Park.

This is one of the closest lodges to the thermal springs (10km/6¼ miles) and bubbling mud pots (5km/3 miles) of Rincón de la Vieja National Park. Hacienda Guachipelin offers up a range of adventure-tour options, including horseback riding, hiking, white-water river inner-tubing, a waterfall canyoning-and-rappeling tour, and a more traditional zip-line canopy tour. The most popular is the hacienda's **One-Day Adventure Pass,** which allows you to choose as many of the hotel's different tour options as you want and fit them into one adventure-packed day.

Almost all the beach hotels and resorts of Guanacaste offer day trips here, or you can book directly through the lodge, including transportation. If you decide to visit this place on your own, be sure to call and make a reservation in advance.

During the high season, there's a bit of a cattle-car feel to the whole operation, with busloads of day-trippers coming in from the beach. Also, I've found the inner-tube adventure to be fairly dangerous when the river is high, particularly during or just after the rainy season.

See map p. 156. Hacienda Guachipelin. 23km (14 miles) northeast of Liberia on the edge of Rincón de la Vieja National Park. To reach the lodge, drive about 5km (3 miles) north of Liberia and turn right on the dirt road to Rincón de la Vieja National Park. The turnoff is well marked. In about 12km (7½ miles), you'll pass through the small village of Curubandé. Continue on this road for another 6km (3¾ miles), until you reach the Hacienda Guachipelin. If you're staying at the lodge or doing a tour here, you shouldn't have to pay the $2 toll collected at the lodge gate. ☎ *2665-3303 for reservations, 2666-8075 at the lodge.* www.guachipelin.com. *Admission: Tours $25–$80 per person; One-Day Adventure Pass $80 per person, including lunch. Tour packages with transportation are available. Open: Daily 7:30 a.m.–5 p.m. (for tours).*

Borinquen Thermal Baths

Another popular day trip from Guanacaste is to visit the mud pots and thermal waters at the Borinquen Mountain Resort & Spa. Set at the foot of a deep valley on the flanks of the Rincón de la Vieja volcano, this place has several natural hot-spring pools of differing temperatures, a natural sauna, and an area for full-body mud baths given with hot volcanic mud, recently collected from steaming volcanic mud pots. After a mud bath and some hot soaking, you can lounge by the large free-form swimming pool. Borinquen is set on the edge of the rain forest beside gentle creeks, with trails to the mud pots and into the forest. There are a couple of pretty waterfalls nearby. Hiking, horseback riding, ATV, and canopy tours can be added on in conjunction with the hot springs and spa treatments offered here.

See map p. 156. Drive 26km (16 miles) north of Liberia along the Interamerican Highway. Take the turnoff toward Cañas Dulces, and follow the signs. The hotel is approximately 22km (14 miles) from the highway along a rough dirt road. ☎ *2690-1900.* www.borinquenresort.com. *Admission: $25 per person for use of the hot pools, sauna, and mud baths; $55–$110 for various adventure tours.*

Rincón de la Vieja National Park

This national park begins on the flanks of the **Rincón de la Vieja volcano** and includes the volcano's active crater. Fumaroles, geysers, and hot pools can all be observed here. In addition to hot springs and mud pots, you can explore waterfalls, a lake, and volcanic craters. The bird-watching is excellent, and the views across the pasturelands to the Pacific Ocean are stunning.

Several excellent trails run inside the Rincón de la Vieja National Park. More-energetic hikers can tackle the 8km (5 miles) up to the **summit** and explore the several craters and beautiful lakes up here. On a clear day, you'll be rewarded with a fabulous view of the plains of Guanacaste and the Pacific Ocean below. The easiest hiking is the gentle **Las Pailas loop.** This 3km (1¾-mile) trail is just off the Las Espuelas Park entrance and passes by several bubbling mud pots and steaming fumaroles. This trail crosses a river, so you'll have to either take off your shoes or get them wet. The entire loop takes around two hours.

My favorite hike here is to the **Blue Lake** and **La Cangrejo waterfall.** This 5km (3-mile) trail passes through several different life zones, including dry forest, transitional moist forest, and open savanna. A variety of birds and mammals are commonly sighted. Pack a lunch; at the end of your two-hour hike in, you can picnic at the aptly named Blue Lake, where a 30m (98-ft.) waterfall empties into the small pond with crystal-blue hues that are amazing.

You can visit Rincón de la Vieja National Park as part of a guided tour or with a four-wheel-drive rental vehicle.

See map p. 156. The Las Espuelas park entrance is 25km (16 miles) northeast of Liberia, down a badly rutted dirt road. To reach the park entrance, drive about 5km (3 miles) north of Liberia and turn right on the dirt road to the park. The turnoff is well marked. In about 12km (7½ miles), you'll pass through the small village of Curubandé. Continue on this road for another 6km (3¾ miles) until you reach the Hacienda Lodge Guachipelin. The lodge is private property, and the owners charge a $2 toll to pass through their gate and continue on to the park. Pay the toll, pass through the lodge's gate, and continue for another 4km (2½ miles) until you reach the park entrance. ☎ **2661-8139.** *Admission: $10. Open: Daily 7 a.m.–3 p.m.*

Rio Corobicí Rafting

This class II river makes for very gentle rafting, although you'll also find a few mild rapids. The *put-in* (spot where the rafting starts) is located just off the Interamerican Highway beside the Restaurant Rincón Corobicí, about 40km (25 miles) south of Liberia. Along the way, you may see many of the area's more exotic animal residents: howler monkeys, iguanas, caimans, coatimundis, otters, toucans, parrots, motmots, trogons, and many other bird species. Aside from your binoculars and camera, a bathing suit and sunscreen are the only things you'll need.

All the tour agencies and tour desks in the area can book this for you, or you can call **Safaris Corobicí** (☎/fax **2669-6191;** www.nicoya.com) and set it up for yourself. These folks offer a variety of options, including separate trips on the Bebedero River. For a much wetter and wilder ride, the folks at **Hacienda Guachipelin** (see listing later in this chapter) offer white-water inner-tube trips on the narrow Río Negro, near their lodge.

Safaris Corobicí. Main office is on the Interamerican Highway, KM193, 40km (25 miles) south of Liberia, and about 1km (⅔ mile) south of the Restaurant Rincón Corobicí. ☎/fax **2669-6191.** www.nicoya.com. *Admission: $38 for a 2-hour float, $62 for a half-day trip including lunch. Open: Daily 8 a.m.–4 p.m.*

Sea Turtle Nesting

Giant leatherback sea turtles nest on Playa Grande between late September and late February. The turtles come ashore to lay their eggs only at night. During the nesting season, you'll be inundated with opportunities to sign up for the nightly tours, which usually cost around $35 to $60 per person.

Do-it-yourselfers can drive over to Playa Grande and book a tour directly with the **National Parks Service** (☎ **2653-0470;** $25). The Parks Service operates out of a small shack next to the turtle museum and opens each evening at around 6 p.m. to begin taking reservations. However, spots fill up fast, and you'll be competing with the local tour operators who tend to snap up the prime spots first. If you don't have a reservation, you may have to wait until really late, and may not be able to go out onto the beach at all.

Between July and November, the smaller Olive Ridley sea turtles nest on several other beaches in Guanacaste, including the northern beaches inside Santa Rosa National Park, and the more southern beach of Ostional. When the Olive Ridley are nesting, tours are available to these beaches as well. The Olive Ridley *arribadas* (nestings) are unique because they come ashore in massive numbers, even during the daytime. ***Note:*** No flash photography is allowed because any sort of light can confuse the turtles and prevent them from laying their eggs; guides must use red-tinted flashlights.

Turtle nesting is a natural, unpredictable, and rare event. Moreover, things have gotten worse in recent years. The number of nesting turtles on Playa Grande was severely down a couple of years ago. All indications are that excessive building and lighting close to the beach are the culprits. Even during heavy nesting years, you sometimes have to wait your turn for hours, hike quite a ways, and even accept the possibility that no nesting mothers will be spotted that evening.

*See map p. 156 for Playa Grande. Located on the main beach access road to Playa Grande 200m (2 blocks) before it hits the ocean, 100m (1 block) before the hotel Las Tortugas. ☎ **2653-0470.** Admission: $15. Open: 6 p.m.–2 a.m. (roughly) during turtle season (late Sept–late Feb).*

More Cool Things to See and Do

All the options listed in this section are probably best done on your own, either in a rental car or by taxi. However, most of the hotel tour desks and independent tour operators can book you almost any of the tours or adventures listed here as well.

Visiting some of the lesser-known beaches

Although none of the beaches in Guanacaste ever gets truly crowded, it is still possible and profoundly rewarding to find your own patch of sand on one of the more isolated or less developed beaches in this area.

An interesting stop on your way to Liberia

If you're driving to or from Guanacaste, be sure to take a brief break to check out the **Catholic Church** in Cañas. Well-known painter, installation artist, and local prodigal son Otto Apuy has designed and directed the envelopment of the entire church in colorful mosaic. The work uses whole and broken tiles in glossy, vibrant colors to depict both religious and abstract themes. The church is located in the center of town, just a few blocks off the Interamerican Highway.

✔ At the northern end of the province, the Papagayo Peninsula has a number of very remote and undeveloped beaches to choose from. **Playa Nacascolo,** which sits within the property of the Four Seasons, is one of the top beaches in this area. All beaches in Costa Rica are public property and open to anyone, and the Four Seasons provides parking and access for people visiting Playa Nacascolo.

✔ Farther south, **Playa Panamá** is a long and lovely beach with just one or two simple restaurants and a couple of hotels.

✔ You'll find a real treasure trove of remote beaches around the Playa Flamingo and Playa Conchal area. From these popular spots, several largely unexplored beaches lie in either direction, including **Playa La Penca, Playa Prieta, Playa Pan de Azúcar, Playa Real,** and a few that are, for all intents and purposes, unnamed.

✔ Although Tamarindo is easily the most developed and crowded beach in the area, just to the north of it, **Playa Grande** is seldom crowded, and to the south, such beaches as **Playa Avellanas, Playa Negra,** and **Playa Junquillal** are known to only a few cognoscenti.

✔ If you head to Playa Avellanas, be sure to have a drink or lunch at **Lola's** (☎ 2652-9097).

If you're feeling really adventurous, rent an ATV. These rugged and easy-to-drive vehicles are available to rent at all the major beach destinations and cost $60 to $90 for the day.

Going under: Scuba diving

Some of Costa Rica's best diving can be had around the offshore islands and underwater rock formations of Guanacaste. Most hotel and tour desks can arrange a dive trip for you. Many also offer certification courses or shorter resort courses, the latter of which will get you some basic instruction and a controlled dive in the shortest amount of time.

A two-tank dive should run between $70 and $140 per person, depending primarily on the distance traveled to the dive sites.

If you don't set up your dive trip through your hotel, several very reputable dive operations are in the area. The best of these are

- **Diving Safaris de Costa Rica** (☎ 2672-1259; www.costarica diving.net) in Playa Hermosa. These folks have a large shop and offer a wide range of trips to numerous dive spots. They also offer night dives, multiday packages, certification classes, and Nitrox dives, which are done with specialized oxygen-enriched tanks.

- **Resort Divers** (☎ 2672-0106; www.resortdivers-cr.com) has set up shop at several of the hotels in this area.

- **Rich Coast Diving** (☎ 800-434-8464 in the U.S. and Canada, 2670-0176 in Costa Rica; www.richcoastdiving.com) is an excellent operator based in Playa del Coco.

Hoisting sail

The winds off Costa Rica's Pacific coast are somewhat fickle and can often be slight to nonexistent. However, from December through March, they can be quite strong, with impressive gusts. Still, plenty of sailing options abound if you want to head to sea here.

A host of different boats take out day charters ranging from a few hours to a full day. Many include some food and drinks, as well as a break or two for some swimming or snorkeling. Some will take you to a deserted beach, and others let you throw a line overboard for fishing.

Rates run around $35 to $55 per person for a few hours or a sunset cruise, $60 to $120 per person for longer outings.

If your hotel can't line up a sail for you, here are a few good boats to check out:

- *Blue Dolphin* (☎ 2653-0446; www.sailbluedolphin.com), a 12m (40-ft.) catamaran based out of Tamarindo

- *Samonique III* (☎ 8388-7870; www.costarica-sailing.com), a 15.6m (52-ft.) ketch sailing out of Playa Flamingo

- *Shannon* (☎ 8827-5533; www.flamingobeachcr.com), a 15.6m (52-ft.) cutter working out of Playa Flamingo

- *Kuna Vela* (☎ 8301-3030; www.kunava.com), a 14.3m (47-ft.) ketch plying the waters off Playa del Coco

Hanging ten: Surfing and surf lessons

The Guanacaste coast is home to some of Costa Rica's best and most consistent surf breaks. Whether you're already a pro or you're looking to get your feet wet, you'll find beaches and breaks that are just right for you.

- Tamarindo is by far the best place for those looking to learn how to surf. There are several good surf schools in town, as well as a variety of surf shops where you can rent a board. Check out **Tamarindo Surf School** (☎ 2653-0923; www.tamarindosurf school.com) or **Witch's Rock Surf Camp** (☎ 2653-1262; www.witchsrocksurfcamp.com).

- Experienced surfers will probably want to rent a car and head to the less crowded beaches south of Tamarindo, including **Playa Avellanas** and **Playa Negra,** or just north of Tamarindo to **Playa Grande.**

- Another option is to take a boat trip to the isolated point breaks of **Witch's Rock** and **Ollie's Point,** which are deep inside the remote Santa Rosa National Park. **Diving Safaris de Costa Rica** (☎ 2672-1259) and **Aqua Sport** (☎ 2672-0050) offer trips for up to six surfers for around $250, including lunch, leaving from Playa Hermosa.

Landing a big one

The waters off Guanacaste's coast are teaming with fish and world-class sportfishing opportunities. Anglers can land marlin and sailfish, as well as tuna, dorado, roosterfish, and more.

A half-day of fishing, with boat, captain, food, and tackle, should cost between $200 and $600 for two to four passengers; a full day should run between $500 and $1,600. The wide range in prices reflects a wide range in the size of the boats, equipment, and distance traveled.

Although fishing is good all year, the peak season for billfish is between mid-April and August.

A host of boats and captains dot the Guanacaste coast. The Flamingo Marina, the area's largest marina, is currently closed, but, at press time, it was due to open soon. Another marina will be built in the coming years on the Papagayo Peninsula. Here are some of the better operators:

- **Capullo Sportfishing** (☎ 2653-0048; www.capullo.com) in Tamarindo

- **Oso Viejo** (☎ 8827-5533; www.flamingobeachcr.com) in Playa Flamingo

- **Tamarindo Sportfishing** (☎ 2653-0090; www.tamarindosport fishing.com) in Tamarindo

- **Tranquilamar** (☎ 8814-0994; www.tranquilamar.com) in Playa del Coco

Teeing off: Golf in Guanacaste

Golf is just beginning to take off in Costa Rica, but you'll find three of the country's best courses in Guanacaste.

The **Paradisus Playa Conchal** (☎ 888-336-3542 in the U.S. or 2654-4123 in Costa Rica; www.solmelia.com) is home to an excellent golf course featuring a few wonderful views of the ocean. This Robert Trent Jones–designed resort course is currently still open to the walk-in public, but as the all-inclusive resort itself gets more popular, it may restrict public access.

Currently, it costs $200 in greens fees for as many rounds as you can squeeze into one day, including a cart. If you tee off after 1 p.m., it's just $160.

South of Tamarindo, **Hacienda Pinilla** (☎ 2680-7000; www.hacienda pinilla.com) is a beautiful, 18-hole, links-style course. The course is currently accepting golfers staying at hotels around the area, with advance reservations. The course is very convenient for folks staying at the JW Marriott resort. Greens fees run around $185 for 18 holes, including a cart.

Finally, the most impressive course in the country is the Arnold Palmer–designed course at the **Four Seasons Resort** (☎ 800-819-5053 in the U.S., 2696-0000 in Costa Rica; www.fourseasons.com/costarica). This stunning and challenging course features ocean views from 15 of its 18 holes. However, the course is only open to hotel guests.

Canopy tours

If you want to try one of the zip-line canopy tours, your best bet in this area is the **Canyon Tour** operation at **Hacienda Guachipelin** (☎ 2665-3303; www.guachipelin.com). This tour has a little bit of everything, with treetop platforms as well as cables crisscrossing a deep mountain canyon, some suspended bridges, a couple of pendulum swings, and two rappels.

However, if you don't want to head that far afield, several other options are spread around Guanacaste, including the following:

- ✔ **Congo Trail Canopy Tour** (☎ 2200-5176) is located near Playa del Coco and Playa Hermosa, and has 11 platforms connected by a series of cables.

- ✔ **Witch's Rock Canopy Tour** (☎ 2667-0661) is located just before the entrance to the Four Seasons (see Chapter 13). The two-and-a-half-hour tour covers 3km (1¾ miles) of cables and suspended bridges touching down on 24 platforms.

Canopy tours are no longer available right in Tamarindo, but the **Santa Rosa Canopy Tour** (☎ 2653-0926) and **Cartagena Canopy Tour** (☎ 2675-0801) are nearby. Of these two, I recommend the Cartagena tour, which has a much more lush forest setting.

Horseback riding

If you don't want to take one of the full-day tours to one of the remote lodges listed under "The Top Attractions," earlier in this chapter, you can still ride a horse for an hour or more at most beach destinations in Guanacaste. Rates run from $10 to $30 per hour.

Be careful, many of the folks offering horseback riding, especially those plying the beaches themselves, are using poorly trained and poorly kept animals. Be sure you feel comfortable with the condition and training of your mount.

If your hotel tour desk can't arrange this for you, the following companies are all reputable, with good horses:

- **Casagua Horses** (☎ 2653-8041)
- **Brasilito Excursions** (☎ 2654-4237)
- **Flamingo Equestrian Center** (☎ 2654-4089)

Shopping for Local Treasures

Simply put, the shopping scene in Guanacaste is disappointing. Mostly, you'll find hotel gift shops and simple souvenir stands. A couple of large souvenir shops, catering to large-scale tourist traffic, have popped up along the highway between the Guanacaste beaches. The best of these is **Kaltak Arts and Craft Market** (☎ 2667-0696), located on the main road between Liberia and the beach towns 19km (11¾ miles) from Liberia, 5km (3 miles) from the airport.

The ceramic wares produced in the small village of **Guaitil** are a notable exception to Guanacaste's standard trinkets. These low-fired works feature locally produced dyes and traditional indigenous design motifs. You'll find plates and bowls and a variety of functional pieces here.

Guaitil is located 12km (7½ miles) inland from the city of Santa Cruz. The road is paved the entire way. Many of the hotels and tour desks around Guanacaste offer tours to Guaitil.

However, if you don't take the trip out to the village itself, be sure to stop at one or more of the many roadside stands selling Guaitil pottery all along the road between Liberia and the Guanacaste beaches.

Living It Up After Dark

All the various beach towns and large resorts have their own bars and dance-club scenes throughout most of the high season. If you want to venture away from your hotel or resort, Tamarindo is by far the most raucous town on this coast.

The most happening bar and club in Tamarindo is **Bar 1** (☎ 2653-2586), an open-air, second-floor affair. Other popular spots include the **Crazy Monkey Bar** (☎ 2653-0114), at the Best Western Vista Villas; **Aqua** (☎ 2653-2782), on the main road into town; and the bar at the **Hotel Pasatiempo** (see Chapter 13), which has a giant television for sporting events and sometimes features live music.

Popular with Ticos, Playa del Coco is another of Costa Rica's livelier beach towns after dark. **Cocomar** (☎ 2670-0167) is the main dance club in town. It's located just off the little park right on the beach. (If these directions don't get you there, just follow the loud music.) However, for a more sophisticated scene, head to **Café de Playa** (☎ 2670-1621), a beachfront club, restaurant, and bar that sometimes has live music, or **Zouk Santana** (☎ 2670-0191; www.zouksantana.com), a hip, Euro-style nightclub with local and visiting DJs spinning dance tunes most nights. For a mellower scene, try the **Lizard Lounge** (☎ 2760-0307), which has a pool table and a laid-back tropical vibe.

In quiet Playa Hermosa, I recommend the **Upper Deck Sports Bar** (☎ 2672-1276), just off the main road.

If you're into gaming, you'll be interested in the several casinos around Guanacaste. In Playa del Coco, you can head to the small casino at the **Coco Bay Hotel & Casino** (☎ 2670-0494). In Playa Flamingo, **Amberes** (☎ 2654-4001) has a small casino as well. The best casinos in the area are in Tamarindo, where you'll find the popular **Jazz Casino** (☎ 2653-0406) in downtown Tamarindo and another out in Playa Langosta at the **Barceló Langosta Beach** resort (☎ 2653-0363).

Part V

Manuel Antonio
and Environs

"Since we lost the dolphins, business hasn't been quite the same."

In this part . . .

*I*n addition to being home to Costa Rica's most popular national park, Manuel Antonio National Park, Manuel Antonio is the heart of Costa Rica's central Pacific coast. This part gives you the lowdown on the highlights to be found in the Manuel Antonio area. Then I tell you about other interesting options to be found up and down this coast, from the breathtaking luxury of the hillside villas at Villa Caletas, to the remote beaches and small hotels south of Dominical.

Chapter 15

Enjoying Magnificent Manuel Antonio

In This Chapter

▶ Arriving in Manuel Antonio

▶ Finding your way around Manuel Antonio

▶ Deciding where to stay and dine in Manuel Antonio

▶ Enjoying the nights in Manuel Antonio

▶ Having fun and adventures in Manuel Antonio

Manuel Antonio is Costa Rica's single most-popular destination. It's a virtual one-stop shop of the best that Costa Rica has to offer: beautiful beaches, lush rain forests, abundant wildlife, oodles of adventure opportunities, excellent restaurants, and romantic boutique hotels.

The compact Manuel Antonio National Park is the crowning jewel of this area. Its several nearly perfect small beaches are connected by gentle trails that meander through a rain forest that's home to endangered squirrel monkeys, three-toed sloths, purple-and-orange crabs, and hundreds of other species of birds, mammals, and plants.

However, Manuel Antonio's popularity means it tends to be more crowded than most of Costa Rica's other beach destinations. Development here is leaving a noticeable footprint. What was once a smattering of small hotels tucked into the forested hillside has become a seemingly unbroken string of lodgings, souvenir shops, restaurants, bars, and adventure outfitters lining the winding road between Quepos and the national park entrance.

Still, this remains one of the most beautiful locations in the entire country. Gazing down on the blue Pacific from high on the hillsides of Manuel Antonio, it's almost impossible not to sit in awe of the surrounding beauty — from the offshore, rocky islands dotting the vast expanse of blue ocean to the rich, deep green of the rain forest sweeping down to the water.

Getting There

You can fly, drive, or be driven to Manuel Antonio. The small airstrip in Quepos is served by a host of daily commuter flights from San José, and this is, by far, the easiest means of getting there. If you want the independence of your own car, you can drive to Quepos and Manuel Antonio in about four hours along paved roads. Finally, you can take a bus or private minivan service. I list more details about all these options in the following sections.

By air

Nature Air (☎ **800-235-9272** in the U.S. and Canada, 2299-6000 in Costa Rica; www.natureair.com) and **Sansa** (☎ **877-767-2672** in the U.S. and Canada, 2290-4100 in Costa Rica; www.flysansa.com) have several daily flights from San José to the small Quepos airport. Nature Air flies from the Tobías Bolaños International Airport in Pavas, while Sansa leaves from San José's Juan Santamaría International Airport. The flight takes just 30 minutes and costs between $75 and $80 each way.

Both Sansa and Nature Air provide airport-transfer service coordinated with their arriving flights. The service costs around $9 per person each way, depending on exactly where your hotel is located. Speak to your airline's agent when you arrive to confirm your return flight and to coordinate a pickup at your hotel for that day, if necessary.

Private cars and official taxis, which are painted red, will also be waiting outside the airport to be hailed. Expect to be charged between $8 and $12 per car for up to four people, depending on the distance to your hotel and your bargaining abilities.

Both Nature Air and Sansa have direct flights between Quepos and other popular destinations in Costa Rica, including Liberia, Tamarindo, Arenal and the southern Zone.

By car

There are several routes to Manuel Antonio.

The traditional and most popular route from San José is a narrow and winding two-lane road, the "old highway," over and through mountains. This road is equal parts scenic and harrowing — it's not uncommon to encounter buses and trucks passing on blind curves, or to find yourself at the back of a long line of cars stuck behind a slow-moving truck, crawling up one of the steep hills.

Begin this route by taking the Interamerican Highway west out of San José and exiting just west of Alajuela near the town of Atenas. Follow any of the numerous signs to any hotel in Jacó or Manuel Antonio. The old highway meets the Costanera (Coastal) highway a few kilometers west of Orotina. From here it's a straight and flat shot down the coast. You'll hit Playa Herradura first, and then Jacó, before getting to Manuel Antonio.

However, this route may soon be obsolete. Thirty years in the planning, and almost endlessly delayed, a new highway is being built connecting San Jose with Orotina, via the western suburbs of Santa Ana and Ciudad Colón. When completed, this new toll highway is expected to substantially reduce the drive time to Manuel Antonio and the rest of the Central Pacific coast. The highway is slated to open in late 2009, but given its history, I wouldn't be surprised if it's somewhat delayed.

If you're coming from anywhere in northern Costa Rica, your best option is to take the Interamerican Highway, get off at the Puntarenas exit, and follow signs to Caldera. From there, head south on the Costanera Highway.

Whichever way you come, you'll first hit the small port city of **Quepos** when you finally get close to Manuel Antonio. To continue on to Manuel Antonio, cross the bridge into town and take the lower road (to the left of the high road). In 4 blocks, turn left; you'll be on the road to Manuel Antonio. This road winds through Quepos a bit for about 10 to 15 minutes before starting over the hill to all the hotels and the national park.

See Chapter 16 for advice on a good crocodile sightseeing stop during your drive.

By bus

Express and **local buses** (☎ **2223-5567** in San José, 2777-0263 in Quepos) to Manuel Antonio leave San José throughout the day from the Coca-Cola bus terminal at Calle 16 between avenidas 1 and 3.

The ride takes around three and a half hours and costs $5.50 on the express bus. The local buses cost a little less but take a bit longer. They're also usually older buses and much less comfortable. I highly recommend taking an express bus.

The express buses go all the way to the national park entrance and will drop you off at any of the hotels along the way. The local buses will drop you off at the main bus terminal in Quepos.

Gray Line (☎ **2220-2126;** www.graylinecostarica.com) and **Interbus** (☎ **2283-5573;** www.interbusonline.com) have regular service to Quepos and Manuel Antonio. The fare with Gray Line is $35; with Interbus, it's $39.

In the busy winter months, tickets sell out well in advance, especially on weekends. If you can, purchase your ticket several days in advance. However, you must buy your Quepos-bound tickets in San José and your San José return tickets in Quepos.

If you're staying in Manuel Antonio, you can buy your return ticket for a direct bus in advance in Quepos. The main bus station is in downtown Quepos, next to the main market. If you've bought your ticket in advance, you can wait along the road to be picked up. No particular bus stop exists; just make sure you're out to flag down the bus and give it time to stop — you don't want to be standing in a blind spot when the bus comes flying around some tight corner.

Orienting Yourself in Manuel Antonio

Manuel Antonio is a bucket term that often refers to one or more of the following: the small city of Quepos, Manuel Antonio National Park, and the winding road that connects these two.

Quepos is a small fishing and port city at the mouth of the Boca Vieja Estuary. A 7km (4⅓-mile) road connects Quepos to Manuel Antonio National Park. All along the road, you'll find the many hotels, restaurants, and shops that are considered part of Manuel Antonio — as opposed to Quepos. For all intents and purposes, the road ends at the national park entrance, although a small side street branches off it here, where you'll find some more hotels and restaurants.

The Costanera Highway South that connects Jacó to Quepos passes through the town and continues on toward Dominical. Just outside the city center, you'll find the small Quepos airstrip, as well as the local hospital.

Manuel Antonio and Quepos don't have official tourist information offices, but a few tour-booking agencies masquerade as such. Most hotels have a knowledgeable front desk staff, concierge, or in-house tour desk that can answer any questions. Also, keep an eye out for *Quepolandia,* a free, bimonthly, local tourist magazine that is loaded with information, articles, and advertisements; it's available at a host of local souvenir shops, restaurants, and hotel lobbies.

Getting Around Manuel Antonio

Getting around and between Quepos and Manuel Antonio is easy. Taxis are plentiful, and regular local bus service runs throughout the day.

The bus between Quepos and Manuel Antonio takes 15 minutes each. way and runs roughly every half-hour from 6 a.m. to 7 p.m. daily, with one late bus leaving Quepos at 10 p.m. and returning from Manuel Antonio at 10:25 p.m.

The buses, which leave from the main bus terminal in Quepos, near the market, go all the way to the national park entrance before turning around and returning. You can flag down these buses from any point on the side of the road. The fare is 60¢.

A taxi between Quepos and Manuel Antonio (or any hotel along the road toward the park) costs between $4 and $6. Taxis are supposed to use meters, although this isn't always the case. If your taxi doesn't have a meter, or the driver won't use it, try to negotiate in advance. Ask your hotel desk what a specific ride should cost, and use that as your guide. At night, or if the taxi must leave the main road (for hotels such as La Mariposa and Makanda-by-the-Sea) the charge is a little higher. If you need to call a taxi, dial ☎ **2777-3080** or 2777-0425.

You can also rent a car from **Adobe** (☎ **2777-4242**), **Alamo** (☎ **2777-3344**), **Economy** (☎ **2777-5260**), **Hertz** (☎ **2777-3365**), or **Payless** (☎ **2777-0115**) for around $50 to $90 a day. All have offices in downtown Quepos, but with advance notice, they'll have someone meet you at the airport with your car for no extra charge.

There's little reason to rent a car in Quepos and Manuel Antonio because taxis are cheap and plentiful. Moreover, most tours and many attractions include transportation in their outings and admissions. The only good reason to rent a car in town is if you want to explore the coastline north and south of Quepos. In that case, a rental car is your best option.

Car break-ins are common here. If you rent a car, never leave anything of value in it unless you intend to stay within sight of the car at all times. Instead, park in one of the parking lots just outside the park entrance that cost around $3 for the entire day. Although these lots are your safest bet, you still shouldn't leave anything of value exposed in the car's interior. Instead, use the trunk or bring your valuables with you.

Spending the Night

Manuel Antonio's growing popularity has brought increased development and ever-expanding crowds of beachgoers. This means that you'll find scores of hotels, in all sizes and price ranges. The best (and most expensive hotels) usually boast rooms with private balconies, featuring the classic Manuel Antonio forest-to-ocean views.

Getting a bewitching view of the Manuel Antonio forest has its own set of drawbacks. If you want this great view, you probably can't stay on the beach — in fact, you probably won't be able to walk to the beach. This means that you'll be driving back and forth, taking taxis, or riding the public bus a lot.

Also, keep in mind that it's hot and humid here, and it rains a lot. Of course, the rain is what keeps Manuel Antonio lush and green, and this wouldn't be the tropics if things were otherwise.

If you're traveling on a rock-bottom budget or you're mainly interested in sportfishing, you may want to stay in Quepos instead of Manuel Antonio.

Arenas del Mar
$$$$–$$$$$ **Manuel Antonio**

This hotel is the complete package — with direct beach access, rain-forest setting and surroundings, fabulous views, and luxurious accommodations. Designed and built by the folks behind Finca Rosa Blanca (see p. 102), this place features seven three-story buildings, with large, luxurious one- and two-bedroom rooms and apartments. Not all have ocean views, so be sure to specify if you want one. The top-floor rooms of the highest building (no. 7) would be my top choice, while buildings 1, 2, and 3 are closest to the beach. All rooms are very large and most have outdoor Jacuzzi tubs on their private balconies. The apartments are immense two-bedroom/three-bathroom affairs with a kitchenette, perfect for families and longer stays.

The restaurant, lobby, and main pool are set on the highest point of land here, and there are several spots with fabulous views of Manuel Antonio's Cathedral Point. A second pool and snack bar are located down near the beach. The owners are truly concerned about the environment and promoting sustainable tourism. Free daily yoga classes and loads of relaxing treatments can be enjoyed at the hotel's spa, and free Wi-Fi access is available throughout the hotel.

See map p. 189. Manuel Antonio. ☎/fax **2777-2777**. www.arenasdelmar.com. *Rack rates: $260 double, $430 suite, $690 apartment. Rates include full breakfast. Rates lower in the off season. AE, MC, V.*

Gaia Hotel & Reserve
$$$$–$$$$$ **Manuel Antonio**

This high-end hotel features chic, postmodern, minimalist design and décor. Rooms and suites are large and well-equipped, and they come with tons of amenities and personalized service. Set on a hilly patch of land, with its own private reserve, the hotel is comprised of a series of tall, blocky buildings. Rooms feature wooden floors, contemporary furnishings, plasma-screen televisions with complete home theater systems, Wi-Fi Internet access, and elaborate bathrooms with stone floors and walls and massive Jacuzzi tubs. Each guest is assigned a personal concierge. The deluxe suites have private rooftop terraces, with reflecting pools and shaded lounge chairs. The spa here is extensive and well-run, with a wide range of treatment options and free daily yoga classes. The restaurant serves excellent fusion cuisine.

See map p. 189. Manuel Antonio. ☎ **800-226-2515** *in the U.S. and Canada, 2777-9797 in Costa Rica. Fax: 2777-9126.* www.gaiahr.com. *Rack rates: $260–$330 double, $350–$495 suite, $840 Gaia suite. Rates include full breakfast. Rates lower in the off season, higher during peak periods. AE, MC, V.*

Manuel Antonio

ACCOMMODATIONS ■
Arenas del Mar **31**
Gaia Hotel & Reserve **13**
Hotel Costa Verde **24**
Hotel Malinche **8**
Hotel Plinio **10**
Hotel Si Como No **21**
Hotel Verde Mar **26**
Makanda-by-the-Sea **30**
Villas Nicolás **20**

DINING ◆
Agua Azul **19**
Café Milagro **2, 17**
El Avión **23**
El Gran Escape **4**
El Patio Bistro Latino **3**
Kapi Kapi **14**
La Hacienda **12**
Plinio Restaurant **10**
Restaurante Marlin **27**
Sunspot Bar & Grill **30**

ATTRACTIONS ●
Fincas Naturales/
   The Nature Farm
   Reserve **22**
Manuel Antonio
   National Park
   Entrance **28, 29**

SHOPPING ▲
Guacamole **12**
La Buena Nota **25**
Regálame **21**

NIGHTLIFE ★
Arco Iris **1**
Bambu Jam **11**
Barba Roja **16**
Billfish Sportbar & Grill **18**
Casino Byblos **18**
Casino Kamuk **5**
Fish Head Bar **4**
Los Pescadores **6**
Salsipuedes **15**
Sargento Garcia's **9**
Si Como No **21**
Wacky Wanda's **7**

Hotel Costa Verde
$$–$$$ Manuel Antonio

Located more than halfway down the hill to Manuel Antonio, about a ten-minute walk from the beach, Costa Verde has rooms in a wide range of sizes and prices. Some of the buildings are quite a hike from the hotel's reception and restaurants, so be sure you know exactly what type of room you'll be staying in and where it's located. The best rooms here have ocean views, kitchenettes, private balconies, and loads of space. Though some of these don't have air-conditioning, that's not a problem because they feature huge screened walls to encourage cross ventilation. If you want to splurge, try the enormous penthouse suite with a commanding view of the spectacular surroundings.

Three small pools are set into the hillside, with views out to the ocean, and the hotel has a couple of miles of private trails through the rain forest. Costa Verde is located more than halfway down the hill to Manuel Antonio, about a ten-minute walk from the beach.

See map p. 189. Manuel Antonio. ☎ **866-854-7958** *in the U.S. and Canada, 2777-0584 in Costa Rica. Fax: 2777-0560.* www.costaverde.com. *Rack rates: $115–$350 double. Rates lower in the off season, higher during peak weeks. AE, MC, V.*

Hotel Malinche
$ Quepos

This downtown Quepos hotel is the best budget choice in town. Look for the Hotel Malinche's arched brick entrance on the first street to your left as you come into Quepos. Inside, you'll find bright rooms with louvered windows. The rooms are small but have hardwood or tile floors and clean bathrooms. Although it's almost always very warm, if not downright hot, in Quepos, be forewarned that most of the rooms have cold-water showers. The more expensive rooms are larger and have air-conditioning, TVs, and on-demand heated showerheads.

See map p. 189. Quepos. ☎ **2777-0093.** *Fax: 2777-1833. Rack rates: $30–$60 double. AE, MC, V.*

Hotel Plinio
$ Manuel Antonio

This hotel is built into a steep hillside, and it's a bit of a climb from the parking lot up to the guest rooms and restaurant. When you're up top, though, you'll think you're in the forest, or some sort of treehouse. The rooms feature floors and walls of polished hardwood, and you'll even find rooms with tree-trunk pillars. The suites, built on either two or three levels, are the best value. The three-story suites have rooftop decks. My favorite room is known as the "jungle house" and is set back in the forest. Behind the hotel rests a private reserve with 15km (9⅓ miles) of trails and, at the top of the hill, a 15m-tall (49-ft.) observation tower with an incredible view. In addition to the popular **Plinio Restaurant** (see later in this chapter), lunches are served at the poolside grill.

See map p. 189. Manuel Antonio. ☎ *2777-0055. Fax: 2777-0558.* www.hotel plinio.com. *Rack rates: $65–$75 double, $85–$110 suite or house. Rates include breakfast buffet in high season. Rates lower May–Nov, but breakfast is not included. V.*

Hotel Sí Como No
$$$$ Quepos

Sí Como No is a lively midsize resort that offers an array of facilities and modern amenities, all with an ecologically conscious attitude. The wood used here is farm-grown, and although all the rooms have energy-efficient air-conditioning units, guests are urged to use them only when necessary. The standard rooms (housed in the hotel's main building or in the ground floor of a villa) are quite acceptable, but it's worth the splurge for a superior or deluxe room or a suite. Most of these are on the top floors of the two- to three-story villas, with spectacular treetop views out over the forest and onto the Pacific.

This place is unique in that it's equally suited to families traveling with children and to couples looking for a romantic getaway. There are two pools, including one with a long and winding waterslide for kids and another reserved for adults. If they tire of swimming, kids will enjoy the wonderful little butterfly garden and frog farm just across the street. The hotel also has a full-service spa, a large modern theater featuring movies each night, and several dining options.

See map p. 189. Manuel Antonio. ☎ *2777-0777. Fax: 2777-1093.* www.sicomono. com. *Rack rates: $210–$265 double, $305–$340 suite. Extra person $30. Children 5 and under stay free in parent's room. Rates include breakfast. Rates lower in the off season. AE, MC, V.*

Hotel Verde Mar
$$ Manuel Antonio

This hotel is a great choice for close proximity to the national park and the beach. From your room, it's just a short walk to Playa Espadilla via a raised wooden walkway through some scrub forest. All the rooms here have plenty of space; wrought-iron, queen-size beds; tile floors; a desk and chair; and a small porch. All but two of the rooms come with basic kitchenettes. Some of the larger rooms even have two queen-size beds. The hotel has no restaurant, but plenty are within walking distance. You'll even find a small pool here, for when the surf is too rough.

See map p. 189. Manuel Antonio. ☎ *877-872-0459 in the U.S. and Canada, or 2777-1805 in Costa Rica. Fax: 2777-1311.* www.verdemar.com. *Rack rates: $100 double, $110 suite. Rates lower in the off season. AE, MC, V.*

Makanda-by-the-Sea
$$$$–$$$$$ **Manuel Antonio**

Makanda-by-the-Sea is an artfully luxurious collection of studio apartments and private villas. The villas are spread out over several thickly forested hillsides. Each is individually decorated with flair and a sense of style. If you combine villa no. 1 with the three studios, you get one very large four-bedroom villa, great for a family or a small group — although children under 16 are not allowed, unless you rent out the entire hotel. Every studio and villa comes with a full kitchenette, cable television, CD/MP3 player, and either a terrace or a balcony. The grounds are well tended, intermixed with tropical flowers and Japanese gardens. A full breakfast is delivered to your room each morning. The hotel's pool and Jacuzzi combine intricate and colorful tile work with a view of the jungle-covered hillsides and the Pacific Ocean.

See map p. 189. Manuel Antonio. ☎ **888-625-2632** *in the U.S., 2777-0442 in Costa Rica. Fax: 2777-1032.* www.makanda.com. *Rack rates: $265 studio, $400 villa. Rates include full breakfast. Rates lower in the off season, higher during peak periods. AE, MC, V.*

Villas Nicolás
$$–$$$ **Manuel Antonio**

These large villas offer plenty of bang for your buck. Built as terraced units up a steep hill in a deep forest, they really give you the feeling that you're in the jungle. Most are quite spacious and well appointed, with wood or terra-cotta tile floors, throw rugs, and large bathrooms. Suites have separate living rooms and full kitchenettes, which make longer stays comfortable. Still, my favorite feature here is the balconies, which come with sitting chairs and a hammock. Some of these balconies are massive and have incredible views. In fact, the rooms highest up the hill have views that are worth even more money. Only some of the units have air-conditioning, but those without air-conditioning do come with fans. During the high season, the hotel opens a restaurant/bar near the pool that serves breakfast and sometimes lunch and dinner, depending on demand.

See map p. 189. Manuel Antonio. ☎ **2777-0481**. *Fax: 2777-0451.* www.villasnicolas.com. *Rack rates: $168 double, $192 suite. Weekly, monthly, and off-season (May–Nov) rates available. AE, MC, V.*

Dining Locally

Manuel Antonio has the best restaurant scene to be found in Costa Rica outside of San José. Many of the hotel restaurants are quite good, with excellent views. Several restaurants stand out, and you'll find them listed in this section.

I've got two words for you: *Eat fish.* Quepos is a port town with a local fishing fleet, as well as numerous sportfishing boats. The local restaurants are awash in fresh-caught tuna, dorado, and snapper.

Agua Azul
$$–$$$ Manuel Antonio SEAFOOD/INTERNATIONAL

With a fabulous perch and panoramic view, this open-air restaurant is my top choice for sunsets, and a good place to come for great food and views any ole time. Tables by the railing fill up fast, so get here well before sunset if you want to snag one. Start things off with a Tuna Margarita, an inventive version of ceviche with a lime-and-tequila marinade. Main dishes include coconut-crusted mahimahi and Panko-crusted tuna. For lunch there are giant burgers and fresh fish sandwiches. The long wooden bar is a popular hangout, and a good place to order up some appetizers and drinks.

See map p. 189. Manuel Antonio, near Villas del Parque. ☎ **2777-5082.** *Reservations not accepted. Main courses: $9–$18. V. Open: Thurs–Tues 11 a.m.–10 p.m.*

El Avion
$$–$$$ Manuel Antonio SEAFOOD/INTERNATIONAL

Set on the edge of Manuel Antonio's hillside, with a great view of the ocean and surrounding forests, this restaurant is housed under some permanent tents and the right wing of a retired army transport plane — hence, the name El Avion, which means "The Plane." This plane was shot down by the Sandinistas during the Contra War in neighboring Nicaragua. Today you can enjoy seafood and steaks as you take in the unique surroundings and glow of history. Fresh tuna steaks are flash-grilled and served with a teriyaki or fresh fruit sauce. Inside the *fuselage* (the old body of the plane), you'll find a small bar.

See map p. 189. Manuel Antonio. ☎ **2777-3378.** *Reservations recommended. Main courses: $8.50–$35. MC, V. Open: Daily noon to 10 p.m.*

El Gran Escape
$$ Quepos SEAFOOD

The fish here is fresh and expertly prepared, and the prices are reasonable. If that's not enough of a recommendation, the atmosphere is lively, the locals seem to keep coming back, and the service is darn good for a beach town in Costa Rica. Sturdy wooden tables and chairs fill up the large indoor dining room, and sportfishing photos and an exotic collection of masks fill up the walls. If you venture away from the fish, you can sample hearty steaks, giant burgers, and a wide assortment of delicious appetizers, including fresh tuna sashimi. El Gran Escape's Fish Head Bar is usually crowded and spirited, and if there's a game going on, it'll be on the television here.

See map p. 189. On the main road into Quepos, on your left just after the bridge. ☎ *2777-0395. Reservations recommended in the high season. Main courses: $5–$20. MC, V. Open: Wed–Mon 8 a.m.–11 p.m.*

El Patio Bistro Latino
$$$ Quepos   NUEVO LATINO/FUSION

This little restaurant is an outgrowth of the popular coffeehouse and roasting company Café Milagro. By day, you can get a wide range of coffee drinks and specialties, as well as simple breakfasts, fresh baked sweets, and a variety of salads, sandwiches, and light lunch dishes. By night, which is when this place really shines, you'll find a small and regularly changing menu of inventive main dishes that take advantage of local ingredients and culinary traditions. So your fresh mahimahi may come steamed in a banana leaf with a spicy *mojo* (parsley and onion garnish), and your tenderloin could feature a tamarind glaze and be served over some roasted local sweet potatoes, called *camote*.

See map p. 189. Quepos. ☎ *2777-4982. Reservations recommended. Main courses: $8–$22. AE, MC, V. Open: Daily 6 a.m.–10 p.m.*

Kapi Kapi
$$$ Manuel Antonio   ASIAN FUSION/NUEVO COSTA RICAN

This new restaurant features elegant Asian-influenced décor. At night, the ample, open-air dining room is candlelit and romantic. Start things off with the Asian-spice-glazed baby-back ribs or some seared fresh yellowfin tuna. Or, save the seared tuna for your main course, where it comes encrusted in peppercorns and served with a green papaya salad. For a sample of local flavors, order up the grilled shrimp served on sugar-cane skewers, with a glaze made from local rum, tamarind, and coconut. For dessert, try the Mango Foster or a hot chocolate soufflé. These folks have an excellent and very fairly priced wine list.

See map p. 189. On the road between Quepos and Manuel Antonio. ☎ *2777-5049. www.restaurantekapikapi.com. Reservations recommended. Main courses: $14–$21. AE, MC, V. Open: Daily 4–10 p.m.*

La Hacienda
$$$ Manuel Antonio   INTERNATIONAL

Located on a jungle-facing, open-air back patio of the small Plaza Yara shopping center, this place is surprisingly intimate and atmospheric, especially at night. Subdued lighting and vines draping down from the high ceiling almost make you feel as if you're in the jungle. The menu is inventive and eclectic. I recommend starting things off with the quesadilla of caramelized onions, brie, and fresh mango. For a main dish, the mixed seafood grill for two features shrimp, squid, and fresh fish prepared on a wood-fired grill with a tropical fruit salsa on the side. The dessert menu changes regularly but almost always features some rich chocolate concoction, as well as a flavored crème brûlée.

See map p. 189. In the Plaza Yara, on the road between Quepos and Manuel Antonio.
☎ **2777-3473.** *Reservations recommended in the high season. Main courses: $12–$28. AE, MC, V. Open: Daily 11:30 a.m.–10 p.m.*

Plinio Restaurant
$$ Manuel Antonio   INTERNATIONAL

This open-air restaurant is about three stories up from its parking lot, so be prepared to climb some steps. It's worth it, though. The broad menu features an enticing mix of international dishes, with an emphasis on Asian fare. The chef uses locally and organically grown herbs and veggies. Thai, Indian, and Indonesian dishes are all excellently prepared, and vegetarian options are also offered, as well as nightly specials.

See map p. 189. In the Hotel Plinio, 1km (½ mile) out of Quepos toward Manuel Antonio. ☎ **2777-0055.** *Reservations recommended in the high season. Main courses: $7–$20. V. Open: Daily 5–10 p.m.*

Restaurant Marlin
$–$$ Manuel Antonio   SEAFOOD/COSTA RICAN

This casual, open-air affair is the best local restaurant down near the national park entrance. Marlin has been serving fresh fish, hearty *casados,* as well as other Costa Rican and international fare for years. Everything is well-prepared and very reasonably priced. In the evenings, they open the second-floor balcony, which is a great spot with a good view of the ocean.

See map p. 189. Facing Playa Espadilla, near the National Park entrance. ☎ **2777-1134.** *Main courses: $5–$17. MC, V. Open: Daily 7 a.m.–10 p.m.*

Sunspot Bar & Grill
$$$$ Manuel Antonio   INTERNATIONAL

If you want one of the most romantic dining experiences to be had in Manuel Antonio, dine here — you'll eat by candlelight, under a purple canvas tent, at one of a handful of poolside tables. The food is some of the best in town as well. The menu changes regularly but always features a selection of prime meats, poultry, and fresh fish, excellently prepared. The rack of lamb may get a light jalapeño-mint or tamarind glaze, and the chicken breast may be stuffed with feta cheese, Kalamata olives, and roasted red peppers, and topped with a blackberry sauce. Nightly specials and a good selection of salads, appetizers, and desserts round out the menu.

See map p. 189. At Makanda-by-the-Sea (see listing earlier in this chapter). ☎ **2777-0442.** *Reservations required. Main courses: $10–$30. AE, MC, V. Open: Daily 11 a.m.–10 p.m.*

Taking a coffee break

Although the area around Quepos and Manuel Antonio is not well-known as a coffee growing region, you can still get excellent fresh-roasted coffee here from the folks at **Café Milagro** (☎ 2777-0794). These folks have two storefront locations: one in downtown Quepos, just over the bridge, and another about midway along the Manuel Antonio road. Excellent fresh-roasted coffee drinks, baked goods, fruit drinks, and ice cream treats are the main draws here, but you can also get full breakfasts, as well as hearty sandwiches and good fresh salads. My favorite option is the selection of iced coffee drinks. Both shops sell fresh-roasted beans to take home with you and also feature well-stocked gift shops.

Exploring Manuel Antonio

Manuel Antonio offers up a wealth of activities and attractions. You can spend time here doing everything from lazing on the beach or beside a pool, to hiking a rain-forest trail, to trying a zip-line tour through the jungle canopy. If you want to head out or into the sea, you can surf, go scuba-diving, try your hand at sportfishing, or take a sunset cruise.

If you visit the park early in the morning, you can leave when the crowds begin to show up at midday. In the afternoon, you can lounge by your pool or on your patio. If you stay at a hotel partway up the hill from the park entrance, you'll have relatively easy access to the beach, you may get a view, and, best of all, you'll be out of earshot of the nearby nightclub.

 If you steer clear of the peak months in Manuel Antonio (Dec–Mar), you'll miss most of the crowds. If you must come during the peak months, try to avoid the weekends, when the beaches inside and outside the park are packed with families from San José.

Fincas Naturales (The Nature Farm Reserve)

This interesting and educational attraction is just across from (and run by) Hotel Sí Como No (see listing earlier in this chapter). A lovely bi-level **butterfly garden** is the centerpiece attraction here, but other attractions include amphibian ponds, reptile exhibits, and a private reserve with a small network of well-groomed trails through the forest.

See map p. 189. Located across from the Hotel Sí Como No, on the road between Quepos and Manuel Antonio. ☎ *2777-1043.* www.butterflygardens.co.cr. *Admission: $15 for a 1-hour guided tour of the butterfly garden, $35 when combined with a 1-hour guided hike through the forest, $35 for a 2-hour night tour. Open: Daily 8 a.m.–4 p.m., with the night tour leaving every evening at 5:30 p.m.*

Manuel Antonio National Park

Manuel Antonio National Park

Manuel Antonio is a small park with only three major trails. Most visitors come primarily to lie on one of the beaches and check out the white-faced monkeys, which sometimes seem as common as tourists.

Playa Espadilla Sur (as opposed to Playa Espadilla, which is just outside the park) is the first beach within the actual park boundaries. It's usually the least crowded beach in the park and one of the best places to find a quiet shade tree to plant yourself under. However, if there's any surf, this is also the roughest beach in the park.

If you want to explore further, you can walk along Playa Espadilla Sur or follow a trail through the forest parallel to **Playa Manuel Antonio,** which is the most popular beach inside the park. This beach is a short, deep crescent of white sand backed by lush rain forest. The water here is sometimes clear enough to offer good snorkeling along the rocks at either end, and it's usually fairly calm. At low tide, Playa Manuel Antonio shows a very interesting relic: a circular stone turtle trap left by its pre-Columbian residents.

From Playa Manuel Antonio, another slightly longer trail leads to **Puerto Escondido,** where you'll spot a blowhole that sends up plumes of spray at high tide. Be careful when hiking beyond Puerto Escondido: What seems like easy beach hiking at low tide becomes treacherous to impassable at high tide.

From either Playa Espadilla Sur or Playa Manuel Antonio, you can take a circular hike around a high promontory bluff. The farthest point on this hike, which takes about 25 minutes round-trip, is **Punta Catedral,** where the view is spectacular. The trail is a little steep in places, but anybody in average shape can do it. I've done it in sturdy sandals, but you may want to wear good hiking shoes. This is a good place to spot monkeys, although you're more likely to see a white-faced monkey than a rare squirrel monkey.

Another good place to see monkeys is the trail inland from Playa Manuel Antonio. This is a linear trail and mostly uphill, but not too taxing. It's great to spend hours exploring the steamy jungle and then take a refreshing dip in the ocean.

A guide is not essential here, but unless you're experienced in rain-forest hiking, you'll see and learn a lot more with one. A two- or three-hour guided hike should cost $25 to $45 per person. Almost any of the hotels in town can help you set up a tour of the park. Bird-watchers might want to book a tour with **Ave Natura** (☎ 2777-0973), a local tour agency that specializes in birding.

The principal park entrance is at **Playa Espadilla,** the beach at the end of the road from Quepos. To reach the park station, you must cross a small stream that's little more than ankle-deep at low tide but that can be knee- or even waist-deep at high tide. It's even reputed to be home to a crocodile or two. For years there has been talk of building a bridge over this stream; in the meantime, you'll have to either wade it or pay a boatman a small voluntary tip for the very quick crossing. Just over the stream and over a small rise, you'll find a small ranger station.

Another ranger station is located inland at the end of the side road that leads off perpendicular to **Playa Espadilla** just beyond Marlin Restaurant. MINAE, the national ministry that oversees the park has been frustratingly inconsistent about which entrance visitors must use. At this writing, tickets are only being sold at the inland entrance. The trail from here begins with about 20 to 30 minutes of hiking along an often muddy access road before you get to the beach and principal park trails. If this is still the situation when you visit, I recommend buying your ticket here, and then heading back to the principal beach entrance to begin your exploration of the park. The Parks Service allows only 600 visitors to enter each day, which could mean that you won't get in if you arrive in midafternoon during the high season.

See map p. 189. 5km (3 miles) south of Quepos, 181km (112 miles) southwest of San José. ☎ 2777-5155. Admission: $10. Open: Tues–Sun 8 a.m.–4 p.m.

Enjoying the beaches outside the park

Playa Espadilla, the gray-sand beach just outside the Manuel Antonio National Park boundary, is a wonderful place to enjoy sun, sand, sea, and local scenery. Because no entrance fee is charged, this is the area's most popular beach with locals and visiting Ticos.

This beach is often perfect for board-surfing and bodysurfing, but at times it can be a bit rough for casual swimming. It's actually a better spot to learn how to surf. Several open-air shops rent surfboards and boogie boards along the road fronting this beach. Rates run between $5 and $10 per hour and around $20 to $40 per day. If you want a lesson, check in with the **Manuel Antonio Surf School** (☎ **2777-4842;** www.masurfschool.com).

Some shops by the water also rent beach chairs and beach umbrellas, neither of which is available inside the park. A full-day rental of a beach umbrella and two chaise lounges costs around $10.

As you walk north along the beach, away from the national park entrance, and beyond a rock outcropping, you'll come to a section of the beach that is "clothing optional" and very popular with the local and visiting gay and lesbian population.

Getting muddy on an all-terrain vehicle

If you want to try riding a four-wheel-drive all-terrain vehicle (ATV), check in with the folks at **Fourtrax Adventure** (☎ **2777-1829;** www.fourtraxadventure.com). Their principal tour is a three-hour adventure through African palm plantations, rural towns, and secondary forest to a jungle waterfall, where you stop for a dip. You cross several rivers and a long suspension bridge. Breakfast or lunch is served, depending on the timing. Cost is $95 per ATV. A second rider on the same ATV costs $30.

Getting up close and personal with a mangrove

One of my favorite tours in the area is a mangrove tour of the **Damas Island estuary.** These trips generally include lunch, a stop on Damas Island, and roughly three to four hours of cruising the waterways. You're certain to see loads of wildlife on the tour. Contact **Iguana Tours** (☎ **2777-1262;** www.iguanatours.com) to set up this tour. The cost is $75.

Landing a big one

Quepos is one of Costa Rica's billfish centers, and sailfish, marlin, and tuna are all common in this town's waters. In the past year or so, fresh- and brackish-water fishing in the area's mangroves and estuaries has also become popular.

If you're into sportfishing, try hooking up with **Blue Fin Sportfishing** (☎ **2777-0000;** www.bluefinsportfishing.com), **Blue Water** (☎ **800-807-1585** in the U.S. and Canada, 2777-4841 in Costa Rica; www.sportfishingincostarica.com), or **High Tec Sportfishing** (☎ **2777-3465;** www.hightecsportfishing.com).

A full day of fishing should cost between $400 and $1,800, depending on the size of the boat, distance traveled, tackle provided, and amenities. You'll find a lot of competition here, so it pays to shop around and investigate.

 If you catch some fresh tuna or dorado, many restaurants in the area, including El Gran Escape (see listing earlier in this chapter), will cook your fresh catch for you.

Playing Tarzan

Tarzan never had it so good. Canopy tours involve putting on a climbing harness and a pulley system that lets you ride along a series of zip lines connecting treetop platforms. Sometimes the trip involves a rappel down from the forest heights, while other times the trip ends with the final platform at ground level. Either way, thrills are guaranteed.

The most adventurous canopy tours in the area are offered by **Canopy Safari** (☎ **2777-0100;** www.canopysafari.com). The **Titi Canopy Tour** (☎ **2777-3130;** www.titicanopytours.com) is a mellower setup, better suited to first-timer or timid adventurers. A canopy tour should run you between $50 and $70 per person.

About 20 minutes outside of Quepos is **Rainmaker Nature Refuge** (☎ **2777-3565;** www.rainmakercostarica.org). The main attraction here is a system of connected suspension bridges strung through the forest canopy, crisscrossing a deep ravine. There are six bridges; the longest is 90m (295 ft.) across. There's also a small network of trails and some great swimming holes. A half-day tour, including a light breakfast, full lunch, round-trip transportation from Quepos, and a guide, costs $65 per person. Tours leave every morning, and most hotels in the area can book them for you.

Going local

For a taste of rural Tico culture, mixed in with some fabulous scenery and adventure, sign up for the **Santa Juana Mountain Tour** (☎ **2777-0850**). This full-day tour takes you to a local farming village about an hour outside of Quepos. Depending upon your needs and interests, you can tour coffee and citrus farms, take part in carbon-offset tree planting, hike the trails, swim in rain-forest pools, fish for Tilapia, see how sugar cane is processed, and/or ride horseback. A typical Tico lunch is included.

Playing tropical cowboy

Although you can still sometimes find locals renting horses on the beaches outside the national park, I discourage this, as there are just too many crowds, the beach is too short, and the droppings are a problem. Better yet, head on horseback into the hills and forests.

Both **Finca Valmy** (☎ 2779-1118; www.valmytours.com) and **Brisas del Nara** (☎ 2779-1235; www.horsebacktour.com) offer horseback excursions that pass through primary and secondary forest and feature a swimming stop or two at a jungle waterfall. Full-day tours, including breakfast and lunch, cost between $70 and $90 per person. Finca Valmy also offers an overnight tour for serious riders, with accommodations in rustic but cozy cabins in the Santa Maria de Dota mountains.

Riding the back roads on a mountain bike

If you want to do some mountain-biking while you're here, check in with **Estrella Tour** (☎/fax 2777-1286), in downtown Quepos. Well-maintained bikes rent for around $5 to $30 per day. You can also do a number of different guided tours according to skill level for $50 to $120 per day, as well as multiday expeditions.

Riding the wild white water of a jungle river

The Savegre and Naranjo rivers start in the rain-forested mountains above Quepos. They provide class II through IV white-water river rafting adventures, depending upon which section you run, and how much it's been raining of late.

Several rafting companies ply both these rivers. Among them, **Iguana Tours** (☎ 2777-1262; www.iguanatours.com) and **Rios Tropicales** (☎ 2777-4092; www.aventurash2o.com) are the best. Both offer full-day rafting trips for around $85 to $110. Large multi-person rafts are used during the rainy season, and single-person *duckies* (inflatable kayaks) are broken out when the water levels drop. Both of these companies also offer half-day rafting adventures and sea-kayaking trips.

 Depending on rainfall and demand, they run either the Naranjo or Savegre rivers. I very much prefer the **Savegre River** for its stunning scenery.

Setting out to sea

Among the many boating options available around Quepos and Manuel Antonio are excursions in search of dolphins and sunset cruises. The choice of vessels range from large charter sailboats to comfortable motorized cruisers to jet skis.

Learning Spanish: A school with a view

Escuela D'Amore (☎/fax **2777-1143**; www.escueladamore.com) runs language-immersion programs out of a former hotel with a fabulous view, on the road to Manuel Antonio. A two-week conversational Spanish course, including a home stay and two meals daily, costs $995.

In addition to **Iguana Tours** (see the preceding section), **Planet Dolphin** (☎ **2777-1647**; www.planetdolphin.com) offers a range of boat outings on a range of vessels for $50 to $80 per person, depending upon the size of the group and the length of the cruise. Most of the tours include a snorkel break and, if you're lucky, dolphin sightings.

If you want to add some exhilaration to your sea venture, **Jungle Coast Jets** (☎ **2777-1706**; www.junglecoastjets.com) offers two-hour jet-ski tours for $105 per person. This tour plies the same waters and includes some snorkeling and the possibility of a dolphin encounter.

Snorkeling and scuba-diving

Oceans Unlimited (☎ **2777-3171**; www.oceansunlimitedcr.com) offers scuba-diving and snorkel outings, as well as certification and resort courses. Because of river runoff and often less-than-stellar visibility close to Quepos, the best trips involve some travel time. However, **Isla del Caño** is only about a 90-minute ride (each way) in a fast boat. This is one of the best dive sites in Costa Rica, and I highly recommend it.

Taking a break to rejuvenate body and soul

Quite a few massage therapists and a couple of excellent day spas can be found around Manuel Antonio. The best of these are **Raindrop Spa** (☎ **2777-2880**; www.raindropspa.com), **Spa Uno** (☎ **2777-2607**; www.spauno.com), and **Serenity Spa** at the Hotel Sí Como No. A wide range of treatments, wraps, and facials are available at all of these places.

Sivana Yoga (☎ **2777-5268**; www.sivanayoga.com) has open classes ($12) Monday through Friday at 8 a.m. above the Anaconda restaurant, across from the Hotel Costa Verde. Private classes are also offered.

Shopping for Local Treasures

If you're looking for souvenirs, you'll find plenty of beach towels, beachwear, and handmade jewelry in a variety of small shops in Quepos and at impromptu stalls down near the national park. For a good selection of all the above, and more, try **La Buena Nota** (☎ 2777-1002), which is on the road to Manuel Antonio, fairly close to the national park entrance. This shop is jam-packed with all sorts of beachwear, souvenirs, used books, and U.S. magazines and newspapers.

For higher-end gifts, check out Hotel Sí Como No's **Regálame** (www.regalameart.com) gift shop, which has a wide variety of craft works, clothing and original paintings and prints. Look for handmade batik and tie-dyed clothing at **Guacamole** (☎ 2777-2071), in the small Plaza Yara shopping center.

Living It Up After Dark

Bars and clubs are almost as common in Manuel Antonio as capuchin monkeys. Night owls and dancing fools have a lot to choose from.

The bars at the **Barba Roja** (☎ 2777-0331) restaurant and the **Hotel Sí Como No** (see earlier in this chapter) are good places to hang out and meet people in the evenings. For shooting pool, I head to the **Billfish Sportbar & Grill** (☎ 2777-0411) at the Byblos Resort.

For tapas and local *bocas,* try **Salsipuedes** (☎ 2777-5019), which translates as "get out if you can."

If you want live music, **Bambu Jam** (☎ 2777-3369), located along the road between Quepos and the park entrance, and **Dos Locos** (☎ 2777-1526), in the heart of downtown, are your best bets.

Back in Quepos, **Los Pescadores** (☎ 2777-4130), **Sargento Garcia's** (☎ 2777-2960), **Wacky Wanda's** (☎ 2777-2245), and the **Fish Head Bar** at El Gran Escape (see listing earlier in this chapter) are the most popular hangouts.

For real late-night dance action, the local favorite remains the **Arco Iris** (no phone), which is located just before the bridge heading into town. Admission is usually around $3.

If you enjoy the gaming tables, the **Hotel Kamuk** (☎ 2777-0811) in Quepos and the **Hotel El Byblos** (☎ 2777-0411) on the road to Manuel Antonio both have small casinos and will even foot your cab bill if you try your luck and lay down your money.

If you want to see a flick, check out what's playing at **Hotel Sí Como No's** little theater, although you have to eat at the restaurant or spend a minimum at the bar to earn admission.

Fast Facts: Manuel Antonio

Ambulance

Call ☎ **128.**

ATMs

You'll find several ATMs in Quepos, as well as one at Banca Promerica, which is located about midway along the road to the national park.

Country Code and City Code

The country code for Costa Rica is **506.** Costa Rica doesn't use city or area codes. To call from the United States, dial 011-506 plus the eight-digit number. From within Costa Rica, you simply dial the eight-digit number.

Currency Exchange

Most hotels will exchange money for you at decent rates. To get official rates, head to one of the banks in Quepos or to Banca Promerica, which is located about midway along the road to the national park.

Fire

Call ☎ **118.**

Hospitals

The Quepos Hospital (☎ 2777-0922) is located just outside of town, on the road to the airport and Dominical.

Information

Manuel Antonio and Quepos don't have official information offices. Most hotels have a tour desk, concierge, or helpful front desk where you can ask questions.

Internet Access

Several Internet cafes are located in Quepos, and a few are strung along the road to the national park. Many hotels also have their own in-house Internet cafes or wireless service. Rates run from 50¢ to $3 per hour.

Newspapers

Several gift shops around town and various hotels can get you current or day-late editions of the *Miami Herald, New York Times,* or *USA Today,* as well as all the local papers, such as the *Tico Times.* Also, keep an eye out for *Quepolandia,* a bimonthly tourist magazine that has a wealth of information and local advertising.

Pharmacies

Several well-stocked pharmacies can be found in downtown Quepos. You can even find one among the cluster of shops and restaurants near the national park entrance.

Police

Call ☎ **911** or 2777-2117.

Post Office

You'll find a post office in downtown Quepos (☎ 2777-1471). Alternatively, most hotels can mail your letters and postcards for you.

Taxis

Taxis are plentiful in Quepos and Manuel Antonio. If you don't feel like flagging one down on the street, have your hotel call one for you, or dial ☎ 2777-3080 or 2777-0425.

Chapter 16

Living the Lush Life on the Central Pacific Coast

In This Chapter

▶ Getting to and deciding where to settle on the central Pacific coast

▶ Seeing scarlet macaws in Carara National Park

▶ Dining in style on the central Pacific coast

▶ Heading south to Dominical and the beaches south of Dominical

▶ Exploring isolated beaches south of Dominical

Costa Rica's central Pacific coast is home to some of the closest beaches to San José. In addition to Manuel Antonio (see Chapter 15), this coast boasts the popular fun-in-the-sun **Jacó** and the surfer stalwart **Playa Hermosa.** These two beach destinations are often busy and bustling with Tico weekenders and itinerant surfers, while the rest of the destinations covered in this chapter are rather underdeveloped and uncrowded.

For luxury, you could head to the exclusive resort beach of **Playa Herradura,** which features a large golf and beach resort and full-service marina. In the hills above Playa Herradura sits Villa Caletas, one of the finest and most luxurious boutique hotels in the country.

If you're looking to get away from it all without spending too much, **Dominical** and the **beaches south of Dominical** should be your top choice on this coast. The rain-forested hills and mountains that back these beaches are stunningly beautiful.

This coast is also home to **Carara National Park,** one of the last places in Costa Rica where you can see the disappearing dry forest join the damp, humid forests that extend south down the coast. This park is a prime nesting spot for the endangered scarlet macaw.

The climate here is considerably more humid than that farther north, but it's not nearly as steamy as it is along the Southern Pacific or Caribbean coasts. This area stays lush and green year-round, even during the dry season.

Jacó and Playa Herradura

For all intents and purposes, these beaches are the two closest to San José. Playa de Jacó is also the closest thing in Costa Rica to Fort Lauderdale during spring break — although Tamarindo is making a strong play to share this dubious distinction.

This long stretch of beach is filled with a dense hodgepodge of hotels in all price categories, cheap souvenir shops, seafood restaurants, and pizza joints. The main strip here, which runs parallel to the shoreline, is a congested collection of restaurants, shops, and small strip malls, where pedestrians, bicycles, scooters, cars, and ATVs vie for right of way both day and night.

The number-one attraction in Jacó is the surf, and this is definitely a surfer-dominated beach town. In fact, the beach here is not particularly appealing. It's made of dark-gray sand with lots of rocks, and it's often very rough. Still, young surfers, Tico weekenders, and a regular stream of snowbirds keep this town pretty full during the northern winter months.

Just north of Jacó lies the crescent-shaped beach of Playa Herradura. Like Jacó, the dark-brown-sand beach here is fairly unattractive, although it is calm and protected. South of Jacó lie several other mostly undiscovered and undeveloped beaches, including Playa Esterillos and Playa Bejuco.

Jacó and Playa Herradura can be visited from San José as a day trip. However, you're probably best off dedicating about one or two nights to take full advantage of this area.

Getting there

The best way to get to Jacó and Playa Herradura is to drive. If you don't want to rent a car, frequent bus and minivan services are available. I list the specifics of each in the following sections.

By car

Several routes run to Jacó and Playa Herradura from San José.

The traditional and most popular route is the narrow and winding two-lane road, the "old highway," over and through mountains. This road is equal parts scenic and harrowing — it's not uncommon to encounter buses and trucks passing on blind curves, or to find yourself at the back of a long line of cars stuck behind a slow-moving truck, crawling up one of the steep hills.

Begin this route by taking the Interamerican Highway west out of San José and exiting just west of Alajuela near the town of Atenas. Follow any of the numerous signs to any hotel in Jacó or Manuel Antonio. The old

Central Pacific Playas

ACCOMMODATIONS ■
Arenal Pacífico **6**
Club del Mar Condominiums
& Resort **6**
Hotel Fuego del Sol **8**
Hotel Mar de Luz **6**
Hotel Nine **6**
Marriott Los Sueños Ocean
& Golf Resort **5**
Pochote Grande **6**
Villa Caletas **4**
Villa Lapas **2**
Xandari By The Pacific **9**

DINING ◆
Caliche's Wishbone **6**
El Galeon **5**
El Nuevo Latino **5**
El Pelicano **5**
Lemon Zest **6**
Rioasis **6**

ATTRACTIONS ●
Bijagual Waterfalls **3**
Carara National Park **1**
Chiclets Tree Tour **8**
La Laguna Golf Course **5**
Pura Vida Botanical
Gardens **3**
Rain Forest Aerial Tram
Pacific **7**

SHOPPING ▮
Guacamole **6**
La Galería Heliconia **6**

NIGHTLIFE ★
Clarita's Bar & Grill **6**
Congas **6**
Disco La Central **6**
Ganesha Lounge **6**
Hotel Copacabana **6**
Hotel Poseidon **6**

Jazz Casino **6**
Le Loft **6**
Los Amigos **6**
Stellaris Casino **5**
Tabacón **6**

highway meets the Costanera (Coastal) Highway a few kilometers west of Orotina. From here it's a straight and flat shot down the coast. You'll hit Playa Herradura first, and then Jacó.

However, this route may soon be obsolete. Thirty years in the planning, and almost endlessly delayed, a new highway is being built connecting San Jose with Orotina, via the western suburbs of Santa Ana and Ciudad Colón. When completed, this new toll highway is expected to reduce the drive time to Jacó and the rest of the central Pacific coast substantially. The highway is slated to open in late 2009, but given its history, I wouldn't be surprised if it's somewhat delayed.

Finally, if you're coming from anywhere in northern Costa Rica, you'll need to take the Interamerican Highway and get off at the Puntarenas exit and follow signs to Caldera. From here, head south on the Costanera Highway.

Jaws of death: Looking for killer crocs

The Costanera Highway passes over the Tárcoles River, just outside the entrance to **Carara National Park,** about 23km (14 miles) south of Orotina. The river below this bridge is home to a hearty population of American crocodiles. This spot is a popular one for pulling over and gandering at these gargantuan reptiles. Some can reach up to 4.5m (15 ft.) in length. Anywhere from 10 to 20 are easily visible, either swimming in the water or sunning on the banks.

You'll have to be careful on two counts. First, you'll be walking on a narrow sidewalk along the side of the bridge with cars and trucks speeding by. And, second, car break-ins are common here, although an on-site police post has somewhat reduced the risk. Still, don't leave your car or valuables unguarded for long; better yet, leave someone at the car and take turns watching the crocs.

When you're in Jacó or any of the other nearby beach towns, you'll find several opera-tors who run daily crocodile tours on the Tárcoles River. These tours are simple ones, in open skiffs or Boston Whalers. Most of these companies bring along plenty of freshly killed chicken to attract the reptiles and pump up the adrenaline. Don't expect a highly trained naturalist guide or any semblance of respect for the natural world. Do expect to pay $35 to $55 per person for the trip.

By bus

Transportes Jacó express buses (☎ 2223-1109 in San José, 2643-3135 in Jacó) leave San José daily every two hours between 6 a.m. and 7 p.m. from the Coca-Cola bus terminal at Calle 16 between avenidas 1 and 3. The trip takes between two and a half and three hours; the fare is $3.25. Return buses run on roughly the same schedule. On weekends and holi-days, extra buses are often added, so calling to check is a good idea.

No direct bus runs to Playa Herradura. The Jacó bus will drop you off at the crossroads. From here, it's about 2km (1¼ miles) to the beach.

Gray Line (☎ 2220-2126; www.graylinecostarica.com) has two buses that leave San José for Jacó daily at 7:30 a.m. and 4 p.m. **Interbus** (☎ 2283-5573; www.interbusonline.com) also has two buses that leave San José for Jacó daily at 8:15 a.m. and 2:30 p.m. Both companies charge $27 and will pick you up at most San José–area hotels. Both also have outgoing transportation with connections to most major tourist destinations in the country.

Buses from San José to Quepos and Manuel Antonio also pass by Jacó. (They let passengers off on the highway about 1km/½ mile from town). However, during the busy months, some of these buses will refuse pas-sengers getting off in Jacó or will accept them only if they pay the full fare to Quepos or Manuel Antonio.

Playa Jacó

ACCOMMODATIONS ■
Arenal Pacífico **18**
Club del Mar Condominiums
  & Resort **20**
Hotel Mar de Luz **5**
Hotel 9 **19**
Pochote Grande **1**

DINING ◆
Caliche's Wishbone **9**
Lemon Zest **16**
Rioasis **12**

SHOPPING ▲
Guacamole **15**
La Galería Heliconia **11**

NIGHTLIFE ★
Clarita's Bar & Grill **2**
Congas **3**
Disco La Central **13**
Ganesha Lounge **8**
Hotel Copacabana **4**
Hotel Poseidon **7**
Jazz Casino **17**
Le Loft **14**
Los Amigos **10**
Tabacón **6**

The Jacó bus station is at the north end of town, at a small mall across from the Jacó Fiesta Hotel. Buses returning to San José from Quepos pass periodically and pick up passengers on the highway. Because schedules can change, asking at your hotel about current departure times is wise.

Orienting yourself in and around Jacó and Playa Herradura

Both of these beaches are located about 1km (½ mile) off the Costanera Highway. Aside from the large Los Sueños Marriott resort, marina, and condominium project, which dominates the northern section of the beach here, very little has been developed in Playa Herradura.

Playa de Jacó is much more developed. Still, just one main road runs parallel to the beach, with a host of arteries heading toward and away from the water. You'll find most of the hotels, restaurants, and shops on or just off the main road.

Villa Caletas is located down a private road off the Costanera Highway, on the hillsides above Playa Herradura.

Jacó doesn't have an official tourist information office, although several tour-booking agencies masquerade as such. Most hotels have a knowledgeable front-desk staff, concierge, or in-house tour desk that can answer any questions. Also, keep an eye out for *Jaco's Guide* (www. jacoguide.com), a free, glossy, monthly, local tourist magazine packed with information, articles, and advertisements; it's available at most souvenir shops, restaurants, and hotel lobbies around town.

Getting around

Almost everything is within walking distance in Jacó, but you can rent a bicycle or scooter from several shops on the main street. A bike rental should run you around $8 to $15 per day, and a scooter should cost $30 to $55 per day.

Taxis are plentiful and inexpensive in this area. If you can't flag one down on the street, have your hotel call for you, or dial **Asotaxi** (☎ **2643-2020** or 2643-1919).

For longer excursions, you can rent a car from **Alamo** (☎ **2643-2881**), **Budget** (☎ **2643-2265**), **Economy** (☎ **2643-1098**), **National** (☎ **2643-1752**), **Payless** (☎ **2643-3224**), or **Zuma** (☎ **2643-3207**). Expect to pay approximately $45 to $90 for a one-day rental. You might also consider talking to a local taxi driver, who'd probably take you wherever you want to go for about the same price, saving you some hassle and headache.

Spending the night

Arenal Pacífico
$$–$$$$ Jacó

This hotel is a good midrange option, and it's right on the beach to boot. The rooms are nothing special — and few offer an ocean view — but they are clean and cool, and most are pretty spacious. The grounds are lush by Jacó standards — you have to cross a shady bridge over a little stream to get from the parking lot and reception to the rooms and restaurant. I like the second-floor rooms, which have private balconies. The superior rooms are larger, and come with coffeemakers and minifridges. There are two outdoor pools — one with a little waterfall filling it, another with a round children's pool. The open-air restaurant serves standard Tico and international fare. Free Wi-Fi is provided throughout the hotel.

See map p. 207. Playa de Jacó. ☎ **2643-3419**. *Fax: 2643-3770.* www.arenal pacifico.com. *Rack rates: $99–$137 double, $240 junior suite. Rates include continental breakfast. Rates lower in the off season. AE, MC, V.*

Club del Mar Condominiums & Resort
$$$–$$$$$ Jacó

This has long been my favorite hotel right in Jacó. Club del Mar is at the far southern end of the beach, where the rocky hills meet the sand. Most of the rooms are actually one- or two-bedroom condo units, with full kitchens. All are spacious and feature private balconies or porches. You'll find eight rooms on the second floor of the large main building, as well as two huge and luxurious penthouse suites up on the third floor. All units come with an ocean view, although some are more open and expansive than others. The grounds are lush and chock-full of flowering heliconia and ginger. A midsize, multiuse pool and a good open-air restaurant, as well as some modest spa facilities, are also available. Over the years, this place has prided itself on being a family resort. The full kitchens in the condo units just make it all that much better in this regard. The free Wi-Fi reaches every corner of the resort. I've even checked my e-mail while sitting in the sand here.

See map p. 207. Playa de Jacó. ☎ **866-978-5669** *in the U.S. and Canada, or 2643-3194. Fax: 2643-3550.* www.clubdelmarcostarica.com. *Rack rates: $153 double, $224–$320 condo, $383 penthouse. Rates lower in the off season, higher during peak weeks. AE, DC, MC, V.*

Hotel Fuego del Sol
$$–$$$ Playa Hermosa

This place is located right on the beach and offers up the best rooms in Playa Hermosa, especially if you're looking for a good value, as well as easy access to waves. Most of the rooms are housed in a long, two-story block set perpendicular to the beach. Each comes with a queen-size and a twin bed and a private balcony overlooking the free-form pool. Rooms closest to the water will also give you a glimpse of the sea. About half the rooms have televisions. The suites come with king-size beds, a separate sitting room, and a fully stocked kitchenette, and everything is well maintained. Although the food is pretty standard fare, you get a nice view of the beach from the restaurant here.

See map p. 207. Playa Hermosa. ☎ **800-850-4532** *in the U.S. and Canada, 2289-6060 reservations office in San José, or 2643-7171 at the hotel. Fax: 2288-0123.* www. fuegodelsolhotel.com. *Rack rates: $86–$116 double, $161–$182 suite. Rates include breakfast. Lower rates in the off season. AE, MC, V.*

Hotel Mar de Luz
$$ Jacó

This is one of Playa de Jacó's best deals and a comfortable alternative to the typical string of cut-rate *cabinas* (cheap hotels) you'll see all over this popular beach town. All the rooms are immaculate and comfortable. Some feature stone walls, small sitting areas, and one or two double beds placed on a raised sleeping nook. My only complaint is that the windows in some are too small and mostly sealed, so you're forced to use the air-conditioning. Plus, you're a couple of blocks away from the beach. In the gardens just off the pools, a couple of grills are available for guest use. You'll also find a comfortable common sitting area, with a selection of magazines and books in several languages, and there's free Wi-Fi throughout. These folks also have a sister hotel down the coast a little way at the remote and isolated Playa Bejuco (www.hotelplayabejuco.com).

See map p. 207. Jacó. ☎/*fax 2643-3259.* www.mardeluz.com. *Rack rates: $91 double. Rates lower in the off season, higher during peak weeks. AE, MC, V.*

Hotel Nine
$$$–$$$$ Jacó

This new hotel features contemporary architectural design touches that would be right at home on Miami's South Beach. The look is appropriate, as the L-shaped, two-story building fronts the sand toward the southern end of Jacó beach. Inside, the rooms are decorated in a tropical style with wood and rattan furnishings and bold colors. The premium suites have two separate rooms and a small kitchenette with microwave oven. Laundry service, surfboards, and Wi-Fi are all complimentary. The excellent restaurant here bills itself primarily as a steakhouse, but fresh fish and seafood options are also available.

See map p. 207. Jacó. ☎ **2643-5335**. www.hotelnine.com. *Rack rates: $130–$170 double, $220 suite. Rates lower in the off season, higher during peak weeks. Rates include continental breakfast. AE, DC, MC, V.*

Los Sueños Marriott Ocean & Golf Resort
$$$$–$$$$$ Playa Herradura

This is the closest large-scale resort to San José and is one of the most luxurious hotels in the country. The hotel is a massive, four-story, horseshoe-shaped building facing the beach. The entire thing is decorated in Spanish colonial style, with stucco walls, heavy wooden doors, and red-clay roof tiles. The rooms are all large and tastefully done. They come with one king-size or two queen-size beds, a large armoire, a desk, and a sitting chair with an ottoman. The bathrooms are large and have plenty of counter space. Every room has a balcony, but all are not created equal. Most have only Juliet-style balconies. Those facing the ocean are clearly superior, and a few of the ocean-facing rooms even have large, comfortable balconies with chaise longues and tables and chairs.

The pool is a vast, intricate maze built to imitate the canals of Venice, with private nooks and grottos. Kids love exploring it. The beach here is calm and good for swimming, although it's one of the least attractive beaches on this coast, with a mix of rocks and hard-packed, dark-brown sand. The Ted Robinson–designed 18-hole golf course winds through some of the neighboring forest and is an excellent, if not particularly challenging, resort course. The resort's Stellaris casino is the largest and swankiest to be found at any beach resort in Costa Rica.

See map p. 207. Playa Herradura. ☎ **888-236-2427** *in the U.S., 2928-0844 reservations in San José or 2630-9000 at the hotel. Fax: 2630-9090.* www.marriott.com. *Rack rates: $300–$350 double, $400–$700 suite, $1,300–$1,700 presidential suite. Rates lower in the off season. AE, DC, MC, V.*

Pochote Grande
$$ Jacó

This well-kept hotel is located just off the beach toward the far north end of Jacó. All the rooms are quite large, although sparsely furnished, and they have white-tile floors, one queen-size and one single bed, a small fridge, and a balcony or patio. I prefer the second-floor rooms, which are blessed with high ceilings. The modest restaurant and snack bar serve a mixture of Tico, German, and American meals. (The owners are German by way of Africa.). The grounds here were once shady and lush, but encroaching construction all around has left this place feeling a bit exposed, and ongoing construction can be a nuisance and source of noise.

See map p. 207. Jacó. ☎ **2643-3236.** *Fax: 2220-4979.* www.hotelpochote grande.net. *Rack rates: $80 double. Add $5 for a room with television. Rates lower in the off season, higher during peak weeks. AE, MC, V.*

Villa Caletas
$$$–$$$$$ Above Playa Herradura

Villa Caletas offers up opulent and luxurious rooms and villas with commanding views of the Pacific over forested hillsides. The entire complex is set on the summit and slopes of a steep hilltop. The standard rooms are all elegantly appointed and spacious, but you'll definitely want to stay in a villa or suite here. Each individual villa is situated on a patch of hillside facing the sea or forests. Inside, you'll find a main bedroom with a queen-size bed and a comfortable sitting room with couches that convert into two single beds. The villas feature white-tile floors, modern bathrooms, and a private terrace for soaking up the views. The junior suites are even larger and come with their own outdoor Jacuzzis. The suites and master suites are larger still — they even come with their own private swimming pools. Some of the villas and suites are located a vigorous hike downhill from the main hotel building and restaurants.

Although most guests are happy to lounge around and swim in the free-form infinity pool that seems to blend into the sea below and beyond, Villa Caletas offers hourly shuttle service to its own little private beach, as well as a host of tour options. You'll also find a Greek-style amphitheater that hosts nightly sunset gatherings, as well as periodic concerts of jazz or classical music.

Zephyr Palace is a seven-suite addition, with its own pool, located a little bit below the main hotel and villas. The rooms here are immense and thematically designed — there's an African suite, an Arabian suite, an

Oriental suite, and so on. The Imperial suite has its own gym and sauna. All have beautiful ocean views, home theater systems, Jacuzzis, and private balconies.

See map p. 207. Cuesta Caletas. ☎ **2630-3003.** *Fax: 2637-0404.* www.hotelvilla caletas.com. *Rack rates: $178–$198 double, $230 villa, $300–$470 suite, $450–$600 Zephyr Palace suites. Rates slightly lower in the off season. Extra person $35. AE, MC, V.*

Villa Lapas
$$ Tarcoles

Villa Lapas is a good choice if you're looking to combine a bit of ecoadventure and bird-watching with some beach time. The rooms here are spacious, with two double beds; cool, red-clay tile floors; air-conditioning; ceiling fans; free Wi-Fi; and a shady veranda with wooden benches for taking in the scenery. The hotel's best feature is its massive open-air restaurant and deck overlooking the river, where buffet-style meals are served. Villa Lapas has 217 hectares (536 acres) of land with excellent trails, a series of suspended bridges crossing the river, and its own canopy tour. Across the river, you'll find a small re-creation of a typical Costa Rican rural village of times gone by. This attraction features three massive gift shops, a large open-air restaurant, an atmospheric old-style Costa Rican bar, and a small chapel. Located on a lush piece of property along the Río Tarcolitos and bordering Carara National Park, the hotel is about 15 to 20 minutes north of Jacó. You'll see the signs for Villa Lapas on the left, just after passing Carara National Park.

See map p. 207. Tárcoles. ☎ **2637-0232.** *Fax: 2637-0227.* www.villalapas.com. *Rack rates: $121 double. Rates lower in the off season, higher during peak weeks. AE, MC, V.*

Xandari by the Pacific
$$$–$$$$ Playa Esterillos Centro

If you're looking for a large private villa done in a stunning and contemporary style on a nearly private stretch of beach, this is the place for you. A sister to the upscale boutique hotel Xandari (see p. 107) in Alajuela, this small beachfront resort is very similar in terms of design, style, and aesthetics. All the accommodations here are large private villas, with high curved ceilings and loads of artistic touches. Most feature open, mosaic tile showers that let out onto lush gardens. The Maxima villas here are the top option and come with their own private plunge pool. Most of the villas are beachfront, but those that aren't have large gardens and a wonderful sense of seclusion and romance. In order to encourage the enjoyment of the villas, beach, and surrounding nature, there are no televisions in the rooms, although you can enjoy free Wi-Fi throughout the grounds. The open-air seafront restaurant serves excellent international fare, with an equal emphasis on healthy, fresh ingredients and creative cooking combinations. There's an excellent full-service spa here, similar to their wonderful spa in Alajuela.

See map p. 207. Playa Esterillos Centro. ☎ **866-363-3212** *in the U.S. and Canada, 2778-7070 in Costa Rica. Fax: 2778-7878.* www.xandari.com. *Rack rates: $235–$370 double. Rates include continental breakfast. Rates lower in the off season, higher during peak weeks. AE, MC, V.*

Dining locally

Caliche's Wishbone
$–$$$ Jacó   SEAFOOD/MEXICAN

This casual spot is a bit of an anomaly. It's popular with surfers who come here to carb-load on Tex-Mex standards and homemade pizzas as well as hearty stuffed potatoes and a variety of sandwiches served in homemade pita bread. However, they also serve excellent fresh fish and perfectly prepared seafood dishes, which will please even the most discerning of palates. No matter what you order, the portions are huge. Caliche's almost always has delicious fresh tuna lightly seared and served with a soy-wasabi dressing. The best tables are street-side on a covered veranda. Inside, you'll find more tables, as well as a bar with television sets showing surf videos.

See map p. 207. On the main road in Jacó. ☎ **2643-3406.** *Reservations not accepted. Main courses: $5.50–$27. V. Open: Thurs–Tues 10 a.m.–10 p.m.*

El Galeón
$$$–$$$$ Playa Herradura   FUSION

This is the best restaurant in a complex of restaurants found at the Los Sueños resort and marina. The setting is elegant; the service, refined; and the menu, wide-ranging, creative, and eclectic. Appetizers range from an inventive plate of scallop sliders, to crisp Asian-spiced soft-shell crabs and sea bass ceviche served with avocado and a local salsa. For a main course, I recommend the pumpkin, ricotta, and basil-filled ravioli served with grilled Creole jumbo shrimp.

See map p. 207. At the marina of the Los Sueños Marriott (p. 212). ☎ **2630-4555** *or 2637-8331. Reservations recommended. Main courses: $19–$43. AE, MC, V. Open: Daily 6–10 p.m.*

El Pelicano
$$–$$$ Playa Herradura   SEAFOOD/COSTA RICAN

This is my favorite simple beachfront fish-and-seafood joint in the area. Heavy wooden tables and chairs are spread around a large, open-air dining room facing the beach and boats bobbing at anchor off of Playa Herradura. The menu features a range of ceviche, salad, and main courses, with a heavy — and logical — emphasis on fresh seafood. The *corvina al ajillo* (sea bass in garlic sauce) is excellent here, as is the *arroz con mariscos* (rice with seafood). To get here, drive the Playa Herradura road until you hit the beach, and then turn left on the narrow, sandy access road.

See map p. 207. On the beach in Playa Herradura. ☎ **2637-8910.** *Reservations recommended during high season. Main courses: $7–$45. MC, V. Open: Daily 11:30 a.m.–10 p.m.*

Lemon Zest
$$$–$$$$ Jacó   SEAFOOD/FUSION

Culinary institute graduate and former Cordon Blu instructor, chef Richard Lemon has set up shop in a second-floor space right along Jacó's main strip. The décor is elegant, with subdued lighting and white cloth-covered tables. I recommend starting things off with the lobster and manchego quesadilla, or the Korean BBQ satay skewers served with a homemade banana ketchup. Seafood main courses include macadamia-crusted mahimahi and fresh seared tuna. For a splurge, try the sesame-and-Panko-crusted lobster with a pineapple risotto and sweet chile sauce. There are also daily specials, and some outrageous desserts. The wine list here is well-priced, with several good selections offered by the glass.

See map p. 207. Downtown Jacó. ☎ **2643-2591.** www.lemonzestjaco.com. *Reservations recommended during high season. Main courses: $13–$20. AE, MC, V. Open: Mon–Sat 5–10 p.m.*

Rioasis
$–$$ Jacó   PIZZA/MEXICAN

Popular with visiting and local surfers alike, Rioasis serves hearty burritos, simple pasta dishes, and a wide array of freshly baked wood-oven pizzas. My favorite dish is the Greek pizza, with olives, feta cheese, and anchovies, but the barbecue chicken pizza is also delicious. Both indoor and terrace seating are offered, as well as a bar area complete with pool table, dartboards, and a couple of TVs for sports events and surf videos. This place gets crowded and raucous most nights throughout the high season and on weekend nights year-round.

See map p. 207. On the main road in Jacó. ☎ **2643-3354.** *Main courses: $6–$17. V. Open: Daily noon to 10 p.m.*

Exploring Jacó and Playa Herradura

The attractions listed in this section can easily be combined in a one-day trip. All the hotels in this area can arrange tours to these attractions, or you can book and visit them yourself with the numbers and information provided.

The top attractions

Bijagual Waterfalls

A series of spectacular stepped jungle waterfalls rests near the remote village of Bijagual. The highest waterfall here is 180m (590 ft.). Excellent swimming holes are near the bottom of this impressive waterfall.

You can choose from one of several ways to visit these falls. Various companies run tours from Jacó or from entrances both at the top and bottom of the falls. Try **Gray Line Tours** (☎ **2643-3231;** www.grayline costarica.com) or **Superior Sightseeing** (☎ **2643-0180** www.jagua riders.com). Alternatively, you can drive yourself or take a cab (see "Getting around," earlier in this chapter, for cab information).

Just above the falls, a local family runs the **Complejo Ecológico La Catarata** (no phone), which features a basic restaurant and a campground. They run horseback tours down to the falls for around $45. Alternatively, you can hike in from an entrance lower down. The hike takes about 45 minutes each way, and the entrance is $20 per person. Either way, you'll end up at the base of the tallest fall.

While you're up this way, you can also stop in at the **Pura Vida Botanical Gardens** (☎ **2645-1001**). Entrance to the gardens is $20. The fee includes free run of the gardens and trails, which lead to a couple of smaller local waterfalls.

See map p. 207. To get here, turn off the Costanera Highway at the signs for Hotel Villa Lapas. From here, it's about 5km (3 miles) to the lower entrance and 8km (5 miles) up to the top entrance to the falls. Open: Daily 8 a.m.–4 p.m.

Carara National Park

A little more than 15km (9⅓ miles) north of Jacó is Carara National Park, a world-renowned nesting ground for **scarlet macaws.** It has a few kilometers of trails open to visitors. A loop trail here takes about an hour, and another trail is only open to tour groups. The forests here are lush transitional forests, loaded with wildlife.

The macaws migrate daily, spending their days in the park and their nights among the coastal mangroves. It's best to view them in the early morning, when they arrive, or around sunset, when they head back to the coast for the evening; a good guide can usually find them for you during the day. Regardless of whether you see them, you should hear their loud squawks. Among the other wildlife that you might see here are caimans, coatimundis, armadillos, pacas, peccaries, river otters, kinkajous, and, of course, hundreds of species of birds.

 Be sure to bring along insect repellent, or, better yet, wear lightweight cotton long sleeves and pants. (I was once foolish enough to attempt a quick hike in beach clothes and flip-flops — not a good idea.)

Watching the sun set

Perched on a high hillside overlooking the Pacific Ocean, **Villa Caletas** (see listing earlier in this chapter) is a perfect place to enjoy sunsets. What's more, the Greek-style amphitheater here is set facing the nightly solar sayonara. Even if you're not staying here, you can come for a cocktail and watch the sun sink into the sea.

However, the word has gotten out, and during the high season, hoards of other tourists come here for the same pleasure. When it's crowded, getting a good seat can be difficult and service can be a little slow.

You can hike the trails of Carara independently, but my advice is to take the guided tour; you'll learn a lot more about your surroundings. Several companies offer tours to Carara National Park for around $30 to $50. Check at your hotel.

If you're looking for a more personalized tour, check out **Gray Line Tours** (☎ 2643-3231; www.graylinecostarica.com) or **Superior Sightseeing** (☎ 2643-0180 www.jaguariders.com).

See map p. 207. Located just off the Costanera Highway, a little more than 15km (9⅓ miles) north of Jacó. ☎ 2637-1054. Admission: $10. Open: Daily 7 a.m.–4 p.m.

More cool things to see and do

Although this area has few major attractions, there's plenty to keep you busy. Your choices run from just hanging out on the beach, to taking a zip-line canopy tour, to trying your hand at some deep-sea sportfishing.

Enjoying the beaches in and around Jacó and Playa Herradura

All these beaches are easily reached by car, moped, or bicycle — if you have a lot of energy. Road signs are located at the entrance/access roads to each of the beaches, so you'll have no trouble finding them.

✔ **Playa de Jacó:** Unfortunately, Playa de Jacó has a reputation for dangerous riptides — as do most of the beaches along Costa Rica's Pacific coast. Even strong swimmers have been known to have trouble with the power rips here. In general, the far southern end of the beach is the calmest and safest.

The same waves that often make Playa de Jacó dangerous for swimmers make it one of the most popular beaches in the country with surfers. Those who want to challenge the waves can rent boogie boards and surfboards for around $3 to $5 an hour or $10 to $15 per day from any one of the numerous surf shops along the main road. If you want to learn how to surf, check in with Johnny at **Superior Sightseeing** (☎ 2643-0180; www.jaguariders.com), or ask for him at Club del Mar.

✔ **Playa Herradura:** If you're looking for a calmer beach, head to Playa Herradura. This is a hard-packed, brown-sand-and-rock beach ringed by lush hillsides. Despite the presence of the Los Sueños Marriott resort complex, Playa Herradura still feels a lot more isolated and deserted than Jacó.

✔ **Playa Hermosa:** Experienced surfers will want to head to Playa Hermosa, 10km (6¼ miles) southeast of Jacó. This long, black-sand beach has the most consistent surf along this coast. From July through December, sea turtles nest along Playa Hermosa most nights.

✔ **Playa Esterillos:** For a sense of solitude, check out Playa Esterillos, 22km (14 miles) southeast of Jacó. This beach is long and wide and almost always nearly deserted.

Heading to sea in search of a trophy catch

If you're interested in doing some sportfishing, I recommend that you head on over to the 250-slip marina next to the Los Sùeños Marriott (see listing earlier in this chapter). Dependable operators that have already set up here include **Maverick Sportfishing Yachts** (☎ **866-888-6426** in the U.S., 2637-8824 in Costa Rica; www.maverickyachtscostarica. com), **Costa Rica Dreams** (☎ **732-901-8625** in the U.S. and Canada, 2637-8942 in Costa Rica; www.costaricadreams.com), and **Cuervo Sport Fishing** (☎ **800-656-1859** in the U.S. and Canada; www.costarica-fishingcharters.com). A half-day fishing trip for four people costs around $850 to $1,200; a full day is between $1,000 and $1,800.

Paddling around

Kayak Jacó (☎ **2643-1233;** www.kayakjaco.com) runs a couple of different trips. Tours range from gentle paddles and floats on the Tulin River to a combination ocean-kayaking and snorkel trip on Herradura Bay, to full-on kayak surfing at one of the local beach breaks. You can also do some moderate white-water kayaking in easy-to-use inflatable kayaks or try your hand in the ocean on one of the eight-person outrigger canoes. Most options run around four hours and include transportation to and from the put-in, as well as fresh fruit and soft drinks during the trip. The tours cost between $55 and $70 per person, depending on the particular trip and group size.

Rough riding

Several operators take folks out on ATV tours through the surrounding countryside. Expect to ford rivers and ride over some rough terrain. Tours range in length from two to six hours and cost between $85 and $165 per person. Contact **Four Trax Adventure** (☎ **2643-2373;** www.fourtraxadventure.com) or **Jaguar Riders** (☎ **2643-0180l** www.jaguariders.com).

Saddling up

Horseback-riding tours give you a chance to get away from all the development in Jacó and see a bit of nature. The best operator in the area, with the best horses, is **Discovery Horseback** (☎ **8838-7550,** or 2637-0808) down in Playa Hermosa.

Seeing the sights from on high

You have several ways to enter the forest canopy in this area.

- ✔ The gentlest approach is to take the **Rain Forest Aerial Tram Pacific** (☎ 2257-5961; www.rfat.com). A sister project to the original Rain Forest Aerial Tram, this attraction features modified ski-lift-type gondolas that take you through and above the transitional forests here bordering Carara National Park. The $55 entrance fee includes the guided 40-minute tram ride, as well as a guided 45-minute hike on a network of trails. You can also hike the company's trails at your leisure for as long as you like. These folks also have a zip-line canopy tour on the same grounds, and offer guided tours, including transportation from both San José and any hotel in the area. The Aerial Tram is located a few kilometers inland from an exit just north of the first entrance into Jacó.

- ✔ A few zip-line and harness-style canopy tours are also available if you want more adventure. **Chiclets Tree Tour** (☎ 2643-1880) offers up a canopy adventure ($60 per person) just outside Jacó in nearby Playa Hermosa. This is an adventurous tour, with 13 platforms set in transitional forest, and some sweeping views of the Pacific.

- ✔ **Villa Lapas** (see listing earlier in this chapter) has two different tours through the treetops outside of Jacó. The better option, for my money, is a guided hike on its network of trails and five suspended bridges ($20 per person). The operator also has a relatively low-adrenaline zip-line canopy tour ($35 per person), with seven platforms connected by six cables.

Pampering yourself

Serenity Spa (☎ 2643-1624; www.serenityspacr.net) offers massage, as well as mud packs, face and body treatments, and manicures and pedicures. The spa's Jacó branch is located on the first floor, among a tiny little cul-de-sac of shops next to Zuma Rent-A-Car. These folks also have operations at the Los Sueños Marriott, Villa Caletas, and Club del Mar Condominiums & Resort.

Hitting the links

There's the excellent **La Laguna** 18-hole golf course at the **Los Sueños Marriott Ocean & Golf Resort** (☎ 2630-9000; www.golflaiguana. com). The course is open to all, whether guests of the hotel or not. Greens fees are $160 for a full round; the price drops to $130 if you tee off after noon. Club and shoe rentals are available. Marriott guests pay slightly less to play here.

Shopping for local treasures

If you try to do any shopping in this area, you'll be overrun with shops selling T-shirts, cut-rate souvenirs, and handmade jewelry and trinkets. The two notable exceptions are **Guacamole** (☎ 2643-1120), a small clothing store that produces its own line of batik beachwear, and **La Galería Heliconia** (☎ 2643-3613), a high-end gift shop that carries a good selection of artworks and pottery. Both of these shops are located on the main road in Jacó.

Living it up after dark in Jacó and Playa Herradura

Playa de Jacó is the central Pacific's party town, with tons of bars and several discos. The **Disco La Central** (☎ 2643-3076), just off the beach near the south end of town, is packed every night of the high season and every weekend during the off season. A huge open-air hall features the requisite 1970s flashing lights and suspended mirrored ball, as well as a garden bar in a thatch-roofed building that's a slightly quieter place to have a drink.

For a more refined dance scene, try **Congas** (☎ 2643-1200), which often has live salsa bands and is located toward the south end of town. Both discos charge a nominal cover fee.

For a more casual atmosphere, head to **Los Amigos** (☎ 2643-2961) or **Tabacón** (☎ 2643-3097). Both are located right on the main drag in town.

My favorite bar in town is the new beachfront **Ganesha Lounge** (☎ 2643-3916), which has a laid-back Ibiza-like club vibe, while the similarly new **Le Loft** (☎ 2643-5846) aims to attract a more sophisticated and chic clubbing crowd.

Sports freaks can catch the latest games at **Hotel Copacabana** (☎ 2643-1005), **Hotel Poseidon** (☎ 2643-1642), or **Clarita's Beach Bar & Grill** (☎ 2643-2615).

The **Jazz Casino** (☎ 2643-2316), located at the Hotel Amapola, is a modest casino. If you're into gaming, you should head to the **Stelaris Casino** (☎ 2630-9000) at the Los Sueños Marriott.

Fast Facts: Jacó and Playa Herradura

Ambulance

Call ☎ **128**.

ATMs

You'll find several ATMs around Jacó and at the Los Sueños Marriott in Playa Herradura.

Country Code and City Code

The country code for Costa Rica is **506**. Costa Rica doesn't have city or area codes. To call from the United States, dial 011-506 plus the eight-digit number. From within Costa Rica, you simply dial the eight-digit number.

Currency Exchange

Most hotels will exchange money for you at decent rates. To get official rates, head to the Banco Nacional (☎ 2643-3072) or the Banco de Costa Rica (☎ 2643-3695). Both have branches in town on the main road and are open Monday through Friday from 8:30 a.m. to 3 p.m.

Fire

Call ☎ **118**.

Hospitals

The closest hospitals are located in Quepos and Puntarenas. A decent medical center (☎ 2643-3667) is located at the Municipal Center, toward the southern end of Jacó.

Information

No official information offices are located in Jacó or Playa Herradura. Most hotels have a tour desk, concierge, or helpful front desk where you can ask questions.

Internet Access

Several Internet cafes are located in Jacó, as well as one at the Los Sueños Marriott in Playa Herradura. Many hotels also have their own in-house Internet cafes or wireless service. Rates run between 50¢ and $3 per hour.

Newspapers

Several gift shops around town and various hotels can get you current or day-late editions of the *Miami Herald, New York Times,* or *USA Today,* as well as all the local papers, including the *Tico Times.* Also, keep an eye out for *Jaco's Guide,* a free monthly tourist magazine that has a wealth of information and local advertising.

Pharmacies

Jacó has several well-stocked pharmacies. Farmacia Fischel (☎ 2643-2683), in the El Galeone shopping center, and the Farmacia Jacó (☎ 2643-3205) are both on the main road through town.

Police

Call ☎ **911** or 2643-3011.

Post Office

A post office is located in downtown Jacó (☎ 2643-2175), toward the southern end of town, in the Municipal Center. Alternatively, most hotels can mail your letters and postcards for you.

Taxis

Taxis are plentiful in Jacó, and to a much lesser extent in Playa Herradura and Playa Hermosa. If you can't flag one down on the street, have your hotel call for you, or dial Asotaxi (☎ 2643-2020 or 2643-1919).

Dominical and the Beaches South of Dominical

Dominical and the coastline just south of it are lush and wild. This is an excellent area to find isolated beaches, spectacular views, remote jungle waterfalls, and a wide range of lodgings.

The beach at Dominical itself has consistent right and left beach breaks, which means plenty of surfers are usually in town. In fact, even though the beach at Dominical does get broad, flat, and beautiful at low tide, it's primarily appealing to surfers and is often too rough for casual bathers. However, you'll find excellent beaches for swimming, sunbathing, and strolling just a little farther south.

From Dominical south, the coastline is dotted with tide pools, tiny coves, cliff-side vistas, and some of Costa Rica's most unexplored beaches. Among the beaches you'll find are **Playa Ballena, Playa Uvita, Playa Piñuela, Playa Ventanas,** and **Playa Tortuga.**

Getting there

Whether you're coming from San José, or from Quepos and Manuel Antonio, driving is your best option for reaching this area because bus service is infrequent. However, if you want or need to travel by bus, you can get more information in the following sections.

By car

From San José, head south, toward Cartago, on the Interamerican Highway. Continue on this road all the way to San Isidro de El General, where you'll see an exit for Dominical.

The long and winding stretch of the Interamerican Highway between San José and San Isidro is one of the most difficult sections of road in the country. Not only are the usual car-eating potholes and periodic landslides present, but you must also contend with driving over the 3,300m (10,824-ft.) **Cerro de la Muerte (Mountain of Death).** This aptly named mountain pass is legendary for its dense afternoon fogs, blinding torrential downpours, steep drop-offs, severe switchbacks, and unexpectedly breathtaking views. Drive with extreme care, and bring a sweater or sweatshirt — it's cold up at the top.

Pay attention as you approach San Isidro. The exit for Dominical is marked, but it's a simple right-hand turn onto a busy city street that passes through the center of San Isidro. After passing through the city, continue on this same street until it turns into the winding two-lane road to Dominical and the coast. The entire drive takes about four hours.

You can also drive here from Manuel Antonio and Quepos. Just take the road out of Quepos toward the hospital and airport. Follow the signs for Dominical. It's a straight, albeit bumpy, shot. However, the road has been slated to be paved for a few years now, and if that happens, it should no longer take more than an hour to cover the mere 40km (25 miles).

By bus

To reach Dominical by bus, you must first head to San Isidro de El General or Quepos. Plenty of daily buses will take you to San Isidro. **Musoc** (☎ 2222-2422 in San José, 2771-3829 in San Isidro) buses leave from their modern terminal at Calle Central and Avenida 22 roughly hourly between 5:30 a.m. and 5:30 p.m. **Tracopa** (☎ 2221-4214 or 2771-0468) also runs express buses between San José and San Isidro that leave roughly every hour between 5 a.m. and 6 p.m. from Calle 5 between avenidas 18 and 20. Whichever company you choose, the trip takes a little over three hours, and the fare is roughly $4.40.

From San Isidro de El General, Transportes Blanco buses (☎ 2771-4744) leave for Dominical at 7 a.m., 9 a.m., 1:30 p.m., and 4 p.m. The bus station for Dominical is 1 block south of the main bus station and 2 blocks west of the church. The trip takes one and a half hours and the fare is $1.50.

Buses (☎ 2771-4744) leave Quepos for Dominical daily at 5 a.m., 6:30 a.m., 9:30 a.m., 11:30 a.m., 3:30 p.m., and 5:30 p.m. The trip takes two hours, and the fare is $3.

When you're ready to leave, buses depart Dominical for San Isidro at 6:30 a.m., 7:15 a.m., 2:30 p.m., and 3:30 p.m. Buses leave San Isidro for San José roughly every hour between 5 a.m. and 6 p.m. Still, if you want to get to San José the same day, you should catch the morning bus. Buses to Quepos leave Dominical at approximately 5 a.m., 8 a.m., 11:30 a.m., 1:30 p.m., and 5:30 p.m.

Orienting yourself in and around Dominical

Dominical is a small town on the banks of Río Barú. The dirt road into and through town is to the right after you cross the bridge. It runs parallel to and a bit inland from the beach. As you first come into town, you'll see a *fútbol* (soccer) field and the San Clemente Bar & Grill, which has a couple of public telephones. As you continue on the dirt road, you'll come to a small side street that cuts through and joins the beachfront access road.

On the Costanera Highway heading south, just beyond the turnoff into Dominical is a little strip mall, **Plaza Pacífica,** with a couple of restaurants, gift shops, and the town's main grocery store.

Heading south from Dominical, the Costanera Highway is paved and in beautiful shape all the way to Ojochal and beyond.

You won't find any official tourist information offices in this area. However, most hotels have a helpful and knowledgeable front-desk staff or in-house tour desk. The tour office at San Clemente Bar & Grill (see "Dining locally," later in this chapter) is also a good bet.

Getting around

Taxis congregate around the *fútbol* field in the center of Dominical. If you can't flag one down, or have your hotel call one for you, try **Nelson** (☎ **8835-9528**) or **Erik** (☎ **8881-4220**). The actual town/village of Dominical is very compact and can easily be navigated on foot. If you're heading farther afield, taxis are the best option. Bus service (to the beaches south, to Quepos, and to San Isidro and San José) is infrequent, and not really an option for getting around the area. However, you can rent a car from **Alamo** (☎ **2787-0052**), which has a desk inside the Villas Rio Mar resort.

Spending the night

Cabinas San Clemente
$ **Dominical**

In addition to running the town's most popular restaurant and serving as the social hub for the surfers, beach bums, and expatriates passing through, this place offers basic, but clean, budget rooms just steps from the beach. Some of the newer second-floor rooms have wood floors and wraparound verandas and are a real steal in this price range. The grounds are shady, and you can relax in one of several hammocks strung between coconut palms. The least expensive rooms are housed in a bunk-bed, hostel-style affair in a separate building dubbed the **Dominical Backpacker's Hostel.** All rooms here come with access to a communal kitchen.

Dominical. ☎ *2787-0026 or 2787-0055. Fax: 2787-0158. Rack rates: $10 per person with shared bathroom, $30–$40 double with private bathroom. AE, MC, V.*

Cuna del Angel
$$–$$$ **South of Dominical**

This is the most luxurious hotel you'll find along this stretch of coast. The name translates roughly as "The Angel's Cradle." All the rooms are named after angels, and angel motifs are abundant, as are stained-glass windows and lampshades, carved wood details, tile mosaics, and other artistic touches. The hotel is a bit set in, away from the ocean, but there are pretty good sea views from many rooms and common areas, over the thick forest and gardens here. Rooms come with an open front patio fronting the pool or a private balcony. I prefer the second-floor rooms with the balconies. Free Wi-Fi access covers the entire hotel, and a wide range of treatments are available at the pretty little spa here.

9km (5.5 miles) south of Dominical. ☎ *2787-8436. Fax: 2787-8015.* www.cunadel angel.com. *Rack rates: $97–$178 double. Rates include full breakfast. Rates lower in the off season, higher during peak weeks. AE, MC, V.*

Hotel Roca Verde
$–$$ Dominical

If you want to be right on the beach, this popular hotel offers the best accommodations to be found in Dominical. The setting is superb — on a protected little cove with rocks and tide pools. The rooms are located in a two-story building beside the swimming pool. Each room comes with one queen-size and one single bed and a small patio or balcony. The large open-air restaurant boasts a popular bar that keeps folks dancing most weekend nights. The rooms are a bit close to the bar, so getting an early night's sleep can sometimes be hard, especially on Saturday nights during the high season.

1km (½ mile) south of Dominical, just off the coastal highway. ☎ *2787-0036. Fax: 2787-0013.* www.rocaverde.net. *Rack rates: $65–$85 double. Rates lower in the off season, higher during peak weeks. MC, V.*

La Cusinga Lodge
$$$ Bahía Ballena

This should be a top choice for bird-watchers and those looking for a comfortable room that also feels entirely in touch with the natural surroundings. The individual and duplex cabins here all feature lots of varnished woodwork and large screened windows on all sides for cross ventilation. Most have interesting stone and tile work in their bathrooms. The whole small complex is set on a hill overlooking Ballena National Park and Playa Uvita. Heavy stone paths connect the main lodge to the various individual cabins. With high ceilings, lots of light through large picture windows, and sparkling varnished wood floors and walls, the two dorm rooms here may just be the nicest dorm rooms I've ever seen.

Bahía Ballena. ☎ */fax 2770-2549.* www.lacusingalodge.com. *Rack rates: $135–160 double. Rates include breakfast. MC, V.*

Pacific Edge
$ Dominical

This place isn't that close to the beach, but the views from each individual bungalow are so breathtaking that you may not mind. Spread along a lushly planted ridge on the hillside over Dominical, these comfortable cabins have wood floors, solar-heated water, and solar reading lights. Their best feature is surely the private porch with a comfortable hammock in which to laze about and enjoy the view. A wide range of tours and activities can be arranged here, and a refreshing swimming pool awaits you if you're too tired or lazy to head down to the beach. Pacific Edge is 4km (2½ miles) south of Dominical and then another 1.2km (¾ mile) up a

steep and rocky road; four-wheel-drive vehicles are highly recommended —
I'd say required.

Dominical. ☎*/fax* **2787-8010.** www.pacificedge.info. *Rack rates: $58–$70
double. AE, MC, V.*

Dining locally

Coconut Spice
$$ Dominical   THAI/INDIAN

Housed in a small shopping complex near the river mouth, this place
serves up tasty and reasonably authentic Thai and Indian cuisine. The
lemon-grass soups and pad Thai are both excellent. Chicken, pork and
shrimp are all served up in a selection of red, green, yellow, and Panang
curry sauces. The open-air dining room has wood floors and paneling,
heavy wooden tables and chairs, and a smattering of Asian decorations.

In the Pueblo del Río shopping complex, Dominical. ☎ **2787-0073.** *Reservations rec-
ommended in the high season. Main courses: $7–$14. V. Open: Daily 1:15–9 p.m.*

Exotica
$$–$$$ Ojochal   FRENCH

This little place is tucked away deep along the dirt road that runs through
Ojochal. With polished concrete floors, roll-up bamboo screens for walls,
and only a few tree-trunk slab tables and plastic lawn chairs for furniture,
it is, nonetheless, one of the most popular restaurants in the area. The
chalkboard menu changes regularly but may feature shrimp in a coconut
curry sauce or duck breast à l'orange. The Chicken Exotica is chicken
stuffed with bacon, prunes, and cheese, topped with a red-pepper sauce.
The lunch menu is much more reduced, with a small selection of fresh
salads and a few more-filling mains.

1km (½ mile) inland from the turnoff for Ojochal. ☎ **2786-5050.** *Main courses: $4–$16
lunch, $7–$27 dinner. MC, V. Open: Mon–Sat 8 a.m.–9 p.m.*

Renting a luxurious hillside villa

In addition to the places listed throughout this section, you'll find that a host of beautiful
private homes built on the hillsides above Dominical are regularly rented out. Most
come with several bedrooms and full kitchens, and quite a few have private pools. The
setting and views you'll find here are spectacular.

If you're here for an extended stay and have a four-wheel-drive vehicle (a must for most
of these), check in with **Paradise Costa Rica** (☎ 800-708-4552 in the U.S. and Canada;
www.paradisecostarica.com) or with the folks at **Cabinas San Clemente** or
Hotel Roca Verde (see listings earlier in this chapter).

La Parcela
$$–$$$ Dominical SEAFOOD/INTERNATIONAL

This open-air restaurant has a gorgeous setting on a rocky bluff overlooking the ocean. Try to get one of the tables by the railing and you'll be able to watch the waves crashing on the rocks below. The menu features fresh seafood, meat, and poultry dishes, as well as a selection of pastas. The sauces and presentation are all interesting. Start things off with a tuna tartar tower, and then try either their fresh mahimahi with a mango relish or the filet mignon in a porcini mushroom sauce.

At Cabinas Punto Dominical. ☎ *2787-0016. Reservations recommended. Main courses: $8–$31. V. Open: Daily 7:30 a.m.–9 p.m.*

San Clemente Bar & Grill
$–$$ Dominical SEAFOOD/MEXICAN

The social center of Dominical, this place specializes in massive breakfasts, an extensive menu of hefty sandwiches and tasty Mexican-American food, and nightly specials. The fresh fish, done blackened or simply grilled, is delicious. One unique (and sobering) décor touch here is the ceiling full of broken surfboards. If you break a board out on the waves, bring it in and they'll hang it and even buy you a bucket of beer.

Downtown Dominical. ☎ *2787-0055. Main courses: $3.50–$8. MC, V. Open: Daily 7 a.m.–10 p.m.*

Exploring Dominical and the beaches south of Dominical

All the hotels in the area can arrange tours and visits to the following attractions. You can also book and visit them on your own with the information provided, or contact **Southern Expeditions** (☎ **2787-0100;** www.southernexpeditionscr.com), the largest tour operator in the area.

The top attractions

Ballena Marine National Park

Ballena Marine National Park protects a coral reef that stretches from Uvita south to Playa Piñuela and includes the little Isla Ballena, just offshore. Although the park is predominantly offshore, it does include **Playa Uvita,** an expansive and beautiful beach. Playa Uvita is well protected and good for swimming. At low tide, an exposed sandbar allows you to walk about and explore another tiny island.

This park is named for the whales that are sometimes sighted close to shore in the winter months. If you ever fly over this area, you'll also notice that this little island and the spit of land that's formed at low tide compose the perfect outline of a whale's tail.

You'll find a park's office at the entrance. These folks administer the park and even run a small turtle-hatching shelter and program. Camping is allowed here for around $2 per person per day, with access to a public bathroom and shower.

Located about 16km (10 miles) south of Dominical, the main entrance to the National Park is at Playa Uvita. To get here, drive south on the Costanera Highway until the village of Bahía. Turn right here and drive another 3km (1¾ miles) east along a rough dirt road until you hit the beach. ☎ *2743-8236. Admission: $10. Open: Daily 8 a.m.–4 p.m.*

Hacienda Barú

Hacienda Barú is a private wildlife refuge and tourism project located just north of Dominical, on the other side of the Barú River. These folks offer a variety of hikes and tours, including a walk through mangroves and along the riverbank (for some good bird-watching), a rain-forest hike through virgin jungle, an all-day trek from beach to mangrove to jungle that includes a visit to some Indian petroglyphs, an overnight camping trip, and a combination horseback-and-hiking tour.

They even have tree-climbing tours and a small canopy platform 30m (98 ft.) above the ground. If you're traveling with a group, you'll be charged a lower per-person rate, depending on the number of people in your group.

Hacienda Barú also has six comfortable cabins with two bedrooms each, full kitchens, and even a living room ($60 double, including breakfast).

Hacienda Barú is located 1.5km (1 mile) north of Dominical on the road to Quepos and Manuel Antonio. ☎ *2787-0003. Fax: 2787-0057. www.haciendabaru.com. Tour prices range from $20 for the mangrove hike to $60 for the jungle overnight.*

Nauyaca Waterfall

The Nauyaca waterfall is a two-tiered jungle waterfall with an excellent swimming hole. This waterfall is also called Santo Cristo, and sometimes even Don Lulo's waterfall. The latter name belongs to a local man who pioneered and continues to lead many of the tours here. Most include a mix of hiking, horseback-riding, and hanging out at the falls.

All the hotels in town can arrange a visit to Nauyaca Waterfall, or you can call **Don Lulo** himself at ☎ **2787-8013.** A full-day tour, with both breakfast and lunch, and transportation to and from Dominical costs around $50 per person. This site has become so popular that Don Lulo has set up a little welcome center at the entrance (just off the road into Dominical from San Isidro) and even allows camping here. Round-trip car transportation can be arranged for a nominal charge.

The main entrance to these falls is located 10km (6¼ miles) outside of Dominical, on the road to San Isidro. ☎ *2787-8013. www.cataratasnauyaca.com. Admission: $50 for a full-day tour, with both breakfast and lunch and round-trip transportation. Open: Daily 8 a.m.–4 p.m.*

Parque Reptilandia

Located a few miles outside of Dominical, on the road to San Isidro, this place features over 50 terrariums and open-air exhibits of snakes, frogs, turtles, and lizards, as well as crocodiles and caimans. Be sure to check out the brilliantly colored mottled eyelash viper. These folks even have a Komodo dragon. Although I'm generally disappointed in this type of attraction, the display enclosures here are the best I've seen in Costa Rica.

*Located 7km (4⅓ miles) outside of Dominical, on the road to San Isidro. ☎ **2787-8007**. www.crreptiles.com. Admission: $9. Open: Daily 9 a.m.–4:30 p.m.*

More cool things to see and do

The Dominical area offers visitors a host of adventurous and educational options:

- ✔ **Diving:** If you want to take a scuba-diving trip out to the rocky sites off of Ballena National Park, or all the way out to Caño Island, call **Mystic Dive Center** (☎ 2786-5217; www.mysticdivecenter.com), which has its main office in a small roadside strip mall down toward Playa Tortuga and Ojochal.

- ✔ **Flying:** If you're looking for a bird's-eye view of the area, **Skyline Ultralights** (☎ 2743-8037; www.flyultralight.com) offers a variety of airborne tours. Located near the beach in Uvita, these folks offer options ranging from a 20-minute introductory flight for $65 to a circuit exploring the Ballena Marine National Park and neighboring mangrove forests lasting a bit over an hour for $160.

- ✔ **Learning Spanish:** If you're looking to learn or bone up on your Spanish, **Adventure Education Center** (☎ 2787-0023; www.adventurespanishschool.com) is located right in the heart of Dominical and offers a variety of immersion-style language programs.

Getting wet in Dominical and the beaches south of Dominical

Dominical is a major surf destination, and the long and varied beach break here is justifiably popular. In general, the beach boasts powerful waves best suited to experienced surfers. However, when the waves aren't too big, this is a good place to learn how to surf. Beginners should check in at the **Green Iguana Surf Camp** (☎ 2787-0157 or 8825-1381; www.greeniguanasurfcamp.com), which offers hourly lessons and comprehensive surf camps.

Because the beach in Dominical itself is unprotected, it's often too rough for swimming; however, you can go for a swim in the calm waters at the mouth of the **Río Barú,** or head down the beach a few kilometers to the little sheltered cove at **Roca Verde.**

If you have a car, you should continue driving south, exploring beaches as you go. You'll first come to **Dominicalito,** a small beach and cove that shelters the local fishing fleet and can be a decent place to swim. But I recommend you continue on a bit. You'll soon hit **Playa Hermosa,** a long stretch of desolate beach with fine sand. As in Dominical, this is unprotected and can be rough, but it's a nicer place to sunbathe and swim than Dominical.

Among the beaches you'll find farther south are **Playa Ballena, Playa Uvita, Playa Piñuela, Playa Ventanas,** and **Playa Tortuga.** Of these, Playa Ballena and Playa Uvita (see "The top attractions" earlier in this section) are the best for swimming. Playa Piñuela is made up predominantly of large, smooth stones, especially near the high-tide line. All these beaches have an isolated and undiscovered feel to them.

 Several of the beaches mentioned here are considered part of **Bahía Marine National Park** and charge an entrance fee of $10 per person. If you're visiting several of these beaches in one day, save your ticket, it's good at all of them.

Shopping for local treasures

Aside from your standard souvenir shops, no notable shopping options stand out in this area.

Living it up after dark in Dominical

Nightlife options are extremely limited in Dominical and virtually nonexistent south of Dominical. However, the young surfers who fill up this beach town do like to party, so the available bars are put to good use.

The big party scenes shift from night to night. **Maracutú** hosts an open jam session every Tuesday and a reggae night every Thursday. The loud and late-night dancing scene usually takes place Fridays at **San Clemente Bar & Grill** (☎ 2787-0055) and Saturdays at **Roca Verde.** In addition, **Thrusters** (☎ 2787-0127) is a popular surfer bar with pool tables and dartboards. The bar at **ConFusione** (☎ 2787-0244) also sometimes has live music.

If you want to hang within earshot of the waves, **Tortilla Flats** (☎ 2787-0168) is your best shot.

Fast Facts: Dominical and the Beaches South of Dominical

Ambulance

Call ☎ **128.**

ATMs

You'll only find ATMs in Dominical at the little shopping plaza adjacent to the San Clemente Bar & Grill (see earlier in this chapter), and at Plaza Pacífica, as well as at the Banco Nacional in Uvita.

Country Code and City Code

The country code for Costa Rica is **506.** Costa Rica doesn't use city or area codes. To call from the United States, dial 011-506 plus the eight-digit number. From within Costa Rica, simply dial the eight-digit number.

Currency Exchange

Dominical doesn't have any banks or money-exchange houses. Most hotels and restaurants will exchange money for you at decent rates.

Fire

Call ☎ **118.**

Hospitals

The closest hospitals are Hospital Quepos (☎ 2777-0922) and Hospital San Isidro (☎ 2771-3122).

If you need medical care in Dominical, contact **Dominical Doctor (☎ 2787-0129** or 8865-4064), which is inside the Pueblo del Rio minimall.

Information

Dominical doesn't have any official information offices, nor will you find any at the beaches south of Dominical. Most hotels have a tour desk, concierge, or helpful front-desk staff.

Internet Access

Several Internet cafes are located in Dominical. You can find one in Bahía and another in Ojochal, too.

Newspapers

The hotels and shops in this area only carry the local papers, but this includes the *Tico Times.* Also, keep an eye out for *Dominical Daze,* a free monthly tourist publication that has a wealth of information and local advertising; it's available at a host of hotel lobbies, restaurants, and stores.

Pharmacies

Farmacia Dominical (☎ 2787-0197) is a reasonably well-stocked pharmacy in the Pueblo del Río shopping center.

Police

Call ☎ **911** or 2787-0011.

Post Office

No official post office is located in Dominical. However, a window at the San Clemente Bar & Grill (see earlier in this chapter) functions as one. In addition, most hotels can mail your letters and postcards for you.

Taxis

Taxis congregate around the *fútbol* field in the center of Dominical. Or you can call Nelson (☎ 8835-9528) or Erik (☎ 8881-4220).

Part VI

Monteverde and Environs

"We're entering the Raincoat Forest. The Cloud Forest should be just ahead."

In this part . . .

Much of Costa Rica's natural beauty can be found inland, especially in the northern zone. You'll find everything from active volcanoes and mystical cloud forests to large inland lakes and pristine rivers and jungle waterfalls here. This is also the place to come for high-octane adventure, including mountain biking, canyoning, and riding zip-line canopy tours.

Monteverde, and the cloud forests around it, boast a distinct and unique beauty. The misty cloud forests here are home to the Resplendent Quetzal, one of the most stunning and revered birds of Mesoamerica. And Arenal volcano is one of Costa Rica's most mesmerizing sights. This active volcano regularly spews molten lava from its perfectly conical crater. At the foot of the volcano sit several natural hot springs, as well as Lake Arenal, a mecca for windsurfers, kiteboarders, and bass fishermen alike.

Chapter 17

Visiting the Cloud Forests of Monteverde

In This Chapter

▶ Arriving in Monteverde
▶ Getting around Monteverde
▶ Deciding where to stay and dine in Monteverde
▶ Enjoying the nights in Monteverde
▶ Having fun and adventures in Manuel Antonio

*I*f you're looking for cool mountain air, a taste of rural Costa Rica, and the chance to visit a cloud forest, Monteverde is the place for you. *Monteverde* translates as "green mountain," and that's exactly what you'll find at the end of the steep and winding dirt road that leads here. Perched on a high mountain ridge, this small, scattered village and its surrounding cloud forests are well known among both scientific researchers and ecotravelers.

Monteverde was settled in 1951 by Quakers from the United States who wanted to leave behind the fear of war, as well as an obligation to support continued militarism through paying U.S. taxes. They chose Costa Rica, a country that had abolished its army just a few years earlier, in 1948.

Although Monteverde's founders came here primarily to farm the land, they wisely recognized the need to preserve the rare cloud forests that covered the mountain slopes above their fields, and to that end they dedicated the largest adjacent tract of cloud forest as the Monteverde Cloud Forest Reserve.

Cloud forests are a unique phenomenon. If you think about it, the name says it all. Rain forests get their name from the fact that they receive copious amounts of rainfall, often heavy at times. Cloud forests get their moisture — and their moniker — from being nearly constantly enveloped in a combination of mist and clouds. Cloud forests are formed when moist, warm air sweeping in off the ocean cools as it reaches the cooler temperatures of higher elevation, thus forming clouds.

This constant level of moisture has given rise to an incredible diversity of innovative life-forms and a forest in which nearly every square inch of space has some sort of plant growth. Within the cloud forest, the branches of huge trees are draped with epiphytic plants: orchids, ferns, and bromeliads. This intense botanic competition has created an almost equally diverse population of insects, birds, and other wildlife.

Monteverde Cloud Forest Reserve covers 10,400 hectares (25,688 acres) of forest, including several different life zones that are characterized by different types of plants and animals. Within this small area are more than 2,500 species of plants, including 400 types of orchids, 400 species of birds, and 100 species of mammals. It's no wonder that the reserve has been the site of constant scientific investigations since its founding in 1972.

For many, the primary goal of a visit to Monteverde is a chance to glimpse the elusive and rare Resplendent Quetzal, a bird once revered by the pre-Columbian peoples of the Americas. This beautiful bird is a sight to see, with a bright red breast, iridescent blue-green back feathers, and, in the case of the males, tail feathers that can reach some 2 feet in length.

Getting There

There are no airstrips in or around Monteverde, so you have to arrive by some sort of vehicle. Given the lay of the land here, and the fact that various attractions and activities are spread out, I recommend driving your own rental car. However, bus service to Monteverde is available, and after you're there, taxis are available for getting around. I describe these various options in more detail in the following sections.

By car

Take the Interamerican Highway north toward Nicaragua. About 20km (12 miles) past the turnoff for Puntarenas there will be a marked turnoff for Sardinal, Santa Elena, and Monteverde. From this turnoff, the road is paved as far as the tiny town of Guacimal. From here it's another 20km (12 miles) to Santa Elena. It should take you a little over two hours to reach the turnoff and another one and a half hours or so from there.

An alternative route is to continue on the Interamerican Highway until just before the Río Lagarto bridge. This turnoff isn't always well marked. From the Río Lagarto turnoff, it's 38km (24 miles) to Santa Elena and Monteverde.

Whichever route you take, the final going is slow because the roads into Santa Elena are rough, unpaved, dirt-and-gravel affairs. However, once you arrive, the roads in and around Santa Elena are paved, including all the way to Cerro Plano, and about halfway to the Cloud Forest Preserve.

You don't absolutely need a four-wheel drive vehicle, but you'll appreciate the extra clearance, especially in the rainy season (mid-Apr to Nov).

Just before you enter the town of Santa Elena, you'll be stopped at a little tollbooth collecting 200 colones. The money is ostensibly going to maintain the road, which is sort of ironic. Appropriately, the payment is optional.

By bus

Transmonteverde express buses (☎ **2222-3854** in San José, 2645-5159 in Santa Elena) leave San José daily at 6:30 a.m. and 2:30 p.m. from Calle 12, between avenidas 7 and 9. The trip takes around four hours; the fare is $4.45. Buses arrive at and depart from Santa Elena; if you're staying at one of the hotels or lodges closer to the reserve, you'll want to arrange pickup, if possible, or you'll have to take a taxi or local bus.

Taking a horse, boat, and taxi to La Fortuna, or vice versa

You can travel between Monteverde and La Fortuna by boat and taxi, or on a combination boat, horseback, and taxi trip. A 10- to 20-minute boat ride across Lake Arenal cuts an hour or more of rough driving off the route circling it. It's about a one-and-a-half-hour, four-wheel-drive, taxi ride between Santa Elena and the Río Chiquito dock on the shores of Lake Arenal. It's just a 20-minute taxi ride from the dock on the other side and the city of La Fortuna. These trips can be arranged in either direction for $25 to $50 per person, all-inclusive.

You can also add on a horseback ride on the Santa Elena/Monteverde side of the lake. Several routes and rides are offered. This is most commonly done in the direction of La Fortuna to Monteverde. The steepest route heads up the mountains and through the forest to the town of San Gerardo, which is only a 30-minute car ride from Santa Elena. Other routes throw in mellower and shorter sections of horseback-riding along the lakeside lowlands. With the horseback ride, this trip runs around $50 to $75 per person.

The riding is sometimes rainy, muddy, and steep. Many find it much more arduous than awe-inspiring. Moreover, I've received numerous complaints about the condition of the trails and the treatment of the horses, so be very careful and demanding before signing on for this trip. Find out what route you'll be taking as well as the condition of the horses, if possible. **Desafío Expeditions** (☎ **2645-5874** in Monteverde, 2479-9464 in La Fortuna; www.desafiocostarica.com) is one of the more reputable operators. They'll even drive your car around for you while you take the scenic (and sore) route.

If you're looking to make the ride just by taxi and boat, check in with **Jeep Boat Jeep** (☎ **2479-9955**), which has two daily fixed departures in each direction at 7 a.m. and 4 p.m.

Gray Line (☎ 2220-2126; www.graylinecostarica.com) has a daily bus that leaves San José for Monteverde at 8 a.m.; the fare is $35. **Interbus** (☎ 2283-5573; www.interbusonline.com) has two daily buses that leave San José for Monteverde at 8:15 a.m. and 2:30 p.m.; the fare is $39. These companies will pick you up and drop you off at most San José– and Monteverde-area hotels.

There is a daily bus from Tilarán (Lake Arenal) at 12:30 p.m. The trip duration, believe it or not, is two hours (for a 40km/25-mile trip); the fare is $2.30.

The express bus departs for San José daily at 6:30 a.m. and 2:30 p.m. A bus from Santa Elena to Puntarenas leaves daily at 6 a.m. If you're heading to Jacó, Playa Herradura, or Manuel Antonio, take the Santa Elena/ Puntarenas bus and transfer in Puntarenas for a bus down the coast to any of these destinations.

To reach Liberia, take any bus down the mountain and get off when you hit the Interamerican Highway. You can then flag down a bus bound for Liberia (almost any bus heading north). The Santa Elena–Tilarán bus leaves daily at 7 a.m.

Orienting yourself in Monteverde

As you near the top of the local mountain, you'll approach the small village of **Santa Elena.** Take the right fork in the road if you're heading directly to Monteverde or the reserve.

If you continue straight, you'll hit the center of Santa Elena, which is centered on a block-long triangle of paved streets. Here, you'll find the bus stop, a health clinic, a bank, a small supermarket, a laundromat, and a few restaurants, hotels, souvenir shops, and tour offices.

A marked road heads out of Santa Elena toward the Monteverde Cloud Forest Reserve — where the road ends.

Monteverde is not a village in the traditional sense of the word. There's no center of town — only dirt lanes leading off from the main road to various farms, hotels, and attractions. This main road has signs for all the hotels and restaurants mentioned here.

There are no official tourist information offices in Santa Elena or Monteverde, although several tour-booking agencies masquerade as such. Most hotels have knowledgeable front-desk staffs, concierges, or in-house tour desks that can answer any questions. Also, keep an eye out for *Good Times,* a free local tourist paper that's loaded with information, articles, and advertisements.

Monteverde

ACCOMMODATIONS ■
Arco Iris Lodge **4**
Finca Valverde **6**
Hotel Belmar **20**
Hotel El Establo **16**
Hotel El Sapo Dorado **11**
Hotel Fonda Vela **28**
Hotel Poco a Poco **9**
Monteverde Lodge **8**

DINING ◆
Chimera **15**
Chunche's **3**
Flor de Vida **12**
Morpho's Café **2**
Pizzeria de Johnny **13**
Sophia **14**
Stella's Bakery **22**

ATTRACTIONS ●
Bajo del Tigre Trail **25**
Bat Jungle **21**
Butterfly Garden **19**
Ecological Farm **18**
Frog Pond of Monteverde **10**
Monteverde Cheese Factory **27**
Monteverde Cloud Forest Reserve **30**
Monteverde Serpentarium **7**
Orchid Garden **5**
The Original Canopy Tour **31**
Reserva Sendero Tranquilo **26**
Santa Elena Cloud Forest Reserve **32**
Selvatura Park **32**
Sky Trek **32**
Sky Walk **32**
World of Insects **1**

SHOPPING ■
Casa de Arte **17**
CASEM **24**
Hummingbird Gallery **29**

NIGHTLIFE ★
Flor de Vida **12**
La Taberna **6**
Monteverde Amphitheater **23**

Area of detail

Caribbean Sea

San José
COSTA RICA

PACIFIC OCEAN

0   50 mi
0   50 km

N

0   0.5 km
0   1/2 mi

MONTEVERDE BIOLOGICAL CLOUD FOREST RESERVE

Quebrada Máquina

Gas Station

Río Guacimal

MONTEVERDE

To San Luis →

SANTA ELENA

See inset below

Bus Stop

Santa Elena

To San José ↙

← To San José

Reading up on the early Quaker settlers

If you want an in-depth look into the lives and history of the local Quaker community, try to pick up a copy of the *Monteverde Jubilee Family Album*. Published in 2001 by the Monteverde Association of Friends, this collection of oral histories and photographs is 260 pages of local lore and memoirs. Although it's very simply bound and printed, it's well worth the $20 price.

Getting around

There are a half-dozen or so buses daily between the town of Santa Elena and the Monteverde Cloud Forest Reserve. The buses leave Santa Elena for the reserve beginning at 6 a.m. The last bus returns from the reserve at 4 p.m. The fare is $1.50 each way.

There's also periodic van transportation between the town of Santa Elena and the Santa Elena Cloud Forest Reserve. Ask around town, and you should be able to find the current schedule and book a ride for around $2 per person.

A taxi (☎ **2645-6969** or 2645-6666) between Santa Elena and either the Monteverde Cloud Forest Reserve or the Santa Elena Cloud Forest Reserve costs around $8 to $10 for up to four people. Count on paying $3 to $8 for the ride from Santa Elena to your lodge in Monteverde.

Finally, several places around town rent all-terrain vehicles (ATVs), for around $45 to $70 per day. Hourly rates and guided tours are also available. These vehicles are particularly well suited to the roads up here.

Spending the Night

Arco Iris Lodge
$$–$$$ Santa Elena

This is the best hotel right in Santa Elena proper. The rooms are spread out in eight separate buildings. In fact, most are individual cabins. All have wood or tile floors and plenty of wood accents. My favorites are the honeymoon cabins, which have their own private balconies with a forest view and good bird-watching. The management here is helpful and can arrange a wide variety of tours. Although they don't serve lunch or dinner, there's a daily breakfast buffet, and beer, wine, soft drinks, and other refreshments are available throughout the day and evening.

See map p. 239. Santa Elena. ☎ *2645-5067. Fax: 2645-5022.* www.arcoiris lodge.com. *Rack rates: $60–$180 double. AE, MC, V.*

Finca Valverde
$$ Just Outside Santa Elena

Although this place is located right on the outskirts of Santa Elena, it feels far removed from the hustle and bustle of the town. The standard rooms are set behind the main lodge and restaurant and are reached via a suspension bridge over a small forest creek. Most have one queen-size and two twin beds. All share a broad common veranda and feature free Wi-Fi. The cabins and junior suites are larger and more private, and they feature bathtubs. The junior suites are the highest up the hill and also have televisions, small refrigerators, and coffeemakers. The grounds are lush and well tended. A buffet breakfast and all other meals are served in a large restaurant just off the lobby.

See map p. 239. Monteverde. ☎ **2645-5157.** *Fax: 2645-5216.* www.monteverde.co.cr. *Rack rates: $93–$111 double. Rates lower in the off season. MC, V.*

Hotel Belmar
$$ On the Road to the Monteverde Cloud Forest Reserve

Set on the top of a grassy hill, the Belmar has stunning views of the Nicoya Gulf and the Pacific. Afternoons in the dining room or lounge are idyllic, with bright sunlight streaming in through a west-facing glass wall. Sunsets are spectacular. Most of the guest rooms are fitted with wood paneling, French doors, and little balconies that open onto splendid views. There are actually two buildings here. My favorite rooms are in the main building; those in the separate Swiss-chalet-style building are a bit smaller. The restaurant serves a mix of well-prepared Tico and international cuisine. The Belmar is up a dirt road that passes to the left of the gas station as you come into the heart of Monteverde.

See map p. 239. Monteverde. ☎ **2645-5201.** *Fax: 2645-5135.* www.hotelbelmar.net. *Rack rates: $79–$99 double. Rates lower in the off season. V.*

Hotel El Establo
$$$–$$$$ On the Road to the Monteverde Cloud Forest Reserve

Once a small, family-run budget lodging with rooms in a converted stable, this is now arguably the largest and most luxurious option in Monteverde. However, I think the vision here far exceeds the execution. The design and scale are somewhat out of place with the vibe and aesthetic of Monteverde, and the service and food can fall short. The rooms are housed in a series of large buildings set inland and up a steep hill from the main road. Most have great views. All are quite large and come with a private balcony or patio. The large and luxurious honeymoon suite has a fabulous view and private Jacuzzi. All rooms come with cable television, a rarity in Monteverde. There are two heated pools here, one under the cover of an open-air roof for when it's raining. There's also an on-site canopy tour and extensive spa facility here.

See map p. 239. Monteverde. ☎ **2645-5110.** *Fax: 2645-5041.* www.hotelelestablo.com. *Rack rates: $195 double, $273 suite. Rates include breakfast. AE, MC, V.*

Hotel El Sapo Dorado
$$ Just Outside Santa Elena

Located on a steep hill between Santa Elena and the reserve, El Sapo Dorado offers some of the most charming and comfortable accommodations in Monteverde. The spacious cabins are built of hardwoods both inside and out and are surrounded by a grassy lawn. Big windows let in lots of light, and high ceilings keep the rooms cool during the day. Some of the cabins have fireplaces, which are a welcome feature on chilly nights and during the peak parts of the rainy season. A remodeling in 2008 left most cabins updated, with larger, more modern bathrooms and livelier décor. My favorite rooms are the sunset suites, which have private terraces with views of the Nicoya Gulf and wonderful sunsets. This hotel offers free Wi-Fi in its restaurant, lobby, and common areas.

Not only does El Sapo Dorado own and manage the nearby **Reserva Sendero Tranquilo** (see "More cool things to see and do," later in this chapter), but it also has a network of well-maintained trails into primary forest on-site. To find the hotel and restaurant, watch for the sign on the left-hand side of the main road to the reserve, a few hundred yards outside of the town of Santa Elena.

See map p. 239. Monteverde. ☎ **2645-5010.** *Fax: 2645-5180.* www.sapodorado.com. *Rack rates: $122 double. MC, V. Rates include breakfast and taxes. Lower rates in the off season.*

Hotel Fonda Vela
$$ Monteverde, Close to the Reserve Entrance

This is one of the closer lodges to the Cloud Forest Reserve, an easy 15-minute walk away. And, although it's one of the older hotels here, Fonda Vela remains one of the best choices in Monteverde. Guest rooms are housed in a series of buildings scattered among the forests and pastures of this former farm. Most have views of the Nicoya Gulf. The newer junior suites, some of which have excellent views, are the best rooms in the house, and I prefer them to the older and larger junior suites. All junior suites come with cable television. The dining room has great sunset views, and it sometimes even features live music. Throughout the hotel, you'll see paintings by co-owner Paul Smith, who also handcrafts violins and cellos and is a musician himself.

See map p. 239. Monteverde. ☎ **2257-1413** *or 2645-5125. Fax: 2257-1416.* www.fondavela.com. *Rack rates: $110 double, $130 junior suite. AE, MC, V.*

Hotel Poco a Poco
$$ Santa Elena, close to the Frog Pond of Monteverde

Located just outside of the town of Santa Elena, this hotel provides a host of perks and amenities at a pretty good price. Some of the rooms are on the small size, but the beds are firm and everything is kept neat and contemporary. The best rooms are higher up, away from the road, and have a small balcony. All rooms come with free Wi-Fi, as well as DVD players, and the hotel maintains a movie lending library of over 4,000 titles. There's a heated pool, children's pool, and Jacuzzi on the grounds here, and the small restaurant is excellent.

See map p. 239. Monteverde. ☎ **2645-6000.** *Fax: 2645-6264.* www.hotelpocoa poco.com. *Rack rates: $92 double. Rates include breakfast. Rates lower in the off season, higher during peak periods. MC, V.*

Monteverde Lodge
$$ Just outside Santa Elena

The Monteverde Lodge was one of the first ecolodges to open in Monteverde, and it remains one of the best. Guest rooms are large and comfortable and, thanks to regular remodeling and upkeep, are some of the coziest in town. Most feature angled walls of glass with chairs and a table placed so that avid bird-watchers can do a bit of birding without leaving their rooms.

The gardens and secondary forest surrounding the lodge have some gentle groomed trails and are also home to quite a few species of birds. Perhaps the lodge's most popular attraction is the large hot tub in a big atrium garden just off the lobby. After hiking all day, you can soak your bones under the stars.

The hotel's dining room offers great views, good food, and excellent formal service provided by bow-tied waiters. The adjacent bar is a popular gathering spot and is the setting for regular evening slide shows focusing on the cloud forest. Scheduled bus service to and from San José is available, as is a shuttle to the reserve, horseback-riding, and a variety of optional tours. The excellent guides who work for the owner, Costa Rica Expeditions, have lots of experience with family groups.

See map p. 239. Monteverde. ☎ **2257-0766** *in San José, 2645-5057 at the lodge. Fax: 2257-1665.* www.costaricaexpeditions.com. *Rack rates: $88–$148 double. Rates slightly lower in the off season. AE, MC, V.*

Staying at the reserve

If you don't mind roughing it, you can stay in a simple dormitory room right at the **Monteverde Biological Cloud Forest Reserve** (☎ **2645-5122;** www.cct.or.cr). This is a good way to meet any visiting scientists and get friendly with the local guides and workers. A bunk bed and three meals per day here run $53 per person. For an extra $11 you can get a room with a private bathroom. Admission to the reserve is included in the price.

Dining Locally

Chimera
$$ Cerro Plano   FUSION/TAPAS

Building on the success of Sophia (see listing later in this chapter), Karen Nielsen opened this creative and casual tapas restaurant. The small menu has a broad scope, with options available in the traditional categories of soups, salads, mains, sides, and desserts, and influences ranging from Asia to Latin America to the Old World. Standout dishes include slow-cooked pork with white beans and caramelized onions and the coconut shrimp "lollipops" with a mango-ginger dipping sauce. And, for dessert, don't pass up the chocolate mousse with a sangria syrup. A variety of creative and contemporary cocktails, as well as good wines, are also offered.

See map p. 239. Cerro Plano, on the road between Santa Elena and the reserve, on your right. ☎ *2645-6081. Reservations recommended during high season. Main courses: Tapas $2.50–$8.50. AE, DC, DISC, MC, V. Open: Daily 11:30 a.m.–9:30 p.m.*

Flor de Vida
$$ Just outside Santa Elena   INTERNATIONAL/VEGETARIAN

With large new digs, this long-standing local favorite continues to serve up some of the best and healthiest fare to be found in Monteverde. Large picture windows line the walls, and there's a small lounge area in one corner, with books, magazines, and board games. When it's cold and windy out, I like to start off with a bowl of their pumpkin-almond soup. For lunch, their veggie burger with roasted potatoes is hard to beat, and for dinner I tend to favor the Thai fish curry. In addition to the regular menu, there are always daily specials.

See map p. 239. On the road between Santa Elena and the reserve, on your right. ☎ *2645-6328.* www.flordevida.net. *Reservations recommended during high season. Main courses: $8–$12. MC, V. Open: Daily 7 a.m.–10 p.m.*

Morpho's Café
$ Downtown Santa Elena   COSTA RICAN/INTERNATIONAL

Easily the most popular restaurant in the town of Santa Elena, this simple second-floor affair serves up hearty and economical meals. You'll find soups, sandwiches, and *casados* (plates of the day) for lunch and dinner, and delicious fresh fruit juices, ice cream shakes, and home-baked desserts throughout the day. The tables and chairs are made from rough-hewn lumber and whole branches and trunks, and the place brims with a light convivial atmosphere. This place is a very popular hangout for backpackers and budget travelers.

See map p. 239. In downtown Santa Elena, across from the supermarket. ☎ *2645-5607. Main courses: $4.50–$16. MC, V. Open: Daily 11 a.m.–9 p.m.*

Taking a coffee break

Monteverde and Santa Elena sit in the heart of some prime coffee-growing lands. The area boasts several local coffeehouses where you can sit and enjoy a cup of some locally grown and roasted beans. Moreover, the frequently wet and misty climate here makes this an even more attractive option.

In Santa Elena, **Chunche's** (☎ 2645-5147) is a bookstore with a small coffee shop and espresso bar that also doubles as a laundromat. Along the road to the reserve, **Stella's Bakery** (☎ 2645-5560) is a cheery and long-standing little joint, with a variety of fresh baked goods.

Pizzería de Johnny
$$ **Just outside Santa Elena   ITALIAN/PIZZA**

This perennially popular pizza joint has grown from a little hole in the wall to a downright institution here in Monteverde. The thin-crust, wood-oven pizzas are delicious, and there's a large menu of meat, chicken, and pasta dishes as well. You can start things off with a bruschetta or mussels Parmesan. The signature pizza Traviesa comes with artichoke hearts, onions, mushrooms, garlic, and marinated tomatoes. There's a little gift shop and a quiet bar off the large open dining room. The nicest tables are on the covered veranda out back.

See map p. 239. On the road to the reserve, on your right, just beyond El Sapo Dorado.
☎ 2645-5066. *Reservations recommended during high season. Main courses: $15–$22, pizzas $8–$20. MC, V. Open: Daily 11 a.m.–9:30 p.m.*

Sophia
$$ **Monteverde   COSTA RICAN/FUSION**

This restaurant is the most exciting and eclectic dining option in the Monteverde area. Start everything off with a mango-ginger mojito, and then try one of their colorful and abundant salads. Main courses range from seafood chimichangas to chicken breast served in a guava reduction. The tenderloin comes with a chipotle butter sauce over a bed of mashed sweet potato. Everything is very well prepared and reasonably priced. You'll find two good-size dining rooms here, both with heavy wood furniture. The best seats are close to the large, arched, picture windows overlooking the neighboring forest and gardens.

See map p. 239. Cerro Plano, just past the turnoff to the Butterfly Farm, on your left.
☎ 2645-7017. *Reservations recommended during high season. Main courses: $12–$16. MC, V. Open: Daily 11:30 a.m.–9:30 p.m.*

Exploring Monteverde

Monteverde has an abundance of attractions and activities. All the hotels and lodges in this area offer or can book all the tours and activities listed in this section. If you have your own vehicle, you can also visit all these attractions on your own.

The top attractions

Monteverde Cloud Forest Reserve

The Monteverde Cloud Forest Reserve is one of the most developed and well-maintained natural attractions in Costa Rica. The trails are clearly marked, regularly traveled, and generally gentle in terms of ascents and descents.

The cloud forest here is lush and largely untouched. Still, keep in mind that most of the birds and mammals you've been reading about are rare, elusive, and nocturnal. Moreover, to all but the most trained of eyes, those thousands of exotic ferns, orchids, and bromeliads tend to blend into one large mass of indistinguishable green.

Perhaps the most famous resident of the cloud forests of Costa Rica is the Resplendent Quetzal, a robin-size bird with iridescent green wings and a ruby-red breast. The male Quetzal also has two long tail feathers that can reach nearly 0.6m (2 ft.) in length, making it one of the most spectacular birds on Earth. The best time to see Quetzals is early morning to midmorning, and the best months are February through April, when the birds are mating.

After the Quetzal, Monteverde's most famous resident was the *sapo dorado* (golden toad), a rare native species. However, the golden toad has disappeared from the forest and is feared extinct. Competing theories of the toad's demise include adverse effects of a natural drought cycle, the disappearing ozone layer, pesticides, and acid rain.

Other animals that have been seen in Monteverde, although sightings are extremely rare, include jaguars, ocelots, and tapirs. However, you do have a good chance of seeing one of several different monkey species and an almost innumerable number of bird species.

I highly recommend taking one of the reserve's official guided two- to three-hour hikes; you can see and learn far more than you could on your own. At $17 per person, the reserve's tours may seem like a splurge, especially after you pay the entrance fee, but unless you have a lot of experience in Neotropical forests, it'll be money well spent.

Before venturing off on your tour or self-guided hike, have a look around the information center. Several guidebooks, as well as posters and postcards of some of the reserve's more famous animal inhabitants, are available here.

Monteverde Cloud Forest Reserve

Because only 120 people are allowed into the reserve at any one time, you may be forced to wait for a while before entering. Most hotels can reserve a guided walk and entrance to the reserve for the following day for you, or you can get tickets in advance directly at the reserve entrance.

Some of the trails here can be very muddy, depending on the season, so ask about current conditions. If the mud is heavy, you can rent rubber boots at the reserve entrance for $2 per day. They may make your hike much more pleasant.

Night tours of the reserve leave every evening at 7:15 p.m. The cost is $17 per person, including admission to the reserve, a two-hour hike, and, most important, a guide with a high-powered searchlight. For an extra $2, they'll throw in round-trip transportation to and from your area hotel.

See map p. 239. Located at the end of the dirt road 6km (3¾ miles) from Santa Elena. ☎ _2645-5122._ www.cct.or.cr. _Admission: $17 adults, $9 students and children; $17 per person for a guided or night tour. Open: Daily 7 a.m.–4 p.m. and 7:15–9 p.m._

Getting the most out of a visit to the reserve

Because the entrance fee to the Monteverde Cloud Forest Reserve is valid for a full day, I recommend taking an early-morning tour with a guide and then heading off on your own either directly after that hike or after lunch. A guide will point out and explain a lot, and you're almost assured of seeing more wildlife with a guide. But there's also much to be said for walking quietly through the forest on your own or in very small groups — you'll be able to stray from the more popular paths in the park.

Santa Elena Cloud Forest Reserve

Although the Monteverde Cloud Forest Reserve is the area's most famous and popular attraction, plenty of other areas of cloud forest lie in this region. The **Santa Elena Cloud Forest Reserve** is a 360-hectare (889-acre) reserve located 5km (3 miles) north of the village of Santa Elena. This reserve has a maximum elevation of 1,680m (5,510 ft.), which makes it the highest cloud forest in the Monteverde area.

You'll find 13km (8 miles) of hiking trails, as well as an information center here. Because it borders the Monteverde Reserve, you can find a similar richness of flora and fauna, although Quetzal sightings are not nearly as common. The $12 entry fee at this reserve goes directly to support local schools.

See map p. 239. Located 5km (3 miles) northeast of Santa Elena. ☎ **2645-5390.** *www. reservasantaelena.org. Admission: $12; $15 additional for a 3-hour guided tour. Open: 7 a.m.–4 p.m., with night tours starting at 7 p.m.*

Other attractions in Monteverde

The **Butterfly Garden** (☎ 2645-5512) displays many of Costa Rica's most beautiful butterfly species. Besides the hundreds of preserved and mounted butterflies, you'll find a garden and a greenhouse where you can watch live butterflies, as well as an informative guided tour that takes you through the life cycle of this fascinating insect. The garden is located near the end of the Cerro Plano road and is open daily from 9:30 a.m. to 4 p.m. Admission is $10 for adults and $8 for students and children, including a guided tour. The best time to visit is between 9:30 a.m. and 1 p.m., when the butterflies are most active.

If your taste runs toward the slithery, you can check out the **Monteverde Serpentarium** (☎ 2645-5238; www.snaketour.com), on the road to the reserve. This place features a broad selection of reptiles, including many species of venomous and nonvenomous snakes. It's open daily from 8 a.m. to 8:30 p.m. and charges $8 for admission.

The **Frog Pond of Monteverde** (☎ 2645-6320; www.ranario.com), located a couple of hundred meters north of the Monteverde Lodge, is probably a better bet. The $10 entrance gets you a 45-minute tour, and your ticket is good for two days. A variety of species populate a series of glass terrariums. This place is open daily from 9 a.m. to 8:30 p.m. If you visit first during the daytime, I recommend that you stop by at least once after dark, when the various tree frogs are active.

Another entry in this field is the **World of Insects** (☎ 2645-6859), which features a couple dozen terrariums filled with some of the area's more interesting creepy crawlers. My favorites are the giant horned beetles. This place is located 300m (984 ft.) west of the supermarket in Santa Elena. It's open daily from 9 a.m. to 7 p.m.; admission is $9.

If you've had your fill of birds, snakes, frogs, bugs, and butterflies, you may want to stop at the **Orchid Garden** (☎ 2645-5308; www.monte verdeorchidgarden.com), right in downtown Santa Elena. This small botanical garden boasts more than 450 species of orchids. Admission is $10 for adults, $7 for students. It's open daily from 8 a.m. to 5 p.m.

If you're looking to conquer your fear of bats, head to the **Bat Jungle** (☎ 2645-6566) for an in-depth look into the world, natural history, and habits of these odd, flying mammals. A visit here includes several different types of exhibits, from skeletal remains, to large enclosures where you get to see various live species in action — the enclosures and rooms are kept dark, and the bats have had their biological clocks tricked into thinking it's night. The Bat Jungle is open daily from 9:30 a.m. to 8 p.m. Admission is $10.

Finally, it's also worth stopping by the **Monteverde Cheese Factory** (☎ 2645-5150) to savor some homemade ice cream and to pick up some of the best cheese in Costa Rica. From the little store here, you can watch the process in action. The cheese factory is located right on the main road about midway between Santa Elena and the Reserve. It's open Monday through Saturday from 7:30 a.m. to 4 p.m., and Sunday from 7:30 a.m. to noon. A one-hour tour is offered daily at 9 a.m. and 2 p.m. (this latter tour is not offered on Sunday). The tour costs $10.

Canopy tours and suspended bridges

You have several options for getting up into the cloud forest canopy. There are several zip-line canopy-tour and suspended-bridge options to choose from in this area. I list them here in my order of preference.

Anybody in average physical condition can do any of the adventure tours in Monteverde, but they're not for the faint of heart or acrophobic. Try to book directly with the companies listed here or through your hotel. Beware of agents working the streets of Monteverde — they make a small commission and frequently try to steer tourists to the operator paying the highest percentage.

One of the newer additions to the canopy-tour field is **Selvatura Park** (☎ 2645-5929; www.selvatura.com). The extensive canopy tour here features 15 cables connecting 18 platforms. The canopy tour costs $45; the walkways and bridges cost $25. A number of other attractions are also here, so various packages are available; see the "Visiting the best one-stop adventure and activity spot" sidebar for information.

The sister projects of **Sky Walk** and **Sky Trek** (☎ 2645-5238; www.skyadventures.travel) combine a traditional canopy-tour attraction with a network of forest trails and suspension bridges:

  ✔ **Sky Trek** is one of the more extensive canopy tours in the country, with two very long cables to cross. The longest of these is some 770m (2,525 ft.) long, high above the forest floor. There are no rappel descents here, and you brake using the pulley system for friction. This tour costs $50.

  ✔ **Sky Walk** features a loop trail through primary and secondary forest, with a series of bridges spanning large canyons and ravines. The bridges reach 39m (128 ft.) above the ground at their highest point. The Sky Walk is open daily from 7 a.m. to 4 p.m. Admission is $17, and no reservation is necessary. For an extra $13, a knowledge-able guide will point out the diverse flora and fauna on the walk.

For $60 per person, you can do the Sky Trek canopy tour and then walk the trails and bridges of the Sky Walk. Reservations are recommended for the Sky Trek part of the excursion.

Sky Walk and Sky Trek are located about 3.5km (2¼ miles) outside of the town of Santa Elena, on the road to the Santa Elena Cloud Forest Reserve. These folks will provide round-trip transportation from Santa Elena for just $2 per person.

Visiting the best one-stop adventure and activity spot

Selvatura Park (☎ 2645-5929; www.selvatura.com) is the best one-stop shop for various adventures and attractions in the area. In addition to its extensive canopy tour, it also has a network of trails and suspended bridges, as well as a huge butterfly garden, hummingbird garden, and wonderful insect display and museum. Prices vary depending upon how much you want to see and do. Individually, the canopy tour costs $45; the walkways and bridges, $25; the butterfly garden, $12; and the insect museum, $12. Various combination packages are available. For $121, you get the run of the entire joint, all the tours, lunch, and round-trip transportation from your Monteverde hotel. It's open daily from 8 a.m. to 4 p.m.

One of the oldest canopy tours in the country is run by **The Original Canopy Tour** (☎ 2645-5243; www.canopytour.com), which has an office right in the center of Santa Elena. This is one of the more interesting canopy tours in Costa Rica because you'll climb up the hollowed-out interior of a giant strangler fig during your initial ascent. This tour also has 11 platforms and 2 rappels, making it the most adventurous canopy tour in Monteverde. The three-hour tours run three times daily and cost $45 for adults, $35 for students, and $25 for children 11 and under. Call for reservations and tour schedule.

More cool things to see and do

✔ **Hiking:** In addition to hiking in cloud forests, you can hike the trails and grounds of the **Ecological Sanctuary** (☎ 2645-5869; www.ecologicalsanctuary.com), a family-run wildlife refuge and private reserve located down the Cerro Plano road. This place has four main trails, which run through a variety of ecosystems. Because some of the farm is secondary forest and some is cleared land, the wildlife viewing is often quite good here. In fact, the wildlife viewing is often better than that in Monteverde Cloud Forest Reserve and Santa Elena Cloud Forest Reserve. There are a couple of pretty waterfalls off the trails, and night tours are also offered. The Ecological Farm is open daily from 7:30 a.m. to 5 p.m.; admission is $10 for self-guided hiking on the trails; $25 during the day for a two-hour guided tour; and $20 for the two-hour guided night tour that leaves at 5:30 p.m.

The **Bajo del Tigre Trail** (☎ 2645-5003; www.acmcr.org) is a 3.5km (2¼-mile) trail that's home to several different bird species not usually found within the reserve. You can take several different loops, lasting anywhere from one to several hours. The trail starts a little past the CASEM artisans' shop and is open daily from 8 a.m. to 5 p.m. Admission is $8 for adults and $4 for students and children.

You can also go on guided three-hour hikes at the **Reserva Sendero Tranquilo** (☎ 2645-7711), which has 80 hectares (198 acres) of land, two-thirds of which is in virgin forest. This reserve is located up the hill from the Monteverde Cheese Factory. It charges $35 for its tours and is open daily from 7 a.m. to 3 p.m. seasonally, and night tours are also offered with advance reservations.

✔ **Horseback riding:** The rugged dirt roads, untouched forests, and pasturelands surrounding the protected reserves here provide excellent opportunities for getting in the saddle. **Meg's Riding Stables** (☎ 2645-5560), **La Estrella Stables** (☎ 2645-5075), **Palomina Horse Tours** (☎ 2645-5479), and **Sabine's Smiling Horses** (☎ 2645-6894; www.smilinghorses.com) are the most established operators, offering guided rides for around $10 to $20 per hour.

Another option is to set up a day tour and sauna at **El Sol** (☎ 2645-7214; www.elsolnuestro.com). Located about a ten-minute car ride down the mountain from Santa Elena, these folks take you on a roughly three-hour ride either to San Luis or to an isolated little waterfall with an excellent swimming hole. After the ride back, you'll find the wood-burning traditional Swedish sauna all fired up, with a refreshing and beautiful little pool beside it. The tour costs $60 per person, including lunch. These folks also have two very rustically luxurious private cabins ($95–$125 double), with excellent views.

✔ **Taking a coffee tour:** If you're interests focus on java, you can take a tour of several different local coffee farms. The **Monteverde Coffee Tour** (☎ 2645-5901; www.monteverde-coffee.com) is run by the folks at the Cooperativa Santa Elena, a local fair-trade coffee producer, with a shop right next to CASEM, while **Don Juan Coffee Tour** (☎ 2645-7100; www.donjuancoffeetour.com) is a local, family farm operation. Both offer several types of tours that provide insight into the process and production of fine, high-altitude coffee. Depending upon the tour option you choose, rates run between $22 and $30.

✔ **Learning Spanish:** The **Centro Panamericano de Idiomas** (☎ 2645-5441; www.spanishlanguageschool.com) offers immersion language classes in a wonderful setting. A one-week program, with four hours of class per day and a home-stay with a Costa Rican family, costs $465.

Shopping for Local Treasures

Monteverde may just be one of the best tourist destinations in Costa Rica for shopping. Several good art galleries and gift shops are in the area, and even the locally produced crafts are of a higher quality than in most of the rest of the country.

Perhaps the best-stocked gift shop in Monteverde is the **Hummingbird Gallery** (☎ 2645-5030). You'll find the gallery just outside the reserve entrance. Hanging from trees around it are a series of hummingbird feeders that attract more than seven distinct species of these hyperactive little birds. At any given moment, there may be several dozen hummingbirds buzzing and chattering around the building and your head. Inside you will, of course, find a lot of beautiful color prints of hummingbirds and other local flora and fauna, as well as a wide range of craft items, T-shirts, and other gifts.

Another good option is **CASEM** (☎ 2645-5190). This craft cooperative sells embroidered clothing, T-shirts, posters, and postcards with photos of the local flora and fauna, Boruca weavings, locally grown and roasted coffee, and many other items to remind you of your visit to Monteverde.

CASEM is located about halfway along the road between Santa Elena and the reserve.

Over the years, Monteverde has developed a thriving community of artists. Around town, you'll see paintings by local artists such as Paul Smith and Meg Wallace, among others. You should also check out the **Casa de Arte** (☎ 2645-5275), which has a mix of arts and crafts in many media.

Living It Up After Dark in Monteverde

The most popular after-dark activities in Monteverde are night hikes in one Monteverde Cloud Forest Reserve (see listing for "Monteverde Cloud Forest Reserve" earlier in this chapter).

If you want a taste of the local party scene, head to **La Taberna** (☎ 2645-5157), which is just outside of downtown Santa Elena, before the Serpentarium. This place attracts a mix of locals and tourists, cranks its music loud, and often gets people dancing.

You'll certainly want to check whether any live music or another performance is on offer at the **Monteverde Amphitheater** (☎ 2645-6272), a beautiful open-air performance space, located up a steep driveway across from CASEM. However, be forewarned: The concrete seats here are uncomfortable; try to bring something soft to sit on. Alternatively, the **Flor de Vida** restaurant (☎ 2645-6328) sometimes features live music or open-mic jam sessions.

Fast Facts: Monteverde

Ambulance

Call ☎ **128** or 2645-6128.

ATMs

You'll find an ATM at the Banco Nacional in Santa Elena (☎ 2645-5610).

Country Code and City Code

The country code for Costa Rica is **506**. There are no city or area codes within Costa Rica. To call from the United States, dial 011-506 plus the eight-digit number. From within Costa Rica, simply dial the eight-digit number.

Currency Exchange

Most hotels will exchange money for you at decent rates. To get official rates, head to the Banco Nacional in Santa Elena (☎ 2645-5610).

Fire

Call ☎ **118**.

Hospitals

Neither Santa Elena nor Monteverde has a hospital, although you will find a small medical clinic, Clinica Santa Elena (☎ 2645-5076), that can handle most emergencies.

Information

There's no single official tourist information office in Santa Elena or Monteverde, although several tour booking agencies masquerade as such. Most hotels have tour desks, concierges, or helpful front-desk staffs.

Internet Access

You'll find several Internet cafes in Santa Elena, as well as a few strung along the road to the Santa Elena Cloud Forest Reserve. Many hotels also have their own in-house Internet cafes or wireless service. Rates run between $1 and $3 per hour.

Newspapers

Several gift shops around town and various hotels can get you current or day-late editions of the *Miami Herald, New York Times,* or *USA Today,* as well as all the local papers, including the *Tico Times.* Also, keep an eye out for *Good Times,* a small tourist paper with some good information and local advertising.

Pharmacies

The Farmacia Monteverde (☎ 2645-7110) is located in downtown Santa Elena and is fairly well-stocked.

Police

Call ☎ **911** or 2645-6248.

Post Office

You'll find a post office in Santa Elena (☎ 2645-5042). Alternatively, most hotels can mail your letters and postcards for you.

Taxis

Taxis are usually available in Santa Elena and around Monteverde. If you don't feel like flagging one down on the street, have your hotel call for you or dial ☎ 2645-6969 or 2645-6666 for two reliable, private operators.

Chapter 18

La Fortuna and the Arenal Area

In This Chapter

▶ Getting to and around La Fortuna and the Arenal volcano
▶ Deciding where to stay and dine near the Arenal volcano
▶ Enjoying the volcano viewing, hot springs, and other attractions of this area
▶ Having fun and adventures on the shores of Lake Arenal
▶ Buying arts and crafts at a couple of excellent lakeside shops

*A*t the epicenter of the north-central zone of Costa Rica, Lake Arenal and Arenal volcano — water and fire — are two of the country's most striking natural attractions. In fact, the entire area is a naturalist's dream come true. In addition to the volcano and lake, you'll find rain forests, jungle rivers and waterfalls, smaller mountain lakes, hot springs, and an unbelievable wealth of birds and other wildlife. Small, classy, isolated lodges abound, and the sheer diversity of terrain, flora, and fauna is astounding.

If just enjoying the natural beauty and wonders of this area isn't enough, you'll also find ample opportunities to engage in a wealth of exciting adventure sports and tours.

La Fortuna and the Arenal Volcano

If you've never experienced them firsthand, the sights and sounds of an active volcano erupting are awesome. The **Arenal volcano** is one of the world's most regularly active volcanoes. Frequent powerful explosions send cascades of red-hot lava rocks tumbling down the volcano's steep slopes, and lava flows steam and rumble. Although this is all very impressive during the day, at night the volcano puts on its most mesmerizing show. If you're lucky enough to be here on a clear and active night, you'll see the night sky turned red by lava spewing from Arenal's crater and watch the glowing lava flows stream down its flanks.

La Fortuna and the Arenal Volcano

ACCOMMODATIONS ■
Arenal Kioro **16**
Arenal Observatory Lodge **22**
Hotel La Fortuna **2**
Hotel Boutique Las Colinas **5**
Hotel San Bosco **3**
Montaña de Fuego Inn **15**
The Springs Resort & Spa **14**
Tabacón Grand Spa
  Thermal Resort **18**
Volcano Lodge **13**

DINING ◆
Don Rufino **4**
El Novillo de Arenal **17**
Lava Lounge **7**

ATTRACTIONS ●
Arenal Bungee **1**
Arenal Hanging Bridges **20**
Arenal National Park **21**
Baldi Termae **9**
Eco Termales **11**

Jungla y Senderos Los Lagos **12**
La Fortuna Falls **23**
Sky Tram **24**
Tabacón Grand Spa Hot Springs **19**
Tikokú **10**

NIGHTLIFE ★
Luigi's Casino **6**
Volcano Look Disco **8**

Rising to a steep and well-defined cone — given recent activity, there's actually a double cone near the top — the 1,607m (5,271-ft.) Arenal volcano lay dormant for hundreds of years until July 1968, when a sudden eruption leveled the former town of Tabacón and killed almost 80 of its inhabitants.

At the eastern foot of Arenal volcano is the small rural community of **La Fortuna.** This town has become a magnet for volcano watchers from around the world. You'll find a host of hotels and restaurants in and near La Fortuna, and from here you can arrange night tours to the best volcano viewing spots, which are 17km (11 miles) away on the western slope, on the road to and beyond Tabacón Grand Spa Thermal Resort.

Getting there

This area is best visited in a four-wheel-drive rental car. Although bus transportation to the area is available, the freedom of having your own car really pays dividends. However, the easiest and quickest way to visit the area is to take a commuter plane to La Fortuna and then rent a car after you're in town. You'll find details on all these options in the following sections.

By plane

Nature Air (☎ **800-235-9272** in the U.S. and Canada, 2299-6000 in Costa Rica; www.natureair.com) and **Sansa** (☎ **877-767-2672** in the U.S. and Canada, 2290-4100 in Costa Rica; www.flysansa.com) both have daily flights to Arenal/La Fortuna from San José. The flight duration is 30 minutes; the one-way fare is $68 on Sansa, $94 on Nature Air. Nature Air also has connecting flights between Arenal and other major destinations in the country.

By car

You can take several routes to La Fortuna from San José. The most popular is to head west on the Interamerican Highway and then turn north at Naranjo, continuing north through Zarcero to Ciudad Quesada. From Ciudad Quesada, one route goes through Jabillos, while the other goes through Muelle. The former route is better marked, more popular, slightly shorter, and generally better maintained, but the severe weather and heavy traffic quickly take their toll, and the roads up here can be notoriously bad for long stretches. This route offers wonderful views of the San Carlos Valley as you come down from Ciudad Quesada, and Zarcero, with its topiary gardens and quaint church, makes a good place to stop, stretch your legs, and snap a few photos.

You can also stay on the Interamerican Highway until San Ramón (west of Naranjo) and then head north through La Tigra. This route is also very scenic and passes the hotels Villablanca and Valle Escondido.

The travel time on any of these routes is three to four hours.

By bus

Direct buses (☎ **2255-0567**) leave San José for La Fortuna roughly every two hours between 5 a.m. and 7:30 p.m. from the **Atlántico del Norte** bus station at Avenida 9 and Calle 12. The trip takes four and a half hours. The fare is $3.70.

Some of the direct buses to La Fortuna will be labeled "Tilarán"; others will be labeled just "La Fortuna." All these buses leave from the same terminal. There are two routes to Tilarán — one via Ciudad Quesada and La Fortuna, the other via the Interamerican Highway and Cañas. If you take a bus labeled "Tilarán," be sure to ask the driver beforehand if it passes through Ciudad Quesada. If it doesn't, you'll end up in Tilarán via the Interamerican Highway, a long way from La Fortuna.

However, if there's a long wait until the next direct bus, taking a bus first to Ciudad Quesada and then transferring will get you to La Fortuna a little bit quicker. These buses depart roughly every 30 minutes between

5 a.m. and 7:30 p.m. The fare for the two-and-a-half-hour trip is $3. Local buses between Ciudad Quesada and La Fortuna run regularly through the day, although the schedule changes frequently, depending on demand. The trip lasts one hour; the fare is $1.50.

A bus departs **Monteverde** and **Santa Elena** for Tilarán every day at 7 a.m. This is a journey of only 35km (22 miles), but the trip lasts two and a half hours because the road is in such horrendous condition. People with bad backs should think twice about making this trip, especially by bus. The return bus from Tilarán to Santa Elena leaves at 12:30 p.m. The fare is $2.30.

Buses from Tilarán to La Fortuna depart daily at 8 a.m. and 4:30 p.m. and make the return trip at 7 a.m. and 12:30 p.m. The trip is three to four hours. The fare is $2.75.

Buses depart La Fortuna for San José roughly every two hours between 5 a.m. and 5:30 p.m. In some instances, you may have to transfer in Ciudad Quesada; from there, you can catch one of the frequent buses to San José.

Gray Line (☎ 2220-2126; www.graylinecostarica.com) has two daily buses that leaves San José for La Fortuna at 7 a.m. and 3:30 p.m. **Interbus** (☎ 2283-5573; www.interbusonline.com) also has two buses daily, leaving San José for La Fortuna at 8 a.m. and 2 p.m. The fare is $35 with Gray Line and $39 with Interbus. Both companies will pick you up at most San José–area hotels; they also run routes from La Fortuna with connections to most other major destinations in Costa Rica.

For information on taxi, boat, and horseback transfers between La Fortuna and Monteverde, see Chapter 17.

Orienting yourself in La Fortuna and around the volcano

As you enter La Fortuna, you'll see the massive volcano directly in front of you. La Fortuna is only a few streets wide, with almost all the hotels, restaurants, and shops clustered around the small downtown area, or spread along the main road that leads out of town toward Tabacón and the volcano. You'll find several tour-booking offices, Internet cafes, souvenir shops and laundromats, on the streets that surround the small central park that fronts the Catholic church, La Iglesia de La Fortuna.

From the center of La Fortuna, a road heads toward Lake Arenal. This road passes first through Tabacón and then by the entrance to Arenal National Park, before crossing the dam over Lake Arenal and continuing on around the lake to Nuevo Arenal and Tilarán.

 Many of the hotels with the best views of the Arenal volcano are located along the section of this road between La Fortuna and the Tabacón Grand Spa Thermal Resort.

Getting around and getting information

Tons of taxis can be found in La Fortuna (you can flag one down practically anywhere), and there is always a line of them ready and waiting along the main road beside the central park. A taxi between La Fortuna and Tabacón should cost around $6. Call **Arenal Taxi** at ☎ **2479-9605.**

Another alternative is to rent a car when you get here. **Alamo** (☎ **2479-9090;** www.alamo.com) and **Poás** (☎ **2479-8027;** www.carentals.com) both have offices in La Fortuna.

You'll also find several places to rent scooters and ATVs around town. As long as it's not raining too heavily, this is a good way to get around. Rates run around $35 to $50 per day for a scooter, and $50 to $90 for an ATV.

 If you don't have a car and you want to visit the hot springs or view the volcano's eruptions, you'll need to either take a cab or go on an organized tour.

No official information offices are in this area, although many of the local gift shops and tour agencies advertise themselves as such. Your hotel tour desk, concierge, or front desk will probably be your best source of information (besides this book, of course).

Spending the night

Arenal Kioro
$$$$ Near Lake Arenal

This place is seriously close to the volcano. The views from the hotel's rooms, grounds, pool, and restaurant are astounding. The rooms themselves are massive and opulent, with soaring high ceilings, large picture windows and glass doors, and a private balcony or patio facing the action. Each has its own four-person modern Jacuzzi tub, with sculpted seats and numerous jets. This Jacuzzi is set below a large picture window with a volcano view and is an attempt to compensate for the fact that there are no natural hot springs right on the grounds. The beds are also set to take in the view. The spa here is well designed and offers a wide range of treatment options. There are trails through the grounds, a pretty outdoor pool, and a whole host of tours and activities. The restaurant serves excellent international cuisine in a beautiful setting, with a giant wall of windows strategically set facing the volcano.

See map p. 256. 10km (6 miles) outside La Fortuna on the road to Tabacón. ☎ 888-866-5027 in the U.S. and Canada, 2461-1700 in Costa Rica. Fax: 2461-1710. www.hotel arenalkioro.com. Rack rates: $345 double. Rates include buffet breakfast. Rates lower in the off season, higher during peak periods. AE, DC, MC, V.

Arenal Observatory Lodge
$$–$$$ On the flanks of the Arenal volcano

This hotel is built on a high ridge with a spectacular view of the volcano's cone. Rooms come in a variety of shapes and sizes, and in a variety of locations around the lodge's expansive grounds. The best rooms here are the five junior suites built below the restaurant and main lodge, as well as the four rooms in the Observatory Block, and the White Hawk villa. The Smithsonian rooms are also a good choice; they feature massive picture windows, with a direct view of the volcano. The standard rooms are simple and rustic with no volcano views.

This is one of the better nature lodges for travelers with disabilities, with five rooms truly equipped for wheelchair access and a paved path extending almost a kilometer (½ mile) into the rain forest. When you're not hiking or touring the region, you can hang by the volcano-view swimming pool and Jacuzzi.

To get here, head to the national park entrance, stay on the dirt road past the entrance, and follow the signs to the Observatory Lodge. A four-wheel-drive vehicle used to be required for the 9km (5½-mile) dirt road up to the lodge, but two bridges now eliminate the need to ford any major rivers, and a traditional sedan will usually make it even in the rainy season — although you'll always be better off with the clearance afforded by a four-wheel-drive vehicle.

See map p. 256. On the flanks of Arenal volcano. ☎ **2290-7011** *in San José, 2479-1070 at the lodge. Fax: 2290-8427.* www.arenal-observatory.co.cr. *Rack rates: $73–$98 standard double, $128 Smithsonian, $148 junior suite. Rates include breakfast buffet. Rates lower in the off season. AE, MC, V.*

Hotel Boutique Las Colinas
$–$$ Downtown La Fortuna

Like the Hotel La Fortuna (see the next listing), this long-standing downtown hotel was torn down and rebuilt. Today, Las Colinas sits as the centerpiece of a minimall, which features some shops and a small spa. The rooms range from simple budget accommodations to spiffy junior suites with a private volcano-view balcony and Jacuzzi. The budget rooms come with televisions, but they lack air-conditioning and some of the other amenities found in the rest of the rooms. All come with free Wi-Fi. The best feature of the hotel is its ample rooftop terrace, with a fabulous volcano view, where breakfasts are served. Ecofriendly touches include solar-heated water and an adherence to various sustainable and responsible tourism principles.

See map p. 256. La Fortuna (A.P. 06), San Carlos. ☎ **2479-9305.** *Fax: 2479-9160.* www.lascolinasarenal.com. *19 units. Rack rates: $30 budget room double, $60–$78 double, $70 junior suite. Rates include breakfast and taxes. Rates lower in off season. MC, V (with 5 percent surcharge).*

Hotel La Fortuna
$$ **Downtown La Fortuna**

This budget stalwart burned down a few years ago and was quickly rebuilt as a budget classic. However, it was again razed (intentionally) and replaced with a massive and modern five-story building. Centrally located just 1 block south of the gas station, the Hotel La Fortuna now features large, spiffy rooms with a host of modern amenities, including free Wi-Fi throughout. The best rooms have volcano-view private balconies — ask for one on the fourth or fifth floor with a volcano view. Twelve of the rooms are specially designed for wheelchair accessibility and disabled travelers.

See map p. 256. Downtown La Fortuna, San Carlos. ☎ *2479-9197. Fax: 2479-8563.* www.fortunainn.com. *Rack rates: $75–$85 double. Rates lower in the off season, higher during peak periods. Rates include buffet breakfast. MC, V.*

Hotel San Bosco
$ **La Fortuna**

Located a block off La Fortuna's main street, the San Bosco offers the best rooms to be found right in town. The hotel actually has two styles of rooms. The older units are all well maintained and feature tile floors and fans; however, these are little more than standard budget accommodations. The slightly more expensive rooms are much more attractive and have stone walls, tile floors, reading lights, televisions, and benches on the veranda in front. You'll find an observation deck for volcano viewing on the top floor of the hotel, as well as a helpful front-desk staff. Free Wi-Fi is available throughout the hotel grounds.

See map p. 256. La Fortuna, San Carlos (200m/656 ft. north of the central park). ☎ *2479-9050. Fax: 2479-9109.* www.arenal-volcano.com. *Rack rates: $72–$77 double. Rates include breakfast. Rates lower in the off season. AE, MC, V.*

Montaña de Fuego Inn
$$$ **On the road to Tabacón**

This hotel features a mix of individual cabins and two-story buildings built on stilts over a small artificial lake, which house a handful of suites. The junior suites are the best rooms here, with minifridges. Some even have back balconies overlooking a forested ravine, in addition to the volcano-facing front porch. Behind the hotel are some rolling hills that lead down to a small river surrounded by patches of gallery forest, where they conduct an adventurous horseback, hiking, rappel, and kayak loop tour. These folks have their own zip-line canopy tour, on site.

See map p. 256. 8km (5 miles) outside La Fortuna on the road to Tabacón. ☎ *2460-1220. Fax: 2460-1455.* www.montanadefuego.com. *Rack rates: $128 double, $154–$189 suite. Rates include buffet breakfast. MC, V.*

The Springs Resort & Spa
$$$$$ Off the road to Tabacón

Located well off the main road between La Fortuna and Tabacón, on a large tract of land with a great view of the volcano, this new resort features plush, luxurious rooms, and some fabulous facilities. The five-story main lodge building is massive, with several restaurants, a large, full-service spa, modern exercise room, open-air casino, and much-needed elevator. At its base sit a series of sculpted hot and cold pools of various sizes, and below these you'll find the suites and villas. All the accommodations here are opulently appointed, and all have volcano views. The bathrooms are large, marble affairs with huge Jacuzzi tubs and separate showers. Food and service here are excellent, as you would expect. *Note*: Don't confuse this place with the Arenal Springs Resort, which is far less luxurious.

See map p. 256. 8km (5 miles) off the main road between La Fortuna and Lake Arenal, 10km (6 miles) from La Fortuna. ☎ *954-727-8333 in the U.S. and Canada, 2461-1700 in Costa Rica. Fax: 2401-3313.* www.thespringscostarica.com. *Rack rates: $375–$440 suite, $950–$1,400 villa for 4. Rates lower in the off season. AE, DC, MC, V.*

Tabacón Grand Spa Thermal Resort
$$$$–$$$$$ Between La Fortuna and Lake Arenal

This hotel is built just above and across the street from the spectacular Tabacón hot springs. Many rooms here have excellent, direct views of the volcano. Rooms on the upper floors of the 300-block building have the best vistas. Still, quite a few of the rooms have obstructed, or no, views. Book a standard superior, which comes with a view — it's definitely worth the slight splurge over the straight standard. The newer Forest Deluxe rooms are perhaps some of the plusher rooms here, with a private mosaic tile Jacuzzi and plasma-screen televisions, but, as the name suggests, they come with forest and not volcano views. All rooms are spacious, with heavy wooden furniture; most have a private terrace or balcony with a table and a couple of chairs. All are nonsmoking and feature free Wi-Fi. Nine of the rooms here are designed to be truly accessible to travelers with disabilities, and 11 are suites, with separate sitting rooms; many have private volcano-view Jacuzzis. Guests here enjoy privileges at the hot springs complex and spa across the street, including slightly extended hours. The hotel boasts an excellent restaurant, as well as a large hot-spring-fed pool and separate Jacuzzi.

See map p. 256. On the main road between La Fortuna and Lake Arenal, Tabacón. ☎ *877-277-8291 in the U.S. and Canada, 2519-1900 in Costa Rica, 2460-2020 at the resort. Fax: 2519-1940.* www.tabacon.com. *Rack rates: $230–$310 double, $390–$450 suite. Rates include buffet breakfast. AE, DC, MC, V.*

Villablanca Cloud Forest & Spa
$$$–$$$$ Outside of San Ramón

This venerable, old, mountain retreat received a major facelift and is now part of a group of "green hotels" that includes Sí Como No in Manuel

Antonio. The hotel consists of a series of Tico-style casitas surrounded by 800 hectares (1,976 acres) of farm and forest. Each casita is built of adobe and has tile floors, open-beamed ceilings, and whitewashed walls. Inside, you'll find a fireplace in one corner, comfortable hardwood chairs, and either one queen or two twin beds covered with colorful bedspreads. The deluxe units and suites have separate sitting areas with foldout couches, whirlpool bathtubs, and separate showers. In many rooms, the bathroom tubs look out through a wall of windows onto lush gardens. Some have private patios. Four of the old casitas were converted into a branch of **Serenity Spa.** Adjacent to the lodge are 11km (6¾ miles) of trails through the **Los Angeles Cloud Forest Reserve.** You can also rent horses or take an adventurous swing through the canopy on a canopy tour here.

Villablanca is actually over an hour from La Fortuna, but it's on the way and makes a good overnight stop en route. Villablanca is off the beaten track, but it's relatively close to San José, and if you're interested in bird-watching or exploring a cloud forest and want to avoid the crowds of Monteverde, this is a good choice. If you're driving, head west out of San José to San Ramón and then head north, following the signs to Villablanca. Or you can take a public bus from San José to San Ramón and then take a taxi for around $15.

San Ramón, Alajuela. ☎ *2461-0300. Fax: 2461-0302.* `www.villablanca-costarica.com`. *Rack rates: $170 double, $192 deluxe, $215 suite. Rates include buffet breakfast. AE, DC, MC, V.*

Volcano Lodge
$$ **Between La Fortuna and Lake Arenal**

This lodge is located directly across the road from and facing the volcano. Each of the rooms comes with two double beds, a private bathroom, two wicker chairs inside, and a small terrace with a couple of wooden rocking chairs for volcano viewing outside. The appointments are simple, but the rooms are spacious and get plenty of light through big picture windows. Moreover, the view of the volcano here is top notch, and a wide range of tours is available. The entire complex is wired for Wi-Fi access.

See map p. 256. On the main road between La Fortuna and Lake Arenal. ☎ *866-208-9819 in the U.S. and Canada, 2460-6080 in Costa Rica. Fax: 2460-6020.* `www.volcanolodge.com`. *Rack rates: $125 double. Rates include continental breakfast. Rates lower in the off season. AE, MC, V.*

Dining locally

Don Rufino
$$ **Downtown La Fortuna**   **COSTA RICAN/INTERNATIONAL**

Set on a busy corner in the heart of town, this restaurant is easily the best — and the busiest — option right in town. The front wall and bar area open on to the street and are often filled both with local tour guides and tourists. Try the *pollo al estilo de la abuela* (Grandma's chicken), which is baked and served wrapped in banana leaves, or one of the excellent cuts of meat. It's a good choice for breakfast, and the bar stays open most nights until 2 a.m.

See map p. 256. Downtown La Fortuna. ☎ *2479-9997. Main courses: $6–$34. Reservations recommended during the high season. AE, MC, V. Open: Daily 11 a.m.–11 p.m.*

El Novillo de Arenal

$ **Between La Fortuna and Lake Arenal**   **STEAKHOUSE/COSTA RICAN**

This place is the definition of "nothing fancy." In fact, it's just some lawn furniture (tables and chairs) set on a concrete slab underneath a high, open, zinc roof. Still, it's perennially popular. The steaks are large and well prepared. The chicken and fish portions are large, as well and also nicely done. Meals come with garlic bread, fries, and some slaw. For a real local treat, order some fried yuca as a side. If the night is clear, you can get a good view of any volcanic activity from the parking lot here.

See map p. 256. On the road to Tabacón, 10km (6¼ miles) outside of La Fortuna. ☎ *2479-1910. Main courses: $5.35–$14. MC, V. Open: Daily 10 a.m.–10 p.m.*

Lava Lounge

$–$$ **Downtown La Fortuna**   **INTERNATIONAL**

Californian and Costa Rican cuisine mix in this rustic open-air restaurant. Healthy and hearty sandwiches, wraps, and salads are the main offering here. You can get a traditional burger or one made with fresh grilled tuna. For more substantial fare, there's traditional Costa Rican arroz con pollo and a *casado,* built around a thick pork chop. You can also get several different pasta dishes, and every evening there are dinner specials, which may include some coconut-battered shrimp with mango salsa, or a prime sirloin steak in green pepper or red wine sauce. The simple décor consists of a series of rustic wooden tables with either bench seats or heavy wooden chairs.

See map p. 256. La Fortuna. ☎ *2479-7365. Main courses: $4.50–$20. AE, MC, V. Open: Daily 11 a.m.–11:30 p.m.*

Exploring La Fortuna and the Arenal volcano area

Although the La Fortuna waterfall and various hot springs are easy to visit on your own, the other attractions and activities listed here are best experienced as part of an organized tour or outing.

The top attractions

Arenal Volcano and Arenal National Park

Arenal volcano is an impressive site. It's Costa Rica's most active volcano, regularly spewing lava from its near perfect cone. Still, the first thing you should know is that Arenal volcano borders a region of cloud and rain forests, and the volcano's cone is often socked in by fog. Many people come to Arenal and never get to see the exposed cone. Moreover, the volcano does go through periods when it's relatively quiet.

The second thing you should know is that you can't climb Arenal volcano; it's not safe, due to the constant activity. Several foolish people who have ignored this warning have lost their lives, and others have been severely injured. The most recent fatalities occurred in August 2000.

Still, waiting for and watching Arenal's regular eruptions is the main activity in La Fortuna and is best done at night, when the orange lava glows against the starry sky. Although you can simply look up from the middle of town and see Arenal erupting, the view is best from the north and west sides of the volcano along the road to Tabacón and toward the national park entrance. If you have a car, you can drive along this road, but if you've arrived by bus, you'll need to take a taxi or tour.

Arenal National Park constitutes an area of more than 2,880 hectares (7,114 acres), which includes the viewing and parking areas closest to the volcano. The trails inside the park are gorgeous and fun, running through forest and over old lava flows. However, at night, the view from inside the park is no better than on the roads just outside it.

If you don't have a car and you're staying in La Fortuna, every hotel in town and several tour offices offer night tours to the volcano. The tours usually don't actually enter the park; they stop on the road that runs between the park entrance and the Arenal Observatory Lodge. These tours cost between $10 and $30 per person. Often these volcano-viewing tours include a stop at one of the local hot springs, and the price goes up accordingly.

Although it's counterintuitive, the rainy season is often a better time to see the exposed cone of Arenal volcano, especially at night. I don't know why this is, but I've had excellent volcano-viewing sessions at various points during the rainy season, whereas during the dry season, the volcano can often be socked in solid for days at a time. The bottom line is that catching a glimpse of the volcano's cone is never a sure thing.

See map p. 256. 17km (11 miles) west of La Fortuna. ☎ **2461-8499.** *Admission: $10 per person. Open: Daily 8:30 a.m.–10 p.m.*

Caño Negro National Wildlife Refuge

Caño Negro National Wildlife Refuge is a vast network of marshes and rivers, best known for its amazing abundance of bird life, including roseate spoonbills, jabirus, herons, and egrets, but you can also see caimans and crocodiles. Bird-watchers should not miss this refuge, although keep in mind that the main lake dries up in the dry season (mid-Apr to Nov), which reduces the number of wading birds.

All the hotel tour desks and tour agencies in this area offer tours to Caño Negro. Full-day tours average between $55 and $65 per person. However, most of the trips run out of the La Fortuna area that are billed as Caño Negro tours never really enter the refuge but instead ply sections of the nearby Río Frio, featuring similar wildlife and ecosystems.

About 100km (62 miles) north of La Fortuna, near the town of Los Chiles. Admission: $10 per person. Open: Daily 7 a.m.–4 p.m.

La Fortuna Falls

The La Fortuna waterfall is an impressive jungle torrent plunging in a strong plume from dense rain forest into a perfectly round pool far below. There's a sign in town to indicate the road that leads out to the falls. You can drive or hike to just within viewing distance. It's another 15- to 20-minute hike down a steep and often muddy path to the pool formed by the waterfall. The hike back up will take slightly longer. You can swim, but stay away from the turbulent water at the base of the falls — several people have drowned here. Instead, check out and enjoy the calm pool just around the bend, or join the locals at the popular swimming hole under the bridge on the paved road, just after the turnoff for the road up to the falls. You can hike, drive, or sign up for one of the many horseback or mountain-bike tours out here.

See map p. 256. 5.5km (3½ miles) outside of La Fortuna. ☎ *2479-8360. Admission: $6. Open: Daily 8 a.m.–4 p.m.*

Soaking your weary bones

Arenal volcano has bestowed a terrific fringe benefit on the area around it: several naturally heated thermal springs. **Tabacón Grand Spa Thermal Resort** (☎ 2519-1900; www.tabacon.com) is the most extensive and luxurious spot where you can soak your tired bones. A series of variously sized pools, fed by natural springs, are spread among lush gardens. At the center is a large, warm, spring-fed swimming pool with a slide, a swim-up bar, and a perfect view of the volcano. One of the stronger streams flows over a sculpted waterfall, with a rock ledge underneath that provides a great spot to sit and receive a free hydraulic shoulder massage. The resort also has a spa on the grounds offering professional massages, mud masks, and other treatments at reasonable prices.

In addition to the poolside swim-up bar, you'll find a restaurant and separate snack bar and grill here. You can sign a credit card voucher when you enter and charge your food and drinks throughout your stay. This sure beats pulling soggy bills from your bathing suit.

Entrance fees are $85 for adults and $40 for children 11 and under. This rate includes either a buffet lunch or a dinner, and allows admission for a full day. After 6 p.m., you can enter for $45, not including any meals. The hot springs are open daily from noon to 10 p.m. Spa treatments can be scheduled as early as 8 a.m., and guests at the hotel here can enter at 10 a.m. There's a slight discount for entering after 7 p.m. The management sometimes enforces its policy of limiting the number of visitors at any one time, so reservations are recommended during the high season.

Baldi Termae (☎ 2479-9651), next to the Volcano Look Disco, are the first hot springs you'll come to as you drive from La Fortuna toward Tabacón. This place has grown substantially over the years, with many different pools, slides, and bars and restaurants spread around the expansive grounds. However, I find this place far less attractive than either of the other two options mentioned here. There's much more of a party vibe at Baldi, with loud music often blaring at some of the swim-up bars. Admission is $34.

Just across the street from Baldi Hot Springs is the unmarked entrance of my current favorite local hot spring, **Eco Termales** (☎ 2479-8484). Smaller and more intimate than Tabacón, this series of pools set amid lush forest and gardens is almost as picturesque and luxurious, although there are far fewer pools, the spa services are much less extensive, and there is no view of the volcano. Reservations are absolutely necessary here, and total admissions are limited so that it's never crowded. Admission is $29. These folks have added a restaurant serving basic local fare, but I recommend just coming for the springs.

Finally, the newest entrant in the field is **Tikokú** (☎ 2479-1700), which is located right beside Baldi, and run by the folks at Arenal Kioro. This spot features a row of eight descending sculpted pools. Admission is $24.

Los Lagos

Families with kids may want to head to **Jungla y Senderos Los Lagos.** Children and the young-at-heart love the pool, fountain, and water slide here. I come here more for the network of trails and small lakes that are also on the property. You'll also find a small crocodile hatchery and tilapia farm, a canopy tour, and some basic hot springs here.

See map p. 256. On the road to Tabacón, a few kilometers out of La Fortuna. ☎ 2479-1000. *www.hotelloslagos.com. Admission: $15 for daily use of facilities. Open: Daily 8 a.m.–4 p.m.*

More cool things to see and do

✓ **Canopy tours, bungee-jumping, hanging bridges, and canyoning:** Thrill seekers have plenty of options in this area. The best canopy tour operation in the area is **Sky Tram** (☎ 2479-9944; www.skytrek.com). Every tour at this complex begins with an open, gondola-style ride that takes off near the shores of Lake Arenal and rises up, providing excellent views of the lake and volcano. From here you can hike their series of trails and suspended bridges. In the end, you can either hike down, take the gondola, or strap on a harness and ride their cable canopy tour down to the bottom. The zip-line tour here features several very long and very fast sections, with some impressive views of the lake and volcano. The cost is $60 for the combined tram ride up and zip-line down. It's $50 to ride the tram round-trip. Sky Tram is open daily from 8 a.m. to 4 p.m.

If you'd like a bigger rush than the canopy tours offer, you should go canyoning. This adventure sport is a mix of hiking through and alongside a jungle river, punctuated with periodic rappels through and alongside the faces of rushing waterfalls. **Pure Trek Canyoning** (☎ 866-569-5723 in the U.S. and Canada, 2479-1313 in Costa Rica; www.puretrekcostarica.com) and **Desafío Expeditions** (☎ 2479-9464; www.desafiocostarica.com) both offer canyoning adventures. Pure Trek's trip is probably better for first-timers and families with kids, while Desafio's tour is just a bit more rugged and adventurous. Desafio charges $90; and Puretrek $95, for a half-day canyoning tour, and both offer various combination and full-day tours.

For a mellower means of getting into the forest canopy, you can hike the trails and bridges of **Arenal Hanging Bridges** (☎ **2290-0469;** www.hangingbridges.com). Located just over the Lake Arenal dam, this attraction is a complex of gentle trails and suspension bridges through a beautiful tract of primary forest. It's open daily from 7:30 a.m. to 4:30 p.m.; admission is $22. Guided tours and night tours are also available here.

Finally, you can take a bungee jump in downtown La Fortuna at **Arenal Bungee** (☎ **2479-7440;** www.arenalbungee.com). The bungee jump here is a 40m (130-ft.) fall from a steel tower constructed on the outskirts of downtown La Fortuna. They also offer the opportunity for a water landing, as well as a rocket launch, which is kind of the equivalent of becoming a human sling shot. Jumps, falls, and rocket shots cost $50. Various combination packages are available. This attraction is open from 9:30 a.m. to 9:30 p.m. daily, so you can even partake in the fun after dark.

✔ **Fishing:** Lake Arenal is the largest body of fresh water in Costa Rica, and fishing is a popular activity here. The big action on Lake Arenal is *guapote,* a Central American species of rainbow bass. However, you can also book fishing trips to Caño Negro, where snook, tarpon, and other game fish can be stalked. Most hotels and adventure-tour companies can arrange fishing excursions. Costs run around $150 to $250 for a half-day and $250 to $500 for a full day.

✔ **Horseback-riding:** Horseback-riding is a popular activity in this area, and you'll find scores of good rides on dirt back roads and through open fields and dense rain forest. Volcano and lake views come with the terrain on most rides. Horseback trips to the Río Fortuna waterfall are perhaps the most popular tours sold, but remember, the horse will get you only to the entrance; from there, you'll have to hike a bit. A horseback ride to the falls should cost between $20 and $40, including the entrance fee. Alternately, you can check in with the folks at **Cabalgata Don Tobias** (☎ **2479-1212;** www.cabalgatadontobias.com), which operates its tour on private land (a mix of farmland and forest), with some great views of the volcano.

✔ **Mountain-biking:** This region is very well suited for mountain-biking. Rides range in difficulty from moderate to extremely challenging. You can combine a day on a mountain bike with a visit to one or more of the more popular attractions here. **Bike Arenal** (☎ **866-465-4114** in the U.S. and Canada, 2479-9454 in Costa Rica; www.bikearenal.com) is the only dedicated operator in the field, with an excellent collection of top-notch bikes and equipment, as well as a wide range of tour possibilities.

✔ **White-water rafting:** If you want to get wet and wild, contact **Desafío Expeditions** (☎ 2479-9464; www.desafiocostarica. com) or **Wave Expeditions** (☎ 888/224-6105 in the U.S., or 2479-7262; www.waveexpeditions.com). Both of these companies offer daily raft rides of Class I to II, III, and IV to V on different sections of the Toro, Peñas Blancas, and Sarapiquí rivers. A half-day float trip on a nearby river costs around $65 per person; a full day of rafting on some rougher water costs $85 per person, depending on what section of what river you ride. Both companies also offer mountain-biking and most of the standard local guided trips. If you want a wet and personal ride, try Desafío's tour in inflatable kayaks, or "duckies."

Shopping for local treasures

Most of the shopping you'll find in and around La Fortuna is limited to pretty uninspired tourist fare. One major exception is the shop of a local family that produces a wide range of wood sculptures. As you leave the town of La Fortuna toward Tabacón, keep your eye on the right-hand side of the road. When you see a massive collection of wood sculptures and a building reading **Original Grand Gallery** (no phone), slow down and pull over. A local artisan and his family produce works in a variety of styles and sizes. They specialize in faces, many of them larger than a typical home's front door. You can also find a host of animal figures, ranging in style from purely representational to rather abstract. Another good shop for higher-end arts and crafts is **Galeria Lunática** (☎ 2479-8255), located on the main road in La Fortuna.

You'll also find good options as you drive around the lake. See "Along the Shores of Lake Arenal" later in this chapter for two good craft and gift shops found on the road that circles Lake Arenal.

Living it up after dark in La Fortuna and around the Arenal volcano

Waiting and watching for a volcanic eruption is the most popular after-dark activity in this neck of the woods. Taking a soak in one of the local hot springs runs a close second.

The **Volcano Look Disco** (☎ 2479-9616) is located just out of town on the road to Tabacón. This place is very popular with locals and really gets going on Friday and Saturday nights. There's also a small casino in downtown La Fortuna, **Luigi's Casino** (☎ 2479-9636), although it feels out of place in this rural town and is seldom crowded. For a simple drink and conversation, the open-to-the-street bar at **Don Rufino's** (see "Dining locally," earlier) is my favorite spot.

Fast Facts: La Fortuna and the Arenal Volcano

Ambulance

Call ☎ 128.

ATMs

You'll find ATMs at the Banco Nacional and Banco de Costa Rica in La Fortuna.

Country Code and City Code

The country code for Costa Rica is **506**. There are no city or area codes within Costa Rica. To call from the United States, dial 011-506 plus the eight-digit number. From within Costa Rica, you simply dial the eight-digit number.

Currency Exchange

Most hotels will exchange money for you at decent rates. To get official rates, head to either the Banco Nacional or Banco de Costa Rica in La Fortuna.

Fire

Call ☎ 118.

Hospitals

The closest hospital is Ciudad Quesada hospital (☎ 2401-1200), although there are several doctors and a local clinic (☎ 2479-9142) in La Fortuna.

Information

There are no official information offices in La Fortuna. Most hotels have a tour desk, concierge, or helpful front-desk staff.

Internet Access

Several Internet cafes are located in La Fortuna, and a few are strung along the road to the national park as well. Many hotels also have their own in-house Internet cafes or wireless service. Rates run between $1 and $3 per hour.

Newspapers

Several gift shops around town carry all the local papers, including the *Tico Times*.

Pharmacies

La Fortuna's best pharmacy, Farmacia Catedral (☎ 2479-9518), is on the main street just off the small park in downtown La Fortuna.

Police

Call ☎ **911** or 2479-9689.

Post Office

There is a post office in La Fortuna (☎ 2479-8070). Alternatively, most hotels can mail your letters and postcards for you.

Taxis

Taxis are plentiful in La Fortuna, and they frequently ply the road between La Fortuna and Tabacón Hot Springs. If you can't flag one down on the street, have your hotel call for you, or call Arenal Taxi (☎ 2479-9605).

Along the Shores of Lake Arenal

The area surrounding Lake Arenal is beautiful and serene. A visit here gives you a taste of rural Costa Rica. Rolling hills and virgin forest flank Lake Arenal, the largest lake in Costa Rica. The imposing cone of Arenal volcano lies just beyond the eastern end of the lake, while the small

Along the Shores of Lake Arenal

ACCOMMODATIONS ■
Chalet Nicholas **3**
Hotel Tilawa **8**
Mystica **6**
Villa Decary **1**

DINING ◆
Mystica **6**
Willy's Caballo Negro **2**

ATTRACTIONS ●
Tico Wind **5**
Tilawa Windsurfing Center **7**

SHOPPING ▲
Casa Delagua **4**
The Lucky Bug Gallery **2**

rural towns of Tilarán and Nuevo Arenal anchor the western end. The volcano's barren slopes are a stunning sight from here, especially when reflected in the waters of the lake.

From December through April, strong and steady winds buffet the western end of the lake. Locals used to curse these winds. Today they draw hoards of avid sailboarders and kitesurfers. Lake Arenal's combination of warm, fresh water, steady blows, and spectacular scenery, have made this spot a mecca for practitioners of these water sports.

Although the towns of Tilarán and Nuevo Arenal are little more than quiet rural communities, hotels have sprung up all along the shores of the lake. If you prefer to visit during less windy months, you may enjoy simply hanging out by the lake, hiking in the nearby forests, and catching glimpses of Arenal volcano.

Getting there

This is a region best visited in a rental car. There are no local airstrips, and bus service is infrequent. The drive around Lake Arenal is one of the prettiest in the country, although the road is periodically washed out in places, so a four-wheel-drive vehicle is highly recommended.

By car

From San José, take the Interamerican Highway west toward Puntarenas, and then continue north on this road to Cañas. In Cañas, turn east toward Tilarán. The drive takes four hours. If you're continuing on to Nuevo Arenal, follow the signs in town, which will put you on the road that skirts the shore of the lake. Nuevo Arenal is about a half-hour drive from Tilarán. You can also drive here from La Fortuna, along a scenic road that winds around the lake. From La Fortuna, it's approximately one hour to Nuevo Arenal and one and a half hours to Tilarán.

By bus

Transportes Tilaran express buses (☎ 2258-5792 in San José, 2695-5611 in Tilarán) leave San José for Tilarán several times a day from Calle 20 and Avenida 3. The trip lasts from four to five-and-a-half hours, depending on road conditions; the fare is $5.80.

A bus leaves from **Santa Elena** and **Monteverde** daily at 7 a.m. The fare for the three-hour trip is $2.30. Buses from **La Fortuna** leave for Tilarán daily at 8 a.m. and 4:30 p.m., returning at 7 a.m. and 12:30 p.m. The trip is two to three hours; the fare is $2.75.

From Tilarán, the bus to Santa Elena and Monteverde leaves daily at 12:30 p.m. Buses also leave regularly for Cañas, where you can catch buses north or south along the Interamerican Highway.

Orienting yourself along the shores of Lake Arenal

Nuevo Arenal is about 50km (31 miles) east of La Fortuna. Tilarán is another 35km (22 miles) beyond Nuevo Arenal. If you're coming from the Interamerican Highway, Tilarán is 24km (15 miles) northeast of Cañas.

Both Tilarán and Nuevo Arenal are small rural towns of just a few blocks in any direction. Each has a Catholic church and central plaza at the heart of town.

Getting around and getting information

Having a rental car is a good idea in this area. The road around Lake Arenal, is particularly beautiful and lends itself to some leisurely exploration. A four-wheel-drive vehicle is recommended, mostly for the added clearance.

If you need a taxi to get to a lodge on Lake Arenal, call **Taxis Unidos Tilarán** (☎ 2695-5324) in Tilarán, or **Taxis Nuevo Arenal** (☎ 2694-4415) in Nuevo Arenal.

Spending the night

Chalet Nicholas
$ Nuevo Arenal

This friendly bed-and-breakfast sits on a hill and features great views of the lake from its garden. All three rooms have a view of Arenal volcano in the distance. The upstairs loft room is the largest and comes with its own private deck. Chalet Nicholas is set on 6 hectares (15 acres) of land and has beautiful flower gardens, an organic vegetable garden, and an orchid garden. Behind the property are acres of forest through which you can hike in search of birds, orchids, butterflies, and other tropical treasures. No smoking is allowed in the house or on the grounds. Owners John and Catherine Nicholas go out of their way to make their guests feel at home, although their small pack of Great Danes may intimidate you when you first drive up.

See map p. 271. 2.5km (1½ miles) west of Nuevo Arenal. ☎ **2694-4041.** *www.chalet nicholas.com. Rack rates: $65 double. Rates include full breakfast. No credit cards.*

Hotel Tilawa
$–$$ Between Tilarán and Nuevo Arenal

Built to resemble the Palace of Knossos on the island of Crete, the Hotel Tilawa sits high on the slopes above the lake and has a sweeping vista down to the water. It's primarily a windsurfers' and kiteboarders' hangout. Unusual colors and antique paint effects give the hotel a weathered look; inside there are wall murals and other artistic paint treatments throughout. Rooms have dyed cement floors, Guatemalan bedspreads, big windows, and free Wi-Fi. Some have kitchenettes. Tilawa can arrange windsurfing, kiteboarding, mountain-biking, horseback-riding, and fishing trips. The hotel even boasts a small skate park for radical skateboarders and BMX freestyle bikers, which makes this a good place to bring teenagers. The hotel also has a small spa and one of the few microbrew operations in Costa Rica, both of which will appeal more to the adults.

See map p. 271. On the road between Tilarán and Nuevo Arenal. ☎ **2695-5050.** *Fax: 2695-5766. www.hotel-tilawa.com. Rack rates: $68–$110 double. Rates lower in the off season, higher during peak periods. MC, V.*

Mystica
$$ Between Tilarán and Nuevo Arenal

Set on a high hill above Lake Arenal, this Italian-run joint has simple but spacious and cheery rooms. The painted cement floors are kept immaculate, and the rooms get good ventilation from their large windows. All rooms open onto a long and broad shared veranda with a great view of the lake. There's also a separate private villa, with a kitchenette, fireplace, and large private deck. The owners can help you book a wide range of adventures and tours. There's a large, open-air yoga platform here, and the hotel has begun to host regular classes and retreats. Perhaps the star attraction here is the hotel's excellent Italian restaurant and pizzeria by the same name (see later in this chapter).

See map p. 271. On the road between Tilarán and Nuevo Arenal. ☎ 2692-1001. Fax: 2692-2097. www.mysticalodge.com. Rack rates: $100 double, $145 villa. Rates include continental breakfast. MC, V.

Villa Decary
$$–$$$ Nuevo Arenal

Named after a French explorer, and the rare palm species that he discovered and named, this small bed-and-breakfast is nestled on a hill above Lake Arenal, just outside the town of Nuevo Arenal. Each room comes with one queen-size and one twin bed, large picture windows, and a spacious private balcony with an excellent lake view. The rooms get plenty of light, and the bright Guatemalan bedspreads and white-tile floors create a vibrant look. The separate casitas have full kitchens, more room, and even better views of the lake from their slightly higher perches. Breakfasts are extravagant and memorable, with a steady stream of fresh fruits; fresh juice; strong coffee; homemade pancakes, waffles, or muffins; and usually an excellent omelet or soufflé. There's great bird-watching on the hotel grounds, and howler monkeys are common guests here as well.

See map p. 271. Nuevo Arenal. ☎ 800-556-0505 in the U.S. and Canada, 8383-3012 in Costa Rica, or tel/fax 2694-4330. www.villadecary.com. Rack rates: $99 double, $129–$149 casita for two. Rates include full breakfast. Extra person $15. MC, V.

Dining locally

Mystica
$–$$ Between Tilarán and Nuevo Arenal   ITALIAN/PIZZERIA

The restaurant at this Italian-run hotel has a wonderful setting high on a hill overlooking the lake. The large dining room features rustic wooden chairs and tables, varnished wood floors, colorful tablecloths, and abundant flower arrangements. The most striking features, aside from the view, are the large open fireplace on one end and, on the other, a large brick oven, in the shape of a small cottage, which turns out pizzas and foccacia. The pastas and delicious main dishes are authentically northern Italian. Whenever possible, Mystica uses fresh ingredients from its own organic garden.

See map p. 271. On the road between Tilarán and Nuevo Arenal. ☎ 2692-1001. Main courses: $6.50–$12. MC, V. Open: Daily noon to 9 p.m.

Willy's Caballo Negro
$$ Nuevo Arenal   GERMAN

The German owners of this attractive little roadside cafe serve up two different types of schnitzel, both chicken and veal cordon bleu, and a host of other old-world meat dishes. Try the Zigeuner Schnitzel, a tender veal cutlet in a slightly spicy sauce of onions and bell peppers, served with spaetzle. Despite the emphasis on meats and sausages, vegetarians will find several tasty and filling options here, including stuffed potatoes and eggplant Parmesan. The homemade pesto features locally grown organic macadamia nuts. Wooden tables are set around the edges of the round dining room, with a high peaked roof. Candles and creative lighting give the place a cozy and warm feel.

See map p. 271. Nuevo Arenal (about 3km/1¾ miles out of town on the road to Tilarán). ☎ *2694-4515. Main courses: $6–$14. MC, V. Open: Daily 7 a.m.–8 p.m.*

Exploring along the shores of Lake Arenal

The only true "attraction" in this region is the Arenal Botanical Gardens and Butterfly Sanctuary. However, if you have your own car, the scenic drive around the lake could be considered an attraction in and of itself. Combine a visit to the botanical gardens with a leisurely drive, and stops at the two unique gift shops listed in "Shopping for local treasures," later in this chapter.

Tilawa Windsurfing Center

From early December through April, strong and steady winds kick across the western end of Lake Arenal providing windsurfers and kiteboarders with the primary attraction and activity offered up by this region.

Kiteboarding is an adventure sport, similar to windsurfing, except you're tethered by a harness to a large kite, which you can steer via some control lines. The sport is known for the long and high jumps achieved by experienced practitioners.

If you want to try your hand at either windsurfing or kiteboarding, you can rent equipment from **Tilawa Windsurfing Center,** which has its facilities on one of the lake's few accessible beaches. Boards rent for around $55 per day, and lessons are also available.

Tico Wind (☎ 2692-2002; www.ticowind.com) is also popular with serious sailboarders. It sets up shop on the shores of the lake each year from December 1 to the end of April, which is when the winds here blow most fiercely. Rates run around $78 per day, including lunch, with multiday packages available.

See map p. 271. Located on the lake shore 8km (5 miles) from Tilarán. ☎ *2695-5050. www.windsurfcostarica.com. Open: Daily 7:30 a.m.–5 p.m. Admission: Variable rates for equipment rental and lessons.*

More cool things to see and do

✔ **Fishing:** Ask at your hotel if you want to try your hand at fishing for *guapote*. These large members of the cichlid family are known locally as rainbow bass. Their sharp teeth and fighting nature make them a real challenge. A half-day fishing trip should cost around $150 to $250 per boat, and a full day goes for around $250 to $500. Typically, the boats accommodate up to three people fishing. If you're interested in fishing, I recommend you check in with Captain Ron at **Arenal Fishing Tours** (☎ **2694-4678;** www.arenal fishing.com) or the **Puerto San Luis Yacht Club** (☎ **2695-5750;** www.hotelpuertosanluiscr.com).

✔ **Horseback riding and mountain biking:** The hills, fields, and forests of this area are perfect for exploring on horseback or riding a mountain bike. Any of the hotels in the area can hook you up with a horseback-riding tour for around $10 to $20 per hour. You can rent mountain bikes from the **Hotel Tilawa** (see earlier in this chapter).

✔ **Wakeboarding:** Lake Arenal is a big lake, and there are plenty of calm quiet corners to practice wakeboarding. If you're interested in lessons, or just a reliable pull on a wakeboard or water skis, contact **Fly Zone** (☎ **8339-5876;** www.flyzone-cr.com). Simple pulls behind their specialized boat cost about $85 per hour, including boards, skis, and any other necessary gear.

Shopping for local treasures

If you're in the area, don't miss the **Lucky Bug Gallery,** an excellent little roadside arts-and-crafts and souvenir shop, attached to Willy's Caballo Negro restaurant (see listing earlier in this chapter). This place features a host of functional and decorative pieces. Many of the works here are produced by the owner's triplet daughters.

About halfway between Nuevo Arenal and Tilarán is **Casa Delagua** (☎ **2692-2101)** the studio, gallery, and coffee shop of Costa Rican artist Juan Carlos Ruiz. These folks also have a good used-book and DVD collection on sale.

Fast Facts: Lake Arenal

Ambulance

Call ☎**128** or 2695-5256 in Tilarán.

ATMs

The Banco Nacional branches in both Tilarán and Nuevo Arenal have ATM machines.

Country Code and City Code

The country code for Costa Rica is **506.** There are no city or area codes within Costa Rica. To call from the United States, dial 011-506 plus the eight-digit number. From within Costa Rica, you simply dial the eight-digit number.

Currency Exchange

Most hotels will exchange money for you at decent rates. To get official rates, head to one of the banks in Tilarán or Nuevo Arenal.

Fire

Call ☎ **118.**

Hospitals

The closest hospital is Hospital Enrique Baltodano (☎ **2666-0011)** in downtown Liberia. There are also small health clinics in both Tilarán (☎ 2695-5299) and Nuevo Arenal (☎ 2694-4163).

Information

There are no official information offices in Tilarán or Nuevo Arenal. Most hotels have a tour desk, concierge, or helpful front-desk staff.

Internet Access

You'll find several Internet cafes in both Tilarán and Nuevo Arenal. Many hotels also offer Internet access. Rates run between $1 and $3 per hour.

Pharmacies

There's a pharmacy at the small health clinic in Tilarán (☎ 2695-5299), which is located in the center of town. There's also a pharmacy at the health clinic in Nuevo Arenal (☎ 2694-0405), located on the main street in the center of town.

Police

Call ☎ **911** or 2695-5011 in Tilarán.

Post Office

There are post offices in both Tilarán (☎ 2695-5387) and Nuevo Arenal (☎ 2694-4310). Alternatively, most hotels can mail your letters and postcards for you.

Taxis

Taxis are plentiful in both Tilarán and Nuevo Arenal. If you don't feel like flagging one down on the street, have your hotel call for you, or call Taxis Unidos Tilarán (☎ 2695-5324) in Tilarán or Taxis Nuevo Arenal (☎ 2694-4415) in Nuevo Arenal.

Part VII
Touring the Rest of Costa Rica

The 5th Wave   By Rich Tennant

COSTA RICA'S ESCALATOR FALLS

In this part . . .

This part is the place to turn if you're looking to explore Costa Rica's less-traveled roads and destinations. In this part, you find out all about the beautiful intimate beach resorts and secret getaway spots of the southern Nicoya Peninsula. Nature lovers will want to read up on Corcovado National Park and the remote, and often luxurious, rain-forest lodges of the rich southern zone. Finally, Costa Rica's Caribbean coast, which often gets short shrift, is covered in detail, from the jungle canals and rain forests of Tortuguero, to the sleepy beach towns of Cahuita and Puerto Viejo.

Chapter 19

Seeking Solitude in Southern Nicoya

In This Chapter

▶ Landing a great room in Montezuma
▶ Bathing in the pool of a beautiful jungle waterfall
▶ Enjoying Malpaís before the adoring throngs overrun it
▶ Opting for a romantic and luxurious getaway at Punta Islita

The beaches and resorts of the southern Nicoya Peninsula are more isolated, less developed, and just a bit wilder than those found to the north on Guanacaste's Gold Coast. This is a place to come if you really want to get away from it all.

The two main beach destinations in this area are Montezuma and Malpaís (which is a general term for a string of isolated beaches stretching north from Malpaís itself). Both offer miles of uncrowded beaches and lush forests all around. Montezuma features a couple of gorgeous waterfalls to visit, while Malpaís is becoming one of the country's top surf destinations.

On the northern stretch of the Nicoyan coastline sits Punta Islita, one of the most exclusive and luxurious little resorts in the country.

Montezuma

For decades, Montezuma enjoyed near-legendary status among backpackers, UFO seekers, hippie expatriates, and European budget travelers. Although it still maintains its alternative vibe, Montezuma has matured, and is now a great destination for all manner of travelers looking for a quiet beach retreat surrounded by some stunning scenery. Today the town has a well-tended, somewhat booming feel to it, and there are lodgings of value and quality in all price ranges. After all, the natural beauty, miles of almost abandoned beaches, rich wildlife, and jungle waterfalls first made Montezuma famous, and they continue to make this one of my favorite beach towns in Costa Rica.

Getting there

Flying to Tambor and taking a taxi to Montezuma is the fastest and easiest way to travel out here. Taking a car or bus, however, includes a pretty and relaxing ferry ride.

By air

The nearest airport is in Tambor, 17km (11 miles) away. **Sansa** (☎ **877-767-2672** in the U.S. and Canada, 2290-4100 in Costa Rica; www. flysansa.com) and **Nature Air** (☎ **800-235-9272** in the U.S. and Canada, 2299-6000 in Costa Rica; www.natureair.com) both have a couple of daily flights to Tambor. Flight duration is about 30 minutes, and fares run $94 to $99 each way.

Some of the hotels listed later in this chapter may be willing to pick you up in Tambor for a reasonable fee. If not, you'll have to hire a taxi, which could cost anywhere from $20 to $30. Taxis are generally waiting to meet most regularly scheduled planes.

By car and ferry

The traditional route here is to take the Interamerican Highway from San José to Puntarenas and catch the ferry to Paquera. Montezuma is about 75 minutes south of Paquera.

Naviera Tambor (☎ **2661-2084**) ferries to Paquera leave Puntarenas roughly every two hours between 5 a.m. and 9 p.m. The trip takes one and a half hours. The fare is around $12 for a car and driver, $1.50 or so more for additional adults, 80¢ for children. I recommend arriving early during the peak season and on weekends because lines can be long; if you miss the ferry, you'll have to wait almost two hours or more for the next one. Moreover, the ferry schedule changes frequently, with fewer ferries during the off season, and the occasional extra ferry during the high season to meet demand. Checking in advance is always best.

The car ferry from Paquera to Puntarenas leaves roughly every two hours between 8 a.m. and 9 p.m.

By bus and ferry

Transportes Rodriguez Hermanos (☎ **2642-0219**) runs three daily direct buses between San José and Montezuma. The buses leave from the Coca-Cola bus terminal at Calle 12 and Avenida 5 at 6 a.m. and 2 p.m. The fare is around $12, including the ferry ride, and the trip takes a little over four hours.

Alternatively, it takes two buses and a ferry ride to get to Montezuma. Express buses (☎ **2222-0064**) for Puntarenas leave San José daily every hour, between 6 a.m. and 7 p.m., from Calle 16 and Avenida 12. Trip duration is two and a half hours; the fare is $3.

Montezuma

ACCOMMODATIONS ■
Amor de Mar **11**
El Jardin **7**
Hotel La Aurora **6**
Hotel Los Mangos **9**
Hotel Lucy **10**
Ylang-Ylang Beach Resort **1**

DINING ◆
El Sano Banano Village Cafe **5**
Playa de los Artistas **8**
Ylang-Ylang **1**

ATTRACTIONS ●
Montezuma Waterfall **12**
Waterfall Canopy Tour **13**

NIGHTLIFE ★
Chico's Bar **2**
Hotel Moctezuma **4**
El Sano Banano Village
   Café **5**

SHOPPING ▮
Piedra Colorado **3**

From Puntarenas, you can take one of the car ferries mentioned above or the passenger launch *Paquereña* (☎ 2641-0515), which leaves from the pier behind the market at 11:30 a.m. and 4 p.m. The ferry trip takes one and a half hours; the fare is 90¢. A bus south to Montezuma will be waiting to meet the ferry when it arrives in Paquera. The bus ride takes another 55 minutes; the fare is $2.50.

Be careful not to take the Naranjo ferry — it doesn't meet with regular onward bus transportation to Montezuma.

When you're ready to return, buses for Paquera leave Montezuma daily at regular intervals, timed to meet up with a departing ferry.

Orienting yourself in Montezuma

As the winding mountain road that descends into Montezuma bottoms out, you turn left onto a small dirt road that defines the village proper.

On this 1-block road, you'll find El Sano Banano Village Café and, across from it, a small park with a basketball court and children's playground. The bus stops at the end of this road. From here, hotels are scattered up and down the beach and around the village's few sand streets.

Buses are met by hordes of locals trying to corral you to one of the many budget hotels. *Remember:* They're getting a commission for every body they bring in, so their information is biased.

Getting around and getting information

The town itself is very compact, and you can easily walk from most hotels to the beach and nearby waterfall.

Montezuma doesn't have a huge number of taxis, but you can usually find one hanging around the small central downtown area. Taxis often park in front of the El Sano Banano Village Café. If you can't find one there, you can call **Gilberto** (☎ **2642-0241**) or **Ronald** (☎ **8822-0610**) for a cab.

Montezuma has no official tourist information offices, but several all-purpose tour agencies act as such. **Cocozuma Traveler** (☎ **2642-0911;** www.cocozuma.com) and **Montezuma Travel Adventures** (☎ **2642-0808;** www.montezumatraveladventures.com) can both arrange horseback riding; boat excursions; scuba-dive and snorkel tours; rafting trips; car and motorcycle rentals; airport transfers; international phone, fax, and Internet service; and currency exchange.

Spending the night

Amor de Mar
$–$$ **Montezuma**

It would be difficult to imagine a more idyllic spot in this — or *any* — price range. With its wide expanse of neatly trimmed grass sloping down to the sea, tide pools (one of which is as big as a small swimming pool), and hammocks slung from the mango trees, this is the perfect place for anyone who wants to do some serious relaxing. The rooms are all housed in a beautifully appointed two-story building, which abounds in varnished hardwoods. Most of the rooms have plenty of space and receive lots of sunlight. The big porch on the second floor is a great place for reading or just gazing out to sea. Only breakfast and lunch are served here, but they're served on a beautiful open-air patio overlooking the sea. These folks also rent out a large, fully equipped, two-story, four-bedroom house right next to the hotel.

See map p. 283. Montezuma. ☎ */fax* **2642-0262.** www.amordemar.com. *Rack rates: $50–$60 double with shared bathroom, $70–$95 double with private bathroom, $200 house. Rates lower in the off season. V.*

El Jardin
$ Downtown Montezuma

Set on a steep hill, right on the crossroads leading into "downtown," this is a good choice if you're looking for a comfortable and well-equipped room close to the action. The rooms are located in a series of different buildings spread across the hillside. No. 9 is my favorite, with pretty stonework in the bathroom, a greater sense of privacy than some of the others, and a good view from its private terrace. A two-level pool and Jacuzzi is located in a relaxing little garden area. Although the hotel doesn't have a restaurant, the town and its many dining options are just steps away.

See map p. 283. Montezuma. ☎ **2642-0548.** *tel/fax 2642-0074.* www.hotelel jardin.com. *Rack rates: $65–$75 double. Rates lower in the off season. MC, V.*

Hotel La Aurora
$ Montezuma

It's hard to beat the value and laid-back vibe you'll find at this longstanding budget hotel. Located at the heart of the tiny village, the rooms are spread out over two neighboring buildings fronting Montezuma's small central park and playground. The rooms here are clean and well-kept. I prefer the older rooms, which are located in a spacious, three-story, wooden building. There's even a two-room apartment on the third floor here, with a private balcony and a bit of an ocean view through the treetops. The hotel also features a small lending library, some hammocks and comfortable chairs, a communal kitchen, and flowering vines growing up the walls. In fact, plants and vines are all over La Aurora, which keeps things cool and gives the place a very tropical feel. Fresh coffee, tea, and hearty breakfasts are served each morning.

See map p. 283. Montezuma. ☎/fax **2642-0051.** www.playamontezuma.net. *Rack rates: $45–$70 double. Rates include taxes. Rates lower in the off season. AE, MC, V.*

Hotel Los Mangos
$–$$ Montezuma

Situated across the road from the water, a little bit before the waterfall, on the road toward Cabo Blanco, this place takes its name from the many mango trees under which the bungalows are built. (If mango is your passion, come in May, when it's in season.) The shared-bathroom budget rooms are very basic and a bit worn, but they're a decent value and you do get access to the pool. The roomy, thatch-roofed octagonal bungalows built of Costa Rican hardwoods are the better choice. Each has a small porch with rocking chairs, a thatched roof, a good amount of space, and ceiling fans. Still, even these are pretty spartan. The swimming pool is built to resemble a natural pond — there's even an artificial waterfall flowing into it — and there's a separate Jacuzzi. These folks have a pretty and ample open-air yoga studio, and daily classes are offered.

See map p. 283. Montezuma, Cóbano de Puntarenas. ☎ *2642-0076. Fax: 2642-0259.* www.hotellosmangos.com. *Rack rates: $35 double with shared bathroom, $75 double with private bathroom, $95 bungalow. Rates lower in the off season. AE, MC, V.*

Hotel Lucy
$ Montezuma

Situated on a pretty section of beach, a bit south of town, in front of Los Mangos, this converted two-story home has the best location of any budget lodging in Montezuma. If you can snag a second-floor room with an ocean view, you'll be in budget heaven. The beach here is a bit rough and rocky for swimming, but the sunbathing and sunset views are beautiful.

See map p. 283. Montezuma, Cóbano de Puntarenas. ☎ *2642-0273. Rack rates: $22 double with shared bathroom, $25 double with private bathroom. No credit cards.*

Ylang-Ylang Beach Resort
$$$–$$$$ Montezuma

Set in a lush patch of forest just steps away from the sand, the hotel offers rooms that are about a 15-minute walk northeast of town along the beach. Rooms and cabins come in a variety of shapes and sizes. Coco Joe's Bungalow is the largest cabin and features a luscious wraparound balcony and a small sleeping loft. But I also like the smaller cabins, which are yellow, reinforced-concrete, geodesic domes that look like igloos. Or, you can opt for a "jungalow" — a large tent set on a wooden platform, featuring an indoor sink, small fridge, ceiling fan, and private deck. These units share nearby bathrooms and showers. There's a beautiful little swimming pool with a sculpted waterfall, and the entire operation is set amid untouched forest and lush gardens planted with lots of banana, heliconia, and elephant-ear plants. There is no road to the resort, so arrival and check-in are taken care of at the downtown El Sano Banano Village Café.

See map p. 283. Montezuma. ☎ *2642-0636. Fax: 2642-0068.* www.ylangylang resort.com. *Rack rates: $160–$295 double room. Rates include breakfast and dinner. Rates lower in the off season. AE, MC, V.*

Dining locally

El Sano Banano Village Café
$–$$ Montezuma   VEGETARIAN/INTERNATIONAL

Delicious vegetarian meals, including nightly specials, sandwiches, and salads, are the specialty of this perennially popular Montezuma restaurant. You'll also find a good selection of fresh fish and chicken dishes. Lunches feature hefty sandwiches on whole-wheat bread and filling fish and vegetarian dishes. The yogurt fruit shakes are fabulous, but I like to get a little more decadent and have one of the mocha ice cream shakes. At night, late-run blockbusters and art-house flicks are shown on a large screen here.

See map p. 283. On the main road into the village. ☎ **2642-0944.** *Main courses: $4–$21. AE, MC, V. Open: Daily 6 a.m.–10 p.m.*

Playa de los Artistas
$$ Montezuma   ITALIAN/MEDITERRANEAN

This open-air restaurant is housed in an old house fronting the beach. There are only a few tables, so arrive early. If you don't get a seat and you feel hearty, try the low wooden table surrounded by tatami mats on the sand. Dishes are served in large, broad, wooden bowls set on ceramic-ringed coasters or on fresh banana leaves laid over rough-hewn hunks of wood. The outdoor grill is great for grilled fish and seafood. Every meal comes with plenty of fresh bread for soaking up the sauces. The menu changes nightly but always features several fish and seafood dishes. The fresh grouper in a black pepper sauce is phenomenal, as is the grilled squid.

See map p. 283. Across from Hotel Los Mangos. ☎ **2642-0920.** *Reservations recommended. Main courses: $6.50–$14. No credit cards. Open: Mon–Wed 5–10:30 p.m., Thurs–Sat 11:30 a.m.–10 p.m.*

Ylang-Ylang
$$$ Montezuma   FUSION

A pretty, open-air venue, Ylang-Ylang features a sculpted bar with indigenous and wildlife motifs. The menu is broad with a prominent Asian influence, ranging from fresh sushi to jumbo shrimp in a pineapple and coconut sauce to a vegetarian teriyaki stir-fry. There are also several crepe and pasta options and plenty of fresh seafood dishes. For lunch, you can have a bruschetta or some cool gazpacho and be just a few steps from the sand when you're done.

See map p. 283. At the Ylang-Ylang Beach Resort. ☎ **2642-0402.** *Reservations recommended. Main courses: $10–$25. AE, MC, V. Open: Daily 7 a.m.–9:30 p.m.*

Exploring Montezuma

Both of the major attractions here are easily visited on your own. You can either drive yourself or take a taxi or shuttle to the **Cabo Blanco Absolute Nature Reserve,** while the trailhead for the Montezuma waterfall is just a short walk from the center of town.

The top attractions

Cabo Blanco Absolute Nature Reserve

As beautiful as the beaches around Montezuma are, the beaches at **Cabo Blanco Absolute Nature Reserve** are even more stunning. Located at the southernmost tip of the Nicoya Peninsula, Cabo Blanco is a national park that preserves a nesting site for brown pelicans, magnificent frigate birds, and brown boobies. The main beach here is backed by lush tropical forest that is home to howler monkeys. You can hike through the preserve's lush forest right down to the deserted, pristine Playa Cabo Blanco, which is 4km (2½ miles) away. Or, you can take a shorter 2km (1¼-mile) loop trail through the primary forest here. This is Costa Rica's oldest official biorserve; it was set up thanks to the pioneering efforts of conservationists Karen Mogensen and Nicholas Wessberg.

The trails here are gentle and well-marked. However, if you want to see and learn about the local flora and fauna, you should hire one of the guides who hang out around the park office. A two-hour guided hike should cost around $25 to $35 for a group of up to four people.

Cabo Blanco Absolute Nature Reserve is located 11km (6¾ miles) south of the village, along a rough dirt road. Shuttle buses head from Montezuma to Cabo Blanco roughly every two hours beginning at 8 a.m., and then turn around and bring folks from Cabo Blanco to Montezuma; the last one leaves Cabo Blanco around 5 p.m. The fare is $2 each way. These shuttles often don't run during the off season. Alternatively, you can share a taxi: The fare is around $15 to $20 per taxi, which can hold four or five passengers.

Cabo Blanco Absolute Nature Reserve is located 11km (6¾ miles) south of Montezuma, along the only road out of town. ☎ *2642-0093. Admission: $10. Open: Wed–Sun 8 a.m.–4 p.m.*

Montezuma Waterfall

Located a vigorous 20-minute hike into the rain forest, the Montezuma waterfall is a tropical fantasy, with a large torrent pouring down into a deep, cool pool. A couple of waterfalls are actually located up this stream, but the upper falls are, by far, the more spectacular. This is a popular spot and can get crowded during the high season and on weekends.

Be very careful when climbing close to the rushing water and if you plan on taking any dives into the pools below. The rocks are quite slippery, and several people each year get very scraped up, break bones, and otherwise hurt themselves here.

You'll find the trail to the falls just over the bridge south of the village (on your right, just past Las Cascadas restaurant). At the first major outcropping of rocks, the trail disappears and you have to scramble up the rocks and river for a bit. A trail occasionally reappears for short stretches. Just stick close to the stream and you'll eventually hit the falls.

See map p. 283. 7km (4 ½ miles) southeast of Cóbano, 45km (28 miles) south of Paquera, 18km (11 miles) south of Tambor.

More cool things to see and do

  ✔ **Braving a canopy tour:** The **Waterfall Canopy Tour** (☎ **8823-6111** or 2642-0808; www.suntrailsadventures.com) is built right alongside Montezuma's famous falls. The tour, which features 9 cables connecting 11 platforms, includes a stop to swim at a large pool above the largest drop in the falls. This tour is run several times each day and costs $40 per person.

✔ **Chilling on the beach:** The ocean here is a gorgeous royal blue, and beautiful beaches stretch out along the coast on either side of town. Be careful, though: The waves can occasionally be too rough for casual swimming, and you need to be aware of stray rocks at your feet. Be sure you know where the rocks and tide are before doing any bodysurfing. The best places to swim are a couple hundred meters north of town in front of **El Rincón de los Monos,** or several kilometers farther north at Playa Grande.

If you're driving out to Cabo Blanco, you'll pass through the tiny village of **Cabuya.** You'll find a couple of hidden patches of beach to discover around here, if you poke around some of the deserted dirt roads.

In the center of the village, you'll find some rental shops where you can rent boogie boards and snorkeling equipment (although the water must be very calm for snorkeling).

✔ **Horseback riding:** Several people around the village will rent you horses for around $10 to $20 an hour, although most people choose to do a guided four-hour horseback tour for $30 to $50. The most popular ride is to a second waterfall 8km (5 miles) north of Montezuma. Dubbed **El Chorro,** this waterfall cascades into a tide pool at the edge of the ocean. The pool here is a delightful mix of fresh water and seawater, and you can bathe while gazing out over the sea and rocky coastline. When the water is clear and calm, this is one of my favorite swimming holes in all of Costa Rica. However, a massive landslide in 2004 filled in much of this pool and also somewhat lessened the drama and beauty of the actual falls. Moreover, the pool here is dependent upon the tides — it disappears entirely at very high tide. Luis, whose rental place is down the road that leads from town out to the beach, is a reliable source for horses, as is "Roger, the horse guy" — any local can direct you to him. However, you'll find the best-cared-for and -kept horses at **Finca Los Caballos** (☎ 2642-0124), which is located up the hill on the road leading into Montezuma.

Shopping in Montezuma

Plenty of simple souvenir stores, as well as itinerant artisans selling their wares on the street, rest in Montezuma; most of the offerings are pretty standard fare. However, it's definitely worth stopping in at **Piedra Colorado** (☎ 2642-0612 or 8841-5855) to check out their impressive silver, stone, and polished-shell creations. This place is located in the tiny strip mall in the center of Montezuma.

Living it up after dark in Montezuma

The local action is centered on a couple of bars in downtown Montezuma. Head to either **Chico's Bar** (no phone) or the bar at the **Hotel Moctezuma**

(☎ 2642-0058). Both are located on the main strip in town facing the water. If your evening tastes are mellower, **El Sano Banano Village Café** (☎ 2642-0944) doubles as the local movie house. Nightly DVD releases are projected on a large screen; the selection ranges from first run to quite artsy, and there's a constantly growing library of more than 800 movies. The movies begin at 7:30 p.m. and require a minimum purchase of $5.50.

Fast Facts: Montezuma

Ambulance

Call ☎ 128.

ATMs

You'll find an ATM in downtown Montezuma, as well as at the Banco Nacional in Cóbano.

Country Code and City Code

The country code for Costa Rica is **506**. There are no city or area codes within Costa Rica. To call from the United States, dial 011-506 plus the eight-digit number. From within Costa Rica, you simply dial the eight-digit number.

Currency Exchange

Most hotels will exchange money for you at decent rates. To get official rates, head to the Banco Nacional in Cóbano.

Fire

Call ☎ 118.

Hospitals

The closest hospital is Hospital Monseñor Sanabria in Puntarenas (☎ 2663-0033), although there are several doctors and a local clinic (☎ 2642-0208) in Cóbano.

Information

Montezuma has no official information offices. Most hotels have a tour desk, concierge, or helpful front-desk staff.

Internet Access

Several Internet cafes are located in Montezuma; all are located in the small central downtown area.

Newspapers

Several gift shops around town carry all the local papers, including the *Tico Times*.

Pharmacies

There's no true pharmacy in Montezuma. You can get basic pharmaceutical products at the two minimarts in town. For a better selection, head to the Farmacia Amiga (☎ 2642-0685), located in Cóbano, at the main intersection for Montezuma.

Police

Call ☎ 911 or 2642-0770.

Post Office

There is a post office in Cóbano (☎ 2642-0323). Alternatively, most hotels can mail your letters and postcards for you.

Taxis

Only a limited number of taxis are in Montezuma. Most congregate in the tiny downtown area or park in front of El Sano Banano Village Café. Alternatively, you can call Gilberto (☎ 2642-0241) or Ronald (☎ 8822-0610) for a cab.

Punta Islita

On the northern stretch of coast making up the Nicoya Peninsula sits one of Costa Rica's premier, small, luxury resorts, **Hotel Punta Islita** (☎ 866-446-4053 in the U.S. and Canada, 2231-6122 in Costa Rica, 2661-4044 at the hotel; Fax: 2231-0715; www.hotel puntaislita.com). Nothing else is around, but if you're looking for fabulous rooms, great views, an isolated beach, personalized service, and plenty of amenities and activities to choose from, this spot is perfect.

Punta Islita is isolated on a high bluff between two mountain ridges that meet the sea. The rooms here are done up in a Santa Fe style, with red Mexican floor tiles, Neo-Navajo-print bedspreads, and adobe-colored walls offset with sky-blue doors and trim. Each room has a king-size bed and a private patio with a hammock; a few of these also have Jacuzzis. The suites come with a separate sitting room and a private two-person plunge pool or Jacuzzi; the villas have two or three bedrooms, their own private swimming pools, and full kitchens. The open-air poolside restaurant here serves excellent Continental cuisine with an emphasis on fresh local ingredients.

The beach below the hotel is a small crescent of gray-white sand with a calm, protected section at the northern end. It's about a ten-minute hike, but the hotel will shuttle you down and back if you don't feel like walking. You can take the hotel's small canopy tour, which leaves from just below the small gym and ends just steps from the beach. There's a rancho bar and grill down there, for when you get hungry or thirsty, and a lap pool for when the waves are too rough. The hotel has an excellent little spa offering a full range of spa treatments and services, including regular classes and activities. They even have a 9-hole executive golf course and driving range. Prices run from $300 for doubles, $420 to $480 for suites, and $625 to $920 for villa rooms. Room and suite rates include breakfast.

Although you can drive here from San José or Liberia, I highly recommend flying. The flight takes about 55 minutes, and both **Nature Air** (☎ 800-235-9272 in the U.S. and Canada, 2299-6000 in Costa Rica; www.natureair.com) and **Sansa** (☎ 877-767-2672 in the U.S. and Canada, 2290-4100 in Costa Rica; www.flysansa.com) fly here, as do several charter companies. Nature Air leaves out of the Pavas airport; Sansa leaves out of Juan Santamaría International. Charter companies work out of both. Because Punta Islita is such a luxury resort, with its own little airstrip, letting them book the travel and add it onto your bill is best. Rates run from $115 to $130 per person each way.

Malpaís and Santa Teresa

Malpaís translates as "badlands"; though that moniker may have fit at one time, it's no longer very appropriate. The beach here is a long, wide expanse of light sand, dotted with rocky outcroppings. Sure, it can get rough here, but the surfers love it. The road out here from Cóbano used to be even rougher than the surf, but it's gradually being tamed.

This place is one of Costa Rica's most rapidly developing hot spots, and hotels and restaurants are opening up at a steady pace. Still, it will take some time before this area becomes overly crowded. What you'll find in Malpaís and Santa Teresa today is a scattering of beach hotels and simple restaurants, miles of nearly deserted beach, and easy access to some lush jungle and a host of adventure-tour options.

Getting there

Flying to Tambor and taking a taxi to Malpaís or Santa Teresa is the fastest and easiest way to travel out here. Taking a car or bus, however, includes a pretty and relaxing ferry ride across the Golfo de Nicoya.

By air

The nearest airport is in Tambor, 17km (11 miles) away. **Sansa** (☎ **877-767-2672** in the U.S. and Canada, 2290-4100 in Costa Rica; www.flysansa.com) and **Nature Air** (☎ **800-235-9272** in the U.S. and Canada, 2299-6000 in Costa Rica; www.natureair.com) both have a couple of daily flights to Tambor. Flight duration is about 30 minutes, and fares run $94 to $99 each way.

Some of the hotels listed here may be willing to pick you up in Tambor for a reasonable fee. If not, you'll have to hire a taxi, which could cost anywhere from $40 to $45. **Taxis** are generally waiting to meet most regularly scheduled planes, but if you can't find one, you can call **Gilberto** (☎ **2642-0241**) or **Ronald** (☎ **8822-0610**) for a ride.

By car and ferry

Follow the directions earlier in this chapter to Montezuma. At Cóbano, follow the signs to Malpaís and Playa Santa Teresa. It's another 12km (7½ miles) or so down a very rough dirt road that pretty much requires four-wheel-drive and is sometimes (although rarely) impassable during the rainy season.

By bus and ferry

Follow the directions earlier in this chapter for getting to Montezuma, but get off the Montezuma bus in Cóbano. From Cóbano, there are buses daily for Malpaís and Santa Teresa at 10:30 a.m. and 2:30 p.m.; the fare is $1.50. Buses return daily to Cóbano at 7 a.m., 11:30 a.m., and 3:30 p.m.

These bus schedules are subject to change according to demand, road conditions, and the whims of the bus company. Moreover, as the popularity of this destination grows, more buses are occasionally added, so checking with your hotel in advance is a good idea.

If you miss the bus connection, you can hire a cab in Cóbano for around $20.

Malpaís and Santa Teresa

NICARAGUA

Caribbean Sea

San José

Santa Teresa   COSTA RICA

PACIFIC OCEAN   PANAMA

El Peñon

Santa Teresa

Soccer Field

PACIFIC OCEAN

El Cruce

Playa El Carmen

Malpaís

0   0.5 mi
0   0.5 km

Surfing spots

ACCOMMODATIONS ■
Flor Blanca Resort **9**
Mal País Surf Camp & Resort **3**
Milarepa **8**
Trópico Latino Lodge **6**

DINING ◆
Nectar **9**
Soda Piedra Mar **2**

NIGHTLIFE ★
Frank's Place **4**
La Lora **7**
Mal País Surf Camp **3**
Night & Day **5**

ATTRACTIONS ●
Canopy del Pacifico **1**

Orienting yourself in Malpaís and Santa Teresa

Malpaís and Santa Teresa are two tiny beach villages. In fact, there are no real towns here — just a string of hotels, restaurants, and assorted shops spread along a rough, coastal, dirt road.

As you reach the ocean, the road forks; Malpaís is to your left, Playa Carmen is straight ahead, and Santa Teresa is to your right. If you continue beyond Santa Teresa, you'll come to the even more deserted beaches of Playa Hermosa and Manzanillo (not to be confused with beaches of the same names to be found elsewhere in the country).

Getting around and getting information

This is an area where it's a good idea to have a rental car. **Alamo** (☎ 2640-0526) and **Budget Rent A Car** (☎ 2640-0418) both have offices in Malpais.

Another good option is to rent an ATV. Several hotels and a few shops in the area will rent a rugged ATV for around $45 to $70 per day. If you need a taxi, call **Miguel** (☎ 8819-9021 or 2640-0261) or **Richard** (☎ 8317-7614 or 2640-0003).

Your best bet for information out this way will definitely be your hotel front-desk staff.

Spending the night

Flor Blanca Resort
$$$$$ Playa Santa Teresa

This resort hotel is, hands down, the most luxurious option in this neck of the woods and one of the top hotels in the country. The individual villas are huge, with a vast central living area opening onto a spacious veranda. The furnishings, decorations, and architecture boast a mix of Latin American and Asian influences, with some African adornments thrown in for good measure. Most overlook the lush gardens here, and about half have views through these gardens to the sea. The beachfront villas are the best.

Every villa features a large open-air bathroom with a garden shower and teardrop-shaped tub set amid flowering tropical foliage. You can opt for either a one-bedroom villa with a four-poster king-size bed in the main bedroom or a two-bedroom/two-bathroom villa better suited to families, with two twin beds in a separate upstairs bedroom. You'll find several examples of the resort's namesake tree planted around the grounds.

The restaurant, Nectar, features wonderfully prepared creative fusion cuisine (see listing later in this chapter). There's a full-size and active dojo on grounds, where yoga, kickboxing, and cardio workout classes are regularly offered. The beautiful free-form pool is on two levels, with a sculpted waterfall connecting them and a shady, Indonesian-style gazebo off to one side for lounging around in.

See map p. 293. Playa Santa Teresa. ☎ *2640-0232. Fax: 2640-0226.* `www.flor` `blanca.com`. *Rack rates: $475–$600 double, $650–$750 2-bedroom villa for 4; $850 honeymoon house. Rates include full breakfast. Rates lower during the off season, higher during peak weeks. AE, DC, MC, V. No children 13 or under.*

Mal País Surf Camp & Resort
$–$$ **Malpaís**

Whether you're a wannabe or an experienced wave rider, this is the place to hang out when you're not hanging ten in Malpaís. You'll find a wide range of accommodations here, reflected in the equally wide range of prices. The most basic rooms are open-air ranchos with gravel floors, lathe-and-bamboo walls, bead curtains for doors, and shared bathrooms. From here, your options get progressively more comfortable, ranging from shared-bathroom bunk-bed rooms to new, deluxe, poolside villas to private houses with all the amenities. You can also pitch a tent.

A delightful, free-form tile pool is in the center of the complex, and the large, open main lodge area serves as a combination restaurant/bar/lounge and surfboard storage area. There's satellite TV with surf videos playing most of the day, as well as pool, Ping-Pong, and foosball tables. The overall vibe here is loose and funky, as it should be. The restaurant serves filling, fresh, and, at times, quite creative cuisine, depending on how accomplished the itinerant surf-chef-of-the-month is. Surf rentals, lessons, and video sessions are all available.

See map p. 293. Malpaís. ☎ *2640-0031. Fax: 2640-0061.* `www.malpaissurf` `camp.com`. *Rack rates: $70 double with shared bathroom, $95–$115 double with private bathroom, $10 per person camping. AE, MC, V.*

Milarepa
$$$–$$$$ **Playa Santa Teresa**

Named after a Buddhist sage, this small collection of individual bungalows is spread around shady grounds fronting the beach, just next door to Flor Blanca. The bungalows are simple, roomy, and understated. All have wooden floors, a mix of teak and bamboo furniture, beds with mosquito netting, and private porches. An overhead fan keeps things cool, and there are plenty of windows for cross ventilation. The more expensive units are closest to the beach and have ocean views. All come with free Wi-Fi. There's a midsize pool here for when the surf is too rough, as well as an elegant little restaurant.

See map p. 293. Playa Santa Teresa. ☎ *2640-0023. Fax: 2640-0168.* `www.milarepa` `hotel.com`. *Rack rates: $194–$225 double. Rates include full breakfast and taxes. Rates lower during the off season, higher during peak weeks. AE, MC, V.*

Trópico Latino Lodge
$$–$$$ Playa Santa Teresa

One of the first hotels out here, this small beachfront resort has aged well and is an excellent option. The best accommodations here are the newer private bungalows, which have artistic tile work and décor touches, as well as ocean views. The original rooms here are housed in four duplex units. These are huge — the king-size bamboo bed barely makes a dent in the floor space. There's also a separate sofa bed, as well as a small desk, a wall unit of shelves, and closet space galore. Although none of the older rooms has any ocean view to speak of, each has a private patio with a hammock. The shady grounds are rich in the native *pochote* tree, which is known for its spiky trunk. The small restaurant here has excellent fresh fish and plenty of pasta dishes.

See map p. 293. Playa Santa Teresa. ☎ **2640-0062.** *Fax: 2640-0117.* `www.hotel tropicolatino.com.` *Rack rates: $103–$155 double. Rates lower in the off season. MC, V.*

Dining locally

Nectar
$$$–$$$$ At Flor Blanca Resort FUSION

The dimly lit, open-air setting of this poolside and beachfront restaurant is elegant yet casual. There's a Pacific Rim influence to the fusion cuisine served up here. The menu changes regularly. If you're lucky, you can start things off with a sashimi platter that mixes fresh tuna with thinly sliced beef carpaccio — it's exquisite. In addition to fresh seafood and several vegetarian entrees, you may also find lamb, rabbit, or duck for offer on any given night. The creativity, service, and presentation are some of the best you'll find in Costa Rica.

See map p. 293. At Flor Blanca Resort in Santa Teresa. ☎ **2640-0232.** *Reservations recommended. Main courses: $18–$35. AE, MC, V. Open: Daily 7 a.m. to 9:30 p.m.*

Soda Piedra Mar
$ Malpaís SEAFOOD/COSTA RICAN

This simple, open-air restaurant is set on a rocky outcropping just steps away from the sea. The place is little more than a zinc-roofed shack that seems as if a stiff breeze would quickly level it. There are only a few tables here under the low roof. Weather permitting, more tables are set in the sand under the sun or stars. The fare is simple, but the fish is guaranteed fresh, the portions are hearty, the lobster is very reasonably priced, and the setting and sunsets are wonderful.

See map p. 293. On the beach in Malpaís. ☎ **2640-0069.** *Main courses: $4–$17. No credit cards. Open: Daily 8 a.m.–8 p.m.*

Exploring Malpaís and Santa Teresa

There are no major attractions in this area, but there are plenty of activities and adventures to be had. Join the surfer dudes and catch some waves, or take a hike or horseback ride on solid land. You'll find information and details about the area's most popular options in this section.

The top attraction

Malpaís surfing

Surfing is the main draw in this area. The long beaches of Malpaís, Playa Carmen, and Playa Santa Teresa offer up a steady stream of beach breaks, with enough peaks and points so that it's almost never crowded. If you want to rent a board or take a lesson, check out the **Malpaís Surf Shop** (☎ 2640-0173).

There are rideable waves all along the length of the beaches here, but I like Malpaís best. Open: Daily 24 hours, but I don't recommend surfing at night.

More cool things to see and do

✓ **Embarking on a canopy tour: Canopy del Pacífico** (☎ 2640-0091) is located toward the southern end of Malpaís and inland. A two-hour tour over the nearly 1km (½ mile) of cables touches down on eight platforms, features two rappels, and offers good views of both the forest and the ocean below. The cost is $35.

✓ **Horseback riding and mountain biking:** The hills, fields, and forests of this area are perfect for exploring on horseback or riding a mountain bike. Any of the hotels in the area can hook you up with a horseback-riding tour for around $10 to $15 per hour.

Living it up after dark in Malpaís and Santa Teresa

There's not much in the way of raging nightlife here. Some folks make the long and arduous journey over to Montezuma. The most popular bar in the area is **D&N** (☎ 2640-0353), which stands for Day & Night, and is located about 1 block north of the crossroads into town, off the main road. Surfers and other travelers also tend to gather in the evenings at **Frank's Place** (☎ 2640-0096) and the **Malpaís Surf Camp** (☎ 2640-0031). Out in Santa Teresa, **La Lora** (☎ 2640-0132) is the most happening spot. This is definitely the place to come on Saturday night, to dance some salsa and merengue with the locals.

Fast Facts: Malpaís and Santa Teresa

Ambulance

Call ☎ 128.

ATMs

The closest ATM is at the Banco Nacional in Cóbano.

Country Code and City Code

The country code for Costa Rica is **506**. There are no city or area codes within Costa Rica. To call from the United States, dial 011-506 plus the eight-digit number. From within Costa Rica, you simply dial the eight-digit number.

Currency Exchange

Most hotels will exchange money for you at decent rates. To get official rates, head to the Banco Nacional in Cóbano.

Fire

Call ☎ **118.**

Hospitals

The closest hospital is Hospital Monseñor Sanabria in Puntarenas (☎ 2663-0033), although there are several doctors and a local clinic (☎ 2642-0208) in Cóbano.

Information

There are no official information offices in Malpaís or Santa Teresa. Most hotels have a tour desk, concierge, or helpful front-desk staff.

Internet Access

You'll find several Internet cafes in Malpaís and Santa Teresa.

Newspapers

Several gift shops around town carry all the local papers, including the *Tico Times.*

Pharmacies

There's a well-stocked Farmacia Amiga (☎ 2640-0539) located at the Playa Carmen Centro Comercial in Malpais.

Police

Call ☎ **911.**

Post Office

There is a post office in Cóbano (☎ 2642-0323). Alternatively, most hotels can mail your letters and postcards for you.

Taxis

You'll only find a limited number of taxis in Malpaís and Santa Teresa. The best place to find one is at the crossroads at the entrance to town, in front of Frank's Place. Alternatively, you can call Miguel (☎ 8819-9021 or 2640-0261) or Richard (☎ 8317-7614 or 2640-0003) for a cab.

Chapter 20

Exploring Southern Costa Rica

In This Chapter

▶ Getting to and around Costa Rica's remote southern zone

▶ Hiking and camping in Corcovado National Park

▶ Kayaking with dolphins on the Golfo Dulce

▶ Visiting a couple of bountiful botanical gardens

Costa Rica's southern zone is a place of rugged beauty, with vast expanses of virgin lowland rain forest and few cities or settlements. Lushly forested mountains tumble into the sea, streams run clear and clean, scarlet macaws squawk raucously in the treetops, and dolphins frolic in the Golfo Dulce. This is the place to come for an authentic taste of the tropical rain forest.

This region is home to **Corcovado National Park,** the largest single expanse of lowland tropical rain forest in Central America, and its sister, **Piedras Blancas National Park.** Scattered around the edges of these national parks, on the Osa Peninsula and along the shores of the **Golfo Dulce,** are some of the country's finest nature lodges. These lodges, in general, offer comfortable to quite luxurious accommodations, attentive service, knowledgeable guides, and a wide range of activities and tours, all close to the area's many natural wonders.

This area's beauty doesn't come easy. In many ways, this is Costa Rica's final frontier. The small cities of Golfito and Puerto Jiménez are nearly as wild as the jungles that surround them. Moreover, the heat and humidity are more than many can stand. Some parts of the southern zone receive more than 635cm (250 in.) of rain per year. In addition to producing lush forests, this massive amount of rain produces more than a few disgruntled travelers.

Although most of the lodges listed in this chapter are quite cozy, and some are even spectacular, none of these nature lodges has an in-room television, telephone, or air-conditioning. Although this region is noted for its hot and steamy weather, most of these nature lodges are built with cool tile or wood floors and plenty of shade and ventilation. I never find it uncomfortable, and hoards of satisfied visitors seem to agree. However, if you're particularly sensitive to the heat, or particularly fond of air-conditioning, be sure to book a hotel with in-room A/C.

A flashlight and rain gear are always useful to have on hand in Costa Rica; they're absolutely essential in Drake Bay.

Drake Bay

Located on the northern end of the Osa Peninsula, Drake Bay is named after Sir Francis Drake, who is believed to have anchored here in 1579. Emptying into the bay is the tiny Agujitas River, which acts as a protected harbor for small boats and is a great place to do a bit of kayaking or swimming.

Stretching south from Drake Bay are miles of primary rain forest and deserted beaches, featuring a spread-out collection of isolated lodges catering to naturalists, anglers, scuba divers, and adventure travelers.

Adventurous explorers will find tide pools, spring-fed rivers, waterfalls, forest trails, and some of the best bird-watching in all of Costa Rica. If a paradise such as this appeals to you, Drake Bay makes a good base for exploring the southern zone.

Getting there

Flying directly into the small airstrip in Drake Bay is the preferred means of travel to this remote region. However, you can also get here via a combination of bus, taxi, and boat. I provide detailed information on both of these options in the following sections.

By air

Most visitors fly directly into the little airstrip at Drake Bay, although when demand is high, some are still routed through Palmar Sur. Most lodges in this area include transportation in their packages, so check with them before you book. **Sansa** (☎ 877-767-2672 in the U.S. and Canada, 2290-4100 in Costa Rica; www.flysansa.com) and **Nature Air** (☎ 800-235-9272 in the U.S. and Canada, 2299-6000 in Costa Rica; www.natureair.com) both have regular flights to Drake Bay and Palmar Sur.

If your travels take you to Drake Bay via Palmar Sur, you must then take a 15-minute bus or taxi ride over dirt roads to the small town of Sierpe. This bumpy ride takes you through several banana plantations and quickly past some important archaeological sites. In Sierpe, you board a small boat for a 40km (25-mile) ride to Drake Bay. The first half of this trip snakes through a maze of mangrove canals and rivers before heading out to sea for the final leg to the bay. Entering and exiting the Sierpe River mouth is often treacherous, and I've had several very white-knuckle moments here.

Whichever route you take, have your hotel or lodge arrange final transportation details from the airport to its site.

By bus, taxi, and boat

I recommend arranging your transportation in advance, but if you're really intrepid, you can get to Drake Bay on your own by bus, taxi, and boat.

Tracopa (☎ **2221-4214** or 2258-8939) buses leave San José for Palmar Norte regularly throughout the day between 5 a.m. and 4 p.m. The ride takes six hours. You can also catch any Golfito-bound bus from this same station and get off in Palmar Norte. When you're in Palmar Norte, ask when the next bus goes out to Sierpe. If it doesn't leave for a while (buses aren't frequent), consider taking a taxi.

When you arrive at the Palmar Norte bus station, you'll need to take a taxi to the village of Sierpe. The fare should be around $20. When you get to Sierpe, head to the dock, and try to find space on a boat. This should run you another $20 to $40. If you don't arrive early enough, you might have to hire an entire boat, which usually runs around $90 to $150 for a boat that can carry up to six passengers. Make sure that you feel confident about the boat and the skipper, and, if possible, try to find a spot on a boat from one of the established lodges in Drake Bay.

Orienting yourself in Drake Bay

Until 1997, there was no road into Drake Bay and no airstrip in town. Now that both exist, their effects are palpable. The town is growing and changing at a rapid pace. Legal and clandestine logging is taking place all along the road into Drake Bay and around — and even in — the national park.

Still, because of the bay's remoteness, major development is probably a long way off here. The tiny town itself still has just one dirt road running parallel to the beach along the crescent-shaped namesake bay. Only one lodge listed here is actually in the town of Drake Bay, the rest are across the Río Agujitas or farther south along the coast.

Spending the night

Casa Corcovado Jungle Lodge
$$$$–$$$$$ Osa Peninsula

This isolated lodge is the closest accommodation to Corcovado National Park from the Drake Bay side of the Osa Peninsula. The rooms are all private bungalows built on the grounds of an old cacao plantation on the jungle's edge. The bungalows are all pretty big, with one or two double beds and large tiled bathrooms. Electricity and hot water are supplied by a combination solar and hydroelectric energy system. Family-style meals are served in the main lodge, although most guests take lunch with them to the beach or on one of the various tours available. Late afternoons are usually enjoyed from a high point overlooking the sea and sunset, with your beverage of choice in hand. Access is strictly by small boat here, and

Osa Peninsula

ACCOMMODATIONS ■	Drake Bay Wilderness Resort **2**	ATTRACTIONS ●
Bosque del Cabo	La Paloma Lodge **3**	Caño Island **1**
Rainforest Lodge **6**	Lapa Ríos **7**	Corcovado National Park **5**
Cabinas Jinetes de Osa **2**		Herrera Botanical Gardens **8**
Casa Corcovado	**DINING** ◆	
Jungle Lodge **4**	Juanita's Mexican Bar & Grille **8**	**SHOPPING**
	Soda Carolina **8**	Jagua Arts & Craft Store **8**

sometimes the beach landing can be a bit rough, so it's recommended that guests be in decent physical shape. When the sea is not too rough, the beach is great for swimming; when the sea *is* rough, the beach is a great place to grab a hammock in the shade and read a book. There are two pools here, and a wide range of tours and activities are offered.

See map, above. Osa Peninsula. ☎ **888-896-6097** *in the U.S., 2256-7409 in Costa Rica. Fax: 256-7409.* www.casacorcovado.com. *Rack rates: $855 per person for 3 days/2 nights with 1 tour, $1,105–$1,165 for 4 days/3 nights with 2 tours. Rates are based on double occupancy and include round-trip transportation from San José, all meals, park fees, and taxes. Rates slightly higher during peak weeks, lower in the off season. AE, MC, V.*

Drake Bay Wilderness Resort
$$$–$$$$ Drake Bay

This is one of the best-located lodges at Drake Bay. It backs onto the Río Aguitas and fronts the Pacific. The rooms here are pretty simple, but they're clean and cozy, with ceiling fans, small verandas, and good mattresses on the beds. The best room is the deluxe honeymoon suite, set on a little hill toward the rear of the property, with a great view of the bay. Budget hounds should check out the five cabins that share bathroom and shower facilities. The family-style meals are filling, with an emphasis on fresh seafood and fresh fruits. My favorite treats here are the freshly baked chocolate-chip cookies frequently served for dessert. Because it's on a rocky spit, there isn't a good swimming beach on-site (it's about a 15-minute walk away), but there's a saltwater swimming pool in front of the bay, and, depending on the tide, you can bathe in a beautiful small tide pool formed by the rocks. The resort offers free Wi-Fi, and a wide range of tour options.

See map p. 302. Drake Bay. ☎ 561-762-1763 in the U.S., or ☎/fax 2770-8012 in Costa Rica. www.drakebay.com. Rack rates: $90 per person per day with shared bathroom, $130–$165 per person per day standard and deluxe, $770 per person for 4 days/3 nights with 2 tours. Rates include all meals and taxes. Rates lower in the off season. AE, MC, V.

Hotel Jinetes de Osa
$$–$$$ Drake Bay

Once a budget *cabinas* option, this place has been spruced up, expanded, and turned into a very comfortable option for serious scuba divers and adventure tourists. Although it's now far from a budget lodging, it does offer a reasonable alternative to the more upscale lodges in the area. The wooden construction, attention to detail, free Wi-Fi, and location directly above the beach give Jinetes an edge over other hotels right in the village of Drake Bay. The best rooms here are quite plush and even have a view of the bay. The hotel is pretty close to the docks on the Río Agujitas, which is a plus for those traveling independently or with heavy bags. A wide range of tours and activities is available, as are dive packages, weekly packages, and Professional Association of Diving Instructors (PADI) certification courses.

Drake Bay. ☎ 866-553-7073 in the U.S. and Canada, ☎/fax 2231-5806 in Costa Rica. www.drakebayhotel.com. Rack rates: $132–$176 double. Rates include 3 meals daily. DISC, MC, V.

La Paloma Lodge
$$$$–$$$$$ Drake Bay

Set on a steep hill overlooking the Pacific, with Caño Island in the distance, the bungalows at La Paloma offer expansive ocean views that, combined with the attentive and amiable service, make this my top choice in Drake Bay. All the cabins are spacious and private and are set among lush foliage facing the Pacific. All come with a large balcony or veranda. The large two-story Sunset Ranchos are the choice rooms here: Sliding screen windows and doors keep you in touch with nature and let the ocean breezes blow through, and the views are to die for. The other cabins are a tad smaller but feature luxurious bathrooms and pretty good ocean views as well. The standard rooms, which are located in a row in one long building, are smaller and less private than the cabins, but they're still quite attractive and have good views from their verandas (which, like the cabins, have hammocks).

The main lodge building is a large, open-air structure with a long veranda that has a sitting area and swing chairs, where you can mingle with other guests, or check e-mail on your laptop. The beach is about a seven-minute hike down a winding jungle path, but the swimming pool is located close to all the action and, like everything else here, is set on the edge of the hillside, with great ocean and jungle views. There are single and double kayaks, as well as boogie boards and surfboards free for guests to use. The lodge also offers scuba certification courses.

See map p. 302. Drake Bay. ☎ *2293-7502 or* ☎*/fax 2239-0954.* www.lapaloma lodge.com. *Rack rates: $1,115–$1,470 per person for 4 days/3 nights with 2 tours, $1,310–$1,700 per person for 5 days/4 nights with 2 tours. Rates are based on double occupancy and include round-trip transportation from San José, all meals, park fees, indicated tours, and taxes. Rates slightly lower in the off season. AE, MC, V.*

Dining locally

La Paloma Lodge
$$$$–$$$$$ Drake Bay   CONTINENTAL/COSTA RICAN

Drake Bay is an isolated region, and restaurants are hard to come by. Most resort restaurants tend to have good, tasty, hearty fare, however. The best can be found here at La Paloma. Hearty and delicious meals are served family-style, and the kitchen will accommodate vegetarians or those with special dietary needs, with advance warning. Scrumptious freshly baked bread is served with almost every meal here.

See map p. 302. Drake Bay. ☎ *2293-7502 or* ☎ */fax 2239-0954.* www.lapaloma lodge.com. *Hotel rates include all meals. AE, MC, V. Open: Breakfast, lunch, and dinner daily.*

Exploring Drake Bay

Remember: This is a very remote region, with no cars. All the major attractions here are reached and visited as part of an organized tour. All the hotels in the area arrange tours to these attractions.

The top attractions

Caño Island

One of the most popular excursions from Drake Bay is a trip out to Caño Island and the **Caño Island Biological Reserve.** The island was once home to a pre-Columbian culture about which little is known. A trip to the island includes a short hike to an ancient cemetery, where you'll also be able to see some of the stone spheres that are commonly believed to have been carved by the people who once lived in this area (see "Those mysterious stone spheres," in this chapter). Few animals or birds live on the island, but the beach here is gorgeous, and the coral reefs just offshore teem with life. This is one of Costa Rica's prime scuba spots. Visibility is often quite good, and there's even easily accessible snorkeling right from the beach. It's about a 40-minute boat ride to the island. Trips here usually include a picnic lunch on the beach. All the lodges listed earlier in this chapter offer tours to Caño Island.

See map p. 302. 19km (12 miles) offshore from Drake Bay. Admission: $10 park entrance fee, usually included in the tour price. Open: Daily 8 a.m.–4 p.m.

Those mysterious stone spheres

Although Costa Rica lacks the great cities, giant temples, and bas-relief carvings of the Maya, Aztec, and Olmec civilizations of northern Mesoamerica, its pre-Columbian residents did leave a unique legacy that continues to cause archaeologists and anthropologists to scratch their heads and wonder. Over a period of several centuries, hundreds of painstakingly carved and carefully positioned granite spheres were left by the peoples who lived throughout the Diquís Delta, in southern Costa Rica. The orbs, which range from grapefruit size to more than 2m (6½ ft.) in diameter, can weigh up to 15 tons, and many reach near-spherical perfection.

Archaeologists believe that the spheres were created during two defined cultural periods. The first, called the Aguas Buenas period, dates from around A.D. 100 to A.D. 500. Few spheres survive from this time. The second phase, during which spheres were created in apparently greater numbers, is called the Chiriquí period and lasted from approximately A.D. 800 to A.D. 1500. The "balls" believed to have been carved during this time frame are widely dispersed along the entire length of the lower section of the Terraba River. To date, only one known quarry for the spheres has been discovered, in the mountains above the Diquís Delta, which points to a difficult and lengthy transportation process.

Some archaeologists believe that the spheres were hand-carved in a very time-consuming process, using stone tools, perhaps aided by some sort of firing process. However, another theory holds that granite blocks were placed at the bases of powerful waterfalls, and the hydraulic beating of the water eventually turned and carved the rock into these near-perfect spheres. And more than a few proponents have credited extraterrestrial intervention for the creation of the stone balls.

Most of the stone balls have been found at the archaeological remains of defined settlements and are associated with either central plazas or known burial sites. Their size and placement have been interpreted to have both social and celestial importance, although their exact significance remains a mystery. Unfortunately, many of the stone balls have been plundered and are currently used as lawn ornaments in the fancier neighborhoods of San José. Some have even been shipped out of the country. The **Museo Nacional de Costa Rica** (Chapter 12) has a nice collection, including one massive sphere in its center courtyard. It's a never-fail photo-op. You can also see the stone balls near the small **airports in Palmar Sur** and **Drake Bay**, and on **Caño Island** (which is located 19km/12 miles off the Pacific coast near Drake Bay).

Corcovado National Park

Corcovado National Park is a main attraction in this area. All the lodges in Drake Bay offer day trips and hikes into Corcovado National Park at the San Pedrillo entrance. The trails here are wonderful. One leads to a beautiful jungle waterfall, where you can take a refreshing dip.

If you want to spend a lot of time hiking and camping in Corcovado National Park, Puerto Jiménez is your best base and jumping-off point. (See the Puerto Jiménez section later in this chapter for a much more detailed description of exploring Corcovado National Park.)

See map p. 302. The San Pedrillo entrance to the park is located approximately 15km (9⅓ miles) south of Drake Bay. Admission: $10, usually included in the tour price. Open: Daily 8 a.m.–4 p.m.

More cool things to see and do

In addition to trips to Caño Island and Corcovado National Park, all the lodges in the area offer a host of half-day and full-day tours and activities, including horseback rides, scuba-diving, and sportfishing. In some cases, tours are included in your room rate or package; in others, they must be bought a la carte. Other options include mountain-biking and sea-kayaking. Most of these tours run between $60 and $120, depending on the activity, with scuba-diving ($90–$125 for a 2-tank dive) and sportfishing ($450–$1,500, depending on the size of the boat and other amenities) costing a bit more.

Although the beach fronting Drake Bay itself is acceptable and calm for swimming, it's far from spectacular. The most popular swimming beach is a pretty small patch of sand about a seven-minute hike beyond and down from La Paloma Lodge. The nicest beaches around involve taking a day trip to either Caño Island or San Josesito, a beautiful beach farther south on the peninsula with excellent snorkeling possibilities.

Living it up after dark in Drake Bay

Aside from one weekend disco in the center of town and the small bars at the individual lodges, there is virtually no nightlife in Drake Bay. That is, unless you opt to take the two-hour **Night Tour** (☎ 8382-1619; www.the nighttour.com; $35 per person) offered by Tracie Stice. Tracie is affectionately known as "The Bug Lady." Equipped with flashlights and night-vision glasses, participants get a bug's-eye view of the forest at night (arachnophobes should stay away). You may see the reflection of some larger forest dweller, but most of the tour is a fascinating exploration of the nocturnal insect world. Consider yourself lucky if Tracie finds the burrow of a trap-door spider or large tarantula.

Puerto Jiménez and the Osa Peninsula

Despite its small size and languid pace, Puerto Jiménez is a bustling little burg, where rough jungle gold-panners mix with wealthy ecotourists, budget backpackers, and a surprising number of celebrities seeking a small dose of anonymity and escape. Located on the southeastern tip of the Osa Peninsula, the town itself is just a couple of gravel streets with the ubiquitous *fútbol* (soccer) field, a block of general stores, some inexpensive *sodas* (diner-style restaurants), a butcher shop, and several bars. Scarlet macaws fly overhead, and mealy parrots provide wake-up calls.

Puerto Jiménez is Costa Rica's principal gateway to Corcovado National Park. The national park has its headquarters here, and this town makes an excellent base for exploring this vast wilderness. Although the in-town accommodations are decidedly budget-oriented, you'll find several far-more-luxurious places farther south on the Osa Peninsula.

Getting there

Flying into Puerto Jiménez is the best way to visit this remote region. However, you can get here by car or bus, although both are very long rides. You'll find more information on all these options in the following sections.

By air

Sansa (☎ 877-767-2672 in the U.S. and Canada, 2290-4100 in Costa Rica; www.flysansa.com) and **Nature Air** (☎ 800-235-9272 in the U.S. and Canada, 2299-6000 in Costa Rica; www.natureair.com) both have a few daily flights to Puerto Jiménez from San José. On both airlines, picking up the flight in Quepos and Manuel Antonio, with advance notice, is also often possible.

Note that due to the remoteness of this area and the unpredictable flux of traffic, both Sansa and Nature Air frequently improvise on scheduling. Sometimes this means an unscheduled stop in Quepos or Golfito on the way down from or back to San José, which can add some time to your flight. Less frequently, it may mean a change in departure time, so confirming the time is always best. Also, lodges down here sometimes run charters, so asking them is a good idea.

By car

Take the Interamerican Highway east out of San José (through San Pedro and Cartago) and continue south on this road. In about three hours, you'll reach San Isidro de El General. Although you can continue on the Interamerican Highway all the way south, it is currently faster, smoother, and safer to turn off in San Isidro and head to Dominical, picking up the Southern Highway or Costanera Sur in Dominical. From here, it's a fast and smooth shot down Palmar Norte, where you meet up again with the Interamerican Highway. Take the turnoff for La Palma, Rincón, and Puerto Jiménez. This road is paved at first, but at Rincón it turns to gravel. The last 35km (22 miles) are slow and rough, and, during the rainy season (mid-Apr to Nov), it's too muddy for anything but a four-wheel-drive vehicle.

By bus

Transportes Blanco-Lobo express buses (☎ 2257-4121 in San José, 2771-4744 in Puerto Jiménez) leave San José daily at noon from Calle 12, between avenidas 7 and 9. The trip takes eight hours; the fare is $7.50. The return bus departs Puerto Jiménez for San José daily at 5 a.m.

Orienting yourself in Puerto Jiménez and the Osa Peninsula

Puerto Jiménez is a dirt-lane town on the southern coast of the Osa Peninsula. Actually, a small section of the main road through town is paved for several blocks. The public dock is over a bridge past the north end of the *fútbol* field; the bus stop is 2 blocks east of the center of town. The airstrip runs north–south along the western edge of town.

From Puerto Jiménez, a rough dirt road runs out to Carate, where the road ends and Corcovado National Park begins. This road fords several rivers, which can sometimes be impassable for most vehicles during the rainy season.

Getting around and getting information

You can easily walk anywhere in Puerto Jiménez. Rugged four-wheel-drive taxis are available for trips out to Carate, Corcovado National Park, and the isolated lodges listed later in this chapter.

To travel out to Carate by "public transportation," pick up one of the collective taxis (actually, a four-wheel-drive pickup truck with a tarpaulin cover and slat seats in the back) that leave Puerto Jiménez daily at 6 a.m. and 1:30 p.m., returning at 8 a.m. and 4 p.m. *Remember:* These taxis are very informal and change their schedules regularly to meet demand or avoid bad weather, so always ask in town. The one-way fare is around $8. A small fleet of these pickups leaves from just south of the bus terminal and will stop to pick up anyone who flags them down along the way. Your other option is to hire an entire pickup truck; it costs approximately $70 to $90 each way to Carate, although the taxi can hold as many as ten people.

Several speedboats work as boat taxis between Puerto Jiménez and Golfito. The fare is $5, and the ride takes a little under 30 minutes. These boats leave five or six times throughout the day, or whenever they fill up, beginning at around 5 a.m. and finishing up at around 5 p.m. Ask around town, or at the docks for current schedules.

There is also a daily passenger launch service from Puerto Jiménez to Golfito from the public dock at 6 a.m. Much slower, this trip takes one and a half hours; the fare is $3. The return trip departs at 11:30 a.m. from Golfito's municipal dock.

Puerto Jiménez

ACCOMMODATIONS ■
Bosque del Cabo Office **1**
Lapo Rios Office **4**

DINING ◆
Juanita's Mexican Bar & Grill **2**
Soda Carolina **3**

ATTRACTIONS ●
Corcovado National Park Office **6**
Escondido Trex Office **3**
Herrera Botanical Gardens **7**

SHOPPING ▪
Jagua Arts & Crafts Store **5**

You can also charter a water taxi for the trip across the Golfo Dulce to Golfito. You'll have to pay $40 to $80 for an entire launch, some of which can carry up to 12 people.

If you can't get to your next destination by boat, bus, taxi, commuter airline, or car, **Alfa Romeo Aero Taxi** (☎ **2735-5353** or 2735-5112; www. alfaromeoair.com) runs airline charters to most of the nearby destinations, including Carate, Drake Bay, Sirena, and Golfito. A five-passenger plane costs $200 to $400 one-way, depending on your destination.

The **Corcovado National Park office** (☎ **2735-5036**; Fax: 2735-5276; E-mail: pncorcovado@hotmail.com) is in town here, across from the airstrip. This stop is necessary if you're thinking of camping in the park, and it's a good place to get general info on the park and the area.

Southern Costa Rica

ACCOMMODATIONS ■
Bosque del Cabo
  Rainforest Lodge **5**
Cabinas Jinetes de Osa **10**
Cabinas Los Cocos **3**
Cabinas Sol y Mar **3**
Casa Corcovado
  Jungle Lodge **9**
Casa Roland Marina Resort **2**
Complejo Turístico Samoa
  del Sur **2**
Drake Bay Wilderness Resort **10**
La Paloma Lodge **10**
Lapa Ríos **5**
Playa Nicuesa
  Rainforest Lodge **7**
Tiskita Jungle Lodge **4**

DINING ◆
Bilge Bar, Restaurant & Grill **2**
Juanitas Mexican Bar & Grill **6**
Soda Carolina **6**

ATTRACTIONS ●
Banana Bay Marina **2**
Caño Island **11**
Casa Orquídeas **7**
Corcovado National Park **8**
Golfito Sportfishing **3**
Herrera Botanical Gardens **6**
Pavones **4**
Wilson Botanical Gardens **1**
The Zancudo Lodge **3**

SHOPPING
Jagua Arts & Craft Store **6**

Tapantí National Park
To San José
Cerro de la Muerte
Interamerican Hwy.
Cerro Chirripó
San Isidro de El General
Peñas Blancas
Dominical
Río Pacuare
To Quepos & Manuel Antonio
Punta Uvita
Playa Ballena
BALLENA MARINE NATIONAL PARK
Playa Piñuela
Boca Brava
Ojochal
El Brujo
Ciudad Cortés
Palmar Norte
Coronado Bay
Palmar Sur Airport
CURRÉ INDIAN RESERVATION
Río Sierpe
Sierpe
Sabanilla
Sabalito
Piedras Blancas
San Vito **1**
7 **7**
Drake Bay **10**
Río Chocuaco
La Palma
Playa Cativa
2
Golfito Airport
Río Claro
To Panama
11
Caño Island Biological Reserve
Chocuaco Lake
Rincón
OSA INDIAN RESERVATION
Golfito
Ciudad Neily
9
OSA PENINSULA
Los Patos Ranger Station
El Tigre
6 **6**
Playa Zancudo
2 **2**
3
Río Colorado
Lake Colorado
To Panama
San Pedrillo
Corcovado Lake
Puerto Jiménez
Playa Tamale
Zancudo
CORCOVADO NATIONAL PARK
Playa Sirena
La Leona Ranger Station
Carate
5
Playa Pavones
4
Pavones
Cabo Matapalo
Punta Banco
PANAMA
NICARAGUA
Caribbean Sea
COSTA RICA
San José
PACIFIC OCEAN
Area of detail
PANAMA
PACIFIC OCEAN
Punta Burica
0   100 mi
0   100 km

Airport ✈
Ferry ⛴
Mountain ▲
Ranger Station ⛺

0   50 mi
0   50 km

A couple of Internet cafes are in town. The best of these is **Cafe Net El Sol** (☎ **2735-5719;** www.soldeosa.com), which is a great place to book tours and get information; the cafe is also a Wi-Fi hotspot.

Spending the night

Bosque del Cabo Rainforest Lodge
$$$$$ **Osa Peninsula**

This secluded jungle lodge is a real charmer. The cabins are all spacious and attractively furnished, with wooden decks or verandas to catch the ocean views, and are set amid beautiful gardens. Bosque del Cabo is located 150m (492 ft.) above the water at the southern tip of the Osa Peninsula, where the Golfo Dulce meets the Pacific Ocean. The deluxe cabins come with king-size beds and slightly larger deck space. The Congo cabin is my choice for its spectacular view of the sunrise from your bed. All the cabins have indoor bathrooms, although most have tiled showers set outdoors amid flowering heliconia and ginger. A few also have outdoor garden tubs.

There's a trail down to a secluded beach that has some tide pools and ocean-carved caves. Another trail leads to a jungle waterfall, and several others wind through the rain forests of the lodge's 243 hectares (600-plus-acre) private reserve. The wildlife viewing here is excellent. If you're too lazy to hike down to the beach, you can enjoy the very inviting pool by the main lodge. Surfing is a popular activity here, as are hiking and horseback riding. Attractions include a canopy platform 36m (118 ft.) up a Manu tree, reached along a 90m (295-ft.) zip line, as well as a bird- and wildlife-watching rancho set beside a little lake on the edge of the tropical gardens and surrounded by forest. Trips to the national park or fishing excursions can be arranged, as can guided hikes, sea-kayaking, and a host of other activities and tours.

See map p. 310. Osa Peninsula. ☎ */fax* **2735-5206** *or 8389-2846.* www.bosquedel cabo.com. *Rack rates: $350–$390 double. Rates include 3 meals daily and taxes. $25 round-trip transportation from Puerto Jiménez. MC, V.*

Lapa Ríos
$$$$$ **Osa Peninsula**

This famous ecolodge consists of eight duplex buildings perched along a steep ridge. Each very large room is totally private and oriented toward the view. Walls have open screening, and the ceiling is a high-peaked, thatch roof. Mosquito nets drape languidly over the two queen-size beds. A large deck and small tropical garden, complete with a hammock and outdoor shower, more than double the living space of each room. There's an indoor shower in the room, although this one features open screen walls facing the view, so it's not all that different from being outdoors. It's a bit of a hike back and forth from the main lodge to the rooms located farthest down the ridge.

The centerpiece of the lodge's large open-air dining room is a 15m (49-ft.) spiral staircase that leads to an observation deck tucked beneath the peak of the building's thatched roof. Lapa Ríos is surrounded by its own 400-hectare (988-acre) private rain-forest reserve, which is home to scarlet macaws, toucans, parrots, hummingbirds, monkeys, and myriad other wildlife. However, keep in mind that there are no TVs, no telephones, no air-conditioning, no discos, no shopping, no paved roads, and no crowds.

Moreover, the beach is a good 15-minute hike away, and it's not the best for swimming. In fact, other than a beautiful little pool, miles of hiking trails, an array of adventure tours and activities, and a quiet tropical bar, there is nothing around to distract your attention from the stupendous views of the rain forest all around and the ocean far below.

See map p. 310. Osa Peninsula. ☎ **2735-5130.** *Fax: 2735-5179.* www.laparios. com. *Rack rates: $650 double. Rates include 3 meals daily and taxes. Discounts for children 10 and under; rates lower in the off season, higher during peak periods. AE, MC, V.*

Dining locally

Juanitas Mexican Bar & Grille
$–$$ **Puerto Jiménez MEXICAN**

This place offers good, hearty, California-style Mexican food and fresh local seafood served up in a lively, convivial atmosphere. You can get fajitas with chicken, beef, fish, or even grilled vegetables. They also have pizza by the slice or whole pie, and they will deliver, though I'm not sure how far out the peninsula their drivers will go. There are nightly specials and a popular happy hour. You can either order breakfast a la carte or load up on the abundant breakfast buffet.

See map p. 309. Downtown Puerto Jiménez. ☎ **2735-5056.** *Main courses: $4.80–$15. V. Open: Daily 10 a.m. to midnight.*

Soda Carolina
$ **Puerto Jiménez COSTA RICAN**

Set in the center of the town's main street, and otherwise known as the "Bar, Restaurante y Cabinas Carolina," this is the town's main budget travelers' hangout and also serves as an unofficial information center. The walls are painted with colorful jungle and wildlife scenes. As for the fare, seafood is the way to go. There's good fried fish as well as a variety of ceviches. The black-bean soup is usually tasty, and the *casados* (plates of the day) are filling and cost around $4.30.

See map p. 309. On the main street. ☎ **2735-5185.** *Reservations not accepted. Main courses: $3.50–$14. V. Open: Daily 7 a.m.–10 p.m.*

Exploring Puerto Jiménez and the Osa Peninsula

The main attraction here is the massive and rugged Corcovado National Park. In this section, I offer detailed information on how to best visit and enjoy this park, as well as some suggestions for other activities and attractions around the region.

The top attractions

Corcovado National Park

Corcovado National Park is impressive. It is the single largest expanse of primary lowland tropical rain forest in Central America. Plus, it's home to an amazing amount of tropical flora and fauna and provides one of the few suitable habitats in Costa Rica for maintaining a healthy jaguar population.

Exploring Corcovado National Park is not something to be undertaken lightly, but neither is it the prohibitively arduous expedition that some people make it out to be. The weather is the biggest obstacle to overnight backpacking trips through the park. The heat and humidity are often quite formidable, and frequent rainstorms can make the trails pretty muddy. If you hike along the beach, you'll have to plan your hiking around the tides. Often, there is no beach at all at high tide, and some rivers are impassable at high tide.

Because of its size and remoteness, Corcovado National Park is best explored over several days; however, you can enter and hike a bit of it on a day trip. The best way to plan a trip to the park is to book a tour with your lodge.

The park has four primary entrances, which are really just ranger stations reached by rough dirt roads. When you've reached them, you'll have to strap on a backpack and hike. Perhaps the easiest one to reach from Puerto Jiménez is **La Leona ranger station,** near Carate, which is accessible by car, bus, taxi, or light aircraft. From Carate, it's a 3km (1¾-mile) hike to La Leona.

You can also travel to **El Tigre,** about 14km (8¾ miles) by dirt road from Puerto Jiménez, where there's another ranger station. But note that trails from El Tigre go only a short distance into the park.

The third entrance is in **Los Patos,** which is reached from the town of La Palma, northwest of Puerto Jiménez. From here, there's a 19km (12-mile) trail through the center of the park to **Sirena,** a ranger station and research facility.

The northern entrance to the park is **San Pedrillo,** which you can reach by hiking from Sirena or by taking a boat from Drake Bay or Sierpe (see "Corcovado National Park" under "Drake Bay" earlier in this chapter). It's 14km (8¾ miles) from Drake Bay.

If you're not into hiking in the heat, you can charter a plane in Puerto Jiménez to take you to Carate or Sirena. A five-passenger plane should cost around $200 to $400 one-way, depending on your destination. Contact **Alfa Romeo Aero Taxi** (☎ **2735-5353** or 2735-5112; www.alfaromeoair.com) for details.

Corcovado National Park

Sirena is the park's principal and most fascinating destination. As a research facility and ranger station, it's frequented almost constantly by scientists. One of the longest hikes, from San Pedrillo to Sirena, can be done only during the dry season. Between any two stations, the hiking is arduous and takes all day, so it's best to rest for a day or so between hikes, if possible.

 Remember: This area is quite wild. Unless you're experienced, always hike with a guide. In addition, be especially careful about swimming in any isolated rivers or river mouths because most rivers in Corcovado are home to crocodiles.

 Reservations are essential at the various ranger stations if you plan to eat or sleep inside the park. Make your reservations by contacting the **Park Service** in Puerto Jiménez (☎ **2735-5036;** Fax: 2735-5276; E-mail: pncorcovado@hotmail.com). Its offices are adjacent to the airstrip. Only a limited number of people are allowed to camp at each ranger station, so make your reservations well in advance.

Sirena has a modern research facility with dormitory-style accommodations for 28 people, as well as a campground, *soda,* and landing strip for charter flights. You can also camp at the **La Leona, Los Patos,** and **San Pedrillo** ranger stations. Every ranger station has potable water, but I recommend packing your own supply; whatever you do, don't drink stream water. Campsites in the park are $4 per person per night. A dorm bed at the Sirena station will run you $8 — you must bring your own sheets, and a mosquito net is highly recommended — and meals here are another $40 per day. Everything must be reserved in advance.

See map p. 314. 2.5km (1½ miles) north of Carate. ☎ **2735-5036.** www.corcovado. org. *Admission: $10 per day. Camping: $4 per person per night. Dorm room: $8 per person per night. Open: Daily 24 hours.*

More cool things to see and do

✔ **Adventure tours:** For a real adventure, check in with **Psycho Tours** (☎ 8353-8619; www.psychotours.com). These folks run a variety of adventure tours, but their signature combo trip features a free climb up (with a safety rope attached) the roots and trunks of a 70m-tall (200-ft.) strangler fig. You can climb as high as your ability allows, but most people try to reach a natural platform at around 18m (60 ft.), where you take a leap of faith into space and are belayed down by your guide. This is preceded by an informative hike through primary rain forest, often wading through a small river, and followed by a couple of rappels down jungle waterfalls, the highest of which is around 31m (100 ft.). The five- to six-hour tour costs $120.

✔ **Botanical gardens:** On the outskirts of Puerto Jimenez, you'll find **Herrera Botanical Gardens** (☎ 2735-5210). The project here features over 260 acres of botanical gardens, working permaculture gardens, and secondary forest. There are even a few platforms built high in the trees here and reached by climbing a ladder. A two-and-a-half-hour guided tour of the gardens costs $15, although you can wander the gardens yourself, with a self-guiding map, for just $4.

✔ **Kayaking:** To arrange a kayaking trip around the estuary, up into the mangroves, or out into the gulf, contact **Escondido Trex** (☎ 2735-5210; www.escondidotrex.com). These folks have an office in the Soda Carolina in the center of town. Escondido Trex runs daily paddles through the mangroves, as well as sunset trips out on the gulf, where you can sometimes see dolphins. These folks also do guided rain-forest hikes and can have you rappelling down the face of a jungle waterfall. More-adventurous multiday kayak and camping trips are also available, in price and comfort ranges from budget to luxury (staying at various lodges around the Golfo Dulce and Matapalo). They'll even take you gold panning (although there are no guarantees that your panning will pay for the trip).

✔ **Shopping:** Located right beside the airstrip in town, **Jagua Arts & Craft Store** (☎ 2735-5267) is one of the best gift shops in the country. Owner Karen Herrera has found excellent local and regional art and craft works, including some superb jewelry and blown glass. This store is a great place to head before your departing flight out of Puerto Jimenez. But be sure to give yourself enough time, because they have a wonderful and somewhat extensive collection.

✔ **Sportfishing:** If you're interested in doing some **billfishing** or **deep-sea fishing,** you'll probably want to stay at or fish with **Crocodile Bay Lodge** (☎ **800-733-1115** in the U.S. and Canada, 2735-5631 in Costa Rica; www.crocodilebay.com). This upscale fishing lodge is close to the Puerto Jiménez airstrip.

✔ **Surfing:** Although nearby Pavones gets all the international press and acclaim, three very dependable point breaks are located on the stretch of the Osa Peninsula between Puerto Jiménez and Carate. Matapalo, Pan Dulce, and Backwash are all well-formed right point breaks. These waves are excellent for learning on when they're small. And when the waves are large, they're long and clean. If you want to take lessons, contact **Pollo's Surf School** (☎ **8366-6559;** E-mail: rhoades_gretchen@hotmail.com).

Golfito and the Golfo Dulce

Golfito itself is not a very compelling destination for foreign travelers. Nevertheless, the city's setting is quite pretty, and it serves as the gateway to some truly beautiful isolated lodges located on the shores of the Golfo Dulce, or "Sweet Gulf."

Sportfishing cognoscenti know that Golfito's real draw is the marlin and sailfish just beyond its bay. Arguably one of the best fishing spots in Costa Rica, it provides pleasant, uncrowded surroundings in which die-hard sportfishers can indulge their greatest fantasies of landing the great one to end all great ones.

In its prime, Golfito was a major banana port, but United Fruit pulled out in 1985 following a few years of rising taxes, falling prices, and labor disputes. Now Ticos come here in droves on weekends and throughout December to take advantage of cheap prices on name-brand goods and clothing sold in the duty-free zone, and sometimes all these shoppers make finding a room in town difficult.

In 1998, much of the rain forest bordering the Golfo Dulce was officially declared the **Piedras Blancas National Park,** which includes 12,000 hectares (29,640 acres) of primary forests, as well as newly protected secondary forests and pasturelands.

Along the southern shores of the Golfo Dulce, accessible either by boat or car from Golfito, are the two tiny beach towns of Playa Zancudo and Pavones. The former is a laid-back tropical getaway and sportfishing center, while the latter is one of the prime surf spots on the planet.

Getting there

Flying is the fastest and easiest way to get to Golfito and the Golfo Dulce region. You can drive or take a bus, although in each of these cases, it's a very long ride. You'll find more information on all these options in the following sections.

By air

Sansa (☎ **877-767-2672** in the U.S. and Canada, 2290-4100 in Costa Rica; www.flysansa.com) and **Nature Air** (☎ **800-235-9272** in the U.S. and Canada, 2299-6000 in Costa Rica; www.natureair.com) both fly to Golfito from San José. Taxis meet all incoming flights and can take you into downtown or to the boat docks for under $2.

By car

Take the Interamerican Highway east out of San José (through San Pedro and Cartago) and continue south on this road. In about three hours, you'll reach San Isidro de El General. Although you can continue on the Interamerican Highway all the way south, it's currently faster, smoother, and safer to turn off in San Isidro and head to Dominical, picking up the Southern Highway or Costanera Sur in Dominical. From here, it's a fast and smooth shot down Palmar Norte, where you meet up again with the Interamerican Highway. When you get to Río Claro, you'll notice a couple of gas stations and quite a bit of activity. Turn right here and follow the signs to Golfito. If you end up at the Panama border, you've missed the turnoff by about 32km (20 miles). The drive takes about six hours.

If you're heading to either Playa Zancudo or Pavones, you'll see the turn-off at El Rodeo, about 4km (2½ miles) outside of Golfito, on the road in from the Interamerican Highway. About 20 minutes past the turnoff, you'll have to wait and take a small diesel-operated crank ferry (fare is $1 per vehicle). The ferry generally operates from around 5 a.m. until 10 p.m. However, the hours can be erratic. Moreover, at very low tides, the ferry can't run, so sometimes you have to wait a couple hours. After the ferry, you should make a left at every major intersection; the road is fairly well marked. Follow the flow of traffic if there is any, or stick to the most well-worn route whenever in doubt, to reach either Playa Zancudo or Pavones. In each case, it takes about one hour when the road is in good condition and about two hours when it's not.

On most of the Interamerican Highway, you'll have to contend with pot-holes of sometimes gargantuan proportions. Just remember, if the road is suddenly smooth and in great shape, you can bet that around the next bend there will be a bottomless pothole that you can't swerve around. Take it easy.

By bus

Tracopa express buses leave San José daily at 7 a.m. and 3:30 p.m. from the Tracopa station on the Plaza Viquez at Calle 5, between avenidas 18 and 20 (☎ **2221-4214**). The trip takes seven and a half hours; the fare is $7.50. Buses depart Golfito for San José daily at 5 a.m. and 1:30 p.m. from the bus station near the municipal dock.

Orienting yourself in Golfito and along the Golfo Dulce

Golfito is set on the north side of the Golfo Dulce, at the foot of lush green mountains. The *bomba* (gas station) is the heart of Golfito, and just off this you'll find the municipal dock and compact downtown section.

Farther in along the bay and slightly inland, you come to the old United Fruit Company housing, the duty-free zone, and Golfito's small airstrip. In this area, you'll find well-maintained wooden houses painted bright colors and surrounded by neatly manicured gardens.

However, most of the hotels and lodges listed here are located along the shores of the Golfo Dulce, either north of Golfito where the only access is by boat, or down south in the beach towns of Playa Zancudo and Pavones.

This area is isolated and remote; your best bet for information will invariably be the front desk at your hotel or lodge.

Getting around

With most of the lodges listed here, arranging transportation in advance is best. If you're staying at one of the lodges accessible only by boat and you miss your connection, you can always hire a boat at the Golfito *muellecito* (public dock). Depending on which lodge you're going to, the cost could range from $40 to $80.

There are a couple of daily buses to Playa Zancudo and Pavones leaving from in front of the gas station in downtown Golfito. Alternatively, taxis can be hired for around $40 to $60. There's a steady supply of taxis constantly cruising the one main road through town. Or you can call **Taxi Golfito** (☎ **2775-1170**).

If you can't get to your next destination by boat, bus, commuter airline, or car, **Alfa Romeo Aero Taxi** (☎ **2735-5353** or 2735-5112; www.alfa romeoair.com) runs charters to most of the nearby destinations, including Carate, Drake Bay, Sirena, and Puerto Jiménez.

Spending the night

Cabinas Los Cocos
$ **Playa Zancudo**

If you've ever pondered throwing it all away and setting up shop in a simple house by the beach, these fully-equipped cabins are a good place for a trial run. Set under the trees and only a few meters from the beach, the four cabins are quiet and semi-isolated from one another. Two of them served as banana-plantation housing in a former life, until they were salvaged and moved here. These wood houses have big verandas and bedrooms and large, eat-in kitchens. Bathrooms are down a few steps in back and have hot water. The two newer cabins also offer plenty of space, small kitchenettes, and private verandas, as well as comfortable sleeping lofts. If you plan to stay in Zancudo for a while, this is a perennially good choice. The owners, Susan and Andrew Robertson, also run **Zancudo Boat Tours,** so if you want to do some exploring or need a ride into Golfito or Puerto Jiménez, they're the folks to see.

See map p. 310. Playa Zancudo. ☎ */fax* **2776-0012.** www.loscocos.com. *$60 double. Rates lower in the off season; weekly discounts available. No credit cards.*

Cabinas Sol y Mar
$ **Playa Zancudo**

This friendly, owner-run establishment is one of the most popular lodgings in Zancudo. There are two individual bungalows and two rooms in a duplex building with a shared veranda, but I prefer the individual rooms for their privacy. The bathrooms in these have unusual showers that feature a tiled platform set amid smooth river rocks. There's also a small budget cabin that is quite a good deal, as well as a fully equipped house for longer stays. You can even camp here for a few bucks per night. All the options are just steps away from the sand. The hotel's open-air restaurant is one of the best and most popular places to eat and drink in Zancudo, and there's free Wi-Fi throughout the complex.

See map p. 310. Playa Zancudo. ☎ **2776-0014.** www.zancudo.com. *Rack rates: $25–$45 double. Rates lower in the off season. MC, V.*

Casa Roland Marina Resort
$$$–$$$$ **Golfito**

This new mini-resort offers the best rooms in Golfito proper. Located in the old banana company housing area, near the airport and duty-free zone, this place is geared equally toward business travelers, vacationers, and sport fishermen. However, the hotel is several blocks from the water, so I find the use of *marina* in the name a bit misleading. Still, the rooms are large and well equipped, with interesting art works and comfortable, heavy wood furnishings. The standard or corporate rooms only come with ceiling fans, and in this climate, that's a real handicap, so you'll want to upgrade to a luxury room or suite, which have air-conditioning.

See map p. 310. Old American zone, near the duty-free zone, Golfito. ☎ **2775-0180.** *Fax: 2775-3406.* www.fishingmarinaresort.com. *Rack rates: $125–$165 double, $215–$260 suite. Rates include continental breakfast. AE, MC, V.*

Complejo Turístico Samoa del Sur
$ Golfito

If you have to spend the night in Golfito, this is a good choice. The hotel is well located right on the waterfront near the center of town. The rooms are spacious and clean. Varnished wood headboards complement two firm and comfortable double beds. With red-tile floors, modern bathrooms, and carved-wood doors, the rooms all share a long, covered veranda that's set perpendicular to the gulf, so the views aren't great. If you want to watch the water, you're better off grabbing a table at the popular restaurant and bar here. The hotel's amenities include a swimming pool and volleyball court, as well as a small marina. If you're driving down this way and heading to a lodge out on the Golfo Dulce, these folks will watch your car for around $10 per day.

See map p. 310. 1 block north of the public dock, Golfito. ☎ **2775-0233**. *Fax: 2775-0573.* www.samoadelsur.com. *Rack rates: $60–$95 double. AE, MC, V.*

Playa Nicuesa Rainforest Lodge
$$$$ Golfo Dulce

Set on its own private bay, with a large stretch of black-sand beach, and accessible only by boat, this lodge is the most luxurious and impressive option on the shores of the Golfo Dulce. Although the four Mango Manor rooms are certainly very comfortable, you'll definitely want to snag one of the four individual cabins. These are all set amidst dense forest and are made almost entirely of wood, with large open-air showers, private verandas, and a true sense of being in touch with nature. The huge main building is open aired with an abundance of varnished wood and a relaxed, inviting vibe that induces you to grab a book, play a board game, or chat with other guests. There's an excellent network of trails on the lodge's 66 hectares (165 acres), and a host of tours and activities is offered. Guests have unlimited use of the lodge's kayaks, windsurfers (also called sailboards), and snorkeling and fishing gear.

See map p. 310. Golfo Dulce. ☎ **866-504-8116** *in the U.S., 2258-8250 in Costa Rica. Fax: 2735-5043.* www.nicuesalodge.com. *Rack rates: $360–$400 double. Rates include all meals, taxes, and transfers to and from Golfito or Puerto Jiménez. MC, V.*

Tiskita Jungle Lodge
$$$$ Pavones

This small ecolodge is nearly on the Panamanian border, with the beach on one side and rain-forest-clad hills behind. Originally an experimental fruit farm growing exotic tropical fruits from around the world, Tiskita has become a great place to get away from it all. The lodge itself is set on a hill a few hundred meters from the beach and commands a superb view of the ocean. There's a dark-sand swimming beach, tide pools, jungle waterfalls, a farm and forest to explore, and great bird-watching — 285 species have been sighted. Of the 160 hectares (395 acres) here, 100 hectares (247 acres) are in primary rain forest; the rest are in secondary forest, reforestation projects, orchards, and pastures.

Accommodations are in deluxe rustic cabins with screen walls and verandas. Constructed of local hardwoods, the cabins have a very tropical feel. If you're a bird-watcher, you can just sit on the veranda and add to your life list. My favorite cabin is no. 6, which has a great view and large deck space. Some of the cabins have two or three rooms, making them great for families. Most of the bathrooms are actually outdoors, although they're private and protected, allowing you to take in the sights and sounds as you shower and shave.

Meals are served family style in the open-air main lodge. Although they're not fancy, they're certainly tasty and filling, and you'll be eating plenty of ingredients straight from the organic gardens.

The lodge is well over eight hours from San José by car, so most guests take advantage of the package tours, which include air transportation to Tiskita's private landing strip. If you've already driven all the way to Pavones, Tiskita is only 6km (3¾ miles) farther down the road.

See map p. 310. Pavones. ☎ **2296-8125.** *Fax: 2296-8133.* www.tiskita-lodge. co.cr. *Rack rates: $272 double. Rates include 3 meals, 1 guided walk daily, and all taxes. Packages with transportation to and from Golfito or Puerto Jiménez are available. AE, MC, V.*

Dining locally

Bilge Bar, Restaurant & Grill
$$–$$$ Golfito   INTERNATIONAL/SEAFOOD

This open-air restaurant attached to the Banana Bay Marina is easily the best restaurant in Golfito. The seafood is fresh and excellently prepared, but you can also get hearty steaks and great burgers. I personally recommend the fresh fish burger. Grab a table toward the water and watch the boats bob up and down while you enjoy your meal.

At the Banana Bay Marina, on the waterfront in downtown Golfito. ☎ **2775-0838.** *Main courses: $6–$18. AE, MC, V. Open: Daily 7 a.m.–9 p.m.*

Exploring Golfito and the Golfo Dulce

Most of the attractions and activities available in this region involve getting on or in the waters of the Golfo Dulce. The exception to this rule is Wilson Botanical Gardens, which is located about an hour's drive inland from Golfito. You'll find detailed information about all the various attractions and activities in this section.

The top attractions

Casa Orquídeas

Casa Orquídeas is a private botanical garden lovingly built and maintained by Ron and Trudy MacAllister. The gardens, located on an isolated cove about 30 minutes by boat out of Golfito, feature a broad array of tropical flowers and trees. During the tour, you'll sample a load of fresh fruits picked right off the trees.

Most hotels and lodges in the area offer trips here, including transportation and a two-hour tour of the gardens. If your hotel doesn't offer a tour, you can book a trip out of Golfito with the folks at **Land Sea Tours** (☎ 2775-1614). The entrance and guided tour is only $5 per person, but it will cost you $50 to $60 to hire a boat for the round-trip ride.

See map p. 310. 30 minutes by boat from Golfito, up along the Golfo Dulce. ☎ *2775-1614. Admission: $5 per person. Tours: Sat–Thurs 8:30 a.m.*

Wilson Botanical Gardens

If you have a really serious interest in botanical gardens or bird-watching, consider an excursion to Wilson Botanical Gardens at the Las Cruces Biological Station.

The gardens are owned and maintained by the Organization for Tropical Studies and include more than 7,000 species of tropical plants from around the world. Among the plants grown here are many endangered species, which make the gardens of interest to botanical researchers. Despite the scientific aspects of the gardens, there are so many beautiful and unusual flowers amid the manicured grounds that even a neophyte can't help but be astounded. And all this luscious flora has also attracted at least 360 species of birds.

If you'd like to stay the night here, there are 12 well-appointed rooms on-site. Rates, which include one guided walk, three meals, and taxes, run around $84 per person; you definitely need to make reservations beforehand if you want to spend the night, and it's usually a good idea to make a reservation for a simple day visit and hike.

To get here from Golfito, drive back out to the Interamerican Highway and continue south toward Panama. In Ciudad Neily, turn north. A taxi from Golfito should cost around $40 each way.

See map p. 310. Located 65km (40 miles) northeast of Golfito, just outside the town of San Vito. ☎ *2524-0607 in San José, 2773-4004 at the gardens.* www.threepaths. co.cr. *Admission: $22 for a half-day guided hike, $41 for a full-day guided hike (lunch included). Open: Daily 7:30 a.m.–5 p.m.*

More cool things to see and do

- ✔ **Sailboat charters:** There's no steady charter fleet here, but itinerant sailors often set up shop during the high season. If you're looking to charter a sailboat, you should check with **Banana Bay Marina** (☎ 800-245-1635 in the U.S. and Canada, 2775-0838 in Costa Rica; www.bananabaymarina.com).

- ✔ **Sportfishing:** The waters off Golfito also offer some of the best sportfishing in Costa Rica. If you'd like to try hooking into a possible world-record marlin or sailfish, contact **Banana Bay** (see preceding bullet). These folks have a full-service marina, a few waterside rooms for guests, and a fleet of sportfishing boats and captains. A full-day fishing trip costs $800 to $2,000.

> You can also try **The Zancudo Lodge** (☎ **800-854-8791** in the U.S. and Canada, 2776-0008 in Costa Rica; www.thezancudolodge. com), which is based in Playa Zancudo.

> ✔ **Surfing:** Pavones is one of the world's top surfing destinations. When the swell is working, this point break is reputed to be the longest rideable break left in the world. Even if you don't surf, the seemingly endless rides that this wave provides are impressive.

Fast Facts: Southern Costa Rica

Ambulance

Call ☎ **128.**

ATMs

You'll find ATMs at Banco Nacional and Banco de Costa Rica locations in Puerto Jiménez and Golfito.

Country Code and City Code

The country code for Costa Rica is **506.** There are no city or area codes within Costa Rica. To call from the United States, dial 011-506 plus the eight-digit number. From within Costa Rica, you simply dial the eight-digit number.

Currency Exchange

Most hotels will exchange money for you at decent rates. To get official rates, you'll need to head to one of the banks in Puerto Jiménez or Golfito.

Fire

Call ☎ **118.**

Hospitals

The closest hospital is Hospital Golfito (☎ 2775-1001), although there are several doctors and a local clinic (☎ 2735-5029) in Puerto Jiménez.

Information

There are no official information offices in southern Costa Rica. Most hotels have a tour desk, concierge, or helpful front-desk staff.

Internet Access

There are Internet cafes in Puerto Jiménez and Golfito. Few of the isolated lodges down here provide Internet access for their guests.

Newspapers

This is a very isolated region, although most lodges here receive local newspapers, including the *Tico Times.*

Pharmacies

Farmacia Puerto Jiménez (☎ 2735-5458) is located in the center of town, across from the Soda Carolina.

Farmacia Golfito (☎ 2775-2442) and Farmacia Mendez (☎ 2775-0416) are two well-stocked pharmacies in downtown Golfito.

Police

Call ☎ **911.**

Post Office

There is a post office in Golfito (☎ 2775-1911) and another in Puerto Jiménez (☎ 2735-5045). Alternatively, most hotels can mail your letters and postcards for you.

Taxis

There are numerous taxis in Puerto Jiménez and Golfito. Try Taxi Golfito (☎ 2775-1170) in Golfito. In Puerto Jiménez, call Federico (☎ 2735-5678) or Orlando (☎ 8836-8241).

Chapter 21

Chilling on Costa Rica's Caribbean Coast

In This Chapter

▶ Visiting a remote and rustic mountain lodge in the Talamanca Mountains
▶ Enjoying some of the country's best beaches
▶ Snorkeling and scuba-diving on Costa Rica's Caribbean reefs
▶ Digging the nightlife in Puerto Viejo
▶ Cruising the jungle canals and watching sea turtles lay eggs in Tortuguero

*A*lthough this region was visited by Columbus in 1502, until relatively recently it has remained historically and geographically isolated from the rest of the country. Today, you still feel as if you've entered another world, or at least another country, when you visit Costa Rica's Caribbean coast.

So remote was the Caribbean coast from Costa Rica's population centers in the Central Valley that it has developed a culture all its own. More than half of this coastline is still inaccessible except by boat or small plane. And the Guápiles Highway between San José and Limón was not completed until 1987.

The original inhabitants of the area included people of the Bribri, Cabécar, and Kéköldi tribes, and these groups maintain their cultures on indigenous reserves in the Talamanca Mountains. In fact, until the 1870s, few non-Indians resided in this area.

However, when Minor Keith built the railroad to San José and began planting bananas, he brought in black laborers from Jamaica and other Caribbean islands to lay the track and work the plantations. These workers and their descendants established fishing and farming communities up and down the coast. Today, dreadlocked Rastafarians, reggae music, Creole cooking, and the English-based patois of this Afro-Caribbean culture give this region a quasi-Jamaican flavor.

Cahuita

Cahuita is a sleepy Caribbean beach village with just a few dirt streets and no buildings over two stories high. Nonetheless, it is the first "major" tourist destination you'll reach heading south out of Limón.

Cahuita is one of the most laid-back villages in Costa Rica. After a short time, you'll undoubtedly find yourself slipping into the heat-induced torpor that affects anyone who ends up here.

Most people come to Cahuita for its miles of pristine beaches, which stretch both north and south of town. The southern beaches, the forest behind them, and the coral reef offshore (one of just a handful in Costa Rica) are all part of **Cahuita National Park.**

The village traces its roots to Afro-Caribbean fishermen and laborers who settled in this region in the mid-1800s. Today, the population is still primarily English-speaking blacks, whose culture and language set them apart from other Costa Ricans.

Getting there

There's a commuter flight between San José and Limón, but most visitors to this region still come by car, van, or bus. The drive here is quite beautiful, passing through the massive rain forest of **Braulio Carillo National Park.** Driving a rental car gives you independence and a certain level of convenience. However, if you want to leave the driving to others, several bus and minivan services are available. You'll find information on all these options in the following sections.

By air

Nature Air (☎ 800-235-9272 in the U.S. and Canada, 2299-6000 in Costa Rica; www.natureair.com) flies from San José to Limón on Monday, Wednesday, Saturday, and Sunday. Taxis are always waiting for arriving flights and can take you the final leg down to Cahuita.

By car

The Guápiles Highway heads north out of San José on Calle 3 before turning east and passing close to Barva volcano and through the rain forests of Braulio Carrillo National Park, en route to Limón. The drive takes about two and a half hours and is spectacularly beautiful in parts, especially when it's not raining or misty.

As you enter Limón, about 5 blocks from the busiest section of downtown, watch for a marked intersection, with signs pointing toward Cahuita and Puerto Viejo on your right, just before the railroad tracks. Take this road south to Cahuita, passing the airstrip and the beach on your left as you leave Limón. Alternatively, there's a turnoff with signs for Sixaola and La Bomba several miles before Limón. This winding shortcut skirts the city and puts you on the coastal road several miles south of town.

By bus

MEPE express buses (☎ 2257-8129) leave San José five times throughout the day from the Gran Terminal del Caribe (Caribbean bus terminal) on Calle Central, 1 block north of Avenida 11. The trip's duration is four hours; fare is $7. During peak periods, extra buses are sometimes added. However, checking ahead of time is smart because this bus line is one of the most fickle.

Alternatively, you can catch one of the frequent buses to Limón from the same station and then transfer to a Cahuita- or Puerto Viejo–bound bus (☎ 2758-1572) in Limón. These latter buses leave roughly every hour between 6 a.m. and 7 p.m. from Radio Casino, which is 1 block north of the municipal market.

Gray Line (☎ 2220-2126; www.graylinecostarica.com) and **Interbus** (☎ 2283-5573; www.interbusonline.com) both have daily buses to Cahuita from San José. The fare is $35 to $39. Both companies will pick you up and drop you off at most area hotels in San José and Cahuita.

Orienting yourself in Cahuita

There are only about eight dirt streets in Cahuita. The highway runs inland and parallel to the coast, with three main access roads running perpendicular. The northernmost of these bypasses town and brings you to the northern end of Playa Negra. It's marked with signs for the Magellan Inn and other hotels up on this end. The second road in brings you to the southern end of Playa Negra, 0.8km (½ mile) closer to town. Look for signs for Atlántida Lodge. The third road is the principal entrance into town. The village's main street in town, which runs parallel to the highway, dead-ends at the entrance to the national park (a footbridge over a small stream).

Buses drop their passengers at the main bus terminal, located on the main access road just before it hits the town. At the main intersection in town there's a tiny public park. Across from the park, you'll find a helpful large-scale map of the town. For all intents and purposes, this is the epicenter of Cahuita. If you come in on the bus and are staying at a lodge on Playa Negra, head north out of town on the street that runs between Coco's Bar and the small park. This road curves to the left and continues a mile or so out to Playa Negra.

The local chamber of tourism businesses has set up a small information booth at the **Mariposario Cahuita** (☎ 2755-0361). You can also get good information and set up a range of tours at **Cahuita Tours and Adventure Center** (☎ 2755-0000), **Roberto Tours** (☎ 2755-0117), or

Cahuita

CARIBBEAN SEA

Playa Negra

Soccer Field

San José

COSTA RICA

PACIFIC OCEAN

Cahuita

0   50 mi
0   50 km

Playa Blanca

Trail

To Puerto Viejo and
Parque Vargas Entrance

Río Suárez

CAHUITA NATIONAL PARK

ACCOMMODATIONS ■
Alby Lodge **1**
El Encanto Bed & Breakfast **11**
Magellan Inn **13**

DINING ◆
Cha Cha Cha **9**
Restaurant Edith **10**
Sobre Las Olas **12**

ATTRACTIONS ●
Cahuita National Park Entrance **2**
Bus Stop **5**

SHOPPING ▣
Bodhi's Books & Gifts **7**
Boutique Coco Miko **5**
Boutique Bambata **4**
Cahuita Tours **8**

NIGHTLIFE ★
Coco's Bar **6**
National Park Restaurant **3**

Turística Cahuita Information Center (☎/fax **2755-0071**), all located on the village's main street.

Getting around

Downtown Cahuita is very compact and easily navigable by foot. However, some of the hotels located out toward Playa Negra are a good kilometer or more away from the center. You'll usually spot a few taxis cruising around town. If you can't find one on the street, try calling **Alejandro** (☎ **8875-3209**), **Wayne** (☎ **2755-0078**), or **Dino** (☎ **2755-0012**).

Spending the night

Alby Lodge
$ **Cahuita**

There are just four small private cabins here. The entire complex was hand-built by its German owners. Although close to the center of town and the national park entrance, Alby Lodge has the feel of being its own small village. The cabins are quintessentially tropical, with thatch roofs, mosquito nets, hardwood floors and beams, big shuttered windows, tile bathrooms, and a hammock slung on the front porch. They're surrounded by a large lawn and gardens. There's no restaurant here, but there is a communal kitchen area, if you want to cook your own meals. The turnoff for the lodge is on your right just before you reach the national-park entrance; the hotel is located about 136m (446 ft.) down a narrow, winding lane from here. Free Wi-Fi is available here.

See map p. 327. Cahuita. ☎/fax 2755-0031. www.albylodge.com. *Rack rates: $40 double. Children 11 and under stay free in parent's room. No credit cards.*

El Encanto Bed and Breakfast
$–$$$ Cahuita

Despite being close to the center of town, this place feels far removed. The individual bungalows are set in from the road, on spacious and well-kept grounds. The bungalows themselves are also spacious and have attractive touches that include wooden bed frames, arched windows, Mexican-tile floors, Guatemalan bedspreads, and framed Panamanian *molas* hanging on the walls. There is a separate two-story, three-bedroom, two-bathroom house with a full kitchen at the rear of the grounds, as well as a separate deluxe room. Hearty breakfasts are served in the small open dining room surrounded by lush gardens. Added amenities here include a small kidney-shaped pool, a meditation hall, a covered garden gazebo, and an open-air massage room.

See map p. 327. Just outside of town on the road to Playa Negra, Cahuita. ☎ 2755-0113. Fax: 2755-0432. www.elencantobedandbreakfast.com. *Rack rates: $70–$185 double. Rates include full breakfast. Rates slightly lower in the off season, higher during peak weeks. MC, V.*

Magellan Inn
$$ Playa Negra

This small inn is intimate and cozy. The rooms are carpeted and have French doors, vertical blinds, tiled bathrooms with hardwood counters, and two joined single beds. Although there's a ceiling fan over each bed, the non-air-conditioned rooms could use a bit more ventilation. However, more than half of the rooms here have air-conditioners, and they plan to add A/C to the remaining rooms at the rate of one per year. Each room has its own tiled veranda with a Persian rug and bamboo sitting chairs. The combination bar/lounge and dining room features even more Persian-style rugs and bamboo and rattan furniture. The best features here are the hotel's sunken pool and lush gardens, both of which are built into a crevice in the ancient coral reef that underlies this entire region — which leads to good bird-watching. The entire hotel features free Wi-Fi.

See map p. 327. At the far end of Playa Negra (about 2km/1¼ miles north of downtown), Cahuita. ☎/fax 2755-0035. www.magellaninn.com. *Rack rates: $79 double, $89 double with A/C. Rates include continental breakfast. AE, MC, V.*

Selva Bananito Lodge
$$$–$$$$ **Bananito**

This remote nature lodge is a great stop either before or after you spend some serious beach time in Cahuita or Puerto Viejo. The individual raised-stilt cabins are large and comfortable, with an abundance of varnished woodwork. Inside, you'll find two double beds, a desk and chair, and some fresh flowers, as well as a large private bathroom. Outside there's a wrap-around veranda with a hammock and some chairs. Half the cabins have views of the Bananito River and a small valley; the other half have views of the Matama Mountains, part of the Talamanca mountain range.

There are no electric lights at Selva Bananito and the hot water is provided by a passive solar system. Each evening as you dine by candlelight, your cabin's oil lamps are lit for you. Tasty family-style meals are served in the large, open rancho, which is also a great spot for morning bird-watching. The lodge offers a wide range of tours and activities, including rain-forest hikes and horseback rides in the jungle, tree-climbing, self-guided trail hikes, and even the opportunity to rappel down the face of a jungle waterfall.

The owners are very involved in conservation efforts in this area, and approximately two-thirds of the 840 hectares (2,100 acres) here are primary forest managed as a private reserve. You'll need a four-wheel-drive vehicle to reach the lodge itself, although most folks leave their rental cars in Bananito and let the lodge drive them the final leg. You can also arrange to be picked up in San José.

Bananito. ☎ **2253-8118.** *Fax: 2280-0820.* www.selvabananito.com. *Rack rates: $260–$280 double. Rates include 3 meals daily and all taxes. Rates lower in the off season. No credit cards.*

Dining locally

Cha Cha Cha
$$–$$$ **Cahuita SEAFOOD/INTERNATIONAL**

Fresh seafood and grilled meats, simply and expertly prepared are served here. What more could you ask from a casual, open-air restaurant in a funky beach town? In addition to the fresh catch of the day and filet mignon, the menu here is an eclectic mix, including everything from jerk chicken and Thai shrimp salad to pasta primavera and fajitas. The grilled squid salad with a citrus dressing is one of the house specialties and a great light bite. The restaurant occupies the ground floor of an old wooden building. Everything is painted pure white, with some blue trim and accents. There are only a half-dozen or so tables, and this place fills up fast.

See map p. 327. On the main road in town, 3 blocks north of Coco's Bar. ☎ **8368-1725.** *Reservations recommended during the high season. Main courses: $6–$22. MC, V. Open: Tues–Sun 2–10 p.m.*

That rundown feeling

While on the Caribbean coast, be sure to try some "rondon" soup or stew. It's not roadkill, but rondon, which comes from "run down" and is a spicy coconut-milk stew made with anything the cook can run down. Ingredients usually include some fresh seafood, as well as a mix of local tubers, roots, and vegetables.

Restaurant Edith
$–$$$ Cahuita   CREOLE/SEAFOOD

This place is a local landmark, and deservedly so. If you want a taste of the local cuisine in a homey, sit-down environment, this is the place. While one of Miss Edith's daughters takes the orders, Mom and more daughters cook up a storm out back. The menu, when you can get hold of it, is long, with lots of local seafood dishes and Creole combinations such as yuca in coconut milk with meat or vegetables. The sauces here have spice and zest and are a welcome change from the typically bland fare served up throughout the rest of Costa Rica. Hours can be erratic; it sometimes closes without warning, and service can be slow and gruff at times. After you've ordered, it's usually no more than 45 minutes until your meal arrives. It's often crowded here, so don't be bashful about sitting down with total strangers at any of the big tables.

See map p. 327. By the police station, Cahuita. ☎ **2755-0248**. *Main courses: $3.50–$25. No credit cards. Open: Mon–Sat 11:30 a.m.–10 p.m. Opening hours vary.*

Sobre Las Olas
$$ Cahuita   ITALIAN/SEAFOOD

Set on a slight rise of rocks above a coral cove and breaking waves, this place has the best location in Cahuita. The funky wooden building housing the restaurant features full walls of large picture windows letting out onto the sea view. The Italian owners serve a mix of local and Italian fare. They serve excellent fresh squid or shrimp in a tangy local coconut milk sauce, as well as a host of pasta dishes. The fresh grilled snapper is also always a good way to go. I especially like this place for lunch, when you can really take advantage of the view of the clear blue Caribbean Sea. If the weather permits, grab one of the outdoor tables set in the shade of coconut palms. After you finish eating, you can slide over and into one of the hammocks strung between those palms.

See map p. 327. Just north of town on the road to Playa Negra. ☎ **2755-0109**. *Main courses: $5–$30. MC, V. Open: Wed–Mon noon to 10 p.m.*

Exploring Cahuita

The main attraction in this area is **Cahuita National Park**, which is located right where the main street in town ends. The other major attraction, **Aviarios del Caribe and the Buttercup Sloth Rescue Center,** is located a few miles north of town. You'll find detailed information about visiting and enjoying both of these places in this section.

Top attractions

Aviarios del Caribe and the Buttercup Sloth Rescue Center

This place is becoming one of the world's foremost research and rescue centers for two- and three-toed sloths. A visit here will feature a tour of their natural history center, as well as their sloth rehabilitation facilities. They also offer canoe tours through the surrounding estuary, where more than 330 species of birds have been spotted. And you can even hike their compact series of rain-forest and island trails.

*Located 9km (5½ miles) north of Cahuita. ☎/fax **2750-0775.** www.slothrescue. org. Admission: $15 for 1½-hour canoe-tour combination that includes a visit to the sloth rehabilitation center and self-guided hike on its trails; $30 for a 3½-hour canoe tour. Open: Daily 6 a.m.–4 p.m.*

Cahuita National Park

Cahuita National Park stretches south from the edge of town. The park features a long, beautiful curve of white sand backed by dense lowland rain forest. Although the soft white sand, lush coastal forest, and picture-perfect palm lines are a tremendous draw, the park was actually created to preserve the 240-hectare (787-acre) **coral reef** just offshore. The reef contains 35 species of coral and provides a haven for hundreds of brightly colored tropical fish.

The trail behind the beach stretches a little more than 6.4km (4 miles) to the southern end of the park at **Puerto Vargas,** where you'll find another beautiful white-sand beach, the park headquarters, and a basic camp-ground with showers and outhouses. It's a nice, flat walk, but a rewarding one because there's good wildlife viewing and access to the beach. The loud grunting sounds you hear off in the distance are the calls of howler monkeys, which can be heard from more than a kilometer away. Nearer at hand, you're likely to hear crabs scuttling amid the dry leaves on the forest floor — there are half a dozen or so species of land crabs living in this region.

The main **in-town park entrance** to the park is just over a footbridge at the end of the village's main street. It has bathroom facilities, changing rooms, and storage lockers. This is the best place to enter if you're just interested in spending the day on the beach and maybe taking a little hike in the bordering forest. The official park entrance is at the southern end of the park in **Puerto Vargas.** This is where you should come if you plan to camp at the park or if you don't feel up to hiking a couple of hours to reach the good snorkeling spots. The road to Puerto Vargas is approximately 5km (3 miles) south of Cahuita on the left.

There is an extra $2-per-person charge for **camping.** The 50 campsites at Puerto Vargas stretch along for several kilometers and are either right on

or just a few steps from the beach. My favorite campsites are those farthest from the entrance. There are basic shower and bathroom facilities
at a small ranger station, but these can be a bit far from some of the
campsites.

*See map p. 327. Located south of Cahuita village. The primary public entrance to the
park is at the southern edge of the village. The official park entrance and campsites
are at Puerto Vargas 7km (4⅓ miles) south of Cahuita.* ☎ **2755-0060.** *Admission: $10
per day at the Puerto Vargas entrance; voluntary donation at the town entrance.
Open: Daily 6 a.m.–5:30 p.m.*

More cool things to see and do

✔ **Horseback riding: Brigitte** (☎ 2755-0053; www.brigitte
   cahuita.com) rents horses for $20 per hour (you must have expe-
   rience) and offers guided horseback tours for $35 to $55. She also
   rents mountain bikes for $8 per day.

✔ **Butterfly-watching:** If you want to see a wide variety of butterflies,
   and learn about their fascinating natural history, head to
   Mariposario Cahuita (☎ 2755-0361). This place is located on the
   main highway just outside of town and is open daily from 8:30 a.m.
   to 3:30 p.m. Admission is $8.

✔ **Snorkeling:** Although there's snorkeling right from the beach at
   Puerto Vargas inside Cahuita National Park, the nicest coral heads
   are located several hundred meters offshore, and it's best to have a
   boat take you out. A three-hour **snorkel trip** should cost between
   $20 and $30 per person with equipment. These can be arranged
   by your hotel or with **Cahuita Tours and Adventure Center**
   (☎ 2755-0000).

Shopping for local treasures in Cahuita

For a wide selection of beachwear, local crafts, souvenirs, and batik
clothing, try **Boutique Coco** or **Boutique Bambata.** The latter is a good
place to have your hair wrapped in colorful threads and strung with
beads. Right in the center of town, **Bodhi's Books & Gifts** is a good new
option. Handmade jewelry and crafts are sold by local and itinerant artisans in makeshift stands near the park entrance.

Ask around town, and you may be able to pick up a copy of Paula
Palmer's *What Happen: A Folk-History of Costa Rica's Talamanca Coast.*
The book is a history of the region, based on interviews with many of
the area's oldest residents. Much of it is in the traditional Creole language, from which the title is taken. It makes fun and interesting reading,
and you just might bump into someone mentioned in the book.

If you're interested in the local music scene, you should definitely pick
up a disc by Walter "Gavitt" Ferguson. The local 88-year-old calypso
singer and songwriter is a living legend and has released two separate

CDs of his original songs, *Babylon* and *Dr. Bombodee*. Ask around town, and you should be able to find a copy. If you're lucky, you may even bump into Walter as well.

Living it up after dark in Cahuita

Coco's Bar (no phone), a classic Caribbean watering hole located at the main crossroads in town, has traditionally been the place to spend your nights (or days, for that matter) if you like cold beer and very loud reggae and soca music. Toward the park entrance, the **National Park Restaurant** has a popular bar and disco on most nights during the high season and on weekends during the off season. Check them both out; on any given night, you may be more drawn to one or the other.

Puerto Viejo and the Southernmost Beaches

Although Puerto Viejo is farther down the road from Cahuita, it's much more popular and has a livelier vibe, due in part to the many surfers who come here from around the country (and around the world) to ride the village's famous Salsa Brava wave.

As you head still farther south, you'll come to the most beautiful beaches on this coast, with white sand and turquoise seas. When it's calm (Aug–Oct), the waters down here are some of the clearest anywhere in the country, with good snorkeling among the nearby coral reefs. Paving of the road, all the way to Manzanillo, has made these beaches much more accessible, and a slew of small, moderately priced and budget hotels have been built along this stretch of coast.

This is the end of the line along Costa Rica's Caribbean coast. After the tiny town of Manzanillo, some 15km (9⅓ miles) south of Puerto Viejo, a national wildlife reserve stretches a few final kilometers to the Panamanian border.

Getting there

As with Cahuita, driving a rental car in Puerto Viejo gives you independence and the ability to explore the region on your own. However, if you want to leave the driving to others, bus and minivan services are available. You can also fly into Limón and take a taxi the rest of the way. You'll find information on all these options in the following sections.

By air

Nature Air (☎ **800-235-9272** in the U.S. and Canada, 2299-6000 in Costa Rica; www.natureair.com) flies from San José to Limón on Monday, Wednesday, Saturday, and Sunday. Taxis are always waiting for arriving flights and can take you the final leg down to Puerto Viejo.

By car

To reach Puerto Viejo, continue south from Cahuita for another 16km (10 miles). Watch for a prominent fork in the highway. The right-hand fork continues on to Bribri and Sixaola. The left-hand fork (it actually appears to be a straight shot) takes you into Puerto Viejo on 5km (3 miles) of paved, but very potholed and washed out, road.

By bus

MEPE express buses (☎ **2257-8129** in San José, 2750-0023 in Puerto Viejo) to Puerto Viejo leave San José several times a day from the Gran Terminal del Caribe (Caribbean bus terminal) on Calle Central, 1 block north of Avenida 11. The trip's duration is four and a half to five hours; fare is $8. During peak periods, extra buses are sometimes added. Always ask whether the bus is going into Puerto Viejo (you don't want to end up getting dropped off at the turnoff for Sixaola) and whether it's continuing on to **Manzanillo** (especially helpful if you're staying in a hotel south of town).

Alternatively, you can catch one of the frequent buses to Limón from the same station and then transfer to a Puerto Viejo–bound bus in Limón. These latter buses (☎ **2758-1572**) leave roughly every hour between 5 a.m. and 6 p.m. from Radio Casino, which is 1 block north of the municipal market. Buses from Limón to Manzanillo also stop in Puerto Viejo and leave daily at 5 a.m., 10:30 a.m., 3 p.m., and 6 p.m.

 If you arrive by bus, be leery of hucksters offering you hotel rooms. In most cases, they just work on a small commission from whatever hotel or *cabina* is hiring, and, in some cases, they'll steer you away from one of my recommended hotels or falsely claim that it's full.

Gray Line (☎ **2220-2126;** www.graylinecostarica.com) and **Interbus** (☎ **2283-5573;** www.interbusonline.com) both have daily bus service between San José and Puerto Viejo. The fare is $35 to $39. Both companies will pick you up and drop you off at most hotels, both in San José and in Puerto Viejo.

Orienting yourself in Puerto Viejo and the southernmost beaches

The road in from the highway heads right toward the ocean and then runs parallel to Playa Negra (Black Sand Beach) for a couple hundred meters before entering the village of Puerto Viejo, which has one paved road through the center of town and about ten dirt streets around it. The sea will be on your left and forested hills on your right as you come into town. It's another 15km (9⅓ miles) south to Manzanillo. Along this road, you'll pass the beaches of Playa Cocles, Playa Chiquita, and Punta Uva. Aside from some short sections of gravel, this road is paved all the way to Manzanillo, although heavy rains and traffic have taken their toll.

The **Asociación Talamanqueña de Ecoturismo y Conservación** (Talamancan Association of Ecotourism and Conservation, or ATEC), across the street from the Soda Tamara (☎ **2750-0398** or tel/fax 2750-0191; www.greencoast.com), is concerned with preserving both the environment and the cultural heritage of this area and promoting ecologically sound development. In addition to functioning as the local **information center,** Internet cafe, and traveler's hub, ATEC runs a little shop that sells T-shirts, maps, posters, and books. If you're looking to stay in Puerto Viejo for an extended period of time and would like to contribute to the community, you can ask here about volunteering.

Getting around

You can rent bicycles at almost every hotel or corner around Puerto Viejo; they make an excellent means of getting around.

The town's main **taxi** driver is named **Bull** (☎ **2750-0112** or 8836-8219). You may find him hanging around the *parquecito* (little park), or you can ask a local to point you to his house. If Bull's not around or he's busy, you could try **Delroy** (☎ **2750-0132**).

Spending the night

Azania Bungalows
$$ **Playa Cocles**

This collection of individual bungalows is an excellent option for those seeking a quiet, romantic, tropical getaway. The spacious bungalows are set apart from each other amid the hotel's high flowering gardens, giving each a sense of seclusion. All come with one queen-size bed and one double bed downstairs and another double bed in the small loft. The thatch roofs are high-pitched and, combined with large, screened windows, allow for good cross ventilation. The lounge area features a television with DirecTV, a small lending library, a collection of board games, and free Wi-Fi. There's also a small, refreshing free-form swimming pool with a sculpted waterfall, and an open-air, thatch-roofed, poolside restaurant.

See map p. 341. Playa Cocles. ☎ *2750-0540. Fax: 2750-0371.* www.azania-costa rica.com. *Rack rates: $85 double. Rates include full breakfast. Rates lower in the off season, higher during peak weeks. AE, DC, MC, V.*

Cariblue Bungalows
$$–$$$$ **Playa Cocles**

This Italian-run miniresort is a wonderful choice. The rooms are spread around well-tended and lush grounds. My favorites are the individual raised-stilt wood bungalows. The beds are covered with mosquito nets, and there's a small veranda with a hammock. The nicest features here are the bathrooms, with their intricate mosaic-tile designs. The standard rooms are spacious and comfortable but not quite as private or charming as the bungalows. There's also a two-bedroom house with a full kitchen, for families or for longer stays. The resort has a midsize free-form swimming pool with swim-up bar, and large restaurant and lounge area, with free Wi-Fi. Cariblue is located about 90m (295 ft.) or so inland from the southern end of Playa Cocles.

See map p. 341. Playa Cocles. ☎ **2750-0035** *or tel/fax 2750-0057.* www.cariblue. com. *Rack rates: $95–$120 double, $220 house. Rates include breakfast buffet. Rates slightly lower in the off season. AE, MC, V.*

Casa Verde Lodge
$ **Puerto Viejo**

This is my favorite hotel right in the village of Puerto Viejo, regardless of price. Despite being located in the heart of town, a quiet sense of tropical tranquility pervades this place. The rooms with shared bathrooms are housed in a raised building with a wide, covered breezeway between the rooms. The front and back porches of this building are hung with hammocks and surrounded by lush gardens, where you'll find the showers and toilets. The rest of the rooms are spread around the small complex. Most are larger, with high ceilings, tile floors, private bathrooms, and a private veranda. There's also a small separate bungalow with a kitchenette. Everything is very well maintained, and even the shared bathrooms are kept immaculate. There's a small but well-stocked gift shop, a coffee shop, and delightful pool area. Even though it's an in-town choice, there's great bird-watching all around the grounds here.

See map p. 341. Puerto Viejo. ☎ **2750-0015.** *Fax: 2750-0047.* www.cabinas casaverde.com. *Rack rates: $38–$50 double with shared bathroom, $70 double with private bathroom. Rates slightly higher during peak weeks, lower in the off season. AE, MC, V.*

La Costa de Papito
$–$$ **Playa Cocles**

This intimate collection of individual and duplex cabins is located just across from Cocles Beach, about 1.6km (1 mile) south of Puerto Viejo. The wooden bungalows come with one or two double beds, artfully tiled bathrooms, and an inviting private porch with a table and chairs and either a hammock or a swing chair. La Costa de Papito has been steadily expanding over the years, adding new cabins and amenities. There's an excellent restaurant on site, as well as a well-run little spa.

See map p. 341. Playa Cocles. ☎ **2750-0704** *or tel/fax 2750-0080.* www.lacosta depapito.com. *Rack rates: $54–$78 double. Rates include breakfast buffet. Rates lower in the off season. AE, MC, V.*

Playa Chiquita Lodge
$ **Playa Chiquita**

Set amid the shade of large old trees several kilometers south of Puerto Viejo toward Punta Uva (watch for the sign), the lodge consists of several wooden buildings set on stilts and connected by a raised wooden walkway. There are wide verandas with built-in seating and rocking chairs. The spacious rooms are painted in bright colors. A short trail on the grounds leads down to a semiprivate little swimming beach with tide pools and beautiful turquoise water. This stretch of beach is the site of a daily 4 p.m. pickup volleyball game.

The owners have three children, ranging from a young child to a couple of teenagers, and travelers with kids will feel like part of the family. The owners also rent out fully equipped houses for those interested in longer stays or more privacy and independence.

See map p. 341. Playa Chiquita. ☎ *2750-0062 or tel/fax 2750-0408.* www.playa chiquitalodge.com. *Rack rates: $60 double. Rates lower in the off season. Rates include breakfast. AE, MC, V.*

Shawandha Lodge
$$ Playa Chiquita

If you're looking for an isolated and romantic getaway, this small collection of individual bungalows is a great choice. Set in a lush patch of forest about 180m (590 ft.) or so inland from Playa Chiquita, Shawandha has the feel of a small village. Artistic flourishes abound. The thatch-roofed, raised bungalows feature painted exterior murals, high-pitched ceilings, varnished wood floors, and either one king-size bed or a mix of queen-size and single beds.

The bathrooms are practically works of art, each with original, intricate mosaics of hand-cut tile highlighting a large, open shower. Each bungalow has its own spacious balcony, with both a hammock and a couch, where you can lie and look out on the lush, flowering gardens. The beach is easily accessed by a private path, and a host of activities and tours can be arranged.

There's a large open-air restaurant and lounge where meals and drinks are served. The menu is an eclectic mix, featuring fresh fish and meats in a variety of French, Caribbean, and Polynesian sauces.

See map p. 341. Playa Chiquita. ☎ *2750-0018. Fax: 2750-0037.* www.shawandha lodge.com. *Rack rates: $115 double. Rates higher during peak weeks, lower in the off season. Rates include full breakfast. AE, MC, V.*

Tree House Lodge
$$$$–$$$$$ Playa Chiquita

The three individual houses here are the most unique and stylish to be found on the Caribbean coast. All three are distinct, with fluid and fanciful architectural details and loads of varnished hardwoods. The namesake Tree House is built around a large *sangrillo* tree, while the Beach House Suite features a massive and spectacular domed bathroom with scores of different colored skylights.

The property is located on a beautiful piece of beachfront right off Punta Uva, one of the best and most stunning swimming beaches on this coast.

A runner-up hotel

If all the hotels above are full, you might try Banana Azul Guest House, a very good little hotel. Set on the quiet far northern edge of Playa Negra, this place is awash in varnished hardwoods. Service is attentive and friendly. $–$$. Puerto Viejo, Limón. ☎ **2750-2035** or **8351-4582**. www.bananaazul.com.

See map p. 341. Punta Uva. ☎ 2750-0706. www.costaricatreehouse.com. Rack rates: $250–$390 double. Rates higher during peak weeks, lower in the off season. Rates include full breakfast. No credit cards.

Dining locally

Bread & Chocolate
$–$$ Puerto Viejo   AMERICAN/BAKERY

Perfect for breakfast or lunch, this place is almost always bustling and full. Breakfasts feature waffles, French toast, and pancakes served with some namesake fresh chocolate sauce, or egg dishes served with home-baked biscuits, bagels, or whole-wheat bread. For lunch, sandwiches are served on aforementioned homemade bread. Though you can opt for a BLT, grilled cheese, or jerk chicken sandwich, those with kids (or kids at heart) might want to sample the PB&J or PB&Chocolate, with all homemade ingredients. Both breakfast and lunch are served all day. Don't leave without trying or buying some of their brownies and truffles.

See map p. 341. On the main road. ☎ 2750-0723. Main courses: $3.75–$6. MC, V. Open: Wed–Sat 6:30 a.m.– 6:30 p.m., Sun 6:30 a.m.– 2:30 p.m.

El Loco Natural
$$ Puerto Viejo   INTERNATIONAL

A funky, hippie vibe pervades this open-air restaurant. Seating is at simple wooden tables. The short menu features several vegetarian items, as well as fresh fish and some chicken and meat dishes, prepared in curry, Thai, and Mexican sauces. There's often live music here, running the gamut from reggae to jazz to Latin American folk.

See map p. 341. On the main road just south of downtown. ☎ 2750-0530. Main courses: $4–$15. No credit cards. Open: Thurs–Mon 6–10 p.m.

La Pecora Nera
$$$–$$$$ Playa Cocles   ITALIAN

This open-air joint on the jungle's edge has a well-earned reputation as the finest Italian restaurant in the region, if not the country. Owner Ilario Giannoni is a whirlwind of enthusiasm and activity, switching hats all night long from maître d' to chef to waiter to busboy and back in an entertaining blur. Sure, he's got help, including his grandmother making gnocchi, but it sometimes seems like he's doing it single-handedly. The menu has a broad selection of pizzas and pastas, but your best bet is to just ask Ilario what's fresh and special for that day and to trust his instincts and inventions. I've had fabulous fresh pasta dishes and top-notch appetizers every time I've visited. These folks also have a simpler, more casual restaurant, Gatta Ci Cova, on the main road, just beside the entrance to La Pecora Nera, featuring a much more limited menu of pastas, main courses, and panini sandwiches.

See map p. 341. 50m (164 ft.) inland from a well-marked turnoff on the main road south just beyond the fútbol (soccer) field in Cocles. ☎ **2750-0490.** _Reservations recommended. Main courses: $10–$22. AE, MC, V. Open: Tues–Sun 5:30–11 p.m._

Soda Tamara
$–$$$ Puerto Viejo   COSTA RICAN/CREOLE

This little open-air restaurant has long been popular with budget-conscious travelers and has an attractive setting for such an economical place. The multi-colored painted picket fence in front gives the restaurant a homey feel. The menu features standard local fish, chicken, and meat entrees, served with a hefty helping of Caribbean-style rice and beans. You can also get _patacones_ (fried chips made out of plantains) and a wide selection of fresh-fruit juices. At the counter inside, you'll find homemade cocoa candies and unsweetened cocoa biscuits made by several women in town. They're definitely worth a try. Soda Tamara also has a second-floor open-air bar that's open nightly from 6 p.m. until the last straggler calls it quits.

See map p. 341. On the main road. ☎ **2750-0148.** _Main courses: $3.50–$30. AE, MC, V. Open: Daily 11:30 a.m.–10p.m._

Exploring Puerto Viejo and the southernmost beaches

Miles of often deserted beaches backed by thick rain forest are the main attraction of this region, and in this section, I tell you how to best enjoy them.

The top attractions

The Beaches South of Puerto Viejo

The beaches south of Puerto Viejo are arguably some of the best in the country. Here, thick rain forests and coastal coconut palms come right down to the shore, meeting soft white-sand beaches that front clear, blue Caribbean seas.

The first beach you reach as you head south out of town is **Playa Cocles.** This long, white-sand beach is popular with surfers, especially those not up to the challenge of the thick and treacherous Salsa Brava reef break.

Beyond Playa Cocles lies **Playa Chiquita.** This stretch is characterized by small protected patches of swimmable beach and tide pools punctuating a wavy coastline of exposed and shallow reefs. This is a good place to come and search out a little private cove or tide pool.

Perhaps the most popular beach down here is **Punta Uva** (Grape Point), a beautiful and protected curve of soft sand lying in the lee of a small forested hillside and outcropping. There's a short loop trail through the forest and over the rocks of this gorgeous outcropping.

At the end of the road lies **Manzanillo,** a tiny village with only a few basic *cabinas* and funky *sodas.* The town is the gateway to the Manzanillo-Gandoca Wildlife Refuge (see listing later in this section). The beaches just off the town, as well as those inside the refuge, are stellar. The entire area off the town and much of the refuge is protected by coral reef, making these some of the most beautiful beaches on the coastline, as well as some of the best for swimming.

If you have a rental car, you can explore the various beaches down here at your whim and leisure. However, don't fret if you don't have a car. To reach any of these beaches, you can catch the 7:30 a.m. bus from Puerto Viejo down to Manzanillo. There are a couple more buses throughout the day as well. The last bus back leaves Manzanillo at 5 p.m. It's always wise to check with **Asociación Talamanqueña de Ecoturismo y Conservación** (ATEC) about current local bus schedules. Call ☎ **2750-0398** or tel/fax 2750-0191; also visit www.greencoast.com. You could also hire a cab for around $8 to Punta Uva or $12 to Manzanillo. Call **Bull** (☎ **2750-0112** or 8836-8219) or **Delroy** (☎ **2750-0132**).

Alternatively, it should take you less than an hour each way by bicycle, with only two relatively small hills to contend with. However, although the road is ostensibly paved all the way to Manzanillo, much of it is severely potholed and washed out. It's even possible to walk along the beach all the way from Puerto Viejo to Manzanillo, with just a couple of short and well-worn detours inland around rocky points.

See map p. 341. **Playa Cocles** *is 2km (1¼ miles) south of Puerto Viejo,* **Playa Chiquita** *is 5km (3 miles) from town,* **Punta Uva** *is 8km (5 miles) away, and* **Manzanillo** *is about 15km (9⅓ miles) south of town.*

Finca La Isla Botanical Gardens

One of the nicest ways to spend a day in Puerto Viejo is to visit the Finca La Isla Botanical Gardens. Host Peter Kring, and his late wife, Lindy, poured much time and love into the creation of this meandering collection of native and imported tropical flora. There are medicinal, commercial, and just plain wild flowering plants, fruits, herbs, trees, and bushes here. Visitors get to gorge on whatever is ripe at the moment. You're almost guaranteed to see some poison dart frogs here. There is also a rigorous rain-forest loop trail leaving from the grounds.

See map p. 341. A couple hundred meters inland from the Black Sand Beach on the road that leads into town. ☎ *2750-0046 or 8886-8530.* crgarden@mac.com.

Puerto Viejo

ACCOMMODATIONS ■
Azania Bungalows **16**
Banana Azul Guest House **1**
Cariblue Bungalows **15**
Casa Verde Lodge **12**
La Costa de Papito **17**
Playa Chiquita Lodge **19**
Shawandha Lodge **20**
Tree House Lodge **21**

DINING◆
Bread & Chocolate **10**
El Loco Natural **14**
La Pecora Nera **18**
Soda Tamara **9**

ATTRACTIONS ●
Asociación Talamanqueña
de Ecoturismo y
Conservacion (ATEC) **8**

Finca La Isla Botanical
Gardens **2**
Manzanillo-Gandoca
Wildlife Refuge **22**

NIGHTLIFE ★
Baba Yaga **11**
E-Z Times **7**
Johnny's Place **6**
Stanford's **13**

SHOPPING ▣
Color Caribe **4**
Jewelry Factory **5**
Luluberlu **3**

Admission: $5 per person for the garden or loop trail, or $10 per person with the guided tour. Open: Fri–Mon 10 a.m.–4 p.m., but visits can sometimes be arranged for other days with advance notice.

Manzanillo-Gandoca Wildlife Refuge

The Manzanillo-Gandoca Wildlife Refuge encompasses the small village of Manzanillo and extends all the way to the Panamanian border. Manatees, crocodiles, and more than 350 species of birds live within the boundaries of the reserve. The reserve also includes the coral reef offshore — when the seas are calm, this is the best snorkeling and diving spot on this entire coast. Four species of sea turtles nest on one 8.9km (5½-mile) stretch of beach within the reserve between March and July. Three species of dolphin also inhabit and frolic in the waters just off Manzanillo. Many local tour guides and operators offer boat trips out to spot them.

If you want to explore the refuge, you can easily find the single, well-maintained trail by walking along the beach just south of town until you have to wade across a small river. On the other side, you'll pick up the trailhead. Otherwise, you can ask around the village for local guides.

Inside the Manzanillo-Gandoca refuge is the **Punta Mona Center For Sustainable Living & Education** (☎ 2222-4568; www.puntamona.org). With organic permaculture gardens and a distinctly alternative vibe, this place is open for day visits, overnight stays, and work-exchange and educational programs. A day trip to visit the center, its garden, and facilities, including a vegetarian organic lunch, costs $45; overnight stays cost $40, including three meals.

See map p. 341. 10km (6 miles) southeast of Puerto Viejo. ☎ 2750-0398. *Open: Daily 7 a.m.–4 p.m.*

More cool things to see and do

- ✔ **Getting to know the local culture:** The **Asociación Talamanqueña de Ecoturismo y Conservación (ATEC;** ☎ 2750-0398 or tel/fax 2750-0191; www.greencoast.com) offers half-day and full-day tours that focus on nature and either the local Afro-Caribbean culture or the indigenous Bribri culture. These tours pass through farms and forests, and along the way you'll learn about local history, customs, medicinal plants, and mythology. You'll also have an opportunity to see sloths, monkeys, iguanas, keel-billed toucans, and other wildlife.

  You'll find a range of different tours through the nearby Bribri Indians' Kéköldi Reserve, as well as more strenuous hikes through the primary rain forest. Bird walks and night walks will help you spot more of the area wildlife; there are even overnight camping treks. The local guides who lead these tours have a wealth of information and make a hike through the forest a truly educational experience. Half-day walks (and night walks) are $20 to $35, and a full day costs $30 to $65. ATEC can arrange snorkeling trips to the nearby coral reefs, as well as snorkeling and fishing trips in dugout canoes. A half-day of snorkeling or fishing costs around $35 per person.

- ✔ **Scuba-diving and snorkeling:** Scuba divers can check in with **Reef Runners Dive Shop** (☎ 2750-0480; www.reefrunnersdivers. com). This operation frequents about ten different dive sites between Punta Uva and Manzanillo. When the seas are calm and visibility is good, this beach offers some good snorkeling and diving.

- ✔ **Surfing:** Just offshore from Puerto Viejo's tiny village park is a shallow reef where powerful storm-generated waves sometimes reach 6m (20 ft.). **Salsa Brava,** as it's known, is the prime surf break on the Caribbean coast. Even when the waves are small, this spot is recommended only for very experienced surfers because of the danger of the reef. Less-experienced riders should head for the beach break at Playa Cocles. You can rent surfboards and boogie boards from several makeshift roadside stands around town.

✔ **Taking a yoga class or getting a massage:** If either of these options sounds interesting, check in with **Samasati** (☎ **800-563-9643** in the U.S., 2756-8015 in Costa Rica; www.samasati.com), a lovely jungle yoga retreat with spectacular hillside views of the Caribbean Sea and surrounding forests. You can come up for yoga classes ($15), meditations ($5), or private massages ($75–$110) with advance notice. Samasati is located a couple of kilometers before Puerto Viejo (near the turnoff for Bribri) and roughly 1.6km (1 mile) up into the jungle.

For some in-town pampering, try **Pure Jungle Spa** (☎ **2750-0536;** www.purejunglespa.com), which offers a wide range of massage and treatment options.

✔ **Doing a little bit of this and a little bit of that at Cacao Trails** (☎ **2756-8186;** www.cacaotrails.com): Great for families, this is a one-stop attraction featuring botanical gardens, a small serpentarium, an open-air museum demonstrating the tools and techniques of cacao cultivation and processing, and a series of trails. There's also a large open-air restaurant, and a swimming pool for cooling off. You can also take canoe rides on the bordering Carbon River, and even watch sea turtles lay their eggs during the nesting season. Admission to the attraction is $25, including a guided tour. A full-day tour, including lunch and a canoe trip, as well as the guided tour, costs $47. During turtle nesting season, they do night tours to watch sea turtles lay their eggs.

Shopping for local treasures

Puerto Viejo attracts a lot of local and international bohemians, who seem to survive solely on the sale of handmade jewelry, painted ceramic trinkets (mainly pipes and cigarette-lighter holders), and imported Indonesian textiles. You'll find them at makeshift stands set up by the town's *parquecito* (little park), in a line of wooden kiosks fronting the sea between Soda Tamara and Stanford's.

If you venture away from the makeshift artisan stands, **Luluberlu,** located inland across from Cabinas Guaraná, features locally produced craftwork, including shell mobiles and mirrors with mosaic-inlaid frames, as well as imports from Thailand and India. **The Jewelry Factory** and **Color Caribe,** both on the main road into town, sell a wide range of jewelry, crafts, and gift items, as well as Costa Rican hammocks.

Living it up after dark in Puerto Viejo

Puerto Viejo has one of the best nightlife scenes in the country. There are two main discos/bars in town. **Johnny's Place** (☎ **2750-0623**), is near the Rural Guard station, about a block or so north of the ATEC office. You'll find **Stanford's** (☎ **2750-0016**) overlooking the water out near Salsa Brava just as the main road heads south of town. Both have small dance floors with ground-shaking reggae and rap rhythms blaring. The action usually spills out from the dance floor at both joints on most nights. I like the atmosphere better at Johnny's, where they have tables and candles set out on the sand, near the water's edge.

For a more sophisticated ambience, but still with a crowded dance floor, try the downtown **Baba Yaga** (☎ **8388-4359**).

Another place I like, **E-Z Times** (☎ **2750-0663**) has a more relaxed vibe, with occasional live music performances.

Tortuguero

Tortuguero comes from the Spanish name for the giant sea turtles *(tortugas)* that nest on the beaches of this region every year from early March to mid-October. The chance to see this nesting attracts many people to this remote region, but just as many come to explore the intricate network of jungle canals that serve as the region's main transportation arteries. This stretch of coast is connected to Limón, the Caribbean coast's only port city, by a series of rivers and canals that parallel the sea, often running only about 90m (295 ft.) from the beach. This aquatic highway is lined for most of its length with a dense rain forest that is home to howler and spider monkeys, three-toed sloths, toucans, and great green macaws. A trip up the canals is a bit like cruising the Amazon, but on a much smaller scale.

Getting there

Independent travel is not the norm in this area, although it's possible. Most folks rely on their lodge for boat transportation through the canals and into town. At most of the lodges around Tortuguero, almost everything (bus rides to and from, boat trips through the canals, and even family-style meals) is done in groups. Depending on a variety of factors, this group feeling can be intimate and rewarding or overwhelming and impersonal.

By air

Nature Air (☎ **800-235-9272** in the U.S. and Canada, 2299-6000 in Costa Rica; www.natureair.com) and **Sansa** (☎ **877-767-2672** in the U.S. and Canada, 2290-4100 in Costa Rica; www.flysansa.com) both have regular daily flights to the small airstrip in Tortuguero. In addition, many lodges in this area operate charter flights as part of their package trips. Flights take between 35 and 45 minutes and cost $98 each way on Sansa, $107 each way on Nature Air.

By land and water

You can't drive to Tortuguero. If you have a car, your best bet is to leave it in San José and take an organized tour or drive it to Limón or Moín, find a secure hotel or public parking lot, and then follow my directions

Tortuguero

ACCOMMODATIONS ■
Casa Marbella **2**
Laguna Lodge **6**
Manatus Hotel **7**
Mawamba Lodge **5**
Tortuga Lodge **8**

DINING ◆
Miss Junie's Restaurant **3**

ATTRACTIONS ●
Caribbean Conservation
  Corporation's
  Museum **4**
Tortuguero National Park
  Office **1**

for arriving by boat. There is also secure parking in La Pavona, which meets the boats plying the Cariari and La Pavona route outlined here.

Flying to Tortuguero is convenient if you don't have much time, but a boat trip through the canals and rivers of this region is often the highlight of any visit to Tortuguero. However, although this trip can be stunning and exciting, it can also be tiring and uncomfortable. You'll first have to ride by car, bus, or minivan from San José to Moín, Caño Blanco, or one of the other embarkation points; then it's two to three hours on a boat, usually with hard wooden benches or plastic seats.

All the more expensive lodges listed later in this chapter offer their own bus and boat transportation packages, which include the boat ride through the canals. However, if you're coming here independently, you'll have to arrange your own transportation. In this case, you have a few options.

The most traditional option is to get yourself first to Limón and then to the docks in Moín, just north of Limón, and try to find a boat on your own. Buses leave roughly every half-hour throughout the day for Limón from **Gran Terminal del Caribe,** on Calle Central, 1 block north of Avenida 11 (☎ **2222-0610**). If you're coming by car, make sure you drive all the way to Limón or Moín unless you have prior arrangements out of Cariari or Caño Blanco Marina.

From Limón, you can catch one of the periodic local buses to Moín right from the main bus terminal or hire a taxi for around $6. There are always plenty of taxis hanging around the bus terminal and cruising the streets of Limón. **Taxi Limón** is the main cab company (☎ **2758-1539**).

At the docks, you should be able to negotiate a fare of $40 to $70, depending on how many people you can round up to go with you. These boats tend to depart between 8 a.m. and 10 a.m. every day. Usually, the fare you pay covers the return trip as well, and you can arrange with the captain to take you back when you're ready to leave. The trip from Moín to Tortuguero takes three to four hours.

You can also get to Tortuguero by bus and boat from Cariari. This is the cheapest and most adventurous means of reaching Tortuguero from San José, but it's also more work — and if you miss a connection or the boats aren't running, you could get stuck in a backwater banana village. To take this route, begin by catching the 9 a.m. or 10:30 a.m. direct bus to Cariari from the **Gran Terminal del Caribe,** on Calle Central, 1 block north of Avenida 11 (☎ **2222-0610**). The fare is $2.50. This bus will actually drop you off at the main bus terminal in Cariari, from which you'll have to walk 5 blocks north to a separate small bus station. Look for a booth marked "Coopetraca" or "Clic Clic." At these booths you can buy your bus ticket for La Pavona. The bus fare is around $2. Buy a ticket for the noon bus (a later bus leaves at 3 p.m.). A boat or two will be waiting to meet the bus at the dock at the edge of the river at around 1:30 p.m. and again at 4:30 p.m. Check out the boats heading to Tortuguero, and pick the one that looks most comfortable and safe; then pay onboard.

The boat fare to Tortuguero is not regulated, and the price sometimes varies for foreigners. It can be as low as $3 each way, which is what locals pay. However, the boat captains often try to gouge tourists. Stand firm; you should not have to pay more than $5. Return boats leave Tortuguero for La Pavona every day at 6 a.m., 11:30 a.m., and 3 p.m., making return bus connections to Cariari.

Be careful if you decide to take this latter route. I've received reports of unscrupulous operators providing misinformation to tourists. Folks from a company called **Bananera** have set up shop at the Gran Terminal del Caribe and in Cariari, offering to sell you "packaged transportation" to Tortuguero. However, all they're doing is charging you extra to buy the individual tickets described here. Be especially careful if the folks selling you boat transportation aggressively steer you to a specific hotel option, claim that your first choice is full, or insist that you must buy a package with them that includes the transportation, lodging, and guide services. If you have doubts or want to check on the current state of this route, check out www.tortuguerovillage.com, which has detailed directions about how to get to Tortuguero by a variety of routes.

Orienting yourself in Tortuguero

Tortuguero is one of the most remote locations in Costa Rica. There are no roads into this area and no cars in the village, so all transportation is by boat or foot. Most of the lodges are spread out over several kilometers to the north of the village of Tortuguero on either side of the main canal; the small airstrip is at the north end of the beachside spit of land.

Tortuguero Village is a tiny collection of houses connected by footpaths. The village is spread out on a thin spit of land, bordered on one side by the Caribbean Sea and on the other by the main canal. At most points, it's less than 300m (984 ft.) wide. In the center of the village you'll find a small children's playground and a *fútbol* (soccer) field, as well as a kiosk that has information on the cultural and natural history of this area.

There is a private **information center** (☎ **8833-0827**) in front of the Catholic church in the center of town. This is a good place for independent travelers looking to arrange local tours and onward travel.

Getting around

Transportation in and around Tortuguero is either by foot or small boat. If you stay at a hotel on the ocean side of the canal, you'll be able to walk into and explore the village at your leisure; if you're across the canal, you'll be dependent on the lodge's boat transportation.

There are no banks, ATMs, or currency-exchange houses in Tortuguero, be sure to bring sufficient cash in colones to cover any expenses and incidental charges. The local hotels and shops generally charge a bit of a commission to exchange dollars.

Spending the night

Casa Marbella
$ **Tortuguero Village**

This in-town option is a great choice for budget travelers looking for a bit more comfort and care than that offered at most of the more inexpensive options found right in the village. The rooms here all have high ceilings, tile floors, firm mattresses, and white walls with varnished wood trim. The two "superior" rooms have views of the canal. Owner Daryl Loth is a long-time resident and well-respected naturalist guide. Breakfast is served on a little patio facing the main Tortuguero canal in back of the house. A wide range of tours and onward travels can be arranged. A small library with a good selection of natural history books, a lounge and library area, and free Wi-Fi throughout complete the facilities here.

See map p. 345. Tortuguero. ☎ **8833-0827** *or tel/fax* **2709-8011.** http://casa marbella.tripod.com. *Rack rates: $40–$60 double. Rates include breakfast. Rates lower in the off season. No credit cards.*

Laguna Lodge
$$$$ **Tortuguero**

This rustically plush lodge is located 2km (1¼ miles) north of Tortuguero Village, on the ocean side of the main canal (which allows you to walk along the beach and into town, at your leisure). The rooms are all spacious and attractive. Most have wood walls, waxed hardwood floors, and tiled bathrooms with screened upper walls to let in air and light. Each room also has a little shared veranda overlooking flowering gardens.

The large dining room, where basic buffet-style meals are served, is located on a free-form deck that extends out over the Tortuguero Canal. Another covered deck, also over the water, is strung with hammocks for lazing away the afternoons. Several covered *palapa* huts strung with hammocks have also been built among the flowering ginger and hibiscus. A large and inviting pool, with a poolside bar and grill, as well as lush botanical gardens are on-site. All the standard Tortuguero tours are available.

See map p. 345. Tortuguero. ☎ **2272-4943** *in San José, 2709-8082 at the lodge. Fax: 2272-4927.* www.lagunatortuguero.com. *Rack rates: $526 double for 2 days/1 night, $660 double for 3 days/2 nights. Rates include round-trip transportation from San José, tours, taxes, and 3 meals daily. AE, DC, MC, V.*

Manatus Hotel
$$$$$ **Tortuguero**

This intimate hotel offers the most luxurious accommodations in Tortuguero. The large rooms are plush and well-equipped, with two queen-size beds, high ceilings, wood floors, tasteful local furnishings, and a host of amenities you won't find anywhere else in the area. Meals and service are top-notch here, and they have the best little spa of any local hotel, as well as an on-site art gallery. The amoeba-shaped pool is set just off the dark waters of the Tortuguero canal, with a broad deck and plenty of inviting chaise lounges surrounding it. Children 9 and under are not allowed at the hotel.

See map p. 345. Tortuguero. ☎ **2239-4854** *reservations in San José, 2709-8197 at the hotel. Fax: 2239-4854.* www.manatushotel.com. *Rack rates: $780 double for 2 days/1 night, $990 double for 3 days/2 nights. Rates include round-trip transportation from San José, 3 meals daily, taxes, and daily tours. Rates lower in the off season. AE, MC, V.*

Mawamba Lodge
$$$$ **Tortuguero**

Mawamba is quite similar to Laguna Lodge (see the listing earlier in this chapter); in fact, they're owned by brothers. Also located on the ocean side of the canal, Mawamba is even closer to the village. Rooms have brightly painted walls, varnished wood floors, twin beds, hot-water showers, ceiling fans, and verandas with rocking chairs. The gardens are lush and overgrown with flowering ginger, heliconia, and hibiscus. There are plenty of hammocks around for anyone who wants to kick back, and a beach volleyball court for those who don't.

The family-style meals here are above average for Tortuguero. Rates include a four-hour boat ride through the canals and a guided forest hike. These folks have an extensive menu of kayaking tours and excursions, including one package in which you actually kayak part of the way into Tortuguero. There's a small gift shop on the premises, a small butterfly garden, and nightly lectures and slide shows that focus on the natural history of this area.

See map p. 345. Tortuguero. ☎ **2293-8181** *in San José, 2709-8100 at the lodge. Fax: 2239-7657.* www.grupomawamba.com. *Rack rates: $526 double for 2 days/1 night, $660 double for 3 days/2 nights. Rates include round-trip transportation from San José, 3 meals daily, taxes, and some tours. Rates lower in the off season. AE, MC, V.*

Tortuga Lodge
$$$$ Tortuguero

This is one of the oldest hotels in Tortuguero, and still one of the best. My favorite feature here is the long, multilevel deck located off the main dining room, where you can sit and dine, sip a cool tropical drink, or just take in the view as the water laps against the docks at your feet. There's also a lovely little pool built by the water's edge and designed to create the illusion that it blends into Tortuguero's main canal. Most of the rooms have contemporary wood furniture, tropical décor, and loads of freshly varnished hardwood. Each room comes with either one double and one twin bed or one king-size bed, a ceiling fan, and a comfortable private bathroom. There's also a two-bedroom, two-bath, second-floor penthouse suite, great for families or those wanting more space. Run by Costa Rica Expeditions, service here is top-notch, as are the family-style meals. There are several acres of forest behind the lodge, and a few kilometers of trails wind their way through the trees. This is a great place to look for howler monkeys and colorful poison dart frogs.

See map p. 345. Tortuguero. ☎ **2257-0766** *in San José, 2709-8034 at the lodge. Fax: 2257-1665.* www.tortugalodge.com. *Rack rates: $248 double, $338 penthouse. Rates include full meal plan. Rates lower in the off season, slightly higher during peak periods. Package rates with transportation, meals, and tours are available. AE, MC, V.*

Dining locally

Miss Junie's Restaurant
$ Tortuguero Village   CARIBBEAN/COSTA RICAN

There's little in the way of style or flare at this simple, screened-in restaurant with concrete floors and spartan décor. But the food is hearty and well prepared, and Miss Junie is a delightful host. Have the local rice and beans cooked in coconut milk along with some fresh fish or lobster.

See map p. 345. Tortuguero Village. ☎ *2709-8102. Main courses: $3–$9. No credit cards. Open: Daily 6 a.m.–10 p.m.*

Exploring Tortuguero

This is a very remote region, with no cars. All travel around the region is by boat. Most of the hotels include visits to the various attractions here as part of their package prices. If not, they'll certainly offer them as added-on tour options.

The top attractions

Caribbean Conservation Corporation's Visitors Center and Museum

Aside from the national park, the only other real attraction in town is the small Caribbean Conservation Corporation's Visitors Center and Museum. The museum has information and exhibits on a complete range of native flora and fauna, but its primary focus is on the life and natural history of sea turtles. Most visits to the museum include a short, informative video on these turtles. There's a small gift shop here, and all the proceeds go toward conservation and turtle protection.

See map p. 345. ☎ *2709-8091.* www.cccturtle.org. *Admission: $1. Open: Mon–Sat 10 a.m. to noon and 2–5:30 p.m., Sun 2–5 p.m.*

Tortuguero National Park

Tortuguero National Park exists primarily to protect a major nesting site for several species of sea turtles. According to existing records, sea turtles have frequented the beaches here since at least 1592, largely due to the area's extreme isolation. Over the years, turtles were captured and their eggs were harvested by local settlers; by the 1950s, this practice became so widespread that the turtles faced extinction. Regulations controlling this mini-industry were passed in 1963, and in 1970, Tortuguero National Park was established.

Today, four different species of sea turtles nest here: the green turtle, the hawksbill, the loggerhead, and the giant leatherback. The prime nesting period is from **July to mid-October** (with Aug–Sept being the peak months). Nesting takes place at night, and if you're lucky you'll be able to watch one of these mammoth maritime reptiles laboriously dig a deep hole and then deposit scores of eggs into it. (When the nesting is completed, the turtle covers up the hole and heads back to sea.)

When the turtles are nesting, you'll have to arrange a night tour in advance with either your hotel or one of the private guides working in town. These guided tours generally run between $10 and $15. Flashlights and flash cameras are not permitted on the beach at night because the lights discourage the turtles from nesting.

Turtle tour tips

Visitors to the beach at night must be accompanied by a licensed guide. Tours generally last two to four hours.

Sometimes you must walk quite a bit to encounter a nesting turtle. Wear sneakers or walking shoes rather than sandals. The beach is very dark at night, and you can easily trip or step on driftwood or other detritus.

Wear dark clothes. White T-shirts are not permitted.

Flashlights, flash cameras, and lighted video cameras are prohibited on turtle tours.

Smoking is prohibited on the beach at night.

You can also explore the park's rain forest, either by foot or by boat, and look for some of the incredible varieties of wildlife that live here: jaguars, anteaters, howler monkeys, collared and white-lipped peccaries, some 350 species of birds, and countless butterflies, among others. Boat tours are far and away the most popular way to visit this park, although one frequently very muddy trail here starts at the park entrance and runs for about 2km (1¼ miles) through the coastal rain forest and along the beach.

Most people visit Tortuguero as part of a package tour. Be sure to confirm whether the park entrance is included in the price. Moreover, only certain canals and trails leaving from the park station are actually within the park. Many hotels and private guides take their tours to a series of canals that border the park and are very similar in terms of flora and fauna but don't require a park entrance.

See map p. 345. Located at the southern edge of Tortuguero Village. The Tortuguero National Park entrance and ranger station are at the south end of Tortuguero Village. ☎ *2710-2929. Admission: $10 per day. Open: Daily 8 a.m.–4 p.m.*

More cool things to see and do

- ✔ **Canoeing or kayaking on your own:** In the village, you can rent dugout canoes, known in Costa Rica as *cayucos* or *pangas*. Be careful before renting and taking off in one of these; they tend to be heavy, slow, and hard to maneuver, and you may be getting more than you bargained for. **Miss Junie** (☎ 2709-8102) rents more-modern, lighter, fiberglass canoes for around $5 for a half-day.

- ✔ **Enjoying the beach:** Although Tortuguero's beaches are excellent places to watch sea turtles nest, they aren't particularly well suited for swimming. The surf is usually very rough, and the river mouths have a nasty habit of attracting sharks that feed on the turtle hatchlings and many fish that live here.

Fast Facts: The Caribbean Coast

Ambulance

Call ☎ 128.

ATMs

You'll find ATMs in the port city of Limón, and in Cahuita and Puerto Viejo. There are no ATMs in Tortuguero.

Country Code and City Code

The country code for Costa Rica is **506**. There are no city or area codes within Costa Rica. To call from the United States, dial 011-506 plus the eight-digit number. From within Costa Rica, simply dial the eight-digit number.

Currency Exchange

Most hotels will exchange money, although they often either charge a commission or give below the official rate. To get official rates, you'll need to head to one of the banks in Limón, Cahuita, or Puerto Viejo.

Fire

Call ☎ 118.

Hospitals

The closest hospital is Hospital Tony Facio in Limón (☎ 2758-2222), although there are either local doctors or a small clinic in each of the major destinations here — Tortuguero, Cahuita, and Puerto Viejo.

Information

There are few official information offices in southern Costa Rica. Most hotels have a tour desk, concierge, or helpful front-desk staff.

Internet Access

There are Internet cafes in the general "downtown" areas of Cahuita, Puerto Viejo, and even Tortuguero. In addition, a few of the isolated lodges in Tortuguero provide Internet access for their guests.

Newspapers

This is a very isolated region, although most lodges here receive local newspapers, including the *Tico Times*.

Pharmacies

There are pharmacies in Cahuita and Puerto Viejo but none in Tortuguero. The Cahuita pharmacy (☎ 2755-0383) is located in the health clinic on the principal access road into town, about a block before you hit the main crossroad at the center of the village. Farmacia Amiga (☎ 2750-0698) in Puerto Viejo is located in the small shopping center smack-dab in the center of the village.

Police

Call ☎ 911.

Post Office

There is no post office in Tortuguero, but most hotels can mail your letters and postcards for you. There is a post office in Cahuita (☎ 2755-0096) and another in Puerto Viejo (☎ 2750-0404). Alternatively, most hotels can mail your letters and postcards for you.

Taxis

There are numerous taxis in Cahuita and Puerto Viejo. Try calling Alejandro (☎ 8875-3209), Wayne (☎ 2755-0078), or Dino (☎ 2755-0012) in Cahuita. In Puerto Viejo, call Bull (☎ 2750-0112 or 8836-8219) or Delroy (☎ 750-0132). In Tortuguero, you'll either have to walk or tour around by boat.

Part VIII
The Part of Tens

"In Costa Rica everything comes with rice and beans. Just pay the man for your dry cleaning and let's go."

In this part . . .

In this part, I dispel ten myths and misconceptions many folks have about Costa Rica. Then I point you toward my list of ten favorite moments and experiences available to travelers here.

Chapter 22

Ten Myths about Costa Rica

In This Chapter
- ▶ Learning to love bugs
- ▶ Getting a handle on the weather
- ▶ Finding a good cup of joe

Despite its popularity, many misconceptions about Costa Rica exist. This chapter should help dispel a few.

Costa Rica Is Just for the Adventurous

Sure, the country is an adventure traveler's dream, and you can rough it if you want. But you can also choose from a host of very luxurious options, which run the gamut from ultra-exclusive boutique hotels to large luxury resorts run by the Four Seasons and Marriott chains.

Costa Rica Isn't for Families

You won't find many amusement parks or video arcades here, but Costa Rica has a ton of fun and interesting stuff for the entire family. Options that will thrill all ages include educational hikes in the rain forest, rafting trips, zip-line canopy tours, and butterfly gardens. In addition, Costa Rican hotels are increasingly gearing up to meet the needs of families. Children's programs and reliable baby-sitting are becoming more and more common.

Bugs Are Bad

You'll probably encounter far fewer biting bugs in Costa Rica than you'd expect. Moreover, the insect world is one of the most diverse, fascinating, and vitally important elements of all tropical ecosystems. Learn to love the shimmering beetles, long-legged stick bugs, and industrious leaf-cutter ants, and your visit to Costa Rica will be much more enjoyable. Of course, some insect repellent and light, long-sleeved clothing are always good when mosquitoes or sand flies are present.

Costa Rica Is an Ecological Eden

Although this is partially true, Costa Rica nevertheless faces serious challenges and threats from legal and illegal logging, as well as animal hunting and poaching, pollution, overbuilding, poor planning, and rapid development run amok.

You Can't Drink the Water

Some travelers get a bit sick or queasy with any change to their intestinal flora, but in general, the water is safe to drink in most major tourist hotels and destinations in Costa Rica. That said, if you're at all predisposed to a tender tummy, rely on bottled water and drinks.

The Caribbean Coast Is Dangerous

This myth is quite prevalent in Costa Rica, and I blame a few high-profile crimes and basic racism in equal measure. The fact is that the Caribbean coast is no more or less dangerous than any other major tourist destination in Costa Rica.

It's Okay to Feed the Monkeys

Don't listen to any guide or hotel owner who tells you this. **Remember:** It is *not* cool to feed monkeys or any other wild animal. Wild animals are just that: wild. Close contact with humans — especially humans offering food — alters their behavior, survival mechanisms, and immune systems.

It's Always Raining in the Rain Forest

Sure, it rains a lot in the rain forest — over 508cm (200 in.) per year in many cases. However, these rains are often hard and intense for short durations. Apart from the period between early September and mid-November, it's rare for a visit to a rain-forest lodge to be characterized by constant rainfall. Mornings are often clear and sunny. During the months when the rain forests are, well, rainy, the Caribbean coast is generally bathed in sunshine and calm weather, so you're better off staying there. If you do get caught in the rain, remember: This is what makes the rain forest so vibrant and verdant.

Everybody Speaks English

Although most hotel, restaurant, and tour-agency workers have a working knowledge of English, most rural Costa Ricans do not. Knowing a few important Spanish words and phrases can go a long way toward improving your interactions and relationships with Costa Ricans. See Chapter 2 for more information.

Costa Rican Coffee Is the Best

Costa Rica does produce some of the world's finest coffee, but most of the best beans are destined for export. Moreover, Costa Ricans themselves seem to prefer a weak and very sweet brew. Still, you can get good coffee at most of the better restaurants and hotels, as well as in establishments catering to foreigners.

If you're buying coffee to bring home, make sure you get whole beans, and shoot for a reputable brand such as Cafe Britt, or one of the high-end smaller roasters, such as Cafe Milagro or Cafe Monteverde.

Chapter 23

Ten Costa Rican Moments

In This Chapter
▶ Enjoying a true taste of the local cuisine
▶ Setting your clock to the natural sounds and rhythms
▶ Bathing at the foot of a jungle waterfall
▶ Watching an active volcano erupt

*T*he activities, adventures, and attractions listed in this chapter range from the classic to the obscure and from calm and mellow to wet and wild. I outline many more in the various destination chapters of this book. But be sure to try to fit a few of these experiences into your trip to Costa Rica.

Pouring Salsa Lizano on Your Gallo Pinto

Salsa Lizano, a tart but mild sauce made with vinegar, and *gallo pinto* (rice and beans) are both ubiquitous staples of Costa Rican cuisine. So, order up some *gallo pinto* and pour on some tangy *Salsa Lizano.* If you want to really sound like a local, simply ask for some "Lizano para mi pinto." See Chapter 2 for more information on Costa Rican cuisine.

Waking Up to the Sound of Howler Monkeys

You can leave the alarm clock at home. At many jungle lodges, the first sound you'll hear is the deep guttural roar of a howler monkey. First reactions can range from fear to awe to laughter. If they start going off around 4 a.m., you might simply be annoyed. . . .

Catching Your First Wave

Costa Rica's miles of coastline are loaded with wonderful surf spots. Many of these are excellent waves for beginners. Sign up for a class and you could be hanging ten before you know it.

Zipping among Treetops on a Canopy Tour

Canopy tours are the rage in Costa Rica. If you're reasonably fit and not particularly *acrophobic* (afraid of heights), there's no reason not to strap on a climbing harness, hook on your pulley system, and glide off into the void.

Watching a Sea Turtle Come Ashore to Nest

Following ancient rhythms and routes, sea turtles come ashore at various beaches around Costa Rica to dig their nests and lay a clutch of eggs. Tortuguero is the prime destination for observing this phenomenal feat. See Chapter 21 for more information.

Enjoying a Pacific Ocean Sunset

Villa Caletas (☎ **2637-0606;** www.hotelvillacaletas.com) offers up perhaps the most popular sunset spectacle. But you can enjoy the beauty of a sunset over the Pacific Ocean from almost any beach in Guanacaste, as well as from most hotels and lodges in Manuel Antonio and Drake Bay, as well as along the Osa Peninsula. See Chapter 16 for more information on Villa Caletas.

Marveling at the City Lights at a Mirador

If you're spending a night in San José, grab a cab and head for the hills. A *mirador* is the local name for a restaurant with a view. **Mirador Ram Luna** (☎ **2230-3060**), in the town of Asseri, and **Mirador Tiquicia** (☎ **2289-5839**), above Escazú, are two good options. See Chapter 12 for details on each.

Soaking in the Pool of a Jungle Waterfall

If you have to hike a little bit first, it makes the dip that much more refreshing. The waterfall at Montezuma is one of the popular places to take a plunge. But I prefer the lesser-known **La Cangrejo Falls** inside **Rincón de la Vieja National Park.** See Chapter 11 for more information.

Catching the Glint of Sunlight off a Quetzal's Feathers

The iridescent feathers of a Resplendent Quetzal can range from blue to green to turquoise to deep indigo, with various shades in between, depending upon the angle of the light. This, combined with its bright red chest feathers and brilliant yellow beak, make the Quetzal one of the most spectacular birds on the planet.

Watching Arenal Volcano Blow Its Top

It takes patience and luck, but if you get to catch a clear night with active eruptions, you're in for a treat. I recommend getting a room with a view at **Tabacón Grand Spa Thermal Resort** (☎ **877-277-8291** in the U.S. and Canada; www.tabacon.com); that way you can just roll over and watch whenever a loud blast wakes you. See Chapter 18 for more information.

Quick Concierge

Fast Facts

American Express

American Express Travel Services is represented in Costa Rica by ASV Olympia, Oficentro La Sabana, Sabana Sur (☎ 2242-8585; www.asvolympia.com), which can issue traveler's checks and replacement cards and provide other standard services. To report lost or stolen Amex traveler's checks within Costa Rica, call the number above or ☎ 2295-9000, or call collect to 336-393-1111 in the United States.

ATMs

Costa Rica has an extensive network of ATMs. You'll find one or more ATMs in virtually every town and city, and at most tourist destinations around the country. You'll find them at almost all banks and most shopping centers. The two major networks, Cirrus (☎ 800-424-7787; www.mastercard.com) and PLUS (☎ 800-843-7587; www.visa.com), are both present in Costa Rica.

In 2009, in response to a rash of "express kidnappings" in San José, in which people were taken at gunpoint to an ATM to clean out their bank accounts, both Banco Nacional and Banco de Costa Rica stopped ATM service between the hours of 10 p.m. and 5 a.m. Other networks still dispense money 24 hours a day.

Credit Cards

Visa and MasterCard are the most widely accepted cards in Costa Rica, followed by American Express, and to a much lesser extent Diners Club. To report a lost or stolen American Express card from inside Costa Rica, you can call ☎ 0800-012-3211; for MasterCard, call ☎ 0800-011-0184; for Visa, call ☎ 0800-011-0030; and for Diners Club, call Credomatic, ☎ 2295-9898.

Credomatic (☎ 2295-9898) is the local representative of most major credit cards: American Express, Diners Club, MasterCard, and Visa. It has an office in San José across from the Banco de San José on Calle Central, between avenidas 3 and 5. It's open Monday through Friday from 8 a.m. to 7 p.m., and Saturday from 9 a.m. to 1 p.m. You can call Credomatic to report all lost or stolen cards 24 hours a day.

Currency Exchange

You can change money at all banks in Costa Rica. Sometimes, especially at state-run banks, the service and process can be slow and tedious. Private banks have much more agile service.

Hotels will usually exchange money as well. You won't have to wait in line, but they may shave a few colones off the exchange rate.

There's a Global Exchange currency exchange booth just outside the Customs and Immigration area of the Juan Santamaría International Airport in San José, but they give a very anemic exchange rate.

Be very careful about exchanging money on the streets; it's extremely risky. In addition to forged bills and short counts, street money-changers frequently work in teams that can leave you holding neither colones nor dollars.

Customs

Visitors entering Costa Rica are officially entitled to bring in 500 grams of tobacco, 5 liters of liquor, and $500 in merchandise. Cameras, computers, and electronic equipment for personal use are permitted duty free. Customs officials in Costa Rica seldom check tourists' luggage.

For information on what returning U.S. citizens are allowed to bring back from Costa Rica, download the invaluable free pamphlet "Know Before You Go" online at www.cbp.gov, or contact the U.S. Customs & Border Protection (CBP), 1300 Pennsylvania Ave. NW, Washington, DC 20229 (☎ 877-287-8667) and request the pamphlet.

Canadian citizens can send for the booklet "I Declare," issued by the Canada Border Services Agency (☎ 800-461-9999 in Canada; www.cbsa-asfc.gc.ca).

U.K. citizens should contact HM Customs & Excise at ☎ 0845-010-9000 (from outside the U.K., 020-8929-0152), or consult their Web site at www.hmce.gov.uk.

Australian tourists can get "Know Before You Go," a helpful brochure available from Australian consulates or Customs offices,

or contact the Australian Customs Service at ☎ 1300-363-263 or www.customs.gov.au.

New Zealanders can get the New Zealand Customs Guide for Travellers, Notice no. 4 from New Zealand Customs, The Customhouse, 17–21 Whitmore St., Box 2218, Wellington (☎ 04-473-6099 or 0800-428-786; www.customs.govt.nz).

Driving

Driving a car in Costa Rica is no idle proposition. The roads are riddled with potholes, most rural intersections are unmarked, and, for some reason, sitting behind the wheel of a car seems to turn peaceful Ticos into homicidal maniacs.

A current foreign driver's license is valid for the first three months you're in Costa Rica. Seat belts are required for the driver and front-seat passengers.

If you're involved in an accident, you should contact the Instituto Nacional de Seguros (National Insurance Institute, or INS) at ☎ 800-800-8000. You should probably also call the Transit Police (☎ 800-8726-7486 toll-free nationwide, or 2222-9330); if they have a unit close by, they'll send an officer. An official transit police report will greatly facilitate any insurance claim. If you can't get help from any of these, try to get written statements from any witnesses. Finally, you can also call ☎ 911, and they should be able to redirect your call to the appropriate agency.

Electricity

The standard in Costa Rica is the same as in the United States: 110 volts AC (60 cycles). However, three-pronged outlets can be scarce, so bringing along an adapter is helpful.

Embassies and Consulates

The following embassies and consulates are located in San José: U.S. Embassy, in front of Centro Commercial, on the road to Pavas (☎ 2519-2000, or 2220-3127 after hours in case of emergency); Canadian Consulate, Oficentro Ejecutivo La Sabana, Edificio 5 (☎ 2242-4400); and British Embassy, Paseo Colón, between calles 38 and 40 (☎ 2258-2025). There are no Australian or New Zealand embassies in San José.

Emergencies

In case of any emergency, dial ☎ **911** (which should have an English-speaking operator); for an ambulance, call ☎ **128**; and to report a fire, call ☎ **118**. If 911 doesn't work, you can contact the police at ☎ 2222-1365 or 2221-5337, and they may be able to find someone who speaks English.

Information

See "Where to Get More Information," later in this chapter.

Internet Access and Cybercafes

Internet cafes can be found all over San José and at most major tourist destinations in Costa Rica. Rates run between 50¢ and $3 per hour. Many hotels either have their own Internet cafe or have Wi-Fi or in-room high-speed Ethernet service. If your hotel doesn't provide the service and no Internet cafe is close by, you can buy prepaid cards in 5-, 10-, and 15-hour denominations for connecting your laptop to the Web via a local phone call. Some knowledge of configuring your computer's dial-up connection is necessary. Be sure to factor in the phone-call charge if calling from a hotel. These cards are sold at many supermarkets and drugstores around the country, or contact Racsa (☎ 2287-0087; www. racsa.co.cr), the state Internet monopoly, to find out where you can buy one.

Language

Spanish is the official language of Costa Rica. In most tourist areas, many Costa Ricans speak English very well, however. *Frommer's Spanish PhraseFinder & Dictionary* (Wiley) is a good book to bring with you.

Liquor Laws

Alcoholic beverages are sold every day of the week throughout the year, with the exception of the two days before Easter and the two days before and after a presidential election. The legal drinking age is 18, although it's almost never enforced. Liquor — everything from beer to hard spirits — is sold in specific liquor stores, as well as at most supermarkets and even convenience stores.

Maps

The Costa Rican Tourist Board (☎ 800-343-6332; www.visitcostarica.com) can usually provide you with decent maps of both Costa Rica and San José. They have booths at both international airports, as well as in downtown San José.

Other sources in San José for detailed maps include Seventh Street Books, Calle 7, between avenidas Central and 1 (☎ 2256-8251), and Librería Universal, Avenida Central, between calles Central and 1 (☎ 2222-2222).

Police

In most cases, dial ☎ 911 for the police, and you should be able to get someone who speaks English on the line. Other numbers for the Judicial Police are ☎ 2222-1365 and 2221-5337. The numbers for the

Traffic Police (Policía de Tránsito) are ☎ 800-8726-7486 toll-free nationwide, or 2222-9330.

Post Office

A post office is called a *correo* in Spanish. The main post office in San José is on Calle 2, between avenidas 1 and 3 (☎ 800-900-2000 toll-free in Costa Rica; www.correos.go.cr).

Mailing a postcard or letter to the United States costs 170 colones (30¢); 190 colones (35¢) to Europe. Given the Costa Rican postal service's track record, I recommend paying an extra 500 colones (90¢) to have anything of any value certified.

For important documents or goods, you could use one of the international courier services. DHL, on Paseo Colón, between calles 30 and 32 (☎ 2209-0000; www.dhl.com); EMS Courier, with desks at most post offices (☎ 800-900-2000; www.correos.go.cr); FedEx, which is based in Heredia but will arrange pickup anywhere in the metropolitan area (☎ 800-463-3339; www.fedex.com); and UPS, in Pavas (☎ 2290-2828; www.ups.com), all operate in Costa Rica.

Safety

Although Costa Rica is relatively safe, petty crime and robberies are common. And tourists are targeted for robbery across the country. San José is known for its pickpockets, so never carry a wallet in your back pocket. A woman should keep a tight grip on her purse. (Keep it tucked under your arm.) Thieves also target gold chains, cameras, video cameras, prominent jewelry, and nice sunglasses. Be sure not to leave valuables unlocked in your hotel room. Don't park a car on the street in Costa Rica, especially in San José;

there are plenty of public parking lots around the city.

Rental cars generally stick out, and they're easily spotted by thieves, who know that such cars are likely to be full of expensive camera equipment, money, and other valuables. Don't ever leave anything of value in a car parked on the street, not even for a moment. Also, be wary of solicitous strangers who stop to help you change a tire or bring you to a service station. Although most are truly good Samaritans, there have been reports of thieves preying on roadside breakdowns.

Public intercity buses are also frequent targets of stealthy thieves. Never check your bags into the hold of a bus if you can avoid it. If this can't be avoided, keep your eye on what leaves the hold. If you put your bags in an overhead rack, be sure you can see the bags at all times. Try not to fall asleep.

Finally, don't leave anything of value unattended on beaches or park benches or while dining or touring.

Smoking

Although smoking isn't as prevalent as it is in most of Europe, a large number of Costa Ricans smoke, and public smoking regulations and smoke-free zones have yet to take hold. Restaurants are required by law to have nonsmoking areas, but enforcement is often lax, so separate rooms aren't always available and air circulation may be poor. Bars are often very smoke-filled in Costa Rica.

Taxes

There is a 13 percent value-added tax on most goods and services. Restaurants charge 13 percent tax and also add on a

10 percent service charge, for a total of 23 percent more on your dining bill.

There is a $26 departure tax for all visitors leaving by air. This tax must be purchased prior to check-in. There are desks at the main terminal of all international airports where you can pay this tax. Some local travel agencies and hotels offer to purchase the departure tax in advance, as a convenience for tourists. You must give them authorization, as well as your passport number, and pay a small service fee.

Telephone

Costa Rica has an excellent phone system, with a dial tone similar to that heard in the United States.

To call Costa Rica from another country, dial the international access code (011 in Canada and the U.S., 0011 in Australia, 0170 in New Zealand, 00 in the U.K.) followed by the country code **506**, and the local eight-digit number.

To make a direct international call from within Costa Rica, dial the international access code 00, followed by the country code (1 for the U.S. and Canada, 61 for Australia, 64 for New Zealand, 44 for the U.K.), and finally the local number.

To make a call within Costa Rica, simply dial the eight-digit number. There are no area or long-distance codes.

A phone call within Costa Rica costs around 10 colones (20¢) per minute. Pay phones take either a phone card or 5-, 10-, or 20-colón coins. Phone cards are the way to go, as coin-operated phones are getting harder to find. You can purchase phone cards in a host of gift shops and pharmacies. However, there are several competing phone-card companies, and certain cards work only with certain phones. CHIP phone cards work with a computer chip and just slide into specific phones, although these phones aren't widely available. A better bet are the 197 and 199 phone cards, which are sold in varying denominations. These have scratch-off PINs and can be used from any phone in the country. In general terms, the 197 cards are sold in smaller denominations and are used for local calls, while the 199 cards are deemed international and are easier to find in larger denominations. Either card can be used to make any call, however, provided that the card can cover the costs. Another perk of the 199 cards is the fact that you can get the instructions in English. For local calls, calling from your hotel is often easiest, although you'll likely be charged around 100 to 300 colones (20¢–55¢) per call.

Numbers beginning with 0800 and 800 within Costa Rica are toll-free, but calling an 800 number in the States from Costa Rica is not toll-free. In fact, it costs the same as an overseas call.

Time Zone

Costa Rica is on central standard time (same as Chicago and St. Louis), six hours behind Greenwich mean time. Costa Rica does not use daylight saving time, so the time difference is an additional hour April through October.

Water

Although the water in San José is generally safe to drink, water quality varies outside the city. Because many travelers have tender digestive tracts, I recommend playing it safe and sticking to bottled drinks as much as possible. If you're really susceptible, you may also want to avoid ice.

Toll-Free Numbers and Web Sites

Airlines

Air Canada
☎ 888-247-2262 in the U.S. and Canada
www.aircanada.ca

American Airlines
☎ 800-433-7300 in the U.S. and Canada
☎ 2248-9010 in Costa Rica
www.aa.com

British Airways
☎ 800-247-9297 in the U.S. and Canada
☎ 0844-493-0787 in the U.K.
www.ba.com

Continental Airlines
☎ 800-231-0856 in the U.S. and Canada
☎ 0800-044-0005 in Costa Rica
www.continental.com

Delta Air Lines
☎ 800-221-1212 in the U.S. and Canada
☎ 0800-056-2002 in Costa Rica
www.delta.com

Frontier Airlines
☎ 800-432-1359 in the U.S. and Canada
www.frontierairlines.com

Iberia
☎ 800-772-4642 in the U.S. and Canada
☎ 2431-5633 in Costa Rica
www.iberia.com

JetBlue Airways
☎ 800-538-2583 in the U.S. and Canada
www.jetblue.com

Mexicana
☎ 800-531-7921 in the U.S. and Canada
☎ 2295-6969 in Costa Rica
www.mexicana.com

Nature Air
☎ 800-235-9272 in the U.S. and Canada
☎ 2299-6000 in Costa Rica
www.natureair.com

Sansa
☎ 877-767-2672 in the U.S. and Canada
☎ 2290-4100 in Costa Rica
www.flysansa.com

Spirit Air
☎ 800-772-7117 in the U.S. and Canada
☎ 0800-011-1103 in Costa Rica
www.spiritair.com

TACA
☎ 800-400-8222 in the U.S. and Canada
☎ 2299-8222 in Costa Rica
www.taca.com

United Air Lines
☎ 800-538-2929 in the U.S. and Canada
www.united.com

US Airways
☎ 800-622-1015 in the U.S. and Canada
☎ 0800-011-0793 in Costa Rica
www.usairways.com

Car-rental agencies

Adobe
☎ 800-769-8422 in the U.S. and Canada
☎ 2258-4242 in Costa Rica
www.adobecar.com

Alamo
☎ 877-222-9075 in the U.S. and Canada
☎ 800-462-5266 in Costa Rica
www.alamo.com

Avis
☎ 800-331-1212 in the continental U.S.
☎ 800-879-2847 in Canada
☎ 2293-2222 in Costa Rica
www.avis.com

Budget
☎ 800-472-3325 in the U.S. and Canada
☎ 2436-2000 in Costa Rica
www.budget.com

Dollar
☎ 800-800-3665 in the U.S. and Canada
☎ 2257-1585 in Costa Rica
www.dollar.com

Hertz
☎ 800-654-3001 in the U.S. and Canada
☎ 2221-1818 in Costa Rica
www.hertz.com

National
☎ 877-222-9058 in the U.S. and Canada
☎ 2242-7878 in Costa Rica
www.nationalcar.com

Payless
☎ 800-729-5377 in the U.S. and Canada
☎ 2257-0026 in Costa Rica
www.paylesscarrental.com

Thrifty
☎ 800-847-4389 in the U.S. and Canada
☎ 2257-3434 in Costa Rica
www.thrifty.com

Major hotel and motel chains

Best Western International
☎ 800-780-7234
www.bestwestern.com

Clarion Hotels
☎ 877-424-6423
www.choicehotels.com

Comfort Inns
☎ 877-424-6423
www.choicehotels.com

Courtyard by Marriott
☎ 888-236-2427
www.marriott.com/courtyard

Crowne Plaza
☎ 800-227-6963
www.ichotelsgroup.com

Days Inn
☎ 877-424-6423
www.choicehotels.com

Doubletree Hotels
☎ 800-445-8667
www.doubletree.com

Four Seasons
☎ 800-819-5053
www.fourseasons.com

Hampton Inn
☎ 800-445-8667
www.hamptoninn.com

Hilton Hotels
☎ 800-445-8667
www.hilton.com

Holiday Inn & Holiday Inn Express
☎ 800-465-4329
www.holidayinn.com

InterContinental Hotels & Resorts
☎ 800-424-6835
www.ichotelsgroup.com

Marriott Hotels
☎ 888-236-2427
www.marriott.com

Quality Inns
☎ 877-424-6423
www.choicehotels.com

Radisson Hotels & Resorts
☎ 888-201-1718
www.radisson.com

Ramada Worldwide
☎ 800-272-6232
www.ramada.com

Residence Inn by Marriott
☎ 888-236-2427
www.marriott.com/
    residenceinn

Where to Get More Information

You can get a basic packet of information on Costa Rica by contacting the Costa Rican Tourist Board (ICT, or Instituto Costarricense de Turismo; ☎ **800-343-6332**; www.visitcostarica.com). Travelers from the United Kingdom, Australia, and New Zealand will have to rely primarily on this Web site because the ICT does not have offices or a toll-free number in these countries.

In addition to this official site, you'll be able to find a wealth of Web-based information on Costa Rica with a few clicks of your mouse. In fact, you'll do better surfing because the ICT site is rather limited and clunky.

Some good places to start include the *Tico Times* (www.ticotimes.net), which puts up the top story from its weekly print edition, as well as a daily update of news briefs, a business article, regional news, a fishing column, and travel reviews. There's also a link to current currency-exchange rates. The Latin America Network Information Center (http://lanic.utexas.edu/la/ca/cr) is hosted by the University of Texas Latin American Studies Department and houses a vast collection of diverse information about Costa Rica. This is, hands-down, the best one-stop shop for Web browsing. It also has helpful links to a wide range of tourism and general information sites. Finally, Costa Rica Maps (www.mapcr.com) is the best site I've found for online maps. In addition to selling a wonderful waterproof map to the country, this site features several excellent downloadable nationwide, regional, and city maps, and a host of other useful information.

Index

• A •

AARP, 74
Abercrombie & Kent, 62
Above and Beyond Tours, 76
Abya Yala, 136
accommodations. *See also specific accommodations*
 budgeting for, 49
 cutting costs, 51–52
 online reservations, 52, 71
 overview, 67–68
 rate, finding best, 70–71
 room, reserving best, 72
 types, 9–13, 68–70, 367–368
 value, best, 11–12
activities. *See also* attractions
 Arenal and La Fortuna, 267–269, 275–276
 Cahuita, 332
 Dominical, 230–231
 Golfito and Golfo Dulce, 322–323
 Guanacaste, 173–178
 Jacó, 218–221
 Manuel Antonio, 196–202
 Monteverde, 251–252
 Montezuma, 288–289
 Playa Herradura, 218–221
 Puerto Jiménez and Osa Peninsula, 315–316
 Puerto Viejo, 342–343
 recommended, 15–16
 San José, 140–144
 Tortuguero, 351
Adventure Education Center, 230
adventure tours, 15–16, 41–43, 315, 355
Africa Mia, 170
Agua Azul restaurant (Manuel Antonio), 193
agua dulce, 23
air travel
 airfare, getting best, 51, 59–60
 airlines serving Costa Rica, 58–59, 366

Arenal and La Fortuna, 257
 booking online, 60–61
 Cahuita, 325
 Drake Bay, 300–301
 Golfito and Golfo Dulce, 317
 Guanacaste, 148–149
 Malpaís and Santa Teresa, 292
 Manuel Antonio, 184
 Montezuma, 282
 overview, 49, 64–65
 Puerto Jiménez and Osa Peninsula, 307
 Puerto Viejo, 333
 San José, 92–94
 security, 86–87
 Tortuguero, 344
 transportation to hotels, 92–94
Alajuela (San José), 99
Alby Lodge (Cahuita), 327–328
alcohol, 134, 363
Alta Hotel (San José), 107
Amberes bar, 179
American Express, 56, 57, 116, 361
Amor de Mar hotel (Montezuma), 12, 284
Annexation of Guanacaste Day, 33
APREFLOFAS (Association for the Preservation of the Wild Flora and Fauna), 78
Aqua bar, 179
Aqua Sport, 176
architecture, 21
Arco Iris Lodge (Santa Elena), 240
Arenal Kioro hotel (Lake Arenal), 259
Arenal and La Fortuna. *See also* Arenal Volcano; Lake Arenal
 accommodations, 259–263
 attractions and activities, 264–269
 fast facts, 270
 getting to/around, 256–259
 map, 256
 overview, 255–256
 restaurants, 263–264
 shopping, 269
 tourist information, 259

Arenal National Park, 264–265

Arenal Observatory Lodge (Arenal volcano), 12, 260

Arenal Pacifico hotel (Jacó), 210

Arenal volcano, 29, 255–256, 264–265, 360. *See also* Arenal and La Fortuna; Lake Arenal

Arenas del Mar hotel (Manuel Antonio), 10, 188

art, shopping for, 131–132

Asociación Talamanqueña de Ecoturismo y Conservación, 335, 340, 342

Association of British Insurers, 81

Association for the Preservation of the Wild Flora and Fauna (APREFLOFAS), 78

ASVO (Asociación de Voluntarios para el Servicio en las Areas Protegidas), 78

ATMs, 361. *See also* fast facts

attractions. *See also* activities

Arenal and La Fortuna, 264–267, 275

Cahuita, 330–332

Dominical, 228–230

Drake Bay, 304–306

Golfito and Golfo Dulce, 321–322

Guanacaste, 170–178

Jacó, 216–221

Malpaís and Santa Teresa, 297

Manuel Antonio, 196–202

Monteverde, 246–251

Montezuma, 287–288

Playa Herradura, 216–221

Puerto Jiménez and Osa Peninsula, 312–315

Puerto Viejo, 339–342

San José, 121–128

Tortuguero, 350–351

ATV tours, 199, 219

Auditorio Nacional, 136

Ave Natura, 198

Avenida Central (San José), 130

Aventuras Naturales, 142

Aviarios del Caribe and the Buttercup Sloth Rescue Center, 331

Azania Bungalows (Playa Cocles), 335

• *B* •

B&Bs, 69. *See also* accommodations

Baba Yaga bar, 344

Bacchus restaurant (San José), 110

Bahía National Park, 231

Bajo del Tigre Trail, 251

Baldi Termae, 266

Ballena Marine National Park, 228–229

Bambu Jam bar, 203

Banana Azul Guest House, 338

Banana Bay Marina, 322

Bar 1, 179

Barba Roja bar, 203

Barceló Langosta Beach, 179

Barrio Amón (San José), 95

Barrio Escalanta (San José), 98

Barrio Otoya (San José), 95

Barry Biesanz (handicraft store), 132–133

bars. *See* nightlife

Bat Jungle, 249

beaches

Dominical, 228, 230–231

Guanacaste, 148, 149, 151–153, 173–174

Jacó, 218–219

Manuel Antonio, 199

Montezuma, 289

overview, 14–15

Playa Herradura, 218–219

Puerto Viejo, 339–340

Tortuguero, 351

Best Western International, 367

Biesanz Woodworks, 133

Bijagual Waterfalls, 217

Bike Arenal, 268–269

Billfish Sportbar & Grill, 203

Blue Fin Sportfishing, 200

boating, 237, 301, 344–347

bocas, 22–23

Bodhi's Books & Gifts, 332

books, 24–25, 132

Borinquen Thermal Baths, 171

Bosque del Cabo Rainforest Lodge (Osa Peninsula), 13, 77, 311

botanical gardens, 315

Boutique Annemarie, 133

Boutique Bambata, 332

Boutique Coco, 332

boutique hotels, 69
Boutique Kiosco, 133
Brasilito Excursions, 178
Bread & Chocolate restaurant
    (Puerto Viejo), 338
Brisas del Nara, 201
Britain's Consumers' Association, 81
bucket shops, 59–60
budgeting
    costs, average, 48
    costs, cutting, 51–52
    dining, 50
    lodging, 49
    nightlife, 50
    rental cars, 49
    shopping, 50
    sightseeing, 50
    transportation, 48–49
bugs, 84, 249, 355
bungee-jumping, 140, 267–268
bus travel
    Arenal and La Fortuna, 257–258, 272
    Cahuita, 326
    Dominical, 224
    Drake Bay, 301
    Golfito and Golfo Dulce, 317–318
    Guanacaste, 149–150, 155
    Jacó, 208–209
    Malpaís and Santa Teresa, 292
    Manuel Antonio, 185–186
    Monteverde, 237–238
    Montezuma, 282–283
    overview, 66
    Playa Herradura, 208–209
    Puerto Jiménez and Osa Peninsula,
        308
    Puerto Viejo, 334
    San José, 93, 94, 100
business hours, 116
butterflies, 123–126, 248, 332

• C •

Cabalgata Don Tobias, 268
cabinas, 70, 73–74
Cabinas Los Cocos hotel (Playa
    Zancudo), 318–319
Cabinas San Clemente hotel
    (Dominical), 225
Cabinas Sol y Mar hotel (Playa
    Zancudo), 12, 319

Cabo Blanco Absolute Nature
    Reserve, 287–288
Cacao Trails, 343
Café Art Boruca dance club, 137
Café Britt Farm, 126, 134
Café de Playa bar and restaurant
    (Guanacaste), 164, 179
Café del Teatro Nacional restaurant
    (San José), 110
Café Milagro (Manuel Antonio), 196
Café Mundo restaurant (San José),
    111
Café Rica, 134
Cafeteria 1930 restaurant (San José),
    111, 124
Cahuita
    accommodations, 327–329
    attractions and activities, 330–332
    getting to/around, 325–327
    map, 327
    nightlife, 333
    restaurants, 329–330
    shopping, 332–333
Cahuita National Park, 331–332
Cahuita Tours and Adventure Center,
    326, 332
calendar of events, 33–34
Caliche's Wishbone restaurant (Jacó),
    215
Calypso Tours, 142
Camarón Dorado restaurant
    (Guanacaste), 165
canoeing, 351
Canopy del Pacifico, 297
Canopy Safari, 200
canopy tours
    Arenal and La Fortuna, 267
    Guanacaste, 177
    Jacó, 220
    Malpaís and Santa Teresa, 297
    Manuel Antonio, 200
    Monteverde, 249–250
    Montezuma, 288
    overview, 16, 141, 359
    Playa Herradura, 220
Caño Island, 304–305
Caño Negro National Wildlife Refuge,
    265
canyoning, 16, 267–268
Capullo Sportfishing, 176

car rentals
  agency contact information,
    366–367
  budgeting for, 49, 52
  Dominical, 225
  Guanacaste, 154
  Jacó, 210
  La Fortuna, 259
  Malpaís and Santa Teresa, 294
  Manuel Antonio, 187
  overview, 65–66
  Playa Herradura, 210
  San José, 93–94
Carara National Park, 208, 217–218
Caribbean coast, 30, 324, 356. *See also*
    Cahuita; Puerto Viejo;
    Tortuguero
Caribbean Conservation
    Corporation's Visitors Center
    and Museum, 350
Cariblue Bungalows (Playa Cocles),
    335–336
Carnaval, 34
Cartagena Canopy Tour, 177
Casa Corcovado Jungle Lodge (Osa
    Peninsula), 301–302
Casa de Arte, 253
Casa Delagua, 276
Casa Marbella hotel (Tortuguero),
    347–348
Casa Orquideas, 321–322
Casa Roland Marina Resort (Golfito),
    319
Casa Verde Lodge (Puerto Viejo),
    12, 336
Casagua Horses, 178
CASEM craft cooperative, 252–253
cash, carrying, 56
Casino Club Colonial, 140
Casino Del Rey, 140
Castro's dance club, 137
Catedral Nacional, 124
Celebrity Cruises, 61
Centers for Disease Control and
    Prevention (CDC), 82
central Pacific coast, 28, 205, 207, 208,
    217–218. *See also* Dominical;
    Jacó; Playa Hermosa; Playa
    Herradura
Centro Nacional de Arte y Cultura,
    121
Centro Panamericano de Idiomas, 252

Cerro de la Muerte (Mountain of
    Death), 223
Cha Cha Cha restaurant (Cahuita),
    329
Chalet Nicholas bed-and-breakfast
    (Nuevo Arenal), 273
Chelles bar, 138
Chiclets Tree Tour, 220
Chico's Bar, 289–290
Children's Museum, 122
Chimera restaurant (Cerro Plano), 244
Chunche's coffee shop, 245
Church of San Pedro, 139
Cinco Estrellas Taxi, 100
Ciudad Colón (San José), 98
Clarion Amón Plaza hotel (San José),
    102
Clarion Hotels, 367
Clarita's Beach Bar & Grill, 221
climate, 32, 356
Clínica Bíblica, 85
Club del Mar Condominiums & Resort
    (Jacó), 211
clubs. *See* nightlife
Coco Bay Hotel & Casino, 179
Cocomar bar, 179
Coconut Spice restaurant
    (Dominical), 227
Coco's Bar, 333
Cocozuma Traveler, 284
coffee, 23, 196, 245, 252, 357
colón, 53–54
Columbus, Christopher (explorer), 19
Comfort Inns, 367
communication, 85–86
Complejo Ecológico La Catarata, 217
Complejo Turistico Samoa del Sur
    hotel (Golfito), 320
ConFusione bar, 231
Congas dance club, 221
Congo Trail Canopy Tour, 177
consolidators, 59
consulates, 116, 363
Coopeguaria, 100
Coopeirazu, 100
Copa del Café (Coffee Cup), 33
Copacabana dance club, 137
Corcovado National Park, 306, 309,
    313–315
Costa Rica Biking Adventure, 142
Costa Rica Dreams, 219
Costa Rica Expeditions, 62, 140, 143

Costa Rica Experts, 63
Costa Rica Marriott (San José), 9
Costa Rica Sun Tours, 120, 140, 143
Costa Rica Tourist Board, 33
Costa Rican Tourism Institute, 99
costs, 48, 51–52
Courtyard by Marriott, 107–108, 367
Crazy Monkey Bar, 179
credit cards, 55–56, 361
Crocodile Bay Lodge, 316
crowds, avoiding, 33
Crowne Plaza, 108, 367
cruising, 61, 141–142
Cuervo Sport Fishing, 219
cuisine, 21–23, 358. *See also*
    restaurants
Cuna del Angel hotel (south of
    Dominical), 225–226
currency, 53–54, 361–362. *See also*
    fast facts
customs, 362
cybercafes, 363

• D •

D&N bar, 297
Damas Island estuary, 199
Days Inn, 367
Del Río, 134
democracy, 20–21
dentists, 116
Desafio Expeditions, 237, 267, 269
Día de la Paza, 34
diet, 83–84
dining. *See* restaurants; *specific*
    restaurants
disabled travelers, 75
Disco La Central, 221
Discovery Horseback, 220
diving, 175, 176, 230
doctors, 116
Dominical
    accommodations, 225–227
    attractions and activities, 228–231
    fast facts, 231–232
    getting to/around, 223–225
    nightlife, 231
    overview, 223
    restaurants, 227–228
    shopping, 231
Don Juan Coffee Tour, 252

Don Rufino restaurant (La Fortuna),
    263–264
Dos Locos bar, 203
Doubletree Hotels, 367
Dragonfly Bar & Grill (Guanacaste),
    14, 165
Drake Bay
    accommodations, 301–304
    attractions and activities, 304–306
    getting to/around, 300–301
    nightlife, 306
    overview, 300
    restaurants, 304
Drake Bay Wilderness Resort (Drake
    Bay), 302–303
driving
    Arenal and La Fortuna, 257, 272
    Cahuita, 325–326
    cost of gas for, 49
    Dominical, 223–224
    Golfito and Golfo Dulce, 317
    Guanacaste, 150, 154
    Jacó, 206–207
    Malpaís and Santa Teresa, 292
    Manuel Antonio, 184–185
    Monteverde, 236–237
    Montezuma, 282–283
    Playa Herradura, 206–207
    Puerto Jiménez and Osa Peninsula,
        307
    Puerto Viejo, 334
    San José, 94, 100–101
    Tortuguero, 344–347
dry cleaning, 117

• E •

Earthwatch Institute, 78
Eco Termales, 267
ecolodges, 12–13, 69–70
Ecological Sanctuary, 251
ecology, 356
El Avion restaurant (Manuel Antonio),
    193
El Cuartel de la Boca del Monte bar,
    138
El Encanto Bed and Breakfast
    (Cahuita), 328
El Galeón restaurant (Playa
    Herradura), 215
El Gran Escape restaurant (Manuel
    Antonio), 193–194

El Jardin hotel (Montezuma), 285
El Loco Natural restaurant (Puerto Viejo), 338
El Novillo de Arenal restaurant (La Fortuna), 264
El Observatorio bar, 138
El Patio Bistro Latino restaurant (Manuel Antonio), 14, 194
El Pelicano restaurant (Playa Herradura), 215–216
El Pueblo, 131, 137
El Rodeo Country Inn (San José), 108
El Sano Banano Village Café (Montezuma), 286–287, 290
El Sol, 252
El Tobogán dance club, 137
El Tope, 34
El Velero Hotel (Guanacaste), 11, 155
electricity, 362
Else Kientzler Botanical Garden, 126–127
embassies, 116, 363
emergencies, 117, 352, 363–364
Escazú (San José), 98
Escondido Trex, 315
escorted tours, 61–62
Escuela D'Amore, 202
events, calendar of, 33–34
Exotica restaurant (Ojochal), 227
Expedia, 52, 60, 63, 71, 81
Exploradores Outdoors, 142
E-Z Times bar, 344

• *F* •

families, traveling with, 17, 39–41, 73–74, 355
fast facts
  Arenal and La Fortuna, 270, 276–277
  Costa Rica, 361–365
  Dominical, 231–232
  Golfito and Golfo Dulce, 323
  Guanacaste, 168
  Jacó, 222
  Malpaís and Santa Teresa, 297–298
  Manuel Antonio, 204
  Monteverde, 253–254
  Montezuma, 290
  Playa Herradura, 221
  San José, 116–119
  Tortuguero, 352

faxes, 119
ferry travel, 282–283, 292
Festejos Populares (Popular Fiestas), 34
Fiesta Latina dance club, 137
Fiesta of the Virgin of Los Angeles, 33–34
Figueres, Cecilia "Pefi" (artist), 133
films (research), 25
Finca La Isla Botanical Gardens, 340–341
Finca Los Caballos, 289
Finca Rosa Blanca Coffee Plantation & Inn (San José), 10, 102
Finca Valmy, 201
Finca Valverde hotel (Santa Elena), 241
Fincas Naturales, 196
Fish Head Bar, 203
fishing
  Arenal and La Fortuna, 268, 275–276
  Golfito and Golfo Dulce, 322–323
  Guanacaste, 176
  Jacó, 219
  Manuel Antonio, 199–200
  Playa Herradura, 219
  Puerto Jiménez and Osa Peninsula, 316
Flamingo Equestrian Center, 178
Flor Blanca Resort (Santa Teresa), 11, 77, 294–295
Flor de Caña, 134
Flor de Vida restaurant (Santa Elena), 244, 253
Fly Zone, 276
FlyerTalk, 61
Flying Wheels Travel, 75
Four Seasons Resort (Guanacaste), 10, 155, 157
Four Trax Adventure, 199, 219
Frank's Place bar, 297
frequent-flier membership, 61
Friends dance club, 137
Frog Pond of Monteverde, 249
fruit, fresh, 22–23

• *G* •

Gaia Hotel & Reserve (Manuel Antonio), 188
Galería Amón, 132
Galería Jacobo Karpio, 132

Galería Lunática, 269
Galería Namu, 133
Ganesha Lounge, 221
gay travelers, 75–76
Ginger restaurant (Guanacaste), 14, 165
Gold Museum, 122–123, 124
golfing, 176–177, 221
Golfito and Golfo Dulce
    accommodations, 318–321
    attractions and activities, 321–323
    fast facts, 323
    getting to/around, 317–318
    overview, 16, 316
    restaurants, 321
Grano de Oro Restaurant (San José), 13, 111–112
Gray Line Tours, 66
Green Iguana Surf Camp, 230
GSM (Global System for Mobile Communications), 85
Guacamole clothing store, 203, 221
Guanacaste
    accommodations, 155–164
    attractions and activities, 170–178
    beaches, 149, 151–153, 173–174
    car rental, 154
    fast facts, 168
    getting to/around, 148–155
    guided tours, 169–170
    maps, 156, 158, 160, 162
    nightlife, 178–179
    overview, 27, 147
    restaurants, 164–167
    shopping, 178
    tourist information, 153
guided tours, 120, 140, 169–170

• **H** •

Habitat for Humanity International, 78
Hacienda Barú, 229
Hacienda Guachipelin, 170–171, 177
Hacienda Pinilla, 177
Hampton Inn, 367
handicrafts, shopping for, 132–133
hanging bridges, 267–268
Havana Club, 134
Health Canada, 81–82
Heredia (San José), 99
Herrera Botanical Gardens, 315

High Tec Sportfishing, 200
hiking, 251
Hilton Hotels, 367
Hilton Papagayo Resort (Guanacaste), 157
history, 18–21
Holiday Inn Express (San José), 108
Holland America, 61
Holy Week, 33
Horizontes Tours, 120, 140, 143
horseback riding
    Arenal and La Fortuna, 268, 276
    Cahuita, 332
    Guanacaste, 178
    Jacó, 220
    Malpaís and Santa Teresa, 297
    Manuel Antonio, 201
    Monteverde, 237, 251–252
    Montezuma, 289
    Playa Herradura, 220
hospitals. *See* fast facts
Hotel Aranjuez (San José), 11, 103
Hotel Belmar (Monteverde), 241
Hotel Bougainvillea (San José), 108
Hotel Boutique Las Colinas (La Fortuna), 260
Hotel Britannia (San José), 103
Hotel Cacts (San José), 108
Hotel Capitán Suizo (Guanacaste), 158–159
Hotel Copacabana bar, 221
Hotel Costa Verde (Manuel Antonio), 190
Hotel Don Carlos (San José), 103–104
Hotel El Byblos bar, 203
Hotel El Establo (Monteverde), 241
Hotel El Sapo Dorado (Santa Elena), 242
Hotel Fonda Vela (Monteverde), 12, 242
Hotel Fuego del Sol (Playa Hermosa), 211
Hotel Grano de Oro (San José), 11, 104
Hotel Jinetes de Osa (Drake Bay), 303
Hotel Kamuk bar, 203
Hotel La Aurora (Montezuma), 285
Hotel La Fortuna, 261
Hotel Le Bergerac (San José), 11, 104
Hotel Los Mangos (Montezuma), 285–286
Hotel Lucy (Montezuma), 286

Hotel Malinche (Manuel Antonio), 190
Hotel Mar de Luz (Jacó), 211–212
Hotel Milvia (San José), 108
Hotel Moctezuma bar, 289–290
Hotel Nine (Jacó), 212
Hotel Parque del Lago (San José), 109
Hotel Pasatiempo bar, 179
Hotel Playa Hermosa Bosque del Mar (Guanacaste), 159
Hotel Plinio (Manuel Antonio), 190–191
Hotel Poco a Poco (Santa Elena), 242–243
Hotel Poseidon bar, 221
Hotel Presidente (San José), 105
Hotel Punta Islita (Nicoya Peninsula), 11, 77, 291
Hotel Roca Verde (Dominical), 226
Hotel Rosa del Paseo (San José), 109
Hotel San Bosco (La Fortuna), 261
Hotel Santo Tomás (San José), 105
Hotel Sí Como No bar (Manuel Antonio), 191, 203
Hotel Sugar Beach (Guanacaste), 159–160
Hotel Tilawa (Nuevo Arenal), 273
Hotel Verde Mar (Manuel Antonio), 11, 191
Hotel Villa Casa Blanca (Guanacaste), 160–161
Hotel and Villas Cala Luna (Guanacaste), 157–158
hotels, 69. *See also* accommodations
Hotwire, 71
Hummingbird Gallery, 252

• I •

Iguana Tours, 199, 201, 202
illnesses, 82–84
INBio Park, 127
independence, 19–20, 34
InsideFlyer, 61
Instituto Costarricense de Turismo, 99
insurance, 80–81
Interbus, 66
InterContinental Hotels & Resorts, 368
International Association for Medical Assistance to Travelers, 82

International Coastal Cleanup Day, 34
International Gay and Lesbian Travel Association, 76
International Society of Travel Medicine, 82
Internet access, 86, 363. *See also* fast facts
Irazú volcano, 143
Isla del Caño, 202
itineraries, 35–44, 129–130

• J •

Jacó
    accommodations, 210–215
    attractions and activities, 216–221
    beaches, 218–219
    fast facts, 222
    getting to/around, 206–210
    nightlife, 221
    overview, 206
    restaurants, 215–216
    shopping, 221
Jade Museum, 122, 125
Jagua Arts & Craft Store, 315–316
Jaguar Rides, 219
Jazz Café, 139
Jazz Casino, 179, 221
Jeep Boat Jeep, 237
jet skis, 202
jewelry, shopping for, 133–134, 343
Johnny's Place bar, 343
Juanitas Mexican Bar & Grille (Puerto Jiménez), 312
Jungla y Senderos Los Lagos, 267
Jungle Coast Jets, 202
JW Marriott Guanacaste Resort & Spa (Hacienda Pinilla), 10, 161

• K •

Kaltak Arts and Craft Market, 178
Kandari by the Pacific hotel (Playa Esterillos Centro), 214–215
Kandari Resort & Spa (San José), 107
Kapi Kapi restaurant (Manuel Antonio), 194
kayaking, 142–143, 219, 315, 351
Key Largo bar, 138

• L •

La Buena Nota, 203
La Casona, 131
La Cava Grill (San José), 112, 115
La Costa de Papito hotel (Playa Cocles), 12, 336
La Cusinga Lodge (Bahía Ballena), 226
La Estrella Stables, 251
La Fortuna. *See* Arenal and La Fortuna
La Fortuna Falls, 266
La Galería Heliconia, 221
La Hacienda restaurant (Manuel Antonio), 194–195
La Laguna del Cocodrillo Bistro (Guanacaste), 166
La Lora bar, 297
La Luz restaurant (San José), 112
La Mar Cebicheria restaurant (San José), 112–113
La Monastère (San José), 115
La Paloma Lodge hotel and restaurant (Drake Bay), 12, 77, 303–304
La Parcela restaurant (Dominical), 228
La Paz Waterfall Gardens, 17, 128
La Pecora Nera restaurant (Playa Cocles), 14, 338–339
La Sabana (San José), 95, 124
La Taberna, 253
Laguna Lodge (Tortuguero), 348
Lake Arenal. *See also* Arenal and La Fortuna; Arenal volcano
  accommodations, 273–274
  attractions and activities, 275–276
  fast facts, 276–277
  getting to/around, 272
  map, 271
  restaurants, 274–275
  shopping, 276
  tourist information, 272
language, 23, 202, 230, 252, 356–357, 363
Lankester Gardens, 127–128
Lapa Rios hotel (Osa Peninsula), 13, 77, 311–312
Las Tortugas Hotel (Guanacaste), 161
Latin America Network Information Center, 368
laundry, 117

Lava Lounge restaurant (La Fortuna), 264
Le Loft bar, 221
leather goods, shopping for, 134
Lemon Zest restaurant (Jacó), 216
lesbian travelers, 75–76
Liberty Travel, 63
Librería Internacional, 132
Little Theater Group, 136
Lizard Lounge, 179
Lola's restaurant (Guanacaste), 14, 166, 174
Los Amigos bar, 221
Los Pescadores bar, 203
Los Sueños Marriott Ocean & Golf Resort (Playa Herradura), 212–213, 221
Los Yoses (San José), 98, 139
lost wallet, 57
Lucky Bug Gallery, 276
Luigi's Casino, 269
Luluberlu, 343
luxury hotels, best, 9–11. *See also* accommodations

• M •

Machu Picchu restaurant (San José), 113
Magellan Inn (Playa Negra), 328
Mahogany Park, 141
mail, 117
Makanda-by-the-Sea hotel (Manuel Antonio), 10, 77, 192
Malpaís and Santa Teresa
  accommodations, 294–296
  attractions and activities, 297
  fast facts, 297–298
  getting to/around, 292–294
  map, 293
  nightlife, 297
  restaurants, 296
  tourist information, 294
Malpaís Surf Camp & Resort (Malpaís), 295, 297
Manatus Hotel (Tortuguero), 348
mangroves, 199
Manuel Antonio
  accommodations, 187–192
  attractions and activities, 196–202
  beaches, 199

Manuel Antonio *(continued)*
canopy tours, 200
coffee, 196
fast facts, 204
getting to/around, 184–187
maps, 189, 197
nightlife, 203
overview, 17, 27–28, 183
restaurants, 192–196
shopping, 202–203
Manuel Antonio National Park,
197–198
Manzanillo-Gandoca Wildlife Refuge,
340–342
maps
Arenal volcano, 256
Cahuita, 327
central Pacific coast, 207
Corcovado National Park, 314
Guanacaste, 156, 158, 160, 162
Lake Arenal, 271
Malpaís and Santa Teresa, 293
Manuel Antonio, 189, 197
Monteverde, 239, 247
Montezuma, 283
overview, 117–118, 363
Playa Jacó, 209
Puerto Jiménez and Osa Peninsula,
302, 309
Puerto Viejo, 341
San José, 96–97
southern Costa Rica, 310
Tortuguero, 345
Mar y Sol restaurant (Guanacaste),
166
Mariposario Cahuita, 326, 332
Marriott Costa Rica Hotel (San José),
105–106, 368
massage, 202, 343
MasterCard, 56, 57
Maverick Sportfishing Yachts, 219
Mawamba Lodge (Tortuguero),
348–349
medical insurance, 81
Meg's Riding Stables, 251
Melico Salazar Theater, 124
Mena, Lil (artist), 133
Milarepa hotel (Santa Teresa), 295
Mirador Ram Luna (San José),
115, 359
Mirador Tiquicia (San José), 115, 359

Miss Junie's Restaurant (Tortuguero),
349–350
money, 53–57
monkeys, 356, 358
Montaña de Fuego Inn (Tabacón), 261
Monteverde
accommodations, 240–243
attractions and activities, 246–252
coffee, 245
fast facts, 253–254
getting to/around, 236–238, 240
maps, 239, 247
nightlife, 253
overview, 17, 235–236, 2829
restaurants, 244–245
shopping, 252–253
wildlife, 248–249
Monteverde Cloud Forest Reserve,
246–247
Monteverde Jubilee Family Album, 240
Monteverde Lodge (Santa Elena),
12, 243
Montezuma
accommodations, 284–286
attractions and activities, 287–289
beaches, 289
fast facts, 290
getting to/around, 281–284
map, 283
nightlife, 289–290
restaurants, 286–287
shopping, 289
tourist information, 284
Morazán Park, 125
Morpho's Café (Santa Elena), 244
mountain biking, 16, 142, 201,
268, 276, 297
Museo de Arte Costarricense,
121, 124
Museo de Jade Marco Fidel Tristán,
122, 125
Museo de los Niños, 122
Museo de Oro Banco Central,
122–123, 124
Museo Nacional de Arte y Cultura,
125
Museo Nacional de Costa Rica,
123, 124, 305
Museum of Costa Rican Art, 121, 124
music, shopping for, 134–135
Musoc, 224
Mystic Dive Center, 230

Mystica hotel (Nuevo Arenal), 273–274
Mystica restaurant (Nuevo Arenal), 274
myths, 355–357

• *N* •

National Arts and Culture Center, 121, 125
National Cathedral, 124
National Museum, 123, 124
National Orchid Show, 33
national parks. *See specific national parks*
National Symphony Orchestra, 136
National Theater Company, 124, 136
National University, 136
The Nature Farm Reserve, 196
Nauyaca Waterfall, 229
Naviera Tambor, 282
Nectar restaurant (Malpaís), 296
neighborhoods
    Arenal and La Fortuna, 258, 272
    Cahuita, 326–327
    Dominical, 224–225
    Drake Bay, 301
    Golfito and Golfo Dulce, 318
    Guanacaste, 151–153
    Jacó, 209–210
    Malpaís and Santa Teresa, 294
    Manuel Antonio, 186
    Monteverde, 238
    Montezuma, 283–284
    Playa Herradura, 209–210
    Puerto Jiménez and Osa Peninsula, 308
    Puerto Viejo, 334–335
    San José, 94–99
    Tortuguero, 347
newspapers, 222, 270. *See also* fast facts
Nicoya Peninsula, 29–30
nightlife
    Arenal and La Fortuna, 269
    budgeting for, 50
    Cahuita, 333
    casinos, 139–140
    Dominical, 231
    Drake Bay, 306
    Guanacaste, 178–179
    Jacó, 221
    Malpaís and Santa Teresa, 297
    Manuel Antonio, 203
    Monteverde, 253
    Montezuma, 289–290
    Playa Herradura, 221
    Puerto Viejo, 343–344
    San José, 135–140, 137, 138
Norwegian Cruise Line, 61

• *O* •

Obregón, Manuel (pianist), 135
Olio restaurant (San José), 113
one-day itinerary, 129
one-week itinerary, 35–37, 43–44
online reservations, 52, 63, 71
Orbitz, 52, 60, 63
Orchid Garden, 249
Original Canopy Tours, 141, 251
Original Grand Gallery, 269
Orquideas Inn (San José), 109
Osa Peninsula, 302. *See also* Puerto Jiménez; Puerto Jiménez and Osa Peninsula
Oso Viejo, 176
Overseas Adventure Travel, 62

• *P* •

Pacific Edge hotel (Dominical), 226–227
package tours, 62–63
Pacuare River, 16, 142–143
Palomina Horse Tours, 251
Papagayo Peninsula, 151
Papagayo restaurant (Guanacaste), 167
Papaya Music, 135
Paradise Costa Rica, 227
Paradisus Playa Conchal hotel (Guanacaste), 162–163, 177
Park Café (San José), 13, 113–114
Parque España, 125
Parque La Sabana, 124
Parque Morazán, 125
Parque Nacional, 125
Parque Reptilandia, 230
Paseo Colón (San José), 95
passports, 79–80
Peace Lodge (San José), 10, 106

performing arts, 136
pharmacies. *See* fast facts
Picante restaurant (Guanacaste), 167
Pizzeria de Johnny restaurant (Santa Elena), 245
Playa Avellanas beach, 176
Playa Brasilito beach, 149, 152
Playa Chiquita beach, 340
Playa Chiquita Lodge (Playa Chiquita), 336–337
Playa Cocles beach, 339
Playa Conchal beach, 152
Playa de Jacó beach, 209, 218
Playa de los Artistas restaurant (Montezuma), 287
Playa del Coco beach, 149, 152, 160
Playa Espadilla beach, 198
Playa Esterillos beach, 219
Playa Flamingo beach, 149, 152
Playa Grande beach, 153, 174, 176
Playa Hermosa beach, 17, 151, 162, 219
Playa Herradura
    accommodations, 210–215
    attractions and activities, 216–221
    beaches, 218–219
    fast facts, 221
    getting to/around, 206–210
    nightlife, 221
    restaurants, 215–216
    shopping, 221
Playa Junquillal beach, 174
Playa La Penca beach, 174
Playa Manuel Antonio beach, 15
Playa Montezuma beach, 15
Playa Nacascolo beach, 15, 174
Playa Negra beach, 174, 176
Playa Nicuesa Rainforest Lodge (Golfo Dulce), 13, 320
Playa Ocotal beach, 152
Playa Pan de Azúcar beach, 152, 174
Playa Panamá beach, 149, 151, 174
Playa Potrero beach, 149
Playa Prieta beach, 174
Playa Real beach, 174
Playa Tamarindo beach, 15, 17
Playa Uvita beach, 228
Plaza de la Cultura, 124
Plaza de la Democracia, 124, 131
Plaza Esmeralda, 134
Plinio Restaurant (Manuel Antonio), 195

Poás volcano, 144, 259
Pochote Grande hotel (Jacó), 213
Pollo's Surf School, 316
post office, 364. *See also* fast facts
Puerto Escondido, 198
Puerto Jiménez and Osa Peninsula
    accommodations, 311–312
    attractions and activities, 312–316
    getting to/around, 307–309, 311
    map, 309
    restaurants, 312
    shopping, 315–316
    tourist information, 308–309, 311
Puerto San Luis Yacht Club, 276
Puerto Viejo
    accommodations, 335–338
    attractions and activities, 339–343
    beaches, 339–340
    getting to/around, 333–335
    map, 341
    nightlife, 343–344
    restaurants, 338–339
    shopping, 343
Punta Catedral, 198
Punta Coral, 77
Punta Islita, 291
Punta Mona Center For Sustainable Living & Education, 342
Punta Uva, 340
Pura Vida Botanical Gardens, 217
Pure Jungle Spa, 343
Pure Trek Canyoning, 267

• *Q* •

Quality Inns, 368
Quepolandia (magazine), 186

• *R* •

Radisson Europa Hotel (San José), 109, 368
Radisson Seven Seas Cruises, 61
rafting, 16, 142–143, 172, 201, 269
Railbike Tour, 142
rain, 356
Rain Forest Aerial Tram Caribbean, 141
Rain Forest Aerial Tram Pacific, 220
Raindrop Spa, 202
Rainmaker Nature Refuge, 200

Ramada Worldwide, 368
rate, finding best room, 70–71
Real InterContinental San José, 109
Reef Runners Dive Shop, 342
rental cars. *See* car rentals
research, 24–25
Reserva Sendero Tranquilo, 251
reservations, 60–61
Residence Inn by Marriott, 368
resorts, large, 68–69
Restaurant Edith (Cahuita), 330
Restaurant Marlin (Manuel Antonio), 195
Restaurante Nuestra Tierra (San José), 114
restaurants. *See also specific restaurants*
  best, 13–14
  budgeting for, 50
restrooms, 118
Rincón de la Vieja National Park, 153, 171–172
Rioasis restaurant (Jacó), 216
Ríos Tropicales, 142, 201
river trips, 142–143
room, reserving best, 72
Royal Caribbean, 61

• **S** •

Sabine's Smiling Horses, 251
safety, 84, 118, 364
sailing, 175, 201–202, 322
Salsa Brava, 342
salsa lizano, 358
Salsipuedes bar, 203
San Clemente Bar & Grill (Dominical), 228, 231
San José
  accommodations, 101–109
  attractions and activities, 121–128, 140–144
  day trips from, 140–144
  fast facts, 116–119
  getting to/around, 92–101
  guided tours, 120
  itineraries, 129–130
  maps, 96–97
  nightlife, 135–140
  overview, 26–27, 91
  restaurants, 109–115
  shopping, 130–135
  tourist information, 99
San Pedro (San José), 98, 138–139
Santa Ana (San José), 98
Santa Elena. *See* Monteverde
Santa Elena Cloud Forest Reserve, 248
Santa Juana Mountain Tour, 200
Santa Rosa Canopy Tour, 177
Santa Teresa. *See* Malpaís and Santa Teresa
Sargento Garcia's bar, 203
scuba-diving, 174–175, 202, 342
sea turtles, 173, 359
seasons, 31–33
Seasons by Shlomy restaurant (Guanacaste), 167
security, airline, 86–87
Selva Bananito Lodge (Bananito), 13, 329
Selvatura Park, 250
senior travelers, 74
Serenity Spa, 202, 220
Seventh Street Books, 24, 132
Shawandha Lodge (Playa Chiquita), 337
shopping
  Arenal and La Fortuna, 269, 276
  budgeting for, 50
  Cahuita, 332–333
  Dominical, 231
  Guanacaste, 178
  Jacó, 221
  malls, 131, 139
  Manuel Antonio, 202–203
  markets, 130–131
  Monteverde, 252–253
  Montezuma, 289
  Playa Herradura, 221
  Puerto Jiménez and Osa Peninsula, 315–316
  Puerto Viejo, 343
  San José, 130–135
shuttles, 93
sightseeing budget, 50
Silver Seas Cruises, 61
Sivana Yoga, 202
Sky Tram, 267
Sky Trek, 250
Sky Walk, 250
Skyline Ultralights, 230
Small Distinctive Hotels of Costa Rica, 69

smoking, 364
snorkeling, 202, 332, 342
Sobre Las Olas restaurant (Cahuita), 330
soda, 21
Soda Carolina restaurant (Puerto Jiménez), 312
Soda Piedra Mar (Malpaís), 296
Soda Tamara restaurant (Puerto Viejo), 339
Soda Tapia restaurant (San José), 114
Sophia restaurant (Monteverde), 14, 245
southern Costa Rica, 30, 299–300, 310. *See also* Drake Bay; Golfito and Golfo Dulce; Puerto Jiménez
Southern Expeditions, 228
southern Nicoya Peninsula, 281. *See also* Malpaís and Santa Teresa; Montezuma
Spa Uno, 202
Spain Park, 125
Spanish For Dummies (Wald), 23
spas, 202, 220
sportfishing. *See* fishing
The Springs Resort & Spa (Tabacón), 10–11, 262
Stanford's bar, 343
Stelaris Casino, 221
Stella's Bakery, 245
stolen wallet, 57
Studio Metallo, 133–134
Sueño del Mar hotel (Guanacaste), 163
sunsets, 218, 359
Sunspot Bar & Grill (Manuel Antonio), 14, 195
Superior Sightseeing, 217, 218
surfing
    Dominical, 230–231
    Golfito and Golfo Dulce, 323
    Guanacaste, 175–176
    Malpaís and Santa Teresa, 297
    popularity of, 358
    Puerto Jiménez and Osa Peninsula, 316
    Puerto Viejo, 342
Swiss Travel Service, 120

• *T* •

Tabacón bar, 221
Tabacón Grand Spa Thermal Resort (La Fortuna), 19, 262, 266, 360
Tamarindo, 149, 153, 158, 176
taxes, 56–57, 118, 364–365
taxis
    Arenal and La Fortuna, 270, 272, 277
    central Pacific coast, 222
    Dominical, 232
    Golfito and Golfo Dulce, 323
    Guanacaste, 154, 168
    Malpaís and Santa Teresa, 292, 294, 298
    Manuel Antonio, 204
    Monteverde, 237, 240, 254
    Montezuma, 290
    San José, 93, 99–100, 118–119
    Tortuguero, 352
Teatro Melico Salazar, 124, 136
Teatro Nacional, 124, 136
telephone, 365
temperature. *See* seasons
three-day itineraries, 129–130
Thrusters surfer bar, 231
Tica Bus Company, 94
Tico, 18, 23
Tico Times, 368
Tico Wind, 275
Tikokú, 267
Tilawa Windsurfing Center, 275
time zone, 365
Tin Jo restaurant (San José), 114–115
tipping, 92
Tiskita Jungle Lodge (Pavones), 320–321
Titi Canopy Tour, 200
Tortuga Lodge (Tortuguero), 13, 349
Tortuguero
    accommodations, 347–349
    attractions and activities, 350–351
    beaches, 351
    fast facts, 352
    getting to/around, 344–347
    map, 345
    restaurants, 349–350
Tortuguero National Park, 350–351

tourist information
  Arenal and La Fortuna,
      259, 270, 272, 277
  central Pacific coast, 222
  Dominical, 232
  Golfito and Golfo Dulce, 323
  Guanacaste, 153, 168
  Malpaís and Santa Teresa, 294, 298
  Manuel Antonio, 204
  Monteverde, 254
  Montezuma, 284, 290
  overview, 368
  Puerto Jiménez and Osa Peninsula,
      308–309, 311
  San José, 99, 117
  Tortuguero, 352
tours
  canopy, 141
  escorted, 61–62
  guided, 120, 140, 169–170
  package, 62–63
Tracopa, 224, 301, 317–318
Tralapa beach, 149
transportation budget, 48–49
Transportes Blanco-Lobo, 308
Transportes Jacó, 208
Transportes Rodriguez Hermanos, 282
Transportes Tilaran, 272
traveler's checks, 56
Travelocity, 52, 63, 71
Tree House Lodge (Playa Chiquita),
      11, 337–338
trip-cancellation insurance, 81
Trópico Latino Lodge (Santa Teresa),
      296
turtles, 351
Twister dance club, 137
two-day itineraries, 129
two-week itinerary, 35–37

• **U** •

Upper Deck Sports Bar, 179
Urban Canopy Tour, 141

• **V** •

Vaya Con Silla de Ruedas, 75
Vertigo dance club, 137
Villa Alegre hotel (Guanacaste),
      163–164

Villa Caletas hotel (Playa Herradura),
      10, 77, 213–214, 218, 359
Villa Decary (Nuevo Arenal), 274
Villa del Sueño Hotel (Guanacaste),
      164
Villa Lapas (Tarcoles), 214, 220
Villablanca Cloud Forest & Spa (San
      Ramón), 262–263
Villas Nicolás (Manuel Antonio), 192
Visa, 56, 57
Vista del Valle Plantation Inn (San
      José), 106–107
VoIP (Voice over Internet
      Protocol), 86
Volcano Lodge (La Fortuna), 263
Volcano Look Disco, 269
volcano trip, 143–144
volunteer experiences, 77–78
Vonage, 86

• **W** •

Wacky Wanda's bar, 203
wakeboarding, 276
Wald, Susana
      (Spanish For Dummies), 23
walking, 101, 154–155
water, 119, 356, 365
Waterfall Canopy Tour, 288–289
Wave Expeditions, 269
weather. See seasons
Web sites
  car rental agencies, 65
  cruise lines, 61
  currency exchange rates, 53
  disabled travelers, 75
  escorted tours, 62
  gay and lesbian travelers, 76
  online travel agencies, 60, 71
  package tours, 63
  weddings, 77
weddings, 76–77
Western Union, 57
Whappin' restaurant (San José), 115
white-water rafting, 269
wildlife
  Arenal and La Fortuna, 265
  Cahuita, 332
  Guanacaste, 173
  monkeys, 356
  Monteverde, 248–249

wildlife *(continued)*
    Parque Reptilandia, 230
    Puerto Viejo, 341–342
    Quetzal, 359–360
    sea turtles, 359
    Tortuguero, 351
Willy's Caballo Negro restaurant
    (Nuevo Arenal), 274–275
Wilson Botanical Gardens, 322
windsurfing, 275
Witch's Rock Canopy Tour, 177
Witch's Rock Surf Camp, 176
"working" vacations, 77–78
World of Insects, 249
World Wide Cruises, 61
Worldwide Assistance Services,
    Inc., 81

• *Y* •

Ylang-Ylang Beach Resort and
    restaurant (Montezuma),
    286–287
yoga, 202, 343

• *Z* •

The Zancudo Lodge, 323
Zouk Santana bar, 179

BUSINESS, CAREERS & PERSONAL FINANCE

Accounting For Dummies,
4th Edition*
978-0-470-24600-9

Bookkeeping Workbook
For Dummies†
978-0-470-16983-4

Commodities For Dummies
978-0-470-04928-0

Doing Business in China For Dummies
978-0-470-04929-7

E-Mail Marketing For Dummies
978-0-470-19087-6

Job Interviews For Dummies,
3rd Edition*†
978-0-470-17748-8

Personal Finance Workbook
For Dummies*†
978-0-470-09933-9

Real Estate License Exams For Dummies
978-0-7645-7623-2

Six Sigma For Dummies
978-0-7645-6798-8

Small Business Kit For Dummies,
2nd Edition*†
978-0-7645-5984-6

Telephone Sales For Dummies
978-0-470-16836-3

BUSINESS PRODUCTIVITY & MICROSOFT OFFICE

Access 2007 For Dummies
978-0-470-03649-5

Excel 2007 For Dummies
978-0-470-03737-9

Office 2007 For Dummies
978-0-470-00923-9

Outlook 2007 For Dummies
978-0-470-03830-7

PowerPoint 2007 For Dummies
978-0-470-04059-1

Project 2007 For Dummies
978-0-470-03651-8

QuickBooks 2008 For Dummies
978-0-470-18470-7

Quicken 2008 For Dummies
978-0-470-17473-9

Salesforce.com For Dummies,
2nd Edition
978-0-470-04893-1

Word 2007 For Dummies
978-0-470-03658-7

EDUCATION, HISTORY, REFERENCE & TEST PREPARATION

African American History
For Dummies
978-0-7645-5469-8

Algebra For Dummies
978-0-7645-5325-7

Algebra Workbook For Dummies
978-0-7645-8467-1

Art History For Dummies
978-0-470-09910-0

ASVAB For Dummies, 2nd Edition
978-0-470-10671-6

British Military History For Dummies
978-0-470-03213-8

Calculus For Dummies
978-0-7645-2498-1

Canadian History For Dummies,
2nd Edition
978-0-470-83656-9

Geometry Workbook For Dummies
978-0-471-79940-5

The SAT I For Dummies,
6th Edition
978-0-7645-7193-0

Series 7 Exam For Dummies
978-0-470-09932-2

World History For Dummies
978-0-7645-5242-7

FOOD, HOME, GARDEN, HOBBIES & HOME

Bridge For Dummies, 2nd Edition
978-0-471-92426-5

Coin Collecting For Dummies,
2nd Edition
978-0-470-22275-1

Cooking Basics For Dummies,
3rd Edition
978-0-7645-7206-7

Drawing For Dummies
978-0-7645-5476-6

Etiquette For Dummies,
2nd Edition
978-0-470-10672-3

Gardening Basics For Dummies*†
978-0-470-03749-2

Knitting Patterns For Dummies
978-0-470-04556-5

Living Gluten-Free For Dummies†
978-0-471-77383-2

Painting Do-It-Yourself
For Dummies
978-0-470-17533-0

HEALTH, SELF HELP, PARENTING & PETS

Anger Management For Dummies
978-0-470-03715-7

Anxiety & Depression Workbook
For Dummies
978-0-7645-9793-0

Dieting For Dummies, 2nd Edition
978-0-7645-4149-0

Dog Training For Dummies,
2nd Edition
978-0-7645-8418-3

Horseback Riding For Dummies
978-0-470-09719-9

Infertility For Dummies†
978-0-470-11518-3

Meditation For Dummies
with CD-ROM, 2nd Edition
978-0-471-77774-8

Post-Traumatic Stress Disorder
For Dummies
978-0-470-04922-8

Puppies For Dummies,
2nd Edition
978-0-470-03717-1

Thyroid For Dummies,
2nd Edition†
978-0-471-78755-6

Type 1 Diabetes For Dummies*†
978-0-470-17811-9

INTERNET & DIGITAL MEDIA

AdWords For Dummies
978-0-470-15252-2

Blogging For Dummies, 2nd Edition
978-0-470-23017-6

Digital Photography All-in-One Desk Reference For Dummies, 3rd Edition
978-0-470-03743-0

Digital Photography For Dummies, 5th Edition
978-0-7645-9802-9

Digital SLR Cameras & Photography For Dummies, 2nd Edition
978-0-470-14927-0

eBay Business All-in-One Desk Reference For Dummies
978-0-7645-8438-1

eBay For Dummies, 5th Edition*
978-0-470-04529-9

eBay Listings That Sell For Dummies
978-0-471-78912-3

Facebook For Dummies
978-0-470-26273-3

The Internet For Dummies, 11th Edition
978-0-470-12174-0

Investing Online For Dummies, 5th Edition
978-0-7645-8456-5

iPod & iTunes For Dummie 5th Edition
978-0-470-17474-6

MySpace For Dummies
978-0-470-09529-4

Podcasting For Dummies
978-0-471-74898-4

Search Engine Optimizatio For Dummies, 2nd Edition
978-0-471-97998-2

Second Life For Dummies
978-0-470-18025-9

Starting an eBay Business For Dummies, 3rd Edition†
978-0-470-14924-9

GRAPHICS, DESIGN & WEB DEVELOPMENT

Adobe Creative Suite 3 Design Premium All-in-One Desk Reference For Dummies
978-0-470-11724-8

Adobe Web Suite CS3 All-in-One Desk Reference For Dummies
978-0-470-12099-6

AutoCAD 2008 For Dummies
978-0-470-11650-0

Building a Web Site For Dummies, 3rd Edition
978-0-470-14928-7

Creating Web Pages All-in-One Desk Reference For Dummies, 3rd Edition
978-0-470-09629-1

Creating Web Pages For Dummies, 8th Edition
978-0-470-08030-6

Dreamweaver CS3 For Dummies
978-0-470-11490-2

Flash CS3 For Dummies
978-0-470-12100-9

Google SketchUp For Dummies
978-0-470-13744-4

InDesign CS3 For Dummies
978-0-470-11865-8

Photoshop CS3 All-in-One Desk Reference For Dummies
978-0-470-11195-6

Photoshop CS3 For Dummies
978-0-470-11193-2

Photoshop Elements 5 For Dummies
978-0-470-09810-3

SolidWorks For Dummies
978-0-7645-9555-4

Visio 2007 For Dummies
978-0-470-08983-5

Web Design For Dummies, 2nd Edition
978-0-471-78117-2

Web Sites Do-It-Yourself For Dummies
978-0-470-16903-2

Web Stores Do-It-Yourself For Dummies
978-0-470-17443-2

LANGUAGES, RELIGION & SPIRITUALITY

Arabic For Dummies
978-0-471-77270-5

Chinese For Dummies, Audio Set
978-0-470-12766-7

French For Dummies
978-0-7645-5193-2

German For Dummies
978-0-7645-5195-6

Hebrew For Dummies
978-0-7645-5489-6

Ingles Para Dummies
978-0-7645-5427-8

Italian For Dummies, Audio Set
978-0-470-09586-7

Italian Verbs For Dummies
978-0-471-77389-4

Japanese For Dummies
978-0-7645-5429-2

Latin For Dummies
978-0-7645-5431-5

Portuguese For Dummies
978-0-471-78738-9

Russian For Dummies
978-0-471-78001-4

Spanish Phrases For Dummies
978-0-7645-7204-3

Spanish For Dummies
978-0-7645-5194-9

Spanish For Dummies, Audio Set
978-0-470-09585-0

The Bible For Dummies
978-0-7645-5296-0

Catholicism For Dummies
978-0-7645-5391-2

The Historical Jesus For Dummies
978-0-470-16785-4

Islam For Dummies
978-0-7645-5503-9

Spirituality For Dummies, 2nd Edition
978-0-470-19142-2

NETWORKING AND PROGRAMMING

ASP.NET 3.5 For Dummies
978-0-470-19592-5

C# 2008 For Dummies
978-0-470-19109-5

Hacking For Dummies, 2nd Edition
978-0-470-05235-8

Home Networking For Dummies, 4th Edition
978-0-470-11806-1

Java For Dummies, 4th Edition
978-0-470-08716-9

Microsoft® SQL Server™ 2008 All-in-One Desk Reference For Dummies
978-0-470-17954-3

Networking All-in-One Desk Reference For Dummies, 2nd Edition
978-0-7645-9939-2

Networking For Dummies, 8th Edition
978-0-470-05620-2

SharePoint 2007 For Dummies
978-0-470-09941-4

Wireless Home Networking For Dummies, 2nd Edition
978-0-471-74940-0